Patricia Arredondo
Mary L. Fawcett
Dawnette L. Cigrand
Sandra Bertram Grant
Rieko Miyakuni
Dariyan Adams

Counseling With Immigrants, Refugees, and Their Families From Social Justice Perspectives

American Counseling Association
2461 Eisenhower Avenue, Suite 300
Alexandria, VA 22314
www.counseling.org

Counseling With Immigrants, Refugees, and Their Families From Social Justice Perspectives

American Counseling Association
2461 Eisenhower Avenue, Suite 300
Alexandria, VA 22314
counseling.org

Library of Congress Cataloging-in-Publication Data

Names: Arredondo, Patricia, author. | Fawcett, Mary L., author. | Cigrand, Dawnette L., author. | Bertram Grant, Sandra, author. | Miyakuni, Rieko, author. | Adams, Dariyan, author.
Title: Counseling with immigrants, refugees, and their families from social justice perspectives / Patricia Arredondo, Mary L. Fawcett, Dawnette L. Cigrand, Sandra Bertram Grant, Rieko Miyakuni, and Dariyan Adams.
Description: Alexandria, VA: American Counseling Association, [2024] | Includes bibliographical references and index.
Identifiers: LCCN 2023038045 (print) | LCCN 2023038046 (ebook) | ISBN 9781556204180 (paperback) | ISBN 9781394222957 (ebook) | ISBN 9781394222964 (pdf)
Subjects: LCSH: Immigrants—Counseling of—United States. | Children of immigrants—Counseling of—United States. | Immigrants—Family relationships—United States. | Social work with immigrants—United States.
Classification: LCC HV4010 .A76 2024 (print) | LCC HV4010 (ebook) | DDC 362.89/912830973—dc23/eng/20230921
LC record available at https://lccn.loc.gov/2023038045
LC ebook record available at https://lccn.loc.gov/2023038046

Dedication

With appreciation to the immigrant agricultural workers who toil daily to put food on our table.
—Patricia Arredondo

I dedicate this work to my mother Ann Fawcett Pearce.
—Mary L. Fawcett

To my sons, Dillon and Cody, and my grandson, Brantley, who have brought me much joy and inspiration.
—Dawnette L. Cigrand

To my loving parents, José and Sandra. Thank you for always looking forward and for your sacrifice stepping into the unknown. I couldn't have done it without you.
—Sandra Bertram Grant

To my loved ones, comrades in struggle and solidarity, and mentors who have gifted me with the visions for truth and continue to hold me accountable to use my privilege to do the job while teaching me to practice self-compassion.
—Rieko Miyakuni

To my devoted parents, Todd and Tracye, with all my love and appreciation, thank you for believing in me and encouraging me to always pursue my dreams.
—Dariyan Adams

TABLE OF CONTENTS

Preface

Immigrants, refugees, and their families have been a part of the history of the United States for more than 5 centuries. For many Americans, the arrival of immigrants at Ellis Island is the embodiment of the U.S. immigration experience. Nevertheless, this version is in stark contrast to the experience of African people brought as slaves to America. In the 20th and 21st centuries, millions of people have sought freedom and goals for a better life for themselves and their families. Unaccompanied minors, parents separated from their children at the U.S.-Mexico border, refugees fleeing warfare and other forms of violence and natural disasters, and individuals who arrive with documented status are all part of the immigrant and refugee diaspora of the United States and its territories. From Alaska to Florida, in rural and urban areas, in schools, workplaces, mental health agencies, and other settings, counselors are likely to cross paths with immigrants and refugees of different heritages and generations.

The U.S. immigrant population in 2020 was 44.9 million, a downturn because of the drop-off in arrivals from Mexico, the COVID-19 pandemic, and legislation that limited the number of documented entrants during the Trump administration. The refugee population is smaller and based on annual admissions from specific countries. Between 2020 and 2022, roughly 48,794 refugees were settled in the United States. In 2020, the majority came from the Democratic Republic of the Congo, Myanmar, and Ukraine. In 2021, the primary countries of origin of refugees were the Democratic Republic of the Congo, Syria, and Afghanistan (Baugh, 2022). There are other categories of new arrivals during this period who also settled in the United States. Up to 30,000 individuals monthly were granted temporary protective status. They were from Cuba, Haiti, Nicaragua, and Venezuela. Refugees from Afghanistan and Ukraine were granted humanitarian parole (Ward & Batalova, 2023).

This book is motivated by our long-term interest in and experiences with immigrants, refugees, and families of different ages and generations located in different parts of the country, including northern Minneapolis, northern Ohio, Boston, Phoenix, Milwaukee, Chicago, and Winona, Minnesota. In our encounters through community-based research, counseling, and educational settings, we have been inspired by the resilience, goal orientation, and inner fortitude of migrants. At the same time, the hardships of migration demonstrate the mental and physical stressors individuals have suffered and may continue to suffer in the postmigration period in the United States. Managing change is an ongoing process for immigrants and refugees, and these changes are often unpredictable, leading to risks, difficult decisions, and impromptu adaptations to keep moving forward.

A second reason for writing this book is the paucity of literature (e.g., books, research articles, book chapters) on counseling with immigrants. More recent research addresses the postmigration mental health symptoms for specific cultural groups such as unaccompanied minors, identity issues for adolescents, family disharmony because of different rates of acculturation between parents and children, economic stressors, and challenges for Deferred Action for Childhood Arrivals, or DACA, students. However, specific attention to the mental health needs of immigrants and affirmative counseling approaches is minimal at best.

In this book, our goal is to provide a balanced presentation contextualized in the systems that impinge on immigrants, refugees, and their families from the premigration to the postmigration periods, describing how individuals and families persist to meet their goals. The primary theoretical frameworks for this book are cultural competence development (Ratts et al., 2015; Sue et al., 1992), the biopsychosocial model (Engel, 1980), and Bronfenbrenner's (1977) ecological model.

All chapters have learning objectives, a reader self-assessment, and a minimum of one case scenario that is a composite of clients and individuals in research studies. The three elements provide structure and focus to various concepts, principles, literature, research, and applications of culturally responsive counseling. Quotes from immigrant participants and examples from our research experiences in different community settings are included as applicable. The glossary provides a compilation of terms most relevant for counselors when working with immigrants and refugees.

Chapter Overview

In **Part I: Context, Competencies, and Data to Ground Counseling Practices**, we describe an integrated framework, which is then referenced throughout the book chapters. This framework is informed by interdisciplinary research, historical events, and knowledge about contemporary immigrants and refugees.

Chapter 1: Social Justice and Cultural Competency Frameworks for Counseling With Immigrants and Refugees

Frameworks to ground our work as educators, researchers, and clinicians in an increasingly diverse society include the Multicultural Counseling Competencies documents (Arredondo et al., 1996; Sue et al., 1992) and the Multicultural and Social Justice Counseling Competencies (MSJCC; Ratts, et al., 2015) developed by members of the American Counseling Association (ACA) and the Association for Multicultural Counseling and Development. These frameworks continue to be used as anchors by professionals and students alike working in different contexts, domestically and internationally. In Chapter 1, we discuss the application of social justice principles from different global contexts, including South Africa and Guatemala, and practices in the decolonization of counseling theories and practices that support culturally responsive counseling. ACA ethical principles will be referenced as they also provide guiding principles for culturally responsive practices.

Chapter 2: Historical Context, Legislation, and Trends in the Migration Process

Forced and voluntary migration is historical, beginning in the "Americas" in the 15th century. To contribute to the building of counselor knowledge, in Chapter 2, we describe the history and evolution of U.S. immigration and the laws that have been used to support or block entry to this country. We discuss the settler colonialism framework given that it has affected the goals of migrants, particularly those perceived as inferior. Concepts such as xenophobia and their effects are explained historically. This chapter will also help counselors recognize language and terms that marginalize and oppress immigrants and refugees and how such terminology may emerge in the counseling process. Because many counselors have an immigrant history, an opportunity to examine one's personal family migration history is provided.

Chapter 3: Stages of Migration, Acculturation, and Identity Challenges

Research has contributed to our understanding about the different phases and conditions of the migration process and the lifelong effects of acculturation processes. The three-stage model of premigration, migration-specific, and postmigration is introduced and referenced in later discussions about counseling applications. Particular topics reviewed include the push and pull factors for migration and how they may be different for immigrants and refugees. In Chapter 3, we discuss the challenges faced by migrants and their families as well as strengths-based perspectives that need to be considered by counseling professionals. For example, migrants have a planning and risk-taking mindset that fortifies how they negotiate a myriad of challenges during their migration journey and once in their new country of residence. They are planners. Other invisible strengths are protective factors, such as their faith and collectivistic mindset and behavior—what they are doing is for others. Research points to immigrants' optimism, hope, and resilience. It is in the postmigration phase that the acculturation process evolves, introducing multiple stressors and changes to the lives of immigrants, refugees, and their families. The adjustments and cultural adaptations are many. Immigrants and refugees must also negotiate xenophobia, racism, and other forms of discrimination and microaggressions because of their color, language differences, country of origin, and immigrant identity status. In this chapter, readers will gain a comprehensive view of different migration journeys and migrants' persistence to arrive in the United States.

Chapter 4: Immigrant and Refugee Identity and Experiences Across the Life Span

Chapter 4 contains a discussion of different developmental task expectations informed by cultural socialization processes and intersecting identities. Immigrants and refugees of different ages, genders, countries of origin, languages, disability, LGBTQ+ status, socioeconomic backgrounds, educational attainment, and skill sets represent a diverse constellation of individuals with intersecting identities who arrive in the United States. Because most immigrants and refugees arrive as adolescents and adults, their sense of identity has been shaped in their country of origin and informed by their cultural values, gender role expectations, and developmental milestones. Examples of socialization experiences from different countries are introduced. From this contextual discussion, identity and role expectation challenges in the host country are described. For counselors, there is a continuing need to be culturally aware and knowledgeable in order to be culturally responsive.

Chapter 5: Disputing Biases and Assumptions Regarding Immigrants and Refugees

Chapter 5 focuses on employment patterns of immigrant and refugee women and men and the types of employment they typically assume. Historically, immigrants have been a source of cheap labor. In effect, wages of most immigrants are low because of their employment in industries such as agriculture, dairy, meatpacking, fisheries, and the service industry, among others. For example, many Latinx men are found in back-of-the-house restaurant work while others work in landscaping and construction. Women of all nationalities may be found in childcare, hospital service jobs, and hotel cleaning, and, typically, these jobs do not pay benefits, Social Security, or retirement, leaving long-term employees at a deficit when they retire or require disability services.

The prevailing perception is that immigrants are unskilled and therefore cannot do more than manual labor. Another misperception about immigrants is that they are criminals and that they all belong to gangs or drug cartels. Color was the defining factor in limiting access to individuals from Muslim and African countries from 2016 to 2020. Finally, there has always been rhetoric that migrants take away jobs from U.S. citizens although Americans who are White typically do not work in agriculture or in landscaping and other backbreaking jobs. Knowledge about the mischaracterizations of immigrants and refugees in the workforce is necessary in order for counselors to challenge media misinformation and mischaracterizations when they engage with immigrants and refugees working two or more jobs or 16-hour days.

Chapter 6: Mental Health Needs of Immigrants and Refugees

In the previous chapters, the discussion centered on life circumstances, contexts, and the endurance that propels immigrants to seek uncharted territory for a better life. The premigration and migration-specific phases in their journeys leave imprints that do not readily disappear. Thus, it is in the postmigration years that mental and physical health issues will likely emerge for individuals across the life span. In Chapter 6, a biopsychosocial model is referenced to understand symptoms and presenting issues. Emphasized is the identification of strengths, challenges, and resilience that contribute to immigrants' and refugees' abilities to navigate multiple stressors. For the purposes of counselor cultural responsiveness, mental, physical, and spiritual health are described from non-Western perspectives, and relevant theories and models that do not serve as forms of colonization are discussed.

In **Part II: Counseling With Immigrants, Refugees, and Their Families From Generational and Developmental Perspectives**, we provide multiple case examples of counseling with immigrants and refugees across the life span. The case examples are also examined through the integrated framework introduced in Part I.

Chapter 7: Counseling With Immigrant, Refugee, and Birthright Children

In this chapter, we address different developmental needs of immigrant and refugee children from birth to age 12. According to demographic data, the children of immigrants born in the United States are called "birthright" children because, by birth, they have the rights of every person born in the United States and its territories. Technically, they are second generation in the country, and their parents, the immigrants, are first generation; the same can be said of refugees. Birthright and third-generation children and the children of refugees have different mental health needs. There are also children who are born in another country and who are brought or sent by their parents to the United States. These children may have come with their parents but may have been separated at the border as was the practice since 2016–2020, or they may have arrived as unaccompanied minors. However, the majority likely came as adolescents. As discussed in Chapter 6, these children present with different biopsychosocial needs. Birthright children and immigrant and refugee children go to schools, playgrounds, and other settings where children may be taken to or convene. According to the Adverse Childhood Experiences Test (PsychCentral, n.d.), early life stressors leave imprints on children that can then manifest in more concerning ways in relationships at home and school, and through other unpredictable ways—self-harm, isolation, and so forth. Thus, counselors need to recognize the differences among these children and how federal and state immigration policies may also affect their well-being.

Chapter 8: Counseling With Immigrant, Refugee, and Birthright Adolescents

Chapter 8 focuses on the developmental needs of immigrant, refugee, and birthright children ages 13–18. Age-group differences between those who are children of immigrants and refugees (birthright children) and those who are immigrants are discussed. For counselors, knowledge about cultural socialization practices is essential to understand adolescents' issues to determine the appropriate intervention strategies. Erikson (1967) described identity development as the primary task of adolescence. However, for immigrant and refugee adolescents, identity development is just one of several challenges to be negotiated. For immigrant and birthright adolescents, there are likely different factors affecting how they see themselves. Questions about appearance, particularly color and other physical features, family responsibilities, and demands at school may heighten mental health distress and a sense of belonging. Among the issues that emerge is family discord, particularly if an adolescent is held responsible for younger children or if the adolescent is in a family in which members hold different documentation status.

Chapter 9: Counseling With Immigrant, Refugee, and Birthright Adults

The age of immigrant, refugee, and birthright individuals will present a range of issues and priorities in a counseling setting. A 38-year-old woman born in the United States to immigrant parents may now be a parent herself. Her children are third-generation children. The latter may seek services in college counseling centers as they grapple with issues related to identity, particularly intersecting identities. Birthright young adults have only known the United States as their home, but because of a visible difference of color and other physical features, they may be viewed as foreigners and experience harassment and other alienating behaviors. Adult immigrants and refugees are generally the ones who have had to plan and carry out the migratory processes for themselves and their families. Chapter 3 covers the various stages of the migration process, pointing out that all along, individuals are planful, decisive, and goal-oriented but carry enormous responsibilities on behalf of others. The risk and stress levels are enormous and, understandably, strain the mind, body, and spirit. Refugees may have a different means of entry into the United States; however, extended periods in refugee camps and the loss of family and friends during those confinements are also exhausting. Adults generally do not have time to mourn or reflect on the risks and losses, but this does not mean those events evaporate. Chapter 9 explores these factors, and counselors are encouraged to be mindful of the unspoken issues, as illustrated in the case examples provided.

Chapter 10: Counseling With Immigrant and Refugee Families

Immigrants and refugees are in all sectors of society, and it is in these varied settings where counselors will be called upon to deliver culturally responsive and ethical care. In the acculturation process, many unforeseen situations will emerge for families, and these may contribute to spiritual, physical, and mental health stressors. In our chapters on different developmental periods, we introduce how mental health distress may affect individuals differently within the same cultural group and even the same family. The focus of Chapter 10 is on immigrant and refugee families. Family counseling can be a primary approach in addition to the relational-cultural model because of the collectivistic orientation of many immigrant and refugee families. Students with DACA and undocumented status have additional emotional and pragmatic dilemmas depending on their college and their state of residence. More often, career counseling becomes important to high school youth, college-age young adults, and adults. The MSJCC (Ratts et al., 2015) are a valuable reference for counseling with immigrant and refugee families because the competencies elevate social justice concerns in different environments where discrimination and hostility may be occurring. Counselors can inquire about situations that immigrant and refugee adults feel powerless to control and simultaneously affirm that they are taking on the responsibilities needed as parents, employees, and individuals supporting family members back home.

How Will This Book Help You?

Individuals become counselors because of their desire to help others, to make a difference in their lives. With immigrants and refugees, there are many opportunities for counselors to facilitate their processes of change and to be part of their journeys in the country where they want to be. The United States is a country built by immigrants, refugees, enslaved Africans brought involuntarily, and Indigenous peoples, the original dwellers and owners of the land. The migrations trends to the United States over the centuries have not abated and will continue into the foreseeable future. Rather than perceive immigrants and refugees as a monolithic group composed of non-English-speaking individuals, counselors will learn about the foresight, persistence, and resilience of these brave people. Curiosity will be heightened as counselors hear narratives of fear, bravery, and faith to achieve one's goals. Counseling often focuses on individual issues; this is not the case with immigrants and refugees. In this book, we will illustrate the interdependence, collectivism, and care demonstrated by immigrants and refugees as they persevere to make the lives of their families back home and in the United States much better. We will also describe the risk-taking of adolescents and adults as they seek to establish better lives in this country. Many counseling practices such as reflection, restatements, and speaking with confidence may not be relevant when working with immigrants and refugees who are more action oriented for the present and the future. Counselors may experience these clients as shy and reticent, but they seek guidance as they try to solve problems.

This book will be an invaluable resource to counselors who encounter immigrants and refugees of different ages, countries of origin, and multiple identities in their practice. At the same time, counselors will be challenged to adapt their thinking and skills so that they can meet the immigrant and refugee clients "where they are." The case scenarios in the book will provide excellent opportunities for counselors to compare the hypothetical situations with their own experiences. Counseling with immigrants and refugees will also provide opportunities for counselors to examine their family immigration history, opening the door to personal revelations that may suggest counselors are more similar to their clients than they first thought. Counseling with immigrants and refugees is inspirational as one learns about how these individuals continue to contribute to the economic well-being of our country, the country they also claim as theirs.

References

Arredondo, P., Toporek, R., Brown, S. P., Jones, J., Locke, D. C., Sanchez, J., & Stadler, H. (1996). Operationalization of the multicultural counseling competencies. *Journal of Multicultural Counseling and Development, 24*(1), 42–78. https://doi-10.1002/j.2161-1912.1996.tb00288.x

Baugh, R. (2022, March 8). *Fiscal year 2020 refugees and asylees annual flow report.* Office of Immigration Statistics, Department of Homeland Security. https://www.dhs.gov/sites/default/files/2022-03/22_0308_plcy_refugees_and_asylees_fy2020_1.pdf

Bronfenbrenner, U. (1977). Toward an experimental ecology of human development. *American Psychologist, 32*(7), 513–531. https://doi.org/10.1037/0003-066X.32.7.513

Engel, G. L. (1980). The clinical application of the biopsychosocial model. *The American Journal of Psychiatry, 137*(5), 535–544. https://doi.org/10.1176/ajp.137.5.535

Erikson, E. H. (1967). *Identity and the life cycle.* Norton.

PsychCentral. (n.d.). *Adverse Childhood Experiences Test.* https://psychcentral.com/quizzes/ace-test)

Ratts, M. J., Singh, A. A., Nassar-McMillan, S., Butler, S. K., & McCullough, J. R. (2015). *Multicultural and social justice counseling competencies.* Association for Multicultural Counseling and Development. https://www.counseling.org/docs/default-source/competencies/multicultural-and-social-justice-counseling-competencies.pdf?sfvrsn=20

Sue, D. W., Arredondo, P., & McDavis, R. J. (1992). Multicultural counseling competencies and standards: A call to the profession. *Journal of Multicultural Counseling and Development, 20*(2), 64–88. https://doi.org/10.1002/j.2161-1912.1992.tb00563.x

Ward, N., & Batalova, J. (2023). Refugees and asylees in the United States. *Migration Information Source.* https://www.migrationpolicy.org/article/refugees-and-asylees-united-states

About the Authors

Patricia Arredondo, EdD, has dedicated her career to social justice and multicultural counseling. She served as president of the American Counseling Association (ACA) and the Association for Multicultural Counseling and Development and is a founding member of Counselors for Social Justice. Her scholarship interests and publications address immigrant and Latinx mental health; cultural competencies in research, education, and practice; women's leadership; and diversity in the workplace. A daughter of an immigrant father and maternal immigrant grandparents from Mexico, she has had a long-term interest in advancing positive findings about immigrant resiliency. A higher education administrator for 15 years, since 2016 she has been president of the Arredondo Advisory Group, collaborating with organizations to embed diversity, equity, inclusion, and belonging practices.

Mary L. Fawcett, PhD, is a professor of counselor education at Winona State University. She has been engaged in teaching for 24 years, has practiced counseling for 15 years, and has published a variety of articles and a book on multicultural counseling competencies. Dr. Fawcett is past president of the Minnesota Counseling Association and has been an active member of ACA and the Association for Counselor Education and Supervision for 35 years. She has a special interest in multicultural counseling competencies and has conducted research with immigrants and refugees in Minnesota. She received her doctorate at the University of South Carolina. Dr. Fawcett has served as director of counseling services and has provided clinical mental health counseling in a variety of clinical settings and via telehealth.

Dawnette L. Cigrand, PhD, is a professor and department chair of counselor education at Winona State University. She is a licensed school counselor and past president of the Minnesota School Counselor Association. Her volunteerism involves advocating for and supporting the work of school counselors in the state of Minnesota to help K–12 students develop academic, career, and social-emotional competencies. She has conducted research with immigrants and refugees in Minnesota and is a staunch social justice advocate. Her PhD is from the University of Iowa.

Sandra Bertram Grant earned her BA as a double major in psychology and sociology from the University of Kansas. She then completed her MEd in counseling psychology at the University of Missouri before pursuing her PhD in counseling psychology at the University of Denver. She specializes in Latine psychology, reducing inequities in mental health care through clinical practice and advocacy, increasing access to quality services, and growing representation in the field.

Rieko Miyakuni, PhD, is an Okinawan native and has been teaching in the Counselor Education Department at Winona State University since 2019. Her research interests include critical consciousness and consciousness-raising among students of color, counselors-in-training, and counselor educators. She completed her master's degree in counseling from Marshall University and an EdD in counselor education and supervision at Governors State University. She specializes in working with youth and families and supervised intensive outpatient programs in both urban and rural areas of West Virginia. She is a twice F-1 student and H-1B worker who experienced a glimpse of the U.S. immigration complexity.

Dariyan Adams holds a BA in psychology with a minor in family consumer science from Minnesota State University, Mankato. Currently, she is pursuing a master's degree with a dual focus in school counseling and clinical mental health counseling at Winona State University. Her interests include multicultural counseling competencies, racial and ethnic identity development, and the developing of effective school counseling interventions for students of color. She is passionate about advocating for equitable resources and programs for individuals from diverse cultural backgrounds, placing special emphasis on social justice and advocacy.

▪

PART I

Context, Competencies, and Data to Ground Counseling Practices

Chapter 1

Social Justice and Cultural Competency Frameworks for Counseling With Immigrants and Refugees

The mindset for counseling with immigrants and refugees in the United States must be informed by the historical and contemporary inequities and marginalization they experience as individuals and families (Bemak & Chung, 2021). The counseling profession has advanced frameworks to ground our work to address inequities as educators, researchers, and clinicians in an increasingly diverse society. Social justice movements in the United States and in other countries, as well as the Civil Rights Act of 1964, were pivotal to identifying gaps in the preparation and practice of counselors. Concerns about the monocultural nature of counseling and changing demographics in the United States motivated the actions of culture-centered educators (Sue et al., 1992). The Multicultural Counseling Competencies documents of 1992 (Sue et al., 1992) and 1996 (Arredondo et al., 1996) and the Multicultural and Social Justice Counseling Competencies (MSJCC; Ratts et al., 2015) produced by professionals of the Association for Multicultural Counseling and Development (AMCD) and the American Counseling Association (ACA) continue to be used by professionals and students alike working in different contexts, domestically and internationally.

In this chapter, we will discuss the application of social justice principles and practices and the Multicultural Counseling Competencies framework as they apply broadly to the work of mental health practitioners serving immigrants and refugees. ACA ethical principles will be referenced as they also provide guiding principles for culturally responsive practices. The grounding social justice frameworks and theories for the conceptualization of affirmative counseling practices presented in this chapter will inform applications for culturally responsive practices in Part II of the book.

Learning Objectives

- Identify social justice movements as motivators to address inequities for marginalized individuals and communities such as immigrants and refugees.
- Recognize the rationale of the MSJCC to address the limitations of White, Eurocentric models and theories advanced in counselor training.

- Consider how colonizing approaches that take place in counseling practice further oppress immigrants and refugees.
- Identify key aspects of a culturally responsive counseling foundation to support immigrants as clients, including ethical practice.
- Examine the MSJCC framework to self-assess areas of counseling competence, including self-awareness and knowledge of immigrant experiences within sociopolitical contexts.
- Become familiar with social justice practices from South Africa, Latin America, and the United States that inform opportunities for advocacy.
- Recognize key terms associated with immigration, used legally or colloquially, and consider the effects of their use with immigrants, students, the counseling profession, and society at large.
- Review theoretical frameworks that could be applied in counseling with immigrant populations, namely, relational-cultural theory (RCT), the community cultural wealth (CCW) model, critical race theory (CRT), and acculturation theory.
- Discuss the case study of Amelia.

The following section introduces a self-assessment to gauge your existing knowledge of culturally responsive counseling frameworks designed to address inequities and marginalization, ethical considerations in working with immigrant and refugee populations, and the MSJCC needed to do so. This brief assessment aims to explore your current understanding of key concepts and provide a foundation for further learning. Answering the following questions will better equip you to engage with the content.

Self-assessment: Please respond to the following statements by rating yourself on the following Likert scale: *strongly agree*, *agree*, *disagree*, *strongly disagree*, or *unsure*.

1. I strive to be more culturally aware so that I can be an effective and ethical counselor with immigrant and refugee clients.
2. I recognize the social justice movements in this country that have reduced barriers for immigrants and other disenfranchised groups.
3. The MSJCC guide my counseling work.
4. I have considered the social justice issues that impact immigrants and refugees in counseling.
5. I can define key terms used to describe immigrants and refugees.
6. I have incorporated counseling theories and models (e.g., RCT, the CCW model, CRT, acculturation theory) into my practice as recommended for working with marginalized clients.

Social Justice Movements and Civil Rights

Marginalization and disenfranchisement of individuals based on immigrant status, racial and ethnic minority heritage, gender identity, LGBTQ+ identity, disability status, socioeconomic status, and educational attainment persists to this day in the United States even though the Civil Rights Act (1964) legislated open access to employment, education, and housing for African Americans and other groups. Furthermore, Title VII of the Civil Rights Act (1964) serves to protect women from sexual discrimination and harassment, while the Americans with Disabilities Act (1990) ensures access to public transportation, employment, education support, and other resources for individuals with disabilities. When people's rights are abused, social movements have taken form in this country and around the world. We highlight a few movements because of their relevance to multicultural and social justice principles and practices in the counseling profession and their influence on the promulgation of the MSJCC (Ratts et al., 2015).

"Injustice anywhere is a threat to justice everywhere. We are caught in an inescapable network of mutuality, tied in a single garment of destiny. Whatever affects one directly, affects all indirectly." This quote by Dr. Martin Luther King Jr. (1963) heightened awareness and action to counter injustices toward not only African Americans but also other oppressed groups. In the late 1960s, the United Farmworkers movement began to protect immigrant farmworkers, primarily Latinx and Pilipino, from exploitation specific to wages, work hours, housing, and workplace safety. Consciousness-raising led to grape strikes across the country with the leadership of César Chavez and Dolores Huerta (Library of Congress, n.d.). Earning a living wage has been and continues to be a social justice issue for laborers, such as agricultural workers, across the country.

Indigenous groups maintain their own sovereign nations in the United States yet still must mobilize to have treaties with the United States honored (DeLucia et al., 2021). Counselors need to know about the cultural persecution that occurred in 1857 with the Trail of Tears (Confederated Tribes of Grand Ronde, n.d.; Schurr, 2017) and in the boarding schools (Schupman, 2020) where Indian children were removed from their homes "to have the Indian taken out of them." Social justice movements that have more recently emerged include Black Lives Matter, which has expanded into a global network focused on systemic change for racial equality and the eradication of police brutality (Black Lives Matter Transparency Center, n.d.), and the #MeToo movement, which gives voice to victims of sexual harassment and assault for the sake of legal accountability (me too, n.d.). Specific to immigrants, sanctuary cities (American Immigration Council, 2020) across the country have been created through laws, ordinances, regulations, resolutions, policies, or other practices that restrict immigration enforcement and shield undocumented persons from U.S. Immigration and Customs Enforcement; they provide additional evidence of social justice actions in practice today.

Insomuch as counseling programs are established internationally, knowledge of social justice movements occurring around the world is also necessary. South Africa experienced apartheid for decades, but through the leadership of Nelson Mandela and Archbishop Desmond Tutu, there were countrywide actions to eliminate it. One such movement was called the Defiance Campaign, a large-scale nonviolent resistance never before seen in South Africa that united South Africans of all backgrounds who considered apartheid a social justice issue. Later, with the election of Nelson Mandela as the first non-White president of the country, relations began to shift and greater access to education and other basic rights was ensured for Black South Africans. Archbishop Desmond Tutu, a global crusader for South Africa, stated,

> If you are neutral in situations of injustice, you have chosen the side of the oppressor. If an elephant has its foot on the tail of a mouse and you say that you are neutral, the mouse will not appreciate your neutrality. (as cited in Brown, 1984, p. 19)

The quotation remains a call to action to people and professions; we cannot stand silent when individuals' rights are not honored.

Indigenous rights in many Latin American countries have also been attacked for centuries, dating back to the arrival of the European conquerors who enslaved the Indigenous peoples in numerous countries. Historical genocide and oppression have led to contemporary families living in poverty and others who are walking across Mexico to enter the United States to avoid violence and starvation. An internationally known social justice advocate and recipient of the Nobel Peace Prize in 1992 is Rigoberta Menchú Tum

(The Nobel Foundation, n.d.). She is credited with her interventions leading to reconciliation among ethnic groups and her advocacy for the rights of Indigenous groups in Guatemala, specifically the Mayan people (Gossen, 1999).

These domestic and international accounts of social justice movements influenced the development of the MSJCC (Ratts et al., 2015). The rationale for the competency documents dating back to 1992 is grounded in social justice principles and civil rights legislation. These accounts are important historical examples for contemporary counselors to recognize because, as a profession, we stand on the shoulders of social justice actions and advocacy that can be learned from and applied in the 21st century. The antecedents for the cultural and social justice competencies are discussed in the next section.

MSJCC

The Multicultural Counseling Competencies (Sue et al., 1992) were developed by scholars on behalf of AMCD, originally the Association of Non-White Concerns. The authors (and Dr. Thomas Parham, who commissioned the competency document) were attempting to give voice to the inequities experienced primarily by African Americans, American Indians, Asian Americans, and Hispanics/Latinos in different counseling contexts. Their rationale for a multicultural perspective in counseling was based on (a) diversification of the United States, (b) the monocultural nature of training, (c) sociopolitical realities in the United States, (d) multicultural conceptualization and research, and (e) ethical issues. The tripartite model of culture-centered awareness, knowledge, and skills was a call to action for educators, researchers, and practitioners. These competencies and standards were designed to be aspirational as well as guidelines, particularly for practitioners.

The operationalization of the Multicultural Counseling Competencies (Arredondo et al., 1996) provided greater specificity of the 32 Multicultural Counseling Competencies. These competencies were operationalized with 131 explanatory statements. Additionally, this document was inclusive of more identity groups, not just the four racial/ethnic minority groups referenced in the 1992 document. Although both competency documents were informed by social justice principles, they were not overtly discussed. Thus, the development of the MSJCC (Ratts et al., 2015) served to further articulate power dynamics in the counseling relationship and the role of context. It can be said that the MSJCC have opened new ways of understanding the synergistic nature of identities in relationship to one another.

The MSJCC framework (Ratts et al., 2015) integrates current social justice concepts to create a contextual framework that goes beyond the one-to-one counseling relationship. That is, the MSJCC framework recognizes the layers of complexity in counselor-client relationships, synthesizing the intersections of identity with considerations for dynamics of power, privilege, and oppression that exist in all relationships.

The MSJCC framework conceptualizes counselor development through four domains: "(a) counselor self-awareness, (b) client worldview, (c) the counseling relationship, and (d) counseling and advocacy interventions" (Ratts et al., 2015, p. 37). The focus on advocacy extends the previous multicultural model created by Sue et al. (1992). (See Figure 1.1.)

Counselors' MSJCC competency work includes first developing awareness of their own worldview. Awareness of one's worldview requires taking account of one's privileged and marginalized statuses and "values, beliefs, and biases" (Ratts et al., 2015, p. 38). Counselors gain awareness through self-reflection, interpersonal learning, acquiring knowledge through readings, professional development, and other scholarly opportunities in an intentional quest to learn about oneself in a variety of contexts as a part of a larger cultural community (Ratts et al., 2015). Additionally, through recognition of one's own values and unconscious biases that result from one's status, individual counselors can more likely avoid imposing them on their clients (ACA, 2014, Standard A.4.b.).

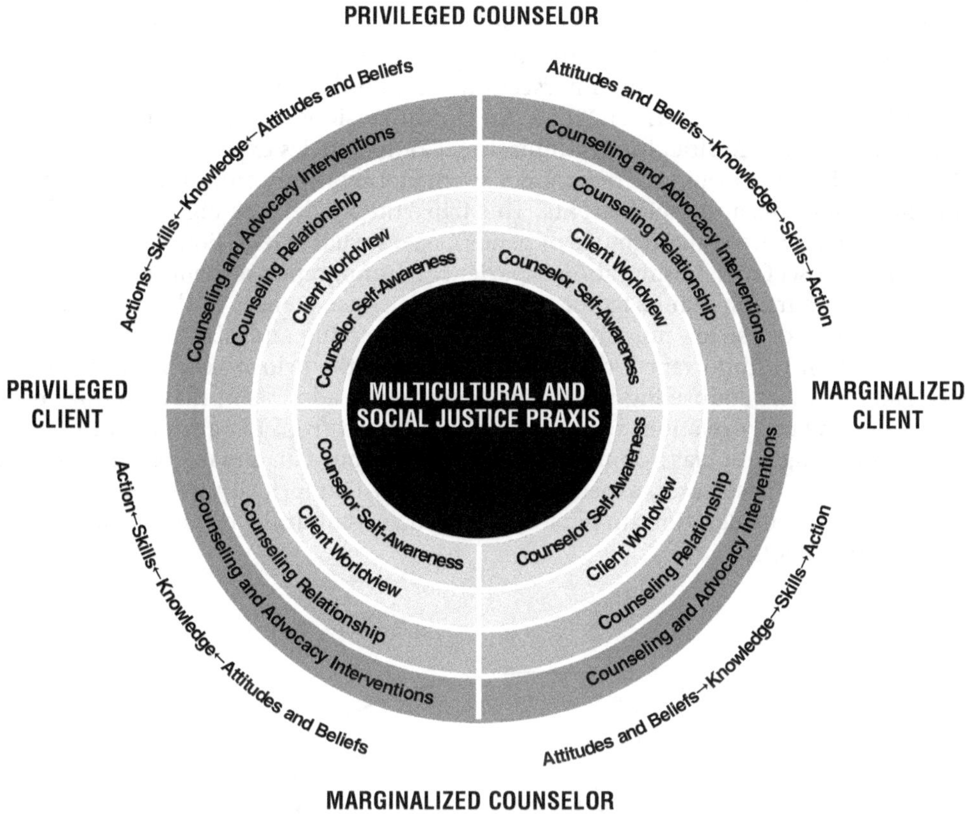

FIGURE 1.1

Multicultural and Social Justice Counseling Competencies

Note. From *Multicultural and Social Justice Counseling Competencies* (p. 4), by M. J. Ratts, A. A. Singh, S. Nassar-McMillan, S. K. Butler, and J. R. McCullough, 2015, Association for Multicultural Counseling and Development (https://www.counseling.org/docs/default-source/competencies/multicultural-and-social-justice-counseling-competencies.pdf). Copyright 2015 by M. J. Ratts, A. A. Singh, S. Nassar-McMillan, S. K. Butler, and J. R. McCullough. Reprinted with permission.

Counselors must also become knowledgeable and aware of their clients' worldview—that is, the sociocultural experiences and intersecting identities of those with whom they work. Here, the MSJCC (Ratts et al., 2015) intersect with counselors' ethical responsibilities. The *ACA Code of Ethics* (ACA, 2014) mandates that counselors learn about clients' perspectives and respect their autonomy, rights, and cultural views (Standard B.1.a.). Thus, counselors are expected to deepen their knowledge about the history of immigration in the United States and associated terminology, the varying experiences immigrant populations from different countries have encountered, and their mental health stressors and needs. In-depth knowledge then informs theoretical perspectives and technical applications that may best support counseling relationships with immigrants, which is crucial to ethical and socially just work. It is also necessary to recognize individuals' developmental status (e.g., child, adolescent, young adult, older adult) and the tasks typically required at these stages.

Immigrants' and refugees' cultural or national heritage identity, and the fluid nature of a person's identity as they navigate new and culturally dissimilar environments, must be assessed as a potential mental health stressor. The intersectionality of the client's identity is also important to consider. Intersectionality, as described by Crenshaw (1989), delineates differentiating aspects of a person's experiences based on the complex interplay of attributes such as race, gender identity, and country of origin. A person's immigration status is only one aspect of their identity, yet the intersections of an individual's identities are inextricably intertwined (Jones & McEwen, 2000). In the dimensions of personal identity model introduced in the 1996 Multicultural Counseling Competencies expansion, Arredondo et al. (1996) described the origins of this model as emanating from counseling research with immigrant adolescents and their parents. This tripartite model (see Figure 1.2) indicates that an individual's personal attributes of gender, age, sexual orientation, and so forth (A Dimensions) intersect with immigration experiences. Immigration is identified as a historical moment. It is a major change factor with multiple consequences in the postmigration period. Although counselors must recognize the intersecting and historical identities of each immigrant, it is important for the client to choose the priority each aspect of their identity takes in their counseling work. For example, an adolescent may say that being gay has upset his family relationships, or a college student from El Salvador may express anxiety about being in a classroom with a professor from Guatemala, fearing political distrust. In each of these cases, aspects of one identity take priority over others, but all are still important considerations in person-centered and culturally responsive counseling with immigrant clients.

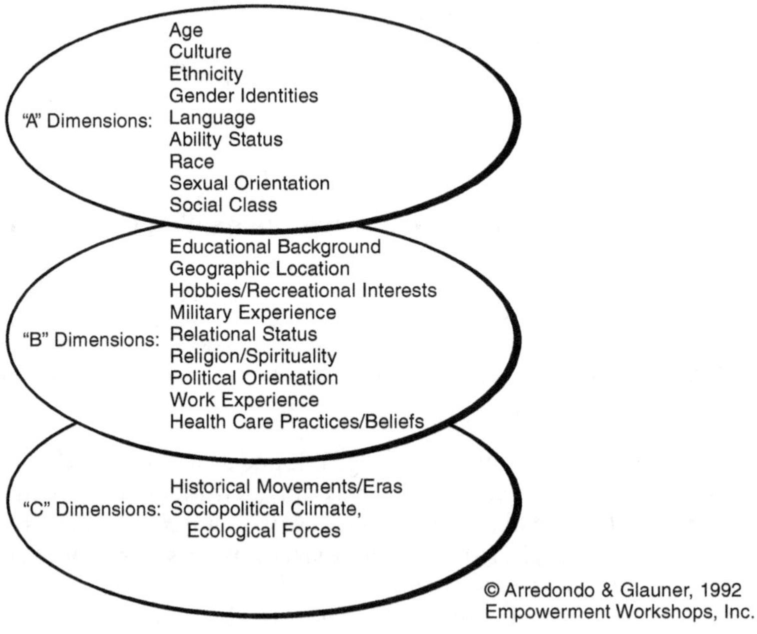

FIGURE 1.2

Dimensions of Personal Identity Model (Arredondo & Glauner, 1992)

Note. From *Personal Dimensions of Identity Model*, by P. Arredondo and T. Glauner, 1992. Copyright 1992 by Empowerment Workshops, Inc. Reprinted with permission.

In line with the MSJCC model (Ratts et al., 2015), counselors also need to explore aspects of an immigrant client's identity and to learn about the systems in which clients have previously experienced and currently navigate. With this information, counselors can respond in systemic ways to support them. It is not enough to work directly with clients in individual counseling. Counselors must consider clients' protective factors and strengths (e.g., collectivistic relationships, spiritual beliefs, resilience) as well as risk factors and contextual barriers (e.g., professional licensing restrictions, language used in school communications, access to insurance benefits). To comprehensively consider systems that impact immigrants, Ratts et al. (2015) referred to five levels of influence in their MSJCC socioecological model: (a) intrapersonal, (b) interpersonal, (c) institutional, (d) community, and (e) public policy. Forms of oppression in each of these levels exist, influencing the development and psychological well-being of clients. It is recommended that counselors explore forms of oppression and support in all systems affecting clients specifically, and then construct layers of intervention according to identified needs, such as setting goals with the individual client, while working in their respective settings like schools, workplaces, community agencies, or family systems to support clients and system change (Singh et al., 2020).

For individuals who are marginalized in various ways across multiple systems, it is important for counselors to be aware of concepts such as minority stress (Meyer, 1995, 2003) and weathering (Geronimus, 1992). Both concepts consider how systemic oppression and discrimination negatively affect marginalized groups and their mental and physical well-being over time. Counselors who consider the impact of systemic forms of oppression on individuals can move from an intrapsychic perspective, which includes focusing treatment planning on change in the individual using "office bound strategies" (Ratts & Greenleaf, 2018, p. 79), to multisystemic intervention models (e.g., the counselor-advocate-scholar model; Ratts & Pedersen, 2014). Thus, the counselor who is knowledgeable about cultural implications for the client works alongside the client as an advocate to intervene with or for the sake of the client. Similar to using a trauma-informed lens (which shifts the question from "What is wrong with you?" to "What happened to you?"), counselors grounded in multiculturalism and social justice recognize that systems of oppression have affected the client and move toward change with the client—and the systems that affect the client—in holistic ways.

Two other components of the MSJCC model require counselors to develop skills and take action to support their clients (Ratts et al., 2015). In addition to using counseling and advocacy skills effectively, counselors are tasked with integrating critical thinking skills into their work to examine disparities in privilege. This means openly considering worldviews different from their own and recognizing their own missteps in counseling relationships. For example, counselors should use their observation and assessment skills to recognize a client's withdrawal behaviors, broach the possibility of the counselor's own missteps, and then work to reconcile any microaggressions they may have committed. For instance, if a counselor refers to a client as African American, and the client corrects them and notes they are from Jamaica or Barbados, the counselor should apologize and take time to explore the client's cultural heritage and what it means to their identity. Because of issues around power, privilege, and oppressive experiences, counselors must be aware that not all immigrant and refugee clients will be forthcoming about microaggressions they have experienced; thus, counselors should periodically create intentional time in session discussions or use other methods (e.g., surveys) to solicit feedback from clients about "how they are doing."

Furthermore, counselors are lifelong learners who intentionally strive to learn from others to develop MSJCC competency and take on part of the social justice work by engaging in social justice advocacy. Social justice advocacy must include joining with immigrant voices to encourage clinics, schools, hospitals, and other community service providers to translate all documents into the preferred languages of all members of the community to make information accessible to all families. Counselors can also connect with cultural leaders to learn about their perceptions of counseling, acknowledge and rectify concerns with the profession (when possible), demystify the counseling process, and destigmatize counseling prevention and intervention practices. When the marginalization of immigrants puts them at risk when self-advocating, counselors advocate for the sake of immigrants (Lewis et al., 2003). For example, counselors can be a voice for undocumented clients who have been victims of specific crimes, in coordination with law enforcement, to be eligible to apply for a U visa (see U.S. Citizenship and Immigration Services, n.d.; Victims of Trafficking and Violence Prevention Act, 2000).

ACA Code of Ethics

Immigrants and their U.S.-born children make up a substantial percentage of the U.S. population at 26%, or approximately 85.7 million people (Ward & Batalova, 2023). Thus, counselors, who strive to provide services to people of all ages and backgrounds, must be ethically and responsibly prepared to work with the immigrant population. The *ACA Code of Ethics* (ACA, 2014) describes clear core values for our profession that inform our work with immigrants. Counselors commit to

1. enhancing human development throughout the life span;
2. honoring diversity and embracing a multicultural approach in support of the worth, dignity, potential, and uniqueness of people within their social and cultural contexts;
3. promoting social justice;
4. safeguarding the integrity of the counselor-client relationship; and
5. practicing in a competent and ethical manner. (ACA, 2014, p. 3)

Ethical practice also includes recognizing diversity and embracing "approaches that support the worth, dignity, potential, and uniqueness of individuals in their historical, cultural, economic, political, and psychosocial contexts" (ACA, 2014, p. 20). Thus, it is important for mental health professionals to recognize that their professions have traditionally oppressed immigrants, including restricting immigration by taking money from the Pioneer Fund to promote the idea of sending Black Americans to Africa, and diminishing educational opportunities (American Psychological Association, 2023). Furthermore, White, Western, and male-dominant perspectives are embedded within the counseling profession (Goodman & Gorski, 2015). In particular, counseling theories are based on North American and European colonist, male ideologies that maintain an intrapsychic focus (Ratts & Greenleaf, 2018) with underlying motives toward power and oppression, which have been perpetuated as counselors told clients "what was wrong with them" without understanding them or their culture (Singh et al., 2020).

Chavez et al. (2016) noted that some traditional theoretical perspectives ignore the subjective experiences of oppressed people, leading to the pathologizing and marginalizing of communities such as immigrants and refugees. For example, Idemudia and Boehnke (2020) provided a critique of attachment theory applications to immigrant populations, given that they do not account for pre- or midmigration contextual factors that may affect the attachment of infants and toddlers to parents who are in the midst of migrating. The problem Chavez et al. (2016) and Singh et al. (2020) identified is that a monocultural legacy still exists in which theory is arbitrarily applied regardless of culture, identity, and experiences, and human behavior is evaluated by comparing it with Eurocentric standards. Thus, marginalization of immigrants and refugees continues.

Instead, counselors must purposefully work to decolonize the profession when integrating theory into practice. Such decolonization requires counselors to critically examine traditional counseling theories that approach work with clients from a White, Eurocentric viewpoint to avoid further marginalization of those clients and to consider alternative theories and counseling practices that may better align with clients' cultural beliefs (Singh et al., 2020).

Decolonization of Counseling

Decolonization can be defined as decentralization of the status quo that perpetuates inequities "maintained by cultural, social, and economic capital of dominant groups" (Hernández-Wolfe, 2011, p. 294). Chavez et al. (2016) provided principles aligned with liberation psychology to do so. In keeping with the MSJCC approach, questioning is an essential part of recognizing marginalization practices. A part of the aforementioned advocacy work includes examining one's own practices as a counselor and the counseling profession for evidence of oppression and marginalization woven into one's education and ongoing professional development.

Recognition of the dynamics of power and privilege is important in all counseling contexts; for counseling relationships with immigrants, this is an essential assessment process (Malott et al., 2023). Traditional counseling theories, almost solely conceptualized by White males from Eurocentric worldviews, have been criticized for "blaming the victim," that is, admonishing the client for their own mental health issues, thereby causing harm (Wendt et al., 2015) to marginalized clients such as immigrants (Sue et al., 1992). Examples in the literature suggest psychoanalysis (Tummala-Narra, 2022), humanism (Chavez et al., 2016), and rational emotive behavior therapy (Terán, 2020) among others should be used with caution with non-White populations. Some authors have gone further to suggest the trend in multicultural, social justice work continues to replicate these Eurocentric frameworks rather than effect real change toward intercultural mental health practices (Goodman & Gorski, 2015). For instance, clinicians still use assessment tools that have not been normed on populations representative of immigrant clients or are in other ways biased against particular racial and ethnic groups, at times leading to inaccurate results and misdiagnoses (Liang et al., 2016; Paalman et al., 2013). Integrating multicultural and social justice concepts into required courses reportedly occurs, but the Council for Accreditation of Counseling and Related Educational Programs, the accrediting body, has not yet raised the bar to require more evidence of multicultural preparation in core courses.

Singh et al. (2020) underscored the importance of decolonizing the counseling profession through critical examination of theories and interventions that continue to victimize marginalized clients. Counselors can learn and include theoretical models containing social justice work as tenets. Singh et al. recommended RCT (Miller, 1976), CRT (Bell, 1995), and intersectionality theory (Crenshaw, 1989, 1991). RCT is highlighted because it focuses on the counseling profession specifically as well as the CCW model, which celebrates strengths in communities of color. Crenshaw (1989, 1991) addressed intersectionality and the importance of including all aspects of the person's identity, similar to what is outlined in the dimensions of personal identity model (Arredondo & Glauner, 1992).

RCT

RCT (Miller, 1976) may give counselors an additional framework to consider how contextual and sociocultural challenges can impact the development of relationships between counselors and clients (Comstock et al., 2008; Duffey & Haberstroh, 2022). With application of RCT, counselors nurture relationship growth by encouraging mutuality and empowerment through empathy, authenticity, and understanding of racial/cultural/social identities along with the particular issues they experience.

When using RCT with immigrant clients, counselors must first consider the needs of the client. Instead of making assumptions about clients' needs, counselors develop authentic relationships by listening to clients' perspectives of their needs and experiences. For example, in one study, 15 Latinx and Asian immigrants and refugees shared their premigration, migration, and postmigration experiences and perceived counseling needs at each stage of their journey (Cigrand et al., 2022). Despite managing difficult decisions and traumatic events, immigrants in this study reported an ability to set goals, persevere toward the achievement of those goals, and maintain resilience throughout the migration process despite life-threatening adversity. One might think these immigrants would require insight-oriented counseling to deal with their experienced traumas. However, a key study finding was that the immigrants reported they may not be interested in seeking counseling support for their trauma (Cigrand et al., 2022). Rather, they indicated they had other more basic and practical needs, such as finding a home, finding a job with stability, and making a livable wage. This feedback from immigrants suggests counselors may need to engage in advocacy more than traditional mental health counseling. Being pragmatic matters.

In addition to identifying ways to advocate for opportunities for immigrants to meet these basic needs, counseling professionals using RCT must ask themselves if there are other reasons that immigrants think counseling relationships are not helpful. Possibly, immigrants have not found connectedness, empathy, empowerment, or respect in counseling, or they do not identify counseling professionals as relational partners and advocates toward mitigation of oppression and social injustices. Immigrants may also be confused about what counselors really do if the term in their preferred language does not explain the meaning well. For example, in many cultures, *psychologist* is more recognized than the term *counselor*. RCT suggests that, to be fully responsive to immigrant populations and their needs, counseling professionals must remain vulnerable in the relationship, broach differences in culture and contextual experiences, and offer space for authentic and honest dialogue rather than reinforce superficial or false stories when clients feel compelled to tell counselors what they believe they want to hear to conform to societal dynamics of power and privilege. As discussed in a later chapter, narrative therapy is often one approach that best engages immigrant clients.

While RCT is focused on relational aspects of counseling, such as connection versus context and assessing individuation and separation (Duffey & Somody, 2011; Jordan, 2001; Miller, 1976), some skill and technical applications have emerged in the literature that can accompany this theoretical approach. Duffey and Somody (2011) suggested using role playing to help clients connect to others by expressing their authentic self through recognition and communication that "their pain matters" (p. 228). Specifically, counselors can help adult clients see that their pain may be similar to the pain experienced by elders, thereby fostering connections across generations through practice and empathy. Similarly, Duffey and Somody recommended revisioning past experiences with clients by reframing relational disconnection as a form of self-preservation. Ruiz (2005) made connections between RCT and Hispanic collectivistic perspectives, noting how *simpatía* (tendency to avoid conflict and confrontation), *respeto* (respect with elements of both emotional dependence and dutifulness), and *personalismo* (use of positive personal qualities to accomplish a task) focus on prosocial behaviors that foster relationships in Hispanic communities and families. Conversely, gender roles of *marianismo* (belief that Latina women should be self-sacrificing and endure suffering for the sake of their families), *hembrismo* (female strength, endurance, courage, perseverance, and bravery), and *machismo* (sense of responsibility Latino men feel for the welfare and protection of their families) can be delimiting, especially between older and newer generations, leading to disconnection. (Term definitions are from the Substance Abuse and Mental Health Services Administration, 2014.) Thus, a counselor must examine clients' perspectives on these values and work with them to consider how they may be creating connection or impasses with individuals inside and outside of the Latinx community.

Fletcher and Ragins (2007) suggested relational mentoring as a method to integrate RCT strategies with mentoring approaches. Different from traditional "gendered" mentoring roles, RCT mentoring approaches focus on seeing interdependency and the self in relation to others as two-directional, growth-fostering interactions, with vulnerability and flexibility. In relational mentoring role playing, the counselor may teach or model behaviors, and then roles are reversed so that the counselor learns from the client. Once modeled, these interactions can be emulated in familial dyads, with multiple generations teaching each other competencies. This approach also has potential for use in group counseling and school and community groups by engaging established immigrants and refugees using RCT tenets with newcomers or those who are having difficulties. Counselors must apply this practice in their work by moving toward vulnerability to recognize how their own privilege or lack of awareness may have negatively affected the development of the counselor-client relationship and subsequently work to examine examples of disconnection they may have induced for the sake of fostering mutual empathy and healing. Counselor educators can focus on empathy and repair of disconnections in microskills development, thereby teaching trainees methods to work through cross-cultural conflicts with clients for the sake of professional and interpersonal growth before entering in real counseling relationships.

CCW Model

Yosso (2005) described a theoretical model that provides counselors with an alternative way of approaching clients. The CCW model identifies six types of capital within communities that may provide counselors with a strengths-based, asset-rich perspective of clients from various cultural groups, including immigrants and refugees. CCW is a combination of assets and resources also known as capital that is aspirational, familial, linguistic, navigational, resistant, and social. Aragon (2018) applied this theory in a research study of Latina youth focusing on counterstories of college-age students to magnify the ways their immigrant parents' work ethic as laborers positively influenced their educational development. Similarly, Anandavalli (2021) made recommendations for using this approach in counseling with international students of color to recognize their strengths, such as their resourcefulness, linguistic abilities, and commitment to education. Additional applications of CCW to specific immigrant populations can be found in Acevedo and Solorzano (2023), Martinez et al. (2021), and Purgason et al. (2020); CCW and RCT are also discussed in other chapters in this book.

CRT

CRT is a methodology of teaching "the truth" about the omissions in law, education, and other systems as these relate to the oppression of persons of color (Delgado & Stefancic, 2023; Salter & Adams, 2013). According to Bell (1995), "critical race theorists strive for a specific, more egalitarian, state of affairs. We seek to empower and include traditionally excluded views and see all-inclusiveness as the ideal because of our belief in collective wisdom" (p. 901). Six basic tenets focus the scholarship on CRT: (a) endemic racism, or recognition that racism is embedded in society and, as such, is invisible to those with privilege; (b) race as a social construction, so it has no biological or genetic reality; (c) differential racialization, meaning that specific groups are assigned particular roles as it benefits the dominant cultural perspective; (d) interest conversion/materialist determinism, fostering material and psychological advantage to the majority race; (e) voices of color, or ignoring historical perspectives of those who are not of the majority race; and (f) antiessentialism, in which other forms of exclusion are utilized to oppress nondominant perspectives (Abrams & Moio, 2009, p. 251).

Tracing the history of mental health, as the American Psychological Association (2023) has done in its self-examination of racial oppression in the profession, is a start toward recognition of illuminating the "truth"—that is, replacing the narrative of a history of doing good work in counseling when oppressed groups often experienced harmful treatment (Lilienfeld, 2007; Wendt et al., 2014). It is also important to recognize that various marginalized groups, including immigrants and refugees, have experienced and continue to experience mental health services that do not take their cultural perspectives into account. To change these harmful patterns in counseling and related professions, counselor education and other professional training programs must implement a step-by-step approach of examining curriculum to include previously left-out perspectives and theories, share past examples of biased and discriminatory practices, and inclusively notice and continue to listen to voices that were previously absent in counselor education training.

Acculturation Theory

Despite attempts to use theories that help counselors make connections to clients across cultures, immigrant and refugees will experience the stressors of acculturation when they have relocated to countries with differing cultural norms, values, languages, and other practices. *Acculturation* is the dual process of cultural and psychological change that takes place as a result of contact between two or more cultural groups and their individual members (Berry, 2007, p. 543). With regard to cultural change, when two or more cultures interact, inevitably change occurs in both groups as they learn about different beliefs and practices. Through acculturation, cross-cultural groups can enjoy each other's food; learn about dress, music, language, and other forms of cultural and artistic expression; and learn to navigate social interactions. Yet, even when both groups are affected and learn from each other, they are not equally impacted. Nondominant groups (i.e., immigrants and refugees) are more likely to be altered than the dominant group (Berry, 2000).

Berry (2005) noted four types of acculturation strategies that align with the attitudes and behaviors of the immigrant and refugee groups but are nonetheless influenced by the receiving culture: integration, assimilation, separation, and marginalization. What follows are theoretical premises about the acculturation strategies; these descriptions should not be viewed as necessarily generalizable. Individuals who *integrate* can maintain relationships and navigate both cultures by compartmentalizing aspects of each culture in specific situations or by meshing both cultures in prosocial ways. When individuals *assimilate*, they move away from their culture of origin and adopt the attitudes and behaviors of the host culture. *Separating* individuals maintain the practices of their culture of origin and reject the expectations of the receiving culture. Finally, those individuals who choose *marginalization* show little interest in maintaining their heritage or making connections in the host culture (Berry, 2005). The effects of acculturation versus enculturation on the mental health of the nondominant group are complex. Yoon et al. (2013), who saw these concepts as unilinear, found positive effects of acculturation on various aspects of mental health, whereas enculturation related to positive self-esteem and life satisfaction but had an unfavorable relationship to anxiety. Once again, immigrants and refugees, as marginalized individuals with little privilege, generally have little real control over the acculturation process (see Chapter 3).

Counselors can serve in an important social justice role here by empowering clients to make their own decisions about how they would like to acculturate and advocating for their right to do so. According to the *ACA Code of Ethics* (ACA, 2014), counselors have a responsibility to advocate for clients; in the micro- through macrosystems, people with power need to stand up for the individual rights of immigrants to maintain their cultural background, replace it with the host culture, integrate the two, or dismiss them all.

Legislative policies, such as various proposals that assert that only English should be spoken in the United States, are examples of systemic microaggressions that threaten immigrants' and refugees' rights and self-determination.

Moving Forward

In essence, counselors can integrate the strengths-based, relational premises of these theories to change the narrative about immigrants by becoming knowledgeable about immigrants as people. Through a stance of cultural humility (Hook et al., 2016), counselors can openly learn about contextual factors that have affected immigrants, their families, and their decisions. Counseling practitioners, counselor educators, and researchers need to recognize the exploitation that has occurred across systems and time. As social justice advocates, counseling professionals can effect change for all people and, in particular, for immigrants and immigrant families. For example, counseling professionals can utilize approaches with immigrants in which they find empowerment to assert their own needs. One technique positions immigrants and refugees as role models through the sharing of their success stories for others to recognize their strengths while countering discriminatory stereotypes (Citkin, 2017). Counselors can also strive to help others see immigrants as role models for our country, our communities, and our children for the sake of reducing oppression of this population. Specifically, immigrants have been noted to have strong character skills, including conscientiousness and openness to experience (Bhai & Dramski, 2018), resilience and perseverance (Cigrand et al., 2022), and adaptability (Ramakrishnan et al., 2018). In line with MSJCC recommendations, counselors aspire to use a strengths-based lens and language to support immigrants.

Defining Terms Associated With Immigrants

Learning about and using cultural and historical terminology accurately to better support and advocate on behalf of immigrant clients (Bonam, 2019; Sue et al., 1992) is an example of cultural competence and respect. Counselors must also recognize how various terms, both legal and colloquial, may be used to depict, delimit, or contribute to the marginalization of individuals or groups (Caicedo, 2016) such as immigrants. The following terms are current with the publication of this book, but it is important to stay up to date with the use of terminologies because they tend to evolve and may become outdated in a short amount of time.

There remains variability worldwide about the terms associated with the migration process and people who embark on these journeys. The United Nations asserts that there is no legal or international definition for migrant, but the International Organization for Migration (IOM, 2019) defines a *migrant* as "any person who is moving or has moved across an international border or within a State away from his/her habitual place of residence, regardless of (1) the person's legal status; (2) whether the movement is voluntary or involuntary; (3) what the causes for the movement are; or (4) what the length of the stay is" (p. 132). Thus, an *immigrant* can be defined "from the perspective of the country of arrival, a person who moves into a country other than that of their nationality or usual residence, so that the country of destination effectively becomes their new country of usual residence" (IOM, 2019, p. 102).

The IOM (1992) also differentiates between voluntary immigrants and forced migration, as well as asylum seekers and refugees. *Forced migration* involves coercion, as with victims of human trafficking "(p .77)". An *asylum seeker* "is a person who has left their country and is seeking protection from persecution and serious human rights violations in another country, but who hasn't yet been legally recognized as a refugee and is waiting to receive a decision on their asylum claim" (Amnesty International, n.d.). A *refugee* has left their country of origin for fear of "persecution, conflict, generalized violence, or other circumstances that have seriously disturbed public order and, as a result, require[s] international protection" (United Nations, 1951). To differentiate between the two, refugees have been granted this legal status of protection, whereas asylum seekers are looking for protection as they enter another country or may have been granted asylee protection temporarily.

At the writing of this book, the war between Russia and Ukraine is occurring. Ukrainians fleeing the war can apply for asylum in countries such as Slovakia as asylum seekers while the country considers legal processes to establish them as refugees. Others can apply for refugee status in countries that have made the legal determination to protect refugees, such as those protections granted by President Biden in the United States to accept 100,000 Ukrainian refugees into the country (U.S. Agency for International Development, n.d.). An additional example includes migrant groups crossing the border in Mexico who are seeking asylum in the United States (Verza et al., 2023).

The term *alien* is a legal term used to describe a person who is not a citizen or national of the United States (U.S. Department of Homeland Security, n.d.) and is considered derogatory (e.g., illegal alien). *Illegal immigrant* is another term that is used but is considered derogatory by many groups. Laurence (2010) commented on the unconstitutional nature of this term, noting that the U.S. Constitution dictates that all people are innocent until proven guilty in a court of law; thus, in actuality, this term should be applied to people in the United States only by a judge. The term *undocumented* is often preferred by immigrants and professional groups (see Kwan, 2022; Laurence, 2010); it refers to a foreign-born individual who has entered the United States without inspection (and has not subsequently obtained any right to remain) or stayed in the United States beyond the expiration date of a visa or other status. Although this term is not currently considered a legal term, it is speculated that the term *undocumented* originated when Chinese people carried certificates of residence (i.e., documents) after the Chinese Exclusion Act of 1882 (Little, 2019). Undocumented immigrants are ineligible for federal, state, and local public benefits covered by welfare reform, unless a specific exception applies (Broder & Lessard, 2023).

Children who are born to undocumented immigrants in the United States are protected by the Fourteenth Amendment (also known as the citizenship clause; Section 1, Clause 1) of the U.S. Constitution and are known as *birthright citizens* or the *birthright generation* (Passel & Taylor, 2010). Compared with the birthright generation, *children of immigrants* is a broadly encompassing expression meant to describe anyone whose parents or guardians define themselves as immigrants. For example, children of immigrants could include individuals who are now adults and whose parents were immigrants. This term should be differentiated from *children in immigrant families*, which includes both first- and second-generation immigrant children (Annie E. Casey Foundation, 2023). The phrase *first-generation immigrant children* refers to foreign-born children with at least one foreign-born parent (Annie E. Casey Foundation, 2023), while *second-generation immigrant children* typically refers to U.S.-born children with at least one foreign-born parent (Annie E. Casey Foundation, 2023).

With the variation in terms and recognition that the colloquial use of terms varies, it is important for counselors to discuss preferred terms with immigrant clients and consider the implications of these terms on their self-identity and on our own perceptions and biases (see Table 1.1 for a listing of commonly used terms, both preferred and pejorative).

Counselors' use of language should reflect the social justice work we are doing with and on behalf of immigrants. The use of correct terminology needs to be incorporated in clinical training specifically because students-in-training will find themselves being prepared in settings that are not necessarily competent when it comes to this matter. Furthermore, counselor educator programs should invite themselves to make presentations to supervisors and administrators about the correct use of terms associated with immigrants.

Table 1.1

Immigrant and Refugee Terms

Term and Definition	Implication of Term
Alien; illegal alien: A legal term used to describe a person who is not a citizen or national of the United States	Pejorative; terms that criminalize migrants
Anchor baby: A child born to a noncitizen parent in a country that has birthright citizenship, which may help a parent or another family member gain legal residency[a]	Pejorative; a term that implies manipulative intention.
Asylum seeker: A person who has left their country and is seeking protection from persecution and serious human rights violations in another country, but who has not yet been legally recognized as a refugee and is waiting to receive a decision on their asylum claim	Preferred
Asylum seeker, affirmative: Asylum Merits Interview with USCIS after a positive credible fear determination, meaning the individual was placed in expedited removal proceeding, received a positive credible fear determination, and USCIS retained the asylum application for further consideration in an Asylum Merits Interview.	Preferred
Asylum seeker, defensive: The individual is facing removal proceedings before an immigration judge.	Preferred
Birthright citizen: A person born to an immigrant who acquires citizenship status in the immigrant's host country	Preferred
Emigration: Leaving one country to move to another	Preferred
External migrant: A person who moves to a different state, country, or continent	Preferred
First generation immigrant child: A foreign-born child with at least one foreign-born parent	Preferred
Illegal immigrant: A colloquial term used to describe a person who is not a citizen or national of the host country	Pejorative; a term that criminalizes migrants
Immigrant: From the perspective of the country of arrival, a person who moves into a country other than that of their nationality or usual residence, so that the country of destination effectively becomes their new country of usual residence	Preferred Preferred
Immigration: Moving into a new country	Preferred
Internal migrant: A person who moves within a state, country, or continent	Preferred Preferred
Migrant: Any person who is moving or has moved across an international border or within a state away from their habitual place of residence, regardless of (a) the person's legal status, (b) whether the movement is voluntary or involuntary, (c) what the causes for the movement are, or (d) what the length of the stay is	Preferred
Naturalized citizen: A migrant person who has completed the process to become a citizen in their host country	Preferred
Refugee: A person who has left their country of origin for fear of "persecution, conflict, generalized violence, or other circumstances that have seriously disturbed public order and, as a result, require international protection," and has been granted legal refugee status by the host country.	Preferred
Return migration: Moving back to the home country where one came from	Preferred
Seasonal migration: Moving with each season or in response to labor or climate conditions	Preferred
Second generation immigrant child: Typically refers to U.S.-born children with at least one foreign-born parent	Preferred
Undocumented: A foreign-born person who does not possess a valid visa or other immigration documentation	

Note. USCIS = U.S. Citizenship and Immigration Services.
[a]Parents of citizen children who have been in the United States for 10 years or more can apply for relief from deportation, though only 4,000 persons a year can receive relief status; having a child in order to gain citizenship for the parent/family member is a long-term and uncertain process.

One of several benefits of this practice is that clinics can change their intake forms and other documents to demonstrate respect and competence.

The following case study of Amelia is provided so that you can apply some of the information you read in this chapter. As you begin counseling relationships with immigrant and refugee clients, consider how a self check-in might be beneficial to look at privileged and nonprivileged statuses within the counselor-client relationship, potential consequences of theoretical applications, and cultural issues that may present themselves based on these relational dynamics.

CASE STUDY

Amelia Gonzalez has called your office to schedule an appointment with you for her first counseling session. A coworker had given her the name of your agency, then Amelia selected you from the list of professionals on the agency's webpage. On the paperwork completed by your administrative assistant, Amelia verbally shared she is an immigrant to the United States and is struggling with relationship issues with her partner. Other areas of concern include difficulty connecting with coworkers and finding venues to develop friendships in the community. She notes feelings of isolation and loneliness when calling to set up the appointment.

In your first session, you learn Amelia is from Spain, is married to a U.S. citizen, and is a professor who teaches global studies at the local university. You decide that RCT may be a good option to focus on Amelia's strengths and coping abilities and to determine how she envisions socially engaging at work or in the community. You also recognize that she may be experiencing some disconnection, so you decide to bring up this topic in the informed consent process, noting your limited experience counseling a person from Spain and your openness to hearing any suggestions she has to make the process positive, especially if you say or do something that would be upsetting to her.

As the counseling relationship develops, Amelia appreciates the discussion of developing self-empathy and creating meaning from problematic experiences she has had since starting at the university. She enjoys the use of visual media, so the two of you discuss constructing a picture collage to depict her experiences contrasting connection and disconnection. She loves the project so much that she decides to make it an assignment in one of her global studies classes and feels empowered to have conversations with others about cross-cultural connections and disconnections with students and university colleagues. Still, Amelia notes continued relational issues with her husband yet is able to recognize feelings of disrespect and guilt she has when she broaches examples of disconnection with her husband. The counselor suggests that, for the next few sessions, they use RCT role-playing approaches to begin work on navigating relationships with men, including her husband and her supervisor.

Reflection Questions and Recommendations for Further Professional Development

1. Using the MSJCC framework, what considerations come to mind in counseling with Amelia?
   a. How did you conceptualize your own worldview, including aspects of privileged or marginalized status and your values, beliefs, and prejudices?
   b. How can you learn about Amelia's worldview and aspects of her identity that are marginalized and privileged?

2. How would you broach the topic of microaggressions or exclusionary behaviors with Amelia so that she feels comfortable sharing her concerns with you regarding your potential cultural missteps?
3. Using RCT or CCW theory, how would you balance counseling conversations on developing supportive relationships, authenticity, and self-empathy, and identifying strengths and social capital, with immigrant and refugee clients with the reality of the exploitation of immigrants in the United States and discriminatory depictions of them?
4. What are the key identity connections between you and Amelia, and how might these be helpful to the counseling relationship?

All counselors are developing their MSJCC competency and are at differing and possibly asynchronous places in their competency regarding various cultures and aspects of individuals' identities. Consider these recommendations to continue to grow to better serve immigrants in socially just ways:

- Think about an immigrant group in your community that you may know less about than others. Identify action steps you can take to become more knowledgeable or aware of that group.
- If you are unfamiliar with RCT or the CCW model, choose one of the resources for this chapter to learn more about it. If you are familiar with these theories, consider how you would integrate them into counseling practice with Amelia, supervision of international students, or counselor education curriculum.

Summary

This chapter underscores the need for mental health professionals to be knowledgeable about social justice movements in history and today, and how they have influenced ethical practices, the MSJCC (Ratts et al., 2015), and theoretical frameworks for effective and just work with immigrant and refugee clients. Additionally, counselor awareness of intersecting aspects of the self and each client in relation to culture, power, and privilege is paramount to the development of relationships with immigrant and refugee clients and their respective communities. This means that counseling and related professions must not only work toward decolonizing counseling through the integration of approaches that value clients' strengths and assets but also recognize systems of oppression that continue to discriminate against them. Finally, mental health professionals such as counselors and counselor educators must work as individuals and as a collective to develop and maintain a strong socially just foundation for the sake of supporting immigrants' and refugees' cultural beliefs and practices, thereby improving opportunities for development and positive mental health outcomes. Simply put, to support and validate this particular demographic, the profession must become more culture centered and responsive.

References

Abrams, L. S., & Moio, J. A. (2009). Critical race theory and the cultural competence dilemma in social work education. *Journal of Social Work Education*, *45*(2), 245–261. https://doi.org/10.5175/JSWE.2009.200700109

Acevedo, N., & Solorzano, D. G. (2023). An overview of community cultural wealth: Toward a protective factor against racism. *Urban Education*, *58*(7), 1470–1488. https://doi.org/10.1177/00420859211016531

American Counseling Association. (2014). *ACA code of ethics*. https://www.counseling.org/resources/aca-code-of-ethics.pdf

American Immigration Council. (2020). *Sanctuary policies: An overview* [Fact sheet]. https://www.americanimmigrationcouncil.org/research/sanctuary-policies-overview

American Psychological Association. (2023). *Historical chronology: Examining psychology's contributions to the belief in racial hierarchy and perpetuation of the inequality for people of color in U.S.* https://www.apa.org/about/apa/addressing-racism/historical-chronology

Americans with Disabilities Act of 1990, 42 U.S.C. § 12101 *et seq.* (1990). https://www.ada.gov/law-and-regs/ada/

Amnesty International. (n.d.). *Refugees, asylum seekers and migrants.* https://www.amnesty.org/en/what-we-do/refugees-asylum-seekers-and-migrants/

Anandavalli, S. (2021). Strengths-based counseling with international students of color: A community cultural wealth approach. *Journal of Asia Pacific Counseling, 11*(1), 111–124. https://doi.org/10.18401/2021.11.1.7

Annie E. Casey Foundation. (2023). *Who are children in immigrant families?* https://www.aecf.org/blog/who-are-the-children-in-immigrant-families

Aragon, A. (2018). Achieving Latina students: Aspirational counterstories and critical reflections on parental community cultural wealth. *Journal of Latinos and Education, 17*(4), 373–385. https://doi.org/10.1080/15348431.2017.1355804

Arredondo, P., & Glauner, T. (1992). *Personal dimensions of identity model.* Empowerment Workshops.

Arredondo, P., Toporek, R., Brown, S. P., Jones, J., Locke, D. C., Sanchez, J., & Stadler, H. (1996). Operationalization of the multicultural counseling competencies. *Journal of Multicultural Counseling and Development, 24*(1), 42–78. https://doi.org/10.1002/j.2161-1912.1996.tb00288.x

Bell, D. A. (1995). Who's afraid of critical race theory? *University of Illinois Law Review, 1995,* 893–910.

Bemak, F., & Chung, R. C.-Y. (2021). A culturally responsive intervention for modern-day refugees: A multiphase model of psychotherapy, social justice, and human rights. In J. D. Aten & J. Hwang (Eds.), *Refugee mental health* (pp. 103–136). American Psychological Association. https://doi.org/10.1037/0000226-005

Berry, J. W. (2000). Sociopsychological costs and benefits of multiculturalism. In J. Dacyl & C. Westin (Eds.), *Governance of cultural diversity* (pp. 297–354). Centre for Research in International Migration and Ethnic Relations.

Berry, J. W. (2005). Acculturation: Living successfully in two cultures. *International Journal of Intercultural Relations, 29*(6), 697–712. https://doi.org/10.1016/j.ijintrel.2005.07.013

Berry, J. W. (2007). Acculturation. In P. D. Hastings & J. E Grusec, (Eds.), *Handbook of socialization* (1st ed., pp. 543–558). Guilford Press.

Berry, J. W. (2015). Acculturation. In J. E. Grusec & P. D. Westin (Eds.), *Handbook of socialization: Theory and research* (pp. 520–540). Guilford Press.

Bhai, M., & Dramski, P. (2018). *The character skills of immigrants.* Social Science Research Network. http://dx.doi.org/10.2139/ssrn.3388352

Black Lives Matter Transparency Center. (n.d.). *Mission.* https://blacklivesmatter.com/transparency/#mission

Bonam, C. M., Nair Das, V., Coleman, B. R., & Salter, P. (2019). Ignoring history, denying racism: Mounting evidence for the Marley hypothesis and epistemologies of ignorance. *Social Psychological and Personality Science, 10*(2), 257–265. https://doi.org/10.1177/1948550617751583

Broder, T., & Lessard, G. (2023). *Overview of immigrant eligibility for federal programs.* National Immigration Law Center. https://www.nilc.org/issues/economic-support/overview-immeligfedprograms/

Brown, J. M. (1984). *Unexpected news: Reading the Bible with third world eyes.* Westminster John Knox Press.

Caicedo, D. A. (2016). *Alien, illegal, undocumented: Labeling, context, and worldview in the immigration debate and in the lives of undocumented youth* [Doctoral dissertation, City University of New York]. CUNY Academic Works. https://academicworks.cuny.edu/cgi/viewcontent.cgi?article=1794&context=gc_etds

Chávez, T.A., Fernandez, I.T., Hipolito-Delgado, C.P. and Rivera, E.T. (2016). Unifying liberation psychology and humanistic values to promote social justice in counseling. *The Journal of Humanistic Counseling, 55*(3), 166–182. https://doi.org/10.1002/johc.12032

Cigrand, D. L., Fawcett, M., Miyakuni, R., Arredondo, P., & Onderak, G. (2022). A phenomenological study of perseverance and resilience through the migration journey. *Journal of Counseling & Development, 100*(2), 157–170. https://doi.org/10.1002/jcad.12413

Citkin, F. (2017, October 28). *Immigrants' integration and American women role models.* HuffPost. https://www.huffpost.com/entry/immigrants-integration-and-american-women-role-models_b_59f4e483e4b06ae9067ab922

Civil Rights Act of 1964, Pub. L. No. 88-352, 78 Stat. 241 (1964). https://www.govinfo.gov/content/pkg/STATUTE-78/pdf/STATUTE-78-Pg241.pdf

Comstock, D. L., Hammer, T. R., Strentzsch, J., Cannot, K., Parsons, J., & Salazar, G., II. (2008). Relational-cultural theory: A framework for bridging relational, multicultural, and social justice competencies. *Journal of Counseling & Development, 86*(3), 279–289. https://doi.org/10.1002/j.1556-6678.2008.tb00510.x

Confederated Tribes of Grand Ronde. (n.d.). *Our story.* https://www.grandronde.org/history-culture/history/our-story/

Crenshaw, K. (1989). Demarginalizing the intersection of race and sex: A Black feminist critique of antidiscrimination doctrine, feminist theory and antiracist politics. *University of Chicago Legal Forum, 1989*(1), Article 8. https://chicagounbound.uchicago.edu/cgi/viewcontent.cgi?article=1052&context=uclf

Crenshaw, K. (1991). Mapping the margins: Intersectionality, identity politics, and violence against women of color. *Stanford Law Review, 43*(6), 1241–1299. https://doi.org/10.2307/1229039

Delgado, R., & Stefancic, J. (2023). *Critical race theory: An introduction* (4th ed.). New York University Press.

Delucia, C., Kiel, D., Phillips, K., & Vigil, K. (2021, March). Histories of Indigenous sovereignty in action: What is it and why does it matter? *The American Historian.* https://www.oah.org/tah/native-american-history-and-sovereignty/histories-of-indigenous-sovereignty-in-action-what-is-it-and-why-does-it-matter/

Duffey, T., & Haberstroh, S. (2022). Multicultural and social justice counseling through relational-cultural theory. In D. Capuzzi & M. D. Stauffer (Eds.), *Counseling and psychotherapy: Theories and interventions* (pp. 29–50). American Counseling Association.

Duffey, T., & Somody, C. (2011). The role of relational-cultural theory in mental health counseling. *Journal of Mental Health Counseling, 33*(3), 223–242. https://doi.org/10.17744/mehc.33.3.c10410226u275647

Fletcher, J., & Ragins, B. R. (2007). Stone Center relational cultural theory: A window on relational mentoring. In B. R. Ragins & K. E. Kram (Eds.), *The handbook of mentoring at work: Theory, research, and practice* (pp. 373–399). Sage Publications.

Geronimus, A. T. (1992). The weathering hypothesis and the health of African-American women and infants: Evidence and speculations. *Ethnicity & Disease, 2*(3), 207–221. https://www.jstor.org/stable/45403051

Goodman, R. D., & Gorski, P. C. (Eds.). (2015). *Decolonizing "multicultural" counseling through social justice.* Springer. https://doi.org/10.1007/978-1-4939-1283-4

Gossen, G. H. (1999). Rigoberta Menchú and her epic narrative. *Latin American Perspectives, 26*(6), 64–69. https://www.jstor.org/stable/2633926

Hernández-Wolfe, P. (2011). Decolonization and "mental" health: A mestiza's journey in the borderlands. *Women & Therapy, 34*(3), 293–306. https://doi.org/10.1080/02703149.2011.580687

Hook, J. N., Farrell, J. E., Davis, D. E., DeBlaere, C., Van Tongeren, D. R., & Utsey, S. O. (2016). Cultural humility and racial microaggressions in counseling. *Journal of Counseling Psychology, 63*(3), 269–277. https://doi.org/10.1037/cou0000114

Idemudia, E., & Boehnke, K. (2020). Theoretical explanations of migrations, mental health, wellbeing and posttraumatic stress disorder. In *Psychosocial experiences of African migrants in six European countries* (pp. 51–81). Springer. https://doi.org/10.1007/978-3-030-48347-0_4

International Organization for Migration. (2019). *Glossary on migration* (No. 34). https://publications.iom.int/system/files/pdf/iml_34_glossary.pdf

Jones, S. R., & McEwen, M. K. (2000). A conceptual model of multiple dimensions of identity. *Journal of College Student Development, 41*(4), 405–414.

Jordan, J. V. (2001). A relational-cultural model: Healing through mutual empathy. *Bulletin of the Menninger Clinic, 65*(1), 92–103. https://doi.org/10.1521/bumc.65.1.92.18707

King, M. L., Jr. (1963). *Letter from Birmingham jail.* https://www.csuchico.edu/iege/_assets/documents/susi-letter-from-birmingham-jail.pdf

Kwan, J. (2022). *Words matter: Illegal immigrant, undocumented immigrant, or unauthorized immigrant?* Santa Clara University, Markkula Center for Applied Ethics. https://www.scu.edu/ethics/focus-areas/immigration-ethics/immigration-ethics-resources/immigration-ethics-blog/words-matter-illegal-immigrant-undocumented-immigrant-or-unauthorized-immigrant/

Laurence, L. E. (2010). The Constitution and use of "illegal immigrant." *Quill, 98*(6), 13.

Lewis, J., Arnold, M. S., House, R., & Toporek, R. L. (2003). *ACA advocacy competencies.* American Counseling Association. https://www.counseling.org/Resources/Competencies/Advocacy_Competencies.pdf

Liang, J., Matheson, B. E., & Douglas, J. M. (2016). Mental health diagnostic considerations in racial/ethnic minority youth. *Journal of Child and Family Studies, 25*(6), 1926–1940. https://doi.org/10.1007/s10826-015-0351-z

Library of Congress. (n.d.). *A Latinx resource guide: Civil rights cases and events in the United States.* https://guides.loc.gov/latinx-civil-rights/united-farm-workers-union

Lilienfeld, S. O. (2007). Psychological treatments that cause harm. *Perspectives on Psychological Science, 2*(1), 53–70. https://doi.org/10.1111/j.1745-6916.2007.00029.x

Little, B. (2019, July 2). *The birth of 'illegal' immigration.* History.com. https://www.history.com/news/the-birth-of-illegal-immigration

Malott, K. M., Barraclough, S., & Yee, T. (2023). Towards decolonizing diagnosis: A critical review and suggested alternatives. *International Journal for the Advancement of Counselling.* Advance online publication. https://doi.org/10.1007/s10447-022-09501-0

Martinez, R. R., Jr., Dye, L., Gonzalez, L. M., & Rivas, J. (2021). Striving to thrive: Community cultural wealth and legal immigration status. *Journal of Latinx Psychology, 9*(4), 299–314. https://doi.org/10.1037/lat0000191

me too. (n.d.). *History & inception.* https://metoomvmt.org/get-to-know-us/history-inception/

Meyer, I. H. (1995). Minority stress and mental health in gay men. *Journal of Health and Social Behavior, 36*(1), 38–56. https://doi.org/10.2307/2137286

Meyer, I. H. (2003). Prejudice, social stress, and mental health in lesbian, gay, and bisexual populations: Conceptual issues and research evidence. *Psychological Bulletin, 129*(5), 674–697. https://doi.org/10.1037/0033-2909.129.5.674

Miller, J. B. (1976). *Toward a new psychology of women.* Beacon Press.

The Nobel Foundation. (n.d.). *Rigoberta Menchú Tum: Biographical.* https://www.nobelprize.org/prizes/peace/1992/tum/biographical

Paalman, C. H., Terwee, C. B., Jansma, E. P., & Jansen, L. M. C. (2013). Instruments measuring externalizing mental health problems in immigrant ethnic minority youths: A systematic review of measurement properties. *PLoS ONE, 8*(5), Article e63109. https://doi.org/10.1371/journal.pone.0063109

Passel, J. S., & Taylor, P. (2010). *Unauthorized immigrants and their U.S.-born children.* Pew Research Center. https://www.pewresearch.org/hispanic/2010/08/11/unauthorized-immigrants-and-their-us-born-children/

Purgason, L. L., Honer, R., & Gaul, I. (2020). Capitalizing on cultural assets: Community cultural wealth and immigrant-origin students. *Professional School Counseling, 24*(1). https://doi.org/10.1177/2156759X20973651

Ramakrishnan, S., Barker, C. D., Vervoordt, S., & Zhang, A. (2018). Rethinking cross-cultural adaptability using behavioral developmental theory: An analysis of different migrant behaviors. *Behavioral Development, 23*(2), 138–152. https://doi.org/10.1037/bdb0000061

Ratts, M. J., & Greenleaf, A. T. (2018). Counselor–advocate–scholar model: Changing the dominant discourse in counseling. *Journal of Multicultural Counseling and Development, 46*(2), 78–96. https://doi.org/10.1002/jmcd.12094

Ratts, M. J., & Pedersen, P. B. (2014). *Counseling for multiculturalism and social justice: Integration, theory, and application* (4th ed.). American Counseling Association.

Ratts, M. J., Singh, A. A., Nassar-McMillan, S., Butler, S. K., & McCullough, J. R. (2015). *Multicultural and social justice counseling competencies.* Association for Multicultural Counseling and Development. http://www.counseling.org/docs/default-source/competencies/multicultural-and-social-justice-counseling-competencies.pdf?sfvrsn=20

Ruiz, E. (2005). Hispanic culture and relational cultural theory. *Journal of Creativity in Mental Health, 1*(1), 33–55. https://doi.org/10.1300/J456v01n01_05

Salter, P., & Adams, G. (2013). Toward a critical race psychology. *Social and Personality Psychology Compass, 7*(11), 781–793. https://doi.org/10.1111/spc3.12068

Schupman, E. (2020). Boarding schools: Struggling with cultural repression. In *Native words, Native warriors*. National Museum of the American Indian. https://americanindian.si.edu/nk360/code-talkers/boarding-schools/

Schurr, N. (2017). *Cherokee removal and the Trail of Tears*. Digital Public Library of America. https://dp.la/primary-source-sets/cherokee-removal-and-the-trail-of-tears

Singh, A. A., Appling, B., & Trepal, H. (2020). Using the multicultural and social justice counseling competencies to decolonize counseling practice: The important roles of theory, power, and action. *Journal of Counseling & Development, 98*(3), 261–271. https://doi.org/10.1002/jcad.12321

Substance Abuse and Mental Health Services Administration. (2014). *Improving cultural competence—Appendix G: Glossary* (Treatment Improvement Protocol [TIP] Series No. 59). https://www.ncbi.nlm.nih.gov/books/NBK248434/

Sue, D. W., Arredondo, P., & McDavis, R. J. (1992). Multicultural counseling competencies and standards: A call to the profession. *Journal of Multicultural Counseling and Development, 20*(2), 64–88. https://doi.org/10.1002/j.2161-1912.1992.tb00563.x

Terán, V. G., Velásquez, E. E., & Fuentes, M. A. (2020). Irrational thinking and psychological distress: A cross-racial/ethnic examination. *Personality and Individual Differences, 164*(8), Article 110102. https://doi.org/10.1016/j.paid.2020.110102

Title VII of the Civil Rights Act of 1964, 42 U.S.C. §§ 2000e–2000e17 (as amended).

Tummala-Narra, P. (2022). Can we decolonize psychoanalytic theory and practice? *Psychoanalytic Dialogues, 32*(3), 217–234. https://doi.org/10.1080/10481885.2022.2058326

United Nations. (1951). *Convention Relating to the Status of Refugees adopted on 28 July 1951 by the United Nations Conference of Plenipotentiaries on the Status of Refugees and Stateless Persons convened under General Assembly resolution 429 (V) of 14 December 1950*. https://www.ohchr.org/sites/default/files/refugees.pdf

U.S. Agency for International Development. (n.d.). *Resources for refugees and asylum-seekers*. https://www.usaid.gov/usaid-response-ukraine/resources-refugees-asylum-seekers

U.S. Citizenship and Immigration Services. (n.d.). *Victims of criminal activity: U nonimmigrant status*. https://www.uscis.gov/humanitarian/victims-of-criminal-activity-u-nonimmigrant-status

U.S. Department of Homeland Security. (n.d.). *Reporting terminology and definitions*. https://www.dhs.gov/immigration-statistics/data-standards-and-definitions/definition-terms

Verza, M., Long, C., & Lee, M. (2023, May 10). *Huge number of asylum seekers at US-Mexico border as COVID-19 restrictions end, new rules begin*. Associated Press. https://apnews.com/article/migrants-mexico-border-asylum-title-42-4a4c55366e42b53f266ff88a8602dd0d

Victims of Trafficking and Violence Prevention Act of 2000, Pub. L. No. 106-386, 114 Stat. 1464 (2000). https://www.govinfo.gov/content/pkg/PLAW-106publ386/pdf/PLAW-106publ386.pdf

Ward, N., & Batalova, J. (2023). *Frequently requested statistics on immigrants and immigration in the United States*. Migration Information Source. https://www.migrationpolicy.org/article/frequently-requested-statistics-immigrants-and-immigration-united-states

Wendt, D. C., Gone, J. P., & Nagata, D. K. (2015). Potentially harmful therapy and multicultural counseling: Bridging two disciplinary discourses. *The Counseling Psychologist, 43*(3), 334–358. https://doi.org /10.1177/0011000014548280

Yoon, E., Chang, C.-T., Kim, S., Clawson, A., Cleary, S. E., Hansen, M., Bruner, J. P., Chan, T. K., & Gomes, A. M. (2013). A meta-analysis of acculturation/enculturation and mental health. *Journal of Counseling Psychology, 60*(1), 15–30. https://doi.org/10.1037/a0030652

Yosso, T. J. (2005). Whose culture has capital? A critical race theory discussion of community cultural wealth. *Race Ethnicity and Education, 8*(1), 69–91. https://doi.org/10.1080/1361332052000341006

Chapter 2

Historical Context, Legislation, and Trends in the Migration Process

The dominant narrative—that the United States of America is a nation of immigrants, as John F. Kennedy called it—obscures the history of settler colonialism, land seizure, and elimination of Indigenous people, as well as immigration and citizenship laws rooted in White supremacy and nationalism that have legalized the discrimination and exclusion of non-White immigrants and racialized others. The United States is a settler colonial state. From the European settlers invading the Western hemisphere in 1492 as empowered by the Doctrine of Discovery, to the first permanent European settlement in St. Augustine, Florida, in 1565, to the Indian Removal Act of 1830 and the annexation of Mexican territory in 1848, European settler colonizers came to stay permanently. White men, of European descent, robbed lands and destroyed them at the most massive genocide scale in history (Stannard, 1993) to create a settler society and continue to occupy the invaded Indigenous lands (Kashyap, 2019; Saito, 2020; Wolfe, 2006).

To achieve their vision of a White nation, since the inception of the country, U.S. citizenship was equated with Whiteness, while non-Whites were subject to elimination, domination, exploitation, or removal, especially when their labors became unnecessary (Gomez, 2018; Kashyap, 2019; Ngai, 2014). European settlers kidnapped Africans from their lands and transported them on slave ships initially to what is today the Caribbean Islands, Central and South America, and Mexico, but then eventually to the southern part of the contemporary United States.

When the Declaration of Independence was signed in 1776, persons of African heritage were not included as "free men." The kidnapping, abuse, and oppression of persons of African heritage persisted, with exploitation and subjugation extending even after slavery was abolished through the Thirteenth Amendment in 1865, except for the punishment of crimes, extending slavery by another name including indentured servants and "runaway slaves" (see Blackmon, 2008). The southern states and counties implemented laws to criminalize free Black people to maintain social and racial controls and labor supplies. What ensued was convict leasing, Jim Crow, and the war on drugs in the 1960s, which created the prison industrial complex and government and corporate entities profiting from criminalization of and mass incarceration of Black and Brown bodies (see Alexander, 2012). In 1941, the federal government finally intervened and ended forced labor and convict leasing (Blackmon, 2008). Because capitalism always prioritizes cheap labor, settlers turned to migrant laborers (e.g., Chinese, Mexican, South and Central American) while excluding them from gaining access to rights for mobility, settlement, and citizenship via naturalization, which was often given to White immigrants. Today, the prison-building business is shifting from locking up Black and Brown people to "illegal immigrants" (Alexander, 2012). U.S. history is replete with events to subjugate any person who is not White.

Before working with immigrants, counselors can learn the history of U.S. immigration, and immigration and citizenship laws and understand that the current issues facing immigrants are not new. Rather, settler colonialism and White supremacy have been codified into the laws and regulations of this country and continue to function in the ways they were designed. Marginalization and privilege, two tenets of the Multicultural and Social Justice Counseling Competencies (MSJCC; Ratts et al., 2015), are embedded in U.S. settler colonization.

This chapter will provide a historical overview of U.S. immigration policy, how these laws and rules changed over time, and the trend in immigration through the settler colonialism framework. Except for Indigenous people and descendants of formerly enslaved Africans, all those living in the United States are immigrants. Some counselors may be newer immigrants of color, and others may be descendants of settlers or European immigrants who benefited from the system. Thus, the application of the MSJCC (Ratts et al., 2015) is suggested when serving the population, given that the model can provide counselors with the opportunities to continuously monitor how the intersections of privilege and oppression manifest in their professional and personal interaction with the immigrant population.

Learning Objectives

- Learn the history and patterns of U.S. immigration.
- Learn the history and evolution of U.S. immigration laws.
- Examine U.S. immigration laws through the settler colonialism framework.
- Engage in personal immigration history exploration to understand one's position and one's family's position in U.S. history.
- Develop the language to explain U.S. immigration history to marginalized and oppressed immigrants/racialized immigrants or immigrants of color as well as nonimmigrants.

The following section introduces a self-assessment to gauge your existing knowledge of the historical context of immigration. These prompts ask counselors to describe their personal immigration history if known; why, when, and under what circumstances their family decided to or were forced to migrate to the United States; and what legal restrictions, if any, they faced during their immigration process. This brief assessment can allow counselors to develop self-awareness, the first step in MSJCC competency, through recognizing and reflecting on the intersection of their privilege and oppression (Singh et al., 2020). Answering the following questions will better equip you to engage with the material.

Self-assessment: Please respond to the following statements by rating yourself on the following Likert scale: *strongly agree*, *agree*, *disagree*, *strongly disagree*, *unsure*, or *not applicable.*

1. I recognize how the Declaration of Independence did not include individuals of African or Indigenous heritage.
2. I know my family's immigration history.
3. Parents of Indigenous children willingly sent them to boarding schools.

4. I am a descendant of African slaves.
5. I have family members who were deported.
6. My ancestors are from Europe.

History of U.S. Migration and Immigration Legislation

The Universal Declaration of Human Rights: Nationality and Freedom of Movement states that migration is a universal right (United Nations, 1948, Articles 13–15). It is the fundamental freedom for all to migrate and ask for asylum. Some immigrants may choose to leave their country of origin because of economic crises, poverty, or lack of meaningful opportunities for education and employment (United Nations High Commissioner for Refugees [UNHCR], 2014). However, when examined from a systemic framework, poverty is the product of long-term civil war and repression, exacerbated by organized violence and government corruption in many countries, and the motivator for leaving one's homeland (Cleaveland, 2011; UNHCR, 2014). In fact, 58% of unaccompanied and separated children who arrived at the U.S. border during and after October 2011 were forced to leave their country because of poverty and potential and actual harm to them (UNHCR, 2014). Furthermore, scholars point out that the root causes of migration stem from historical Western colonization and exploitation (e.g., the North American Free Trade Agreement) and global capitalism that benefits only a few privileged Whites and others, all of which have created economic crises and poverty in immigrants' countries of origin (Cleaveland, 2011). Immigration has presented in waves over the years, fluctuating between peaks and downturns. The following section addresses the four major waves of immigration in the United States.

First Wave (1607–1830): Immigration in the Colonial Era

In 1607, the English founded the first permanent settlement in the present-day U.S. state of Virginia. Virginia was the homeland of a significant number of Indigenous tribes, yet Europeans colonized this area to Christianize the people and open areas for trade. Immigrants came to the United States in the first wave primarily from Northern European countries. While some people chose to leave to practice their religion freely and have better economic opportunities, some did not hold that privilege. The earliest records of slavery in America include Europeans who became indentured servants and Africans who were forcefully placed into servitude and brought to the United States.

Economic opportunities, political freedom, religious freedom, and slavery brought the first wave of immigrants to the United States. In 1798, the first anti-immigrant laws were passed by the Federalist Party, and the Naturalization Act of 1790 increased the eligibility requirement for citizenship from 5 years of residence to 14. Nevertheless, the country grew from an estimated population of 250,000 in 1700 to a population of over 335.8 million in 2023 (U.S. Census Bureau, n.d.).

Second Wave (1830s–1880s): Immigration in the Mid-19th Century

Immigrants perceived the United States as a haven and a country filled with opportunities for those willing to work for them. Ireland went through extreme famine in the mid-19th century, and many Irish people migrated to the United States, making up almost half of the country's immigrants in the 1840s and the largest ethnic group during the second wave (History.com, 2021). Germans also made their way to the present-day Midwest, seeking better economic opportunities. The California Gold Rush lured Asian immigrants and White settlers to California. Asian migrants left their country due to poverty and war, and upon arrival, they realized the tales of gold were only a fantasy. Although Chinese workers found jobs to survive (e.g., the railroad system), they experienced hostility, racism, violence, and legal exclusion.

Improvements in transportation, conflicts (e.g., war, industrialization), and the "American dream" were driving factors for increased migration. Historically, cheap labor was always needed, and persons living in poverty saw the United States as their destination. This surge of newcomers led to the first organized anti-immigrant backlash in the 1850s. Religion, racism, radicalism, and rural and economic resentment drove sentiments of xenophobia, opposing the presence of immigrants. The Civil War defused these oppositions when the United States went through a period of economic depression, and immigration slowed down. It is estimated that 15.3 million immigrants made their way to the United States in the period known as the second wave.

Third Wave (1890s–1920s): European Immigration

The U.S. population increased from 63 million people in 1890 to 106 million in 1920 (History.com, 2021). Immigration hit its peak during a time of industrialization and urbanization. The third wave came with more arrivals and different demographics—in 1880, 87% of immigrants came from Northwestern Europe (e.g., British Isles, Germany, Scandinavia); by 1900, over 80% were from Southern and Eastern Europe (Italy, Greece, Russia, Austro-Hungary). Cultural and socioeconomic diversity quickly increased in size, heightening xenophobia, or the fear/intolerance of people from other countries. Third wave immigrants were often accused of taking jobs, thought to be difficult to "Americanize," and perceived as racially inferior (e.g., Nordicism). Colorism was also a factor because many immigrants from Southern Europe were darker and did not speak English.

World War I and numerical quotas drastically led to declines in migration in the third wave, yet fear and hatred toward U.S. immigrants grew. In the 1920s, the White nationalist movement and eugenics (i.e., the Ku Klux Klan) began to rise, and the Klan's influence on immigration policy was reflected in a key legislation, the Emergency Quota Act (Immigration Restriction Act of 1921), which ended open immigration from Europe and established the National Origin Formula (Jones, 2021; Simins, n.d.). The country-specific quota system restricted future immigration to 3% of the foreign-born population in the United States, as reported in the 1910 census. As racist immigration laws prevailed (e.g., Dred Scott v. Sandford, 1856; Chinese Exclusion Act of 1882 and its extension in 1904, which made the Chinese the only racial group that was explicitly excluded and remained permanently ineligible for citizenship), the favored and older immigrant group, the Northern Europeans, made up most of the new immigrant arrivals. Very few Southern and Eastern Europeans, who were not considered "real" Whites, and far smaller numbers of immigrants such as Jews, Italians, Africans, Middle Easterners, and Asians were admitted (Jones, 2021). In 1924, the U.S. Congress made the Emergency Quota Law permanent; the law set annual quotas for each European country based on the foreign-born population and regulated entry to 2% of the total number of people in each nationality already in America as portrayed by the 1890 national census—a system that favored immigrants from Western Europe and forbade Asian immigrants. The Emergency Quota Law was effective until 1952.

Fourth Wave (1965–Today)

The lowest tide of immigration in U.S. history occurred during the middle of the 20th century (1920s–1960s), partly because of the Great Depression when immigration plummeted. Immigration rose once again after World War II ended. The fourth wave brought with it a shift in immigration patterns. The combination of high poverty, government repression, and the United States' reputation regarding economic opportunities and freedom spurred the fourth wave of immigration. Immigrants came to the United States for multiple reasons, such as escaping communist dictatorships, seeking refuge from wars in their home and neighboring countries, and better financial opportunities. Migration, however, is a complex decision influenced by more than a few reasons. A combination of "push" (encouragement to leave one's place of origin) and "pull" (draw a person to a destination) factors (covered in Chapter 3) is typically involved in the process (Lutheran Immigration and Refugee Service [LIRS], 2021b). The driving forces that prompted immigrants in this wave to migrate were, and still are, numerous and distinct.

Today, people share an immigrant experience of beginning anew in the *perceived* land of opportunity, yet a complicated relationship between newcomers and nonimmigrants exists as has been the situation in the previous waves. The United States welcomed an average of 250,000 immigrants a year in the 1950s, 330,000 in the 1960s, 450,000 in the 1970s, 735,000 in the 1980s, and over 1 million a year since the 1990s (Martin, 2014). Almost a million people arrive at a port of entry and enter the United States daily (U.S. Customs and Border Protection, 2023). The pathways to migration and naturalization, however, are generally limited to employment, family reunification, or humanitarian protection (American Immigration Council, 2021). History continues to document how difficult it can be to find resources and support when leaving one's home country. Notably, whereas migrants may voluntarily relocate, it is critical to recognize that typically, refugees move involuntarily—fleeing war, persecution, and political upheaval. Refugees cross borders seeking safety in another country. The United States admits refugees for resettlement and grants humanitarian protection; however, each fiscal year, the president and Congress set a cap for refugees (Monin et al., 2021). Refugees and immigrants must undertake the complex and expensive process of naturalization to become citizens. We expand on this process and its overall meaning in the following section.

Legislation Affecting Refugees

According to U.S. Citizenship and Immigration Services (n.d.), a refugee is someone who

- Is located outside of the United States
- Is of special humanitarian concern to the United States
- Demonstrates that they were persecuted or fear persecution due to race, religion, nationality, political opinion, or membership in a particular social group
- Is not firmly resettled in another country
- Is admissible to the United States

However, the legal definition of a refugee has fewer requirements and is contained within the Immigration and Nationality Act (1952):

> The term *refugee* means (A) any person who is outside any country of such person's nationality or, in the case of a person having no nationality, is outside any country in which such person last habitually resided, and who is unable or unwilling to return to, and is unable or unwilling to avail himself or herself of the protection of, that country because of persecution or a well-founded fear of persecution on account of race, religion, nationality, membership in a particular social group, or political opinion, or (B) in such special circumstances as the president after appropriate consultation (as defined in section 1157I of this title) may specify, any person who is within the country of such person's nationality or, in the case of a person having no nationality, within the country in which such person is habitually residing, and who is persecuted or who has a well-founded fear of persecution on account of race, religion, nationality, membership in a particular social group, or political opinion. The term *refugee* does not include any person who ordered, incited, assisted, or otherwise participated in the

> persecution of any person on account of race, religion, nationality, membership in a particular social group, or political opinion. For purposes of determinations under this chapter, a person who has been forced to abort a pregnancy or to undergo involuntary sterilization, or who has been persecuted for failure or refusal to undergo such a procedure or for other resistance to a coercive population control program, shall be deemed to have been persecuted on account of political opinion, and a person who has a well-founded fear that he or she will be forced to undergo such a procedure or subject to persecution for such failure, refusal, or resistance shall be deemed to have a well-founded fear of persecution on account of political opinion.

Examples of refugees are persons of Jewish heritage, individuals oppressed in Eastern European countries, survivors of the Vietnam and Afghanistan wars, and more recently, individuals and families from Ukraine.

Racial Requirements for Birthright and Naturalized Citizenship

As previously discussed, U.S. citizenship was equated with Whiteness (Ngai, 2014), and birthright citizenship was not even mentioned in the U.S. Constitution because European settlers, the "founding fathers," saw citizenship to be linked to those who were deemed to be White; there was no need to develop a system to regulate Whiteness (Saito, 2020). However, the extraction of the resources of the stolen lands to develop the settler society required a massive labor force as previously mentioned (e.g., slavery, convict leasing, migrant workers). To maintain White hegemony over increasing numbers of racialized people, settlers established the racial requirement of citizenship and the rule of racial unassimilability (i.e., inability to assimilate) of non-Whites, restricting non-Whites' access to the resources and opportunities of the stolen lands. This laid the foundation of the U.S. citizenship and immigration laws in response to anti-immigration sentiment against immigrants of color from multiple countries (Ngai, 2014).

Until the 1790s, each state defined state citizenship, which guaranteed voting rights. There was no set procedure at the federal level to define citizenship eligibility (Gomez, 2018). The Naturalization Act of 1790 was the first uniform rule for U.S. citizenship eligibility by naturalization, which was limited to "free White people." Nevertheless, the courts struggled to define who qualifies as "White," ultimately ruling that the concept was applicable only to those with European ancestry (Saito, 2020). An exception was made for Mexicans. It is a misconception that Mexicans are new immigrants to the United States (Gomez, 2018). The Mexican-American War moved the border between Mexico and the United States when Mexico ceded the majority of northern Mexico territory (i.e., current Arizona, California, Colorado, Nevada, New Mexico, Texas, Utah, and Wyoming), and more than 115,000 Mexicans were naturalized under the Treaty of Guadalupe Hidalgo of 1848. Because the settler colonial states required Whiteness as a condition of citizenship (Glenn, 2015), the United States deemed Mexicans to be White for the purpose of naturalization (i.e., the 1897 case of *in re Rodríguez*, in which the court upheld Mexicans as White).

While Mexicans were categorized as White merely for the purpose of citizenship, African Americans, Native Americans, and other racialized individuals were excluded. When the *Dred Scott v. Sandford* (1856) lawsuit contested citizenship eligibility for African Americans, the U.S. Supreme Court still denied African Americans citizenship eligibility, citing that African Americans brought to this country as slaves were regarded as "beings of an inferior order . . . they had no rights which the White man was bound to respect" (p. 407); therefore, whether free or enslaved, they could never be citizens but "a separate class of persons" (p. 411). Two years after the Thirteenth Amendment abolishing slavery was eventually ratified in 1868, the Naturalization Act of 1870 extended the right to birthright and naturalized citizenship to all persons "born or naturalized in the United States, including formerly enslaved people" (U.S. Senate, n.d.) as well as the right to naturalize to "aliens of African nativity and to persons of African descent" (Naturalization Act of 1870). This provision did not apply to American Indians or the Indigenous people of Alaska; they were still excluded from birthright and naturalized citizenship until the Indian Citizenship Act of 1924 (Saito, 2020). However, voting rights were governed by state law, and some states barred Native Americans from voting until 1957 (Library of Congress, n.d.-a). This act was part of a "civilizing mission," and conferring citizenship allowed the government to treat them as racial minorities rather than sovereign people (Saito, 2020).

The racial requirements for citizenship of the Naturalization Act of 1870 continued to restrict other immigrants. The racial restriction of birthright citizenship remained true for Chinese immigrants until 1943, for Arabs until 1944, for persons from the Philippines and India until 1946, and for other Asians until 1952. It was in that year that the McCarran-Walter Act (Immigration and Nationality Act of 1952) eliminated racial requirements to citizenship altogether yet replaced the barriers with a numerical quota system, which continued to apply to immigrants from the Western hemisphere (i.e., Central and South America; Saito, 2020).

Often, federal citizenship was inferior to state citizenship, which granted the power of polity or a form of self-governance (Gomez, 2018). For example, the Texas and New Mexico constitutions gave rights to "free Whites" and "citizens of Mexico," whereas the California and Arizona constitutions limited suffrage to "Whites" and "White citizens of Mexico" (Glenn, 2015). By the 1910s, Mexicans were lumped into the "non-White" or "colored" category and branded as "greasers" or "dirty Mexicans" (Glenn, 2015, p. 62). The Supreme Court ruled that state-level restrictions on citizenship and immigration were unconstitutional and designated the federal government to be the sole authority to regulate and restrict immigration (e.g., Passenger Cases of 1849, *Chy Lung v. Freeman* of 1875; Jones, 2021).

Evolving Immigration Policies to Control the Flow of Imported Labor

The U.S. immigration legal system is the contemporary embodiment of ongoing settler colonialism and is the tool for settler colonizers to maintain their power by the elimination of Indigenous people and subordination and exploitation of racialized others and outsiders (Kashyap, 2019; Ngai, 2014; Saito, 2020). To fully understand the evolution of immigration laws and policies in the United States, it is helpful to review the concept of settler colonialism and Indigenous people to challenge the myth that the United States is the land of immigrants. In truth, the country exists on the stolen lands of Indigenous people (López, 2019).

Settler colonial projects are characterized by a mass transfer of people, and their resettlement often involves violence, which can involve genocide (Wolfe, 2006). The purpose of the violence was to remove the Indigenous people who impeded Whites' expansion and permanent settlement. Another settler strategy of invading the lands was the forced removal of Indigenous people (e.g., the Indian Removal Act of 1830 [see Library of Congress, n.d.-b] to accommodate the expansion of plantation lands and claim gold discovered on Cherokee lands). Finally, settlers sought the complete transformation of Indigenous culture through assimilating American Indians into settler society. Eventually, settlers redefined themselves as the "native" inhabitants (Wolfe, 2006).

Another settler colonial project is the subordination and exploitation of racialized others and outsiders, often at settlers' disposal when the demands for labor diminish (Glenn, 2015). Settlers exploited the labors of enslaved Africans to maximize their profits and expansion of the settler society. When slavery was abolished after the Thirteenth Amendment of 1866, outside cheap labor sources became more critical, especially for the states that opposed slavery prior to 1866 (i.e., California and Oregon). A few months before the Mexican-American War (1848) ended, gold was discovered in California, which intensified the U.S. aggression against Mexico because it was critical for the United States to seize the land.

Thousands of men from the East, Midwest, Latin America, and Europe rushed to California. Many of these were Chinese men who worked in railroads, agriculture, mining, manufacturing, and reproductive labor for the largely male Western population (Glenn, 2015). Between 1850 and 1882, over 300,000 Chinese workers were recruited under contract with labor brokers for a fixed term of 7 years. When labor demands started decreasing, White American settlers' resentment toward Chinese workers increased. Chinese people were expelled during the second half of the 19th century when American settlers carried out more than 200 "roundups" (Glenn, 2015). The most notable systematic expulsion and exclusion was the Chinese Exclusion Act of 1882, which barred the legal entry of Chinese laborers for a period of 10 years and prohibited Chinese people already in the United States from becoming naturalized citizens. Since the exclusion, Japanese workers filled the spots until the 1907 Gentlemen's Agreement between the U.S. and Japanese governments limited Japanese immigration (Gomez, 2018). When the flow of Japanese workers was cut, Mexican immigrants were recruited to replace them.

The Immigration Act of 1917 banned immigration from any Asian country but made a temporary exception for Mexican workers (Gomez, 2018) as settler capitalism intentionally sought cheap and exploitable labor. Until the 1930s, the U.S.-Mexico border was not policed, and Mexicans and Americans freely crossed the border. The 2,000-plus U.S.-Mexico border miles were more symbolic than real to those inhabiting the region. After the Chinese Exclusion Act of 1882 and the 1907 Gentlemen's Agreement, Mexican immigrants became the laborer choice of the U.S. agricultural and industrial sectors. When the United States was hit by the Great Depression in the late 1920s and 1930s, competition between White workers and Mexican American workers intensified, and Mexicans became "Mexican problems." The United States hardened immigration laws to restrict Mexican workers from entering the country and carried out a mass deportation of those in the United States. Approximately 350,000 to 600,000 Mexicans, many of whom were U.S. born, were put on trains and sent to Mexico (Glenn, 2015).

Between World War II and the early 1960s, the Migrant Labor Agreement between the United States and Mexico, also known as the Bracero Program (1942–1964), imported Mexican workers on a temporary contract (Ngai, 2014). But simultaneously, the United States carried out "Operation Wetback," and the U.S. Immigration and Naturalization Service (INS) deported over 800,000 undocumented agricultural workers, many of whom were smuggled by U.S. labor contractors (Glenn, 2015; Saito, 2020). The injustices were flagrant. Between 1996 and 2003, a series of new immigration and deportation laws were enacted, elevating the militarization of the U.S.-Mexico border and intensifying surveillance of the interior of the United States as labor demands decreased. "Reduced in settlers' capitalism consciousness, Mexican workers were cheap, exploitable, and disposable goods" (Saito, 2020, p. 120) as Chinese and Japanese migrant workers, as well as enslaved Africans, had been. Today, Mexicans and other racialized immigrants remain the target of restrictive immigration despite labor demands in the agricultural, construction, landscaping, and hospitality industries.

Border State Patrol Responses to "Immigrant Issues"

The Border Patrol is a police force whose central task is racial exclusion; it was established 2 days after the passing of the Immigration Act of 1924 (Jones, 2022). Before 1924, there were customs inspectors at the border to check who was immigrating, but they were not tasked with patrolling crossing points. The current framework of border patrol emerged out of racial profiling and exclusion; the first border patrol was called Mounted Chinese Inspectors. Their job included going into the towns, identifying those who appeared to be Chinese, checking their documents, and removing them if they did not possess the right documents. Unlike the current heavy surveillance and militarization of the U.S.-Mexico border, the border was not policed until the 1930s, which may be attributed to Mexicans and Americans freely crossing the border to work and live. However, Mexicans became lumped into racialized other categories when the supply for cheap labor exceeded the demand. To exercise social and racial control, surveillance of "undesirable people" at the border and the interior of the United States intensified through immigration laws (Gomez, 2018; Saito, 2020).

The institutions that enforced the immigration laws evolved, and their role expanded. In 1891, Congress created the Bureau of Immigration in the Department of Commerce and Labor, the first field organization to enforce the flow of migrant workers (Ngai, 2014). When the department split in 1913, the bureau remained in the Department of Labor. In 1924, Congress established the Border Patrol. In 1932, the Bureau of Immigration and the Bureau of Naturalization merged to create the INS, and Congress moved the INS to the Department of Justice in 1940 (Ngai, 2014).

These institutions have shifted immigration policies and, consequently, the overall process of migration. For example, the number of immigrants who are apprehended or expelled immediately without being held in U.S. custody at the southern border remains the highest in 2 decades (Gramlich, 2022). Some southern border states spent millions of tax dollars to "relocate" immigrants seeking asylum from Latin America primarily. On September 14, 2022, the Florida governor flew 50 migrants, including young children, to Martha's Vineyard, Massachusetts (Zuckoff et al., 2022). On separate occasions, the Texas governor spent more than $12 million sending busloads of immigrants to East Coast cities, including New York City and Washington, DC, and the Naval Observatory, which is the residence of the vice president of the United States (Salhotra, 2022). Fortunately, some immigrant advocacy groups, such as the Migrant Solidarity Mutual Aid Network, met the migrants and provided them with free transportation closer to their original destinations (Heyward, 2022). Combined, these governors' actions resulted in human rights concerns for displaced immigrants because they were left without basic necessities, such as food and water, clothing for the freezing temperatures, or housing (Heyward, 2022). As of August 2023, the "exportation" of migrants continues, fostering inhumane, cruel, and life-endangering practices that affect physical and mental health.

Counselors, mindful of social justice principles, must recognize how the privilege of political leaders further marginalizes immigrants, who are already distressed physically and psychologically. In essence, the goal of this political strategy was to dehumanize and weaponize immigrants, particularly immigrants of color. These acts are sadly not original, and the use of asylum seekers as political pawns has been a tactic drawn directly from the global political playbook for decades (Ramji-Nogales, 2022). According to court documents filed by Lawyers for Civil Rights (2022), one of the plaintiffs in a lawsuit, immigrants stated that they were led to believe that by leaving Texas, they would be provided with permanent housing, stable employment, and help with the immigration process. Instead, immigrants were left homeless, hungry, and abandoned. The second lawsuit, filed by a Democratic state senator of Florida, argued that the state misused state funds to transport the immigrants, given that the individuals were transported from the state of Texas to Massachusetts rather than from their home state of Florida (Kam, 2022). This is one of many examples of how legislators have used immigrants as political pawns as the prevailing oppressive practice.

Interior Surveillance and Overreliance on Deportation as Punishment

The first deportation and expulsion laws were the 1798 Alien Enemies Act and Alien Friends Act (National Archives, n.d.), which empowered the president to expel any noncitizens, or "undocumented" people, who were deemed dangerous (Ngai, 2014). The set of four bills targeted immigrants under the guise of national security and war. Alien refers to the status that belongs to another person or place. In U.S. law, an alien is a person who is not a citizen. The Immigration Act (1891) extended the categories of deportable aliens. The first institutionalized expulsion/exclusion was the Chinese Exclusion Act of 1882. When this law was renewed in 1892 (Geary Act), Chinese people in the United States were required to obtain and carry certification of residency, or they faced deportation. Anti-non-White immigration policies continued to exist in the United States with the government promotion of negative images that immigrants of color are inferior and disposable, using national security justification to expel individuals deemed to threaten national security, which disproportionately targets immigrants of color (Kashyap, 2019). The Immigration and Nationality Act of 1952 was a double-edged sword. Although the provision eliminated racial requirements for entry to the United States and U.S. citizenship eligibility, the act also broadened the definition of deportable and excludable "aliens" and those of "potentially" subversive intent, creating language to validate possible mass detention.

Another recent use of U.S. national security to justify the removal of "undesirable" and "unassimilable" others is the National Security Entry-Exit Registry (NSEER; Kashyap, 2019). In response to 9/11, NSEER was created, and the program required Muslim men to register in the national registry. The registry resembled the Chinese Exclusion Act of 1882, which also required Chinese residents to register or face deportation. NSEER was never tested, and ultimately flaws were found, and it did not result in a single known terrorism-related conviction; however, the program led to the deportation of nearly 14,000 Muslim men after September 11, 2001. Because of the devastating consequences of the NSEER program, the Obama administration completely dismantled it before President Trump took office.

The U.S. Supreme Court has always upheld racist exclusionary acts. In the case of *Chae Chan Ping v. United States* (1889), the Supreme Court upheld the Chinese Exclusion Act on national security grounds. The court ruled that foreigners of different racial backgrounds—non-Whites—were unassimilable and would potentially pose a danger to national security. As a result, Chinese immigrants had no claim for equal protection under the law (Johnson, 2021). Since then, this ruling became the foundation for how the United States controlled immigrants of color, and the Supreme Court has not overturned the case. Furthermore, the Alien Enemies Act of 1798, which affirms the U.S. president's power to detain, deport, and restrict the liberties of any person with whom the United States is at war, is still in effect. Grounding it in military necessity, Franklin D. Roosevelt issued Executive Order 9066 and carried out the indiscriminate mass interment of approximately 110,000 persons of Japanese ancestry, of which 70,000 were U.S. citizens, to concentration camps during World War II (De Genova, 2007). The vast majority were migrant parents who were resident aliens yet ineligible for naturalization on racial grounds until the McCarran-Walter Act (Immigration and Nationality Act of 1952) eliminated racial requirements for citizenship. Fundamentally racist policies toward racialized Japanese were never applied to persons of German and Italian ancestry even though the United States was at war with the dictators of these countries.

Several cases were filed to address racist policies. In the case of *Fred T. Korematsu v. United States* (1944), the Supreme Court upheld the Japanese internment policy as necessary for the military authority to take proper security measures (Kashyap, 2019). In *Rajah v. Mukasey* (2008), the court upheld the post-9/11 NSEER programs as a national security issue, and most recently, in the *Trump v. Hawaii* (2018) case, the Supreme Court upheld the Muslim ban because the policy "has a legitimate grounding in national security concerns" (p. 560). However, it is noteworthy that Trump's Muslim ban was not the first one. In 1522, enslaved Muslims brought via the transatlantic slave trade revolted. After that, English settlers decided to exclude "slaves suspected of Islamic leanings," and the subsequent banning of Muslim slaves followed in 1531, 1543, and 1550 (Kashyap, 2019, p. 566). To expand the restriction of non-White migration and enhance White nationalism, in 2019, Trump declared a national emergency under the National Emergencies Act of 1976 and issued an executive order of the Border Wall Act as a response to the southern border crisis (Brennan Center for Justice, 2020). Support was provided by the Supreme Court, which ruled that Trump could use $2.5 billion in military funding to build a border wall along the southern border (Howe, 2020).

History repeats itself; the U.S. immigration and citizenship laws have legalized discrimination toward Asian Americans and people of Asian ancestry who have been deemed to be perpetual foreigners and enemies. Arab Americans, Muslims, and persons of Arab ancestry and Muslim heritage were viewed as foreign, enemies, and potential terrorists. South and Central Americans and Mexican Americans are viewed as illegal, exploitable/disposable laborers, and thus deportable (De Genova, 2007; Saito, 2001). For counselors aspiring to apply social justice principles and practices, it is imperative to understand that racism and White supremacy have been coded into U.S. immigration laws and across institutions. Counselors also need to recognize that family separations as a result of deportations harm quality of life and mental well-being.

Biden Administration's New Immigration Policies

The prevalence of immigration policy concerns was brought to light when the Biden administration (2021–2024) introduced a new policy regarding Haitian, Cuban, Nicaraguan, and Venezuelan immigrants. Previously, during the COVID-19 pandemic, the Trump administration enforced Title 42, which deals with public health, social welfare, and civil rights (García, 2023). The law empowers federal health authorities to prohibit migrants from entering the country if it is determined that doing so could prevent the spread of contagious diseases (Gramlich, 2022). In March 2020, the Trump administration enacted this clause, which was controversial, and many immigration and humanitarian groups have since accused the Trump administration of using the COVID-19 pandemic as a pretext to deny thousands of migrants the chance for humanitarian relief through asylum (García, 2023).

U.S. settler colonialism has always exploited poor countries. In response to these and other issues, the Biden administration announced new immigration policies in January 2023 that would limit the number of asylum claims at the southern border, while also expanding the use of Title 42 that was put into place during the Trump administration. This clause will allow nationals of Cuba, Haiti, Nicaragua, and Venezuela and their immediate family members to request entry to the United States through a parole program (U.S. Embassy in Cuba, n.d.). Asylum seekers who fail to apply for the parole program and attempt to cross the southern border will be denied entry, will be returned to Mexico, and will be ineligible to apply for the program in the future (U.S. Embassy in Cuba, n.d.). This new policy will be used to push thousands of Cuban, Haitian, Nicaraguan, and Venezuelan immigrants back over the southern border into Mexico while increasing the number of legal pathways for immigrants from these homelands to enter the United States with proper assessment and documentation. It is complicated, however, as most migrants may not be familiar with the program's restriction for future entry. To be accepted through the application process, individuals looking to migrate to the United States had to apply electronically from their homeland for a visa and work permit, show that they had U.S.-based sponsors to support them, have a clean criminal record, undergo a background check, complete vaccinations, and fulfill other public health requirements (U.S. Embassy in Cuba, n.d.).

Sanctuary Cities

In the 1980s, as millions of migrants fled from the civil wars in Central America, a network of religious organizations stepped up to offer safe harbor to immigrants, such as temporary shelter and protection from deportation (National Conference of State Legislatures, 2019). As of March 2021, 11 states claim sanctuary status (LIRS, 2021a). Sanctuary cities are municipal jurisdictions that hold official or unofficial policies that promote human rights and the separation of local and federal laws, encouraging communities to grow with the support of immigrants. These cities discourage closed borders, detention, and deportation, using local resources to solve local problems. A few examples of sanctuary cities include Chicago, New York City, San Franciso, San Jose, and Washington, DC. Sanctuary cities maintain respect for humanity, a fundamental American value.

A specific example is San Jose, California. Like many other sanctuary cities, San Jose has policies that forbid city-level officials from inquiring about immigration status based on actual or perceived immigration status or limit their cooperation with the U.S. Immigration and Customs Enforcement (ICE), although they do not actively prevent the federal officials from carrying out immigration enforcement duties (see American Immigration Council, 2020; "California Is Now a Sanctuary State," n.d.). San Jose became the first city to join other states to sue the Trump administration over the decision to terminate the Deferred Action for Childhood Arrivals (DACA) program (County of Santa Clara, n.d.) and set up a 24-hour rapid response hotline in Santa Clara County that allows people to report ICE raids. Enacting sanctuary jurisdiction is meant to increase wellness and provide a safer environment for undocumented immigrants and their families so that they can better adjust to a new society.

Notably, sanctuary policies have shown positive effects on local jurisdictions (e.g., LIRS, 2021a; Otsu, 2021; Park et al., 2023). For instance, data suggest that crime is statistically lower in sanctuary counties compared with nonsanctuary counties (Kortsha, 2022). A study found that per 10,000 crimes committed, on average, there are 36 fewer in sanctuary counties compared with nonsanctuary counties (Center for American Progress, 2017). Economies are also stronger in sanctuary counties—from less poverty and reliance on public assistance to higher labor force participation and lower unemployment. A study conducted by Houston et al. (2022) found that immigrants regarded sanctuary policies as positive, reducing fear, alleviating stress, and raising awareness about issues immigrants face (e.g., housing, health care). Yet, participants interpreted these benefits with caution, noting the dangers that persist for immigrants within sanctuary cities (Houston et al., 2022).

Many immigration reform advocates say that the immigration system is broken. The system, however, is not broken. Rather, it is working as it is intended to work—to exclude, not include (Walia, 2013). Similarly, the undocumented population was not created by mistake; it is the result of ongoing settler colonialism. Since the inception of the country, the United States has equated Whiteness with citizenship; restrictions have been placed on citizenship, with immigration serving the interests of settlers to maintain White hegemony of the stolen lands from Indigenous groups and the seized lands of Mexico (Saito, 2020). Settler colonialism is not an event but a process that is ongoing (Wolfe, 2006).

Counselors must acknowledge that settlers are not immigrants. Settlers came to take over the land of Indigenous people and create their settler society at the great expense of Indigenous lives and the ongoing subordination and exploitation of racialized others. To accomplish this, counselors, especially those who are White and newly immigrated, should reflect on current immigration enforcement as a settler colonial project. The cruelest form of settler colonialism and immigration policies that affect undocumented immigrants is deportation, with devastating consequences for the individuals who are deported in addition to their families, friends, and employers (Penava, 2022; Ray, 2021).

The Johnson-Reed Act (1924), the first law on national origin quota, introduced the visa system to keep track of the quota. As previously noted, it is critical to remember that undocumented people were not created accidentally; they result from settler capitalism and racist immigration policies.

The following section introduces Pedro. Our aim with this case study is to provide a practical example for readers to apply the information presented in this chapter while considering their roles as therapists and advocates.

CASE STUDY

Pedro migrated to the United States in 2021 when his family fled violence in El Salvador. They moved to the Los Angeles area. He never knew that he was undocumented until his parents broke the news that he lacked legal status when he tried to apply for federal scholarships to pay his college tuition. Only Pedro's closest friends knew about his immigration status. Pedro shares a recent situation in which people speak over him. He experiences excessive performance monitoring in his courses, and people make insensitive jokes and stereotype him. In effect, he is describing acts of racial microaggressions. However, he notes that his biggest fear is deportation, particularly amid a complicated political climate in the United States. He is constantly worried that people will report him and his family to ICE and feels stressed about his financial situation. He worries so much that his grades have started dropping, and because he prefers to stay home, he has avoided spending time with his friends. His family is also concerned about his emotional changes, he reports. He is withdrawn, irritable, and sleeping a lot more than usual.

Reflection Questions and Recommendations for Further Professional Development

1. What is your assessment of Pedro's situation?
2. What do you know about Pedro's home country, El Salvador?
3. How can racism and discrimination impact Pedro's psychosocial adjustment?
4. How will Pedro's legal status affect access to education and employment?
5. What are social and psychological resources that may support Pedro at this time?
6. What are connecting points for you and Pedro as you work to build a counseling relationship?

Additionally,

7. Research and help clients develop critical consciousness by understanding the history of immigration and immigration laws (e.g., Kraut, 2016) because it can equip clients with advocacy skills and knowledge to help them learn the origin of the United States (e.g., American Indian Alliance Law Center, n.d.) and the ongoing settler colonial project of removing racialized others.
8. Reflect on your own migration history, if known. Answer the prompts in the following journal article. Look for and identify your colleagues to create space to reflect together and start building your network of advocates: Kashyap, M. B. (2019). Unsettling immigration laws: Settler colonialism and the U.S. immigration legal system. *Fordham Urban Law Journal, 46(3)*, 548–579. https://ir.lawnet.fordham.edu/cgi/viewcontent.cgi?article=2761&context=ulj

Summary

The focus on historical and contemporary legislation at federal and state levels points to the structural barriers and simultaneously to the oppression of immigrants. As has been described, capitalism and White nationalism led to the settler colonial framework that has disadvantaged and exploited immigrants of color or other undesirable immigrants and refugees for centuries. The contributions of the immigrant labor force drive the economy of the country, but there are many examples of how immigrant workers have been exploited, mistreated, deported, and otherwise not valued as human beings. The majority of counseling students likely know little about immigration history and legislation in the United States because it is not often taught, except perhaps in a multicultural counseling course.

According to the MSJCC (Ratts et al., 2015), "privileged and marginalized counselors intervene with, and on behalf of, clients at the intrapersonal, interpersonal, institutional, community, public policy, and international/global levels" (p. 11). With the accountings in this chapter, counselors may now be better prepared to assess the degree to which historical events contribute to the presenting problems of clients of immigrant heritage (Ratts et al., 2015). It is impossible to fully understand the challenges faced by immigrants without attending to the ways in which the U.S. immigration and citizenship laws have evolved and maintain White hegemony, but there are resources.

Cadenas et al. (2022) developed a three-part webinar training curriculum for counselors, which provides (a) a historical overview of immigration policies and ongoing changes in the policies and its consequences, (b) psychotherapy strategies for working with undocumented immigrants, and (c) strategies for building community support. Incorporating reflective prompts of personal immigration history to increase awareness about attitudes and beliefs with training content that provides knowledge can help privileged and marginalized counselors to develop skills to take social justice action. For instance, the use of inclusive language can be a critical skill when working with an immigrant population that often does not have access to many needed resources. Therefore, say, for example, "You may not be qualified for Medicaid, but this is Access to Care (Access to Care, n.d.) that you can use" rather than "You don't qualify for Medicaid" and leave clients without any access to resources. Counselors working with undocumented students may be able to convey that the students may not be qualified for Free Application for Federal Student Aid, but there are other resources/ways to go to college, such as colleges that provide in-state tuition for DACA students. Counselors can also connect with labor unions that are organized for and by immigrant workers.

Following the *ACA Code of Ethics* (ACA, 2014), counselors have commitments that correspond to their work with immigrants and refugees. For example, counselors commit to "honoring diversity and embracing a multicultural approach in support of the worth, dignity, potential, and uniqueness of people within their social and cultural contexts" (ACA, 2014, p. 3). This chapter presents many examples of contrary behaviors that dehumanize immigrants and diminish their dignity. Thus, counselors also need to draw upon Section E of the MSJCC on public policy: "Privileged and marginalized counselors address public policy issues that impede on client development with, and on behalf of clients" (Ratts et al., 2015, p. 13). As American history shows, the policy change will not happen overnight; however, collective actions among counselors aspiring for social justice will push us closer to a nation that truly embraces multiracial coalition.

References

Access to Care. (n.d.). *Are you eligible for the Access to Care program?* https://accesstocare.org/are-you-eligible/

Acosta, T. P. (2020). *In re Ricardo Rodríguez.* Texas State Historical Association. https://www.tshaonline.org/handbook/entries/in-re-ricardo-rodriguez

Alexander, M. (2012). *The new Jim Crow: Mass incarceration in the age of colorblindness.* New Press.

American Counseling Association. (2014). *ACA code of ethics.* https://www.counseling.org/resources/aca-code-of-ethics.pdf

American Immigration Council. (2020). *Sanctuary policies: An overview.* https://www.americanimmigrationcouncil.org/sites/default/files/research/sanctuary_policies_an_overview.pdf

American Immigration Council. (2021). *Immigrants in the United States* [Fact sheet]. https://www.americanimmigrationcouncil.org/research/immigrants-in-the-united-states

American Indian Alliance Law Center. (n.d.). *Doctrine of discovery.* https://aila.ngo/issues/doctrine-of-discovery/

Blackmon, D. A. (2008). *Slavery by another name: The re-enslavement of Black Americans from the Civil War to World War II.* Doubleday.

Brennan Center for Justice. (2020, October 16). *Border wall emergency declaration litigation.* https://www.brennancenter.org/our-work/court-cases/border-wall-emergency-declaration-litigation

Cadenas, G. A., Neimeyer, G., Suro, B., Minero, L. P., Campos, L., Garcini, L. M., Mercado, A., Paris, M., Silva, M., & Domenech Rodríguez, M. M. (2022). Developing cultural competency for providing psychological services with immigrant populations: A cross-level training curriculum. *Training and Education in Professional Psychology, 16*(2), 121–129. https://doi.org/10.1037/tep0000380

California is now a sanctuary state for undocumented immigrants (n.d.). https://www.sacattorneys.com/california-is-now-a-sanctuary-state-for-undocumented-immigrants.html

Center for American Progress. (2017, January 26). *The effects of sanctuary policies on crime and the economy.* https://www.americanprogress.org/article/the-effects-of-sanctuary-policies-on-crime-and-the-economy/

Chae Chan Ping v. United States (Chinese Exclusion Case), 130 U.S. 581 (1889). https://www.loc.gov/item/usrep130581/

Chinese Exclusion Act of 1882, Pub. L. 47–126; 22 Stat. 58, Chap. 126. (1882).

Cleaveland, C. (2011). Borders, police, and jobs: Viewing Latino immigration through a social spatial lens. *Families in Society, 92*(2), 139–145. https://doi.org/10.1606/1044-3894.4095

County of Santa Clara. (n.d.). *DACA litigation.* https://counsel.sccgov.org/high-profile-matters/daca-litigation

De Genova, N. (2007). The production of culprits: From deportability to detainability in the aftermath of "homeland security." *Citizenship Studies, 11*(5), 421–448. https://doi.org/10.1080/13621020701605735

Dred Scott v. Sandford, 60 U.S. 393 (1856). https://supreme.justia.com/cases/federal/us/60/393/#tab-opinion-1964281

Immigration Restriction Act of 1921, Pub. L. 67-5; 42 Stat. 5.

Fred T. Korematsu v. United States, 323 U.S. 214 (1944). https://www.oyez.org/cases/1940-1955/323us214

García, U. J. (2023, May 8). Here's what you need to know about Title 42, the pandemic-era policy that quickly sends migrants to Mexico. *The Texas Tribune.* https://www.texastribune.org/2022/04/29/immigration-title-42-biden/

Glenn, E. N. (2015). Settler colonialism as structure: A framework for comparative studies of U.S. race and gender formation. *Sociology of Race and Ethnicity, 1*(1), 52–72. https://doi.org/10.1177/2332649214560440

Gomez, L. (2018). *Manifest destinies: The creation of Mexican Americans* (2nd ed.). New York University Press.

Gramlich, J. (2022, April 27). *Key facts about Title 42, the pandemic policy that has reshaped immigration enforcement at U.S.-Mexico border.* Pew Research Center. https://www.pewresearch.org/fact-tank/2022/04/27/key-facts-about-title-42-the-pandemic-policy-that-has-reshaped-immigration-enforcement-at-u-s-mexico-border/

Heyward, G. (2022, December 25). *Busloads of migrants dropped off near Kamala Harris's home on Christmas Eve*. NPR. https://www.npr.org/2022/12/25/1145481615/busloads-of-migrants-dropped-off-at-kamala-harriss-home-on-christmas-eve

History.com. (2021, September 10). *U.S. immigration before 1965*. https://www.history.com/topics/immigration/u-s-immigration-before-1965

Houston, A. R., Da Fonseca, T., Joseph, T. D., & Lincoln, A. K. (2022). Challenging federal exclusion: Immigrant safety, health, and healthcare access in sanctuary cities. *Health & Place, 75*, Article 102822. https://doi.org/10.1016/j.healthplace.2022.102822

Howe, A. (2020, July 31). *Court allows border-wall construction to continue*. SCOTUSblog. https://www.scotusblog.com/2020/07/court-allows-border-wall-construction-to-continue/

Immigration Act of 1917, Pub. L. 64-301, 39 Stat. 874 (1917).

Immigration Act of 1924, Pub. L. 68-139, 43 Stat. 153 (1924).

Immigration and Nationality Act of 1952, 8 U.S.C. §1101(a)(42).

Immigration History. (2019). *Naturalization Act of 1870*. https://immigrationhistory.org/item/naturalization-act-of-1870/

In re Rodriguez, 81 F. 337 (W.D. Tex. 1897).

Indian Citizenship Act of 1924, Pub. L. 68-175, 43 STAT 253.

Jones, R. (2021). *White borders: The history of race and immigration in the United States from Chinese exclusion to the border wall*. Beacon Press.

Jones, R. (2022). *Nobody is protected: How the Border Patrol became the most dangerous police force in the United States*. Counterpoint Press.

Johnson, K. R. (2021). Bringing racial justice to immigration law. *Northwestern University Law Review, 116*, 1–22. https://scholarlycommons.law.northwestern.edu/cgi/viewcontent.cgi?article=1308&conteco=nulr_online

Kam, D. (2022, November 15). *A lawsuit against Florida's migrant flights needs changes, a judge advises*. WUSF Public Media. https://wusfnews.wusf.usf.edu/courts-law/2022-11-15/judge-lawsuit-florida-migrant-flights-needs-changes

Kashyap, M. B. (2019). Unsettling immigration laws: Settler colonialism and the U.S. immigration legal system. *Fordham Urban Law Journal, 46*(3), 548–579. https://ir.lawnet.fordham.edu/cgi/viewcontent.cgi?article=2761&context=ulj

Kortsha, M. (2022, June 13). Sanctuary practices lower counties' crime rates. *UT News*. https://news.utexas.edu/2022/06/13/sanctuary-practices-lower-counties-crime-rates/

Kraut, A. M. (2016, February 8). *Nativism, an American perennial*. Center for Migration Studies. https://cmsny.org/publications/kraut-nativism/

Lawyers for Civil Rights. (2022, September 20). *Immigrants file federal class action against Florida's governor*. http://lawyersforcivilrights.org/our-impact/immigrant-rights/immigrants-file-federal-class-action-against-floridas-governor/

Library of Congress. (n.d.-a). *Indian Citizenship Act*. https://www.loc.gov/item/today-in-history/june-02/#indian-citizenship-act

Library of Congress. (n.d.-b). *Indian Removal Act*. https://guides.loc.gov/indian-removal-act

Lutheran Immigration and Refugee Service. (2021a). *What are sanctuary cities and why do they exist?* https://www.lirs.org/news/what-are-sanctuary-cities-and-why-do-they-exist-lirs/

Lutheran Immigration and Refugee Service. (2021b). *Why do people immigrate? The different causes of immigration*. https://www.lirs.org/causes-of-immigration/

López, J. (2019). CRT and immigration: Settler colonialism, foreign indigeneity, and the education of racial perception. *University of Maryland Law Journal of Race, Religion, Gender & Class, 19*(1), Article 7. https://digitalcommons.law.umaryland.edu/rrgc/vol19/iss1/7

Martin, P. (2014, May 19). *Trends in migration to the U.S.* Population Reference Bureau. https://www.prb.org/resources/trends-in-migration-to-the-u-s/

Monin, K., Batalova, J., & Lai, T. (2021). Refugees and asylees in the United States. *Migration Information Source*. https://www.migrationpolicy.org/article/refugees-and-asylees-united-states-2021

National Archives. (n.d.). *Alien and Sedition Acts (1798)*. https://www.archives.gov/milestone-documents/alien-and-sedition-acts

National Conference of State Legislatures. (2019). *What's a sanctuary policy? FAQ on federal, state and local action on immigration enforcement*. https://www.ncsl.org/immigration/sanctuary-policy-faq

Naturalization Act of 1790, 1 Stat. 103. (1790). https://constitution.congress.gov/browse/essay/artI-S8-C4-1-2-3/ALDE_00013163/

Naturalization Act of 1870, R.S. §2169 (revised from act July 14, 1870, ch. 254, §7, 16 Stat. 256).

Ngai, M. M. (2014). *Impossible subjects: Illegal aliens and the making of modern America.* Princeton University Press.

Otsu, Y. (2021). Sanctuary cities and crime. *Journal of Economic Behavior & Organization, 192,* 600–661. https://doi.org/10.1016/j.jebo.2021.10.020

Park, I. K., von Rabenau, B., & Hong, Z. (2023). The effects of "sanctuary city" policies on the local economy: Empirical evidence from US counties. *International Journal of Urban Sciences, 27*(1), 19–38. https://doi.org/10.1080/12265934.2022.2093261

Penava, E. (2022, October 20). Refocusing deportation law. *The Regulatory Review.* https://www.theregreview.org/2022/10/20/penava-refocusing-deportation-law/

Rajah v. Mukasey, 544 F.3d 449 (2d Cir. 2008). https://www.justice.gov/sites/default/files/eoir/legacy/2014/07/25/3662.pdf

Ramji-Nogales, J. (2022, September 30). *In weaponizing asylum seekers, DeSantis & Abbott unwittingly demonstrate the possibility of safe transit policies for migrants.* Just Security. https://www.justsecurity.org/83280/in-weaponizing-asylum-seekers-desantis-abbott-unwittingly-demonstrate-the-possibility-of-safe-transit-policies-for-migrants/

Ratts, M. J., Singh, A. A., Nassar-McMillan, S., Butler, S. K., & McCullough, J. R. (2015). *Multicultural and social justice counseling competencies.* Association for Multicultural Counseling and Development. https://www.counseling.org/docs/default-source/competencies/multicultural-and-social-justice-counseling-competencies.pdf?sfvrsn=20

Ray, S. B. (2021). Immigration law's arbitrariness problem. *Columbia Law Review, 121*(7), 2049–2118. https://scholarship.law.ua.edu/fac_articles/690?utm_source=scholarship.law.ua.edu%2Ffac_articles%2F690&utm_medium=PDF&utm_campaign=PDFCoverPages

Saito, N. T. (2001). Symbolism under siege: Japanese American redress and the "racing" of Arab Americans as "terrorists." *Asian Law Journal, 8*(1), 1–29. https://doi.org/10.15779/Z38B56V

Saito, N. T. (2020). *Settler colonialism, race, and the law: Why structural racism persists.* New York University Press.

Salhotra, P. (2022, August 31). Gov. Greg Abbott's migrant busing program costs Texas $12 million. *The Texas Tribune.* https://www.texastribune.org/2022/08/31/texas-12-million-migrant-busing-program/

Simins, J. W. (n.d.). *American first: The Ku Klux Klan's influence on immigration policy in the 1920s.* Re-Imagining Migration. https://reimaginingmigration.org/historical-context-the-ku-klux-klan-influence-on-immigration-policy-in-the-1920s/

Singh, A. A., Nassar, S. C., Arredondo, P., & Toporek, R. (2020). The past guides the future: Implementing the multicultural and social justice counseling competencies. *Journal of Counseling & Development, 98*(3), 238–252. https://doi.org/10.1002/jcad.12319

Stannard, D. E. (1993). *American holocaust: The conquest of the New World.* Oxford University Press.

Trump v. Hawaii, 585 U.S. ___ (2018). https://www.oyez.org/cases/2017/17-965

United Nations. (1948). *Universal declaration of human rights.* https://www.un.org/en/universal-declaration-human-rights/

United Nations High Commissioner for Refugees. (2014). *UNHCR global trends 2014: World at war.* https://www.unhcr.org/us/media/unhcr-global-trends-2014

U.S. Census Bureau. (n.d.). *U.S. and world population clock.* https://www.census.gov/popclock/

U.S. Citizenship and Immigration Services. (n.d.). *Refugee.* https://www.uscis.gov/humanitarian/refugees-and-asylum/refugees

U.S. Customs and Border Protection. (2023). *Know before you visit.* https://www.cbp.gov/travel/international-visitors/know-before-you-visit#:~:text=Almost%20a%20million%20individuals%20enter%20the%20U.S.%20daily

U.S. Embassy in Cuba. (n.d.). *Information on the parole application process.* https://cu.usembassy.gov/information-on-the-parole-application-process/

U.S. Senate. (n.d.). *Landmark legislation: The Fourteenth Amendment.* https://www.senate.gov/about/origins-foundations/senate-and-constitution/14th-amendment.htm

Walia, H. (2013). *Undoing border imperialism.* AK Press.

Wolfe, P. (2006). Settler colonialism and the elimination of the native. *Journal of Genocide Research*, 8(4), 387–409. https://doi.org/10.1080/14623520601056240

Zuckoff, E., Clemens, L., Rose, J., Allen, G., & Drew, K. (2022, September 15). *Migrants on Martha's Vineyard flight say they were told they were going to Boston*. NPR. https://www.npr.org/2022/09/15/1123109768/migrants-sent-to-marthas-vineyard

Chapter 3

Stages of Immigration, Acculturation, and Identity Challenges

Research has contributed to our understanding about the different phases and conditions of the migration process and the lifelong effects of the postmigration phase and acculturation processes. In this chapter, we discuss the challenges faced by migrants and their families as well as strengths-based perspectives that counseling professionals need to consider. For example, immigrants and refugees have aspirations and a mindset to plan and take risks that fortify their determination and negotiation in their new country of residence; they take action. In other words, they exercise an internal locus of control (Ciaramella et al., 2022; Hahn et al., 2019). Other invisible strengths include protective factors such as faith and collectivistic mindsets and behaviors—what they are doing is for others, not just for themselves. Research points to immigrant optimism, hope, and resilience (Morales et al., 2023). This calls to mind Multicultural and Social Justice Counseling Competencies (MSJCC) skills statements reminding counselors to "acquire culturally responsive analytical skills to identify the attitudes, beliefs, prejudices, and biases they hold about privileged and marginalized clients" (Ratts et al., 2015, p. 8). In this context, if counselors hold on to negative stereotypes, they may overlook the fortitude and courage of immigrants and refugees, who are generally not privileged.

Empirical data underscore the persistence of immigrants and refugees (Ciaramella et al., 2021; Cigrand et al., 2022). As discussed in this chapter, each phase of the migration process introduces challenges to confront and negotiate. There is no shortage of hardships or difficult decisions to make throughout, yet immigrants and refugees persist to achieve their migration goals. Negative rhetoric about immigrants is often communicated via social media, and no counselor is immune to what they hear; preconceived biases can be barriers to being supportive and fair-minded. When applying the MSJCC (Ratts et al., 2015), counselors need to recognize and address the judgments they may hold. These judgments may include assumptions about immigrants who left children with grandparents or refugees who prefer to live with nonfamily members. Counselors can meet clients where they are by gaining awareness and knowledge, engaging in perspective taking, and suspending judgment.

Learning Objectives

- Analyze the similarities and differences across the three stages of migration.
- Examine decision-making processes in the migration process.
- Recognize the push and pull factors encountered in each migration stage.
- Recognize the unique challenges and changes migrants and their families face in the acculturation/postmigration process.
- Explore the complexity of and highlight the intergenerational differences in the acculturation process.
- Review factors of oppression immigrants and refugees experience, including racism and discrimination in different contexts.
- Assess and apply strengths-based interventions in counseling.

The following section introduces a self-assessment designed to gauge your knowledge on the topic of stages of migration before diving into the forthcoming chapter. This brief assessment aims to explore your existing understanding of key concepts and provides a foundation for further learning. Answering the following questions will better prepare you to engage with the material.

Self-assessment: Please respond to the following statements by rating yourself on the following Likert scale: *strongly agree, agree, disagree, strongly disagree, unsure,* or *not applicable.*

1. Immigrants and refugees have similar aspirations to leave their country of origin.
2. The stressors that push people out of their countries lessen once they arrive in the United States.
3. The three phases of migration are not time bound.
4. Immigrants are planners, goal oriented, and risk takers.
5. Both immigrants and refugees experience trauma.
6. The social justice and cultural competency framework can assist counselors in recognizing their privileges in working with immigrants.
7. Decision-making is a skill applied by immigrants more so than refugees in the premigration phase.

The Multidimensional Immigrant Experience

The three-stage model of premigration, migration specific, and postmigration outlines a framework of processes and behaviors counselors can reference when engaging with clients who are immigrants and refugees. The framework provides an overview of a complex process, decision points, and actions undertaken primarily by adults. Circumstances vary depending on the country of origin and whether the migration is voluntary or involuntary; with children, it is considered involuntary. Although the discussions will not be country specific, this chapter highlights the challenges migrants and their families often face and strengths-based perspectives that counseling professionals need to consider. For example, immigrants have a heightened internal locus of control with a mindset to plan and take risks; this anticipatory planning fortifies how they negotiate a myriad of unplanned events during their migration journey and once in their new country of residence (Ciaramella et al., 2022; Hahn et al., 2019). Refugees who may spend years in camps or must run for their lives because of warfare (as occurred in Vietnam and Ukraine) are always thinking ahead (Cigrand et al., 2022). Natural disasters, such as the earthquakes in Haiti in the last 10 years, have forced people to flee because they have lost everything. Escaping also limits their decision-making power; staying in place is not an option. There are many unforeseen occurrences at all stages of the multidimensional migration experience; thus, social justice considerations need to be recognized by counselors (Ratts et al., 2016) as they conceptualize the realities of clients in their new context.

In Chapter 2, the waves of immigration were outlined. The narrative offered the historical origins of earlier migrants in the United States and the conditions that propelled them to leave their country of origin. In many respects, many of the motivators for leaving described in the first (1607–1830), second (1830s–1880s), and third (1890s–1920s) waves have not substantively shifted, although the countries of origin and sociopolitical dynamics have changed. In the fourth wave (1965–present), the reasons for migrating to the United States point to the country's core pull factors (Armstrong, 2022). Many émigrés perceive international migration as a powerful opportunity to realize aspirations and to change their lives for the better, fulfilling their families' dreams. For instance, immigrants across the globe experience approximately 5% more positive emotions (i.e., enjoyment and laughter) and 7% fewer negative emotions (i.e., worry and sadness) after migrating to a new country (Ray & Esipova, 2018). Better work opportunities, greater security, and access to health care and education may be some pull factors that immigrants look forward to; however, the consequences involved in the three-stage process of migrating to the United States are challenging and not time bound.

Immigrants may plan their departure for a year or more, but their postmigration journey may be fraught with multiple setbacks and lengthy delays. Immigrants experience multiple stressors that affect their overall well-being, such as declines in their mental and physical health; the loss of familiar cultural ways of being, religious customs, and social support systems; and changes in their sense of identity and self-concept (Bhugra & Becker, 2005; Desai, 2023; Muruthi et al., 2023). Despite thoughtful planning, not everything in the migration journey can be controlled.

Three Phases of Migration

Migration is a process that has been broadly conceptualized and described in three phases: premigration, migration specific, and postmigration (e.g., Arredondo, 1986; Bhugra & Jones, 2001; Cigrand et al., 2022). There are motivating factors, hopes, and obstacles in every stage (see Table 3.1). Migration is not a single event but rather a series of complex events and circumstances that contribute to different types of migration experiences in every stage. In her 5-year research study with immigrant high school students who transitioned to college experiences and with adult men seeking employment opportunities, Arredondo-Dowd (1981b, 1984) conceptualized the three phases or stages of migration outlined in Table 3.1, with parallels to contemporary findings. A recent meta-analysis (Garcia & Birman, 2022) documented the stages of youth's migration journeys from making the decision to migrate; the experience during migration including psychological distress and coping upon arrival; adaptation upon arrival in the resettlement country; and the impact of social support and social networks in the resettlement country. Refugees may differ from immigrants in that they are forced to flee their home country, yet their experience is also typically divided into these three stages of migration. In fact, findings show that deleterious effects of premigration and postmigration trauma are notable for both refugees and immigrants (Sangalang et al., 2019).

Table 3.1

Motivating Factors, Hopes, and Obstacles in Phases of Migration

Premigration	Migration Specific	Postmigration
Lifestyle	Method of travel	Acculturative stress
Sense of belonging	Travel companions	Cultural differences
Education	Destination	Stress and health problems
Economic resources and stressors	Number of attempts	Loss and grief
Religious orientation or practices	Traumatic incidents	Identity challenges
Political climate and safety		Safety
War		Goals and dreams to action
Natural disasters		

Words alone do not capture the dynamic nature of the processes and experiences immigrants and refugees face. Themes such as dire decisions, resilience and perseverance, trauma and loss, adopting concealment strategies, routine victimization, and human rights violations (Alessi et al., 2019; Cigrand et al., 2022) are common among immigrants and refugees, and they are more fully discussed in the sections that follow. However, for counselors, this framework is a valuable reference to draw upon when trying to understand what immigrants and their families have gone through and will go through in the postmigration and acculturation process. Working from the MSJCC model (Ratts et al., 2015), culturally responsive counselors can evaluate presenting issues with greater insight, compassion, and their role as privileged professionals.

Premigration Stage

The premigration phase can take years of planning; it is never a snap decision, with the exception of violence, war, and natural disasters that may push individuals out more precipitously. The MSJCC (Ratts et al., 2015) encourage counselors to assess the constellation of identities and experiences that clients and counselors bring to the therapeutic relationship. Counselors should recognize the thought process and push factors that influence the decision and preparation to migrate to the United States, as well as unforeseen factors. Typically, it is not a single reason that leads to this decision, but rather a combination of push and pull factors that persuade individuals to take action. Push factors refer to the conditions or events that lead people to consider a life-changing move. Some common push factors include escaping violence, femicide, poverty, political corruption, lack of employment, environmental degradation, natural disasters, limited access to quality health care and education, drug cartels, and religious oppression (National Immigration Forum, 2019).

On the other hand, pull factors are circumstances in the destination country that make it a more desirable place to live than their home countries (Justice for Immigrants, 2016).

Some examples include safety, a desire for greater stability, freedom, better wages, family reunification, increased quality of life, and availability of basic needs and other services. Immigrants do a cost-benefit analysis in the premigration stage; for instance, they typically ask themselves, "What happens if I stay or leave?" Generally, there is predictability if one stays; leaving is about unknowns. Ultimately, the best choice is to leave with hopes of finding better living conditions and achieving life goals, especially for the family (Cigrand et al., 2022; Lutheran Immigration and Refugee Service, 2021).

For refugees, the circumstances are often out of their control. On the trek to an asylum country, refugees are concerned about improved living conditions compared with what they had in refugee camps. Similar to immigrants, they prioritize basic needs such as food, water, and shelter. They also experience underlying anxiety about the unknown future and their reception and treatment upon arrival (Crowley, 2009). Those who were put in camps as adults have to create a life with their children in these confined spaces. Individuals report being held for 10 years or more, with little control of their future, until someone one day says they will be taken to City X in the United States. Contemporary refugees all have tragic stories about the push conditions that lead them to escape. Cubans get into flimsy boats in the Caribbean, Africans stow away on ships, and Ukrainians fly, when possible, to new countries. The book *Voices of the Border* (Hansen & Robles Robles, 2021) describes migrants' accounts and is an excellent way to better understand their individual and collective experiences crossing the Mexico-U.S. border and highlights a common theme: migration as the road to salvation.

Another migrant group includes those with protected status. Temporary protected status (TPS) is a transitory immigration status for specific countries confronting an ongoing armed conflict or environmental disaster (American Immigration Council, 2023). For example, reports indicate that more than half of the Salvadoran beneficiaries, the largest group to receive TPS, have lived in the United States for at least 20 years. These individuals work, pay taxes, and have raised their families in the United States (Devereaux, 2018). Roughly 7% of Salvadoran immigrants in the Washington, DC, and Baltimore metro areas own businesses (Institute for Immigration Research, 2023). Nearly 3 million Salvadoran immigrants live permanently in the United States (U.S. Census Bureau, n.d.), developing a prominent presence in U.S. society today. However, there are multifaceted complexities around planning for the future when thinking about those who come to the United States under these conditions. Current policies fail to provide assurance of permanent residence, so the uncertainty weighs psychologically on TPS migrants and their children, most of whom were born in the United States.

The push and pull framework (see Table 3.2) offers a guide for counselors to understand some of the basic reasons a person would move their entire life to a different country. Current and historical situations in countries such as Cuba, Venezuela, and Nicaragua with dictatorships; African countries that have experienced economic downturns caused by droughts and ongoing tribal fighting; Middle Eastern or Arab countries with civil wars, such as Syria and Lebanon; and Asian countries with oppression based on religion and ethnic differences as with the Uyghur people all push individuals to leave under less than desirable conditions, often leading them to take risky departures. The MSJCC (Ratts et al., 2015) are helpful in reminding counselors to reflect on their own assumptions, their clients' worldview, their relationship with clients, and interventions that are appropriate, particularly when considering the clients' context. Push factors are all social justice issues (see Table 3.2).

Table 3.2

Push and Pull Factors in Migration (Alchin, 2018)

Factor Type	Push	Pull
Environmental	1. Inaccessibility 2. Harsh climates 3. Natural disasters	1. Safety 2. Fertile soils 3. Lack of natural hazards
Social	1. Discrimination 2. Growth of family 3. Fear 4. Bereavement	1. Good welfare services 2. Relatives and friends 3. Marriage 4. Higher education
Economic	1. Unemployment 2. Poverty 3. Cost of living 4. Taxation	1. Stability 2. Promotions 3. Resource exploitation 4. High living standards
Political	1. Persecution 2. Planning decision 3. Civil unrest	1. Freedom 2. Propaganda 3. Political asylum

During the premigration stage, immigrants thoughtfully assess available options for remaining in or leaving their home country. Emotions also come into play and manifest as fear, anxiety, stress, and physical debilitation. The push factors previously described are an essential part of their decision-making process. Immigrants hold high hopes and expectations for a better life and opportunities, yet they may also feel confused and uncertain because they recognize that they will leave family, friends, and their homeland behind. Research has consistently found that people move to the United States primarily for social and economic benefits (i.e., pull factors); however, more recent reports highlight that fear of the future is pushing them out of their home country despite increased border security and stricter immigration policies in the United States (National Immigration Forum, 2019). For example, where dictatorships persist, agriculture or farming is a reduced option, and access to education is threatened by governmental dictates for those already disenfranchised. Hope turns to desperation for survival.

The premigration phase involves planning, assessing, and hearing narratives of others who have left and are now in the United States. Guidance and advice seeking are required. Individuals turn to family members in the United States, family at home, and even religious leaders. The latter are known to pray with individuals as they contemplate their decision (Hagan & Ebaugh, 2003; Hagan & Straut-Eppsteiner, 2019). The desire and plans to migrate are merely a piece of a larger puzzle. It is impossible to explain with absolute precision the specific factors that drive each individual to come to the United States; however, it is clear that a strong interaction of drivers, including aspirations and hopes, and the push and pull factors are part of a uniquely complex scenario that fuels the final decision to migrate. The MSJCC (Ratts et al., 2015) emphasize that counselors need to be aware of the sociocultural systems in the country of origin that affect their clients' mindset, emotions, and actions in order to intervene in culturally responsive ways and not question the immigrant about their rationale for leaving.

Legislation Affecting the Premigration and Migration-Specific Phases

Getting into the United States with documented status is an expensive and time-consuming process with a roller coaster of events and emotions. For example, at any point in time, particularly in the premigration phase, applicants could receive notice that their request has been rejected, and they are then forced to restart the process all over again. This can make migration unmanageable; in fact, 60,000 people were denied entry at U.S. ports in February 2022 (Transactional Records Access Clearinghouse, 2022).

In 2021, immigrants made up 13.5% of the overall U.S. population with approximately 3.5% living undocumented (U.S. Census Bureau, n.d.). Notably, recent changes in immigration policies have made it particularly dangerous to enter the United States without documentation. Nevertheless, migration across South, Central, and North America is steadily rising as discussed in Chapter 1. For instance, the rate of migrants crossing the U.S.-Mexico border into the United States has grown at a faster pace since the discontinuation of building the border wall and the lifting of various travel bans (U.S. Customs and Border Protection, 2023). Immigration officials reported more than 1.7 million migrations along the U.S. border by the end of 2021, without accounting for those not recorded. In 2022, government agencies had already accounted for 1.2 million encounters by the end of June (McGuire, 2022).

Recently, migrants from countries like Cuba, Haiti, Venezuela, and the Central American triangle countries (El Salvador, Guatemala, Honduras)—as well as migrants fleeing the war in Ukraine and Russia—have tried to cross into the United States despite migration being inherently stressful, especially for those traveling with children. Counselors are often part of resettlement processes and require knowledge about asylum programs, resources that can be made available, and the transporting of migrants from states like Florida and Texas to other states. Although miles away from their entry point, migrants may begin to engage with counselors in New York, Chicago, or other locations. Thus, MSJCC-oriented counselors keep abreast of sociopolitical conditions at the national, state, and local levels in order to identify trauma-inducing situations.

Migration-Specific Stage

The second stage, migration specific, describes the physical activity of leaving one's home country and traveling to the United States. Involved are modes of transportation (e.g., boats, flights, walking), routes taken (e.g., immigrants from Central America leave their homes with the intention of walking across Mexico to get to the U.S. border), travel companions, and number of attempts to cross the border. Migrants from Africa, Russia, Afghanistan, and other non–Latin American countries also follow a similar route. There are reports of this mix of migrants seeking passage through Mexico to the U.S. border (International Rescue Committee, 2023; Isacson, 2022). The migration-specific stage not only captures the process of moving from one country to another but also encompasses the hardships during travel.

Although trauma due to violence, war, and natural disasters is one of the many driving factors that cause people to migrate, counselors should keep in mind that the migration-specific stage is also trauma inducing. For instance, a study found that 13% of migrant and refugee children's parents reported experiencing trauma that posed actual or threatened harm to their families (e.g., physical assault), and 90% of mothers reported fearing for their family and their own safety during migration (Ornelas & Perreira, 2011). Others report heat strokes, lack of sanitary facilities, limited food and water, and other significant threats to their physical health during their journeys (DeLuca et al., 2008). Families may be separated or face trafficking, kidnapping, or sexual violence (Mitra & Hodes, 2019).

In June 2022, a horrific smuggling incident left 46 migrants dead in the back of a tractor trailer in San Antonio, Texas (Hernandez et al., 2022). The report documented that survivors, including children, were "hot to the touch" (p. 1) and suffered from heat stroke and heat exhaustion when they were found. News accounts more regularly report on truckloads of migrants caught en route to the United States in treacherous, packed conditions. In August 2022, for instance, Mexican immigration officials discovered more than 100 migrants crammed into a truck heading for the United States, and in April 2023, border agents in El Paso found 58 migrants crammed in a truck (Eberhart, 2023; Thomas, 2022). These incidents may never come into a migrant's planning process; the trusting and desperate migrants were likely promised passage to the United States, and for some, the outcome was fatal.

"Coyotes" are people who smuggle immigrants across the borders. Migrants often take out loans as high as $16,000 to pay coyotes, often at double-digit interest rates (Janetsky & Stunt, 2020). Threatening harm to family members also occurs to ensure payment. Coyotes gross about $13 billion a year, with crossing fees ranging from $1,500 to $2,500 in Mexico (Rogers, 2022). Sometimes migrants must use their homes as collateral to pay smugglers; unable to work, they risk losing everything. Yet, these are the extreme decisions individuals take for what they hope is a "new" life. It may be tempting for counselors to judge the decisions taken by migrants given the uncertainty and potential harm, including death. Applying the MSJCC (Ratts et al., 2015), counselors should engage in perspective taking: What would they do if they were in the shoes of the migrant? Rather than being judgmental, counselors need to demonstrate empathy and support.

As previously noted, the migration journey introduces many unpredictable events. A report with data obtained from migrants (Revens et al., 2023) revealed a number of traumatic experiences, such as a woman's memory of the dangers she was exposed to with her children. She recalled the fear she felt after being dropped off with her children and people she did not know in an unknown place when it was pitch black and they could not see anything. In their study, Cigrand et al. (2022) heard stories from a mother who had to leave her 2-year-old with a stranger while she learned about travel plans for the next day. Another example is the film *El Norte* (Nava, 1983) in which a brother and a sister face a death-defying journey, navigating tunnels and difficult terrain. The film dramatizes the traumas experienced by the siblings en route to the United States.

The reality is that immigrants must count on the people they paid to lead the way; they are not in control, and they are dependent on these strangers. There are the migrants who leave Syria or Russia, make it to the eastern coast of Mexico, and then begin their journey north. The accounts of refugees from Cuba who enter through Cancún, Mexico, are indicative of the extended migration endeavors some will pursue. Counselors need to be knowledgeable about the terror individuals experience in the migration phase and the consequential trauma that follows. One study (Cohodes et al., 2021) reviewed the effects of migration-related trauma due to these unpredictable events prior, during, and after the migration journey, noting potential negative impacts on nearly all aspects of development, particularly children's physical and mental health.

Often, migrants experience psychological, physical, and spiritual distress and adverse outcomes as a result of their migration journey (Bhugra & Becker, 2005; Djelantik et al., 2020). After the arduous premigration and migration processes, immigrants likely carry with them trauma and exhaustion and, at times, paranoia and a range of physical maladies. As counselors engage with children, adolescents, and parents, they need to assess the circumstances that have contributed to individuals' distress so as not to retraumatize and cause mistrust. Taking a holistic approach about the experiences of migrants in the premigration and migration-specific phases will allow counselors to evaluate the clients' most immediate needs as they move into the very demanding acculturation phase.

Postmigration

The third stage, postmigration, pertains to navigating life in the United States through all the trials and tribulations of the life-changing process in a new and idealized country. Immigrants and their families have unique experiences during this period, a stage that exists without an expiration date. The postmigration process is a continuous adjustment that comprises many changes, including negotiating family structures, overcoming institutional barriers, finding access to services, staying connected with family back home, and managing acculturation-related stressors, in addition to dealing with an array of emotions that range from relief to loss (Arredondo, 2018; Arredondo-Dowd, 1981a; Ornelas & Perreira, 2011). The postmigration phase involves multiple adjustments in a country with new and different social and cultural norms, language differences, weather conditions, interpersonal behaviors of nonimmigrants, and other environmental conditions that are unfamiliar.

Bronfenbrenner's (1977) ecological model suggests that newcomers must engage with numerous systems while pursuing the goals that brought them to the United States. The systems affecting human development are cultural, political, sociocultural, and economic (see Chapter 4 for a discussion of the exosystem, macrosystem, mesosystem, microsystem, and chronosystem). Individuals' autonomy and internal locus of control are often blocked as they encounter macrosystems. These systemic encounters are illustrated in the model (see Figure 3.1) that describes the types of circumstances affecting the migration process.

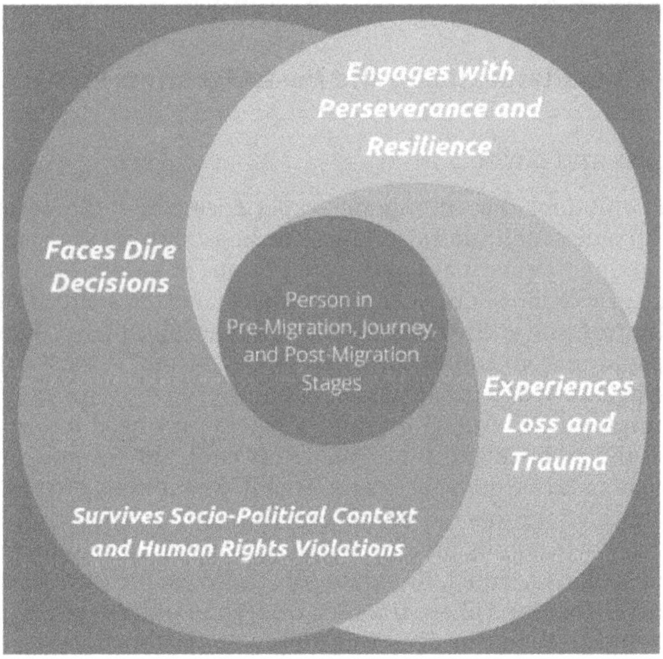

FIGURE 3.1

Process of Person in Migration Journey Over Time

Note. From "A Phenomenological Study of Perseverance and Resilience Through the Migration Journey," by D. L. Cigrand, M. Fawcett, R. Miyakuni, P. Arredondo, & G. Onderak, 2022, *Journal of Counseling & Development, 100*(2), p. 161 (https://doi.org/10.1002/jcad.12413). Copyright 2022 by the American Counseling Association. Reprinted with permission.

The postmigration stage is not typically about the individual experience, but rather one involving family members in one's company and in the home country. Individuals are constantly learning the unspoken rules about adapting to new tasks, such as using public transportation; buying groceries; learning directions; and reading and understanding signage, especially to go home. Each day can be a challenge. Some adults may also prioritize schools and medical clinics for their children. If one is fortunate to have friends or family members in the new location, these individuals can offer support with job-seeking opportunities and guidance on where to go for housing and cultural food staples. It is important for counselors to understand the complexity of the postmigration period and the multiple tasks that must be undertaken. This is the time when immigrant clients and their families may seek assistance for basic needs as well as physical ailments and emotional distress. Counselors should also consider invisible challenges that may affect immigrants' and their family members' well-being.

Several variables affect the acculturation process for migrants and refugees, including their intersecting identities, geographic location and the receptiveness or hostility of people in that community, education history, race and color, and documentation status. In an edited text about immigrants from Spanish-speaking countries, it was found that those who had studied in the United States, were middle class in their home country, and had families in the United States were better prepared to pursue their goals (Arredondo, 2018). Nevertheless, because of their limited English proficiency, color, and lack of support networks, they also faced multiple acculturation challenges about being accepted, as well as losses (Arredondo, 2018).

Considerations in the Postmigration Phase

The Cycles of Loss and Grief

Loss and grief are emotions that immigrants experience across the developmental cycle (from childhood to older adulthood), and these feelings may begin as early as the premigration phase. Planning to leave may engender emotions of sadness for many reasons. For example, one may grieve those one will leave behind and ones already lost to violence, illness, natural disasters, and so forth. In the migration-specific phase, there are unplanned losses, such as separation from family, cultural differences, and, in more extreme instances, the death or disappearance of a traveling companion.

Counselors engaging with immigrants and refugees may need to learn about Oberg's (1960) phases of culture shock and the Kübler-Ross et al. (1972) model to recognize the processes their clients may be going through. At first, newcomers often feel excited about arriving at their destination; this is a big accomplishment. In the next phase, they begin to question and have self-doubts because not all has unfolded as anticipated. They may experience racism, feel disoriented, lose their job, and have pressure to send remittances to family back home. The third phase is a time of deep emotions, anger, frustration, self-blame, and even remorse about the decision to leave. In the fourth stage, immigrants may come to terms with their reality, accept that they are in the United States, and make the best of it. Promises were made to those in the home country and to family members who have come with them; there are high expectations they want to fulfill.

Following MSJCC guidelines (Ratts et al., 2015), counselors need to recognize the stressors associated with meeting expectations, especially for others. Affirming individuals' progress is necessary so that they can accept where they are in the process of achieving promises made. Inherent in the loss and grief process is the feeling of guilt. For example, migrants may experience guilt about leaving others behind, especially children and parents, or survivor guilt for being the fortunate one to have not died during the journey. Guilt is a natural part of grieving (Ward et al., 2012). Migratory grief is a complex and multifaceted process. Migrants often juggle various tangible and intangible losses such as geographic separation, change in status, identity loss, missing support networks, and lack of belonging and sense of place (D. L. Harris, 2019) caused by, for instance, forcible displacement due to increased violent conflict across countries. Displacement may deter appropriate mourning, which, in turn, may contribute to grief reactions that negatively impact migrants' physical and mental health (Jones, 2020). It is possible that openly expressing grief is perceived as unreasonable because of survivor guilt or stigma. During intake, counselors should keep in mind that underlying expressions of sadness and depression may be the feelings of loss, grief, and guilt. Consequently, counselors need to support individuals in the mourning process, be empathic listeners, and remind clients how far they have come in accomplishing their goals.

A combination of socioeconomic status, social variables, interpersonal factors, processes relating to the asylum process, and immigration policies strongly shape immigrants' and refugees' psychological functioning (Ellis et al., 2014; Li et al., 2016). Although their mental health and integration trajectories are large stressors, immigrants and refugees present with low levels of help-seeking behaviors. Structural factors that may act as barriers to seeking support include financial strain, language abilities, unstable housing, lack of trust, and limited understanding of how to access services (Byrow et al., 2020).

According to Bronfenbrenner's (1977) model, these are barriers that emanate in the mesosystem and may be difficult to negotiate. The integration experience is an overall stressor, regardless of legal status. For example, the immigrant mother must manage her acculturation process and that of her children who may not have an easy time in their new school. Thus, the mother must engage with school officials on behalf of her child. She enters the mesosystem where connections are met, but other barriers emerge. For example, if adolescents do not arrive with school records from their home country or school policies require school uniforms, the mother may not know where to turn. Counselor advocacy would be optimal for her.

The Acculturation Journey

In a content analysis of immigrant and refugee research over a 31-year period, Yoon et al. (2023) uncovered that acculturation and enculturation (the process by which an individual learns their traditional culture and assimilates its practices and values) were the variables most often used in the studies they reviewed. Immigrants go through social, psychological, spiritual, and cultural changes in the transition and adjustment period; this is described as acculturation or the acculturation process. Acculturation is a challenging process of cognitive, emotional, and behavioral disequilibrium and unforeseen changes—it is a continuous dance between two cultures that carries considerable tension and stress (Ward & Szabó, 2019). Inherent in the acculturation journey are personal and familial dilemmas. These will be discussed in the following sections. In many respects, acculturative stress encompasses most of the challenges experienced in the postmigration phase.

Although research continues to document patterns in the acculturation process, a one-size-fits-all norm does not accurately depict individual cultural adjustments because of the many variables (e.g., motivation, push and pull factors, method of migration, country of origin, laws, identity variables) that influence how one settles in, feels received, experiences a sense of belonging or not, and adjusts to a new environment. Nevertheless, regardless of the acculturation framework or model, research findings consistently indicate that immigrants undergo an extended period of stress when adjusting to a new culture (e.g., Erazo, 2018; Sims & Hinton, 2022; Zhan et al., 2022).

Counselors need to take into consideration that acculturation rates will vary within the same family (K. M. Harris & Chen, 2022; Titzmann & Lee, 2022; Toro & Nieri, 2018).

Children and adolescents more quickly acclimate and even learn English more readily than their parents and grandparents. In an unfamiliar social world, young people want to fit in and more readily learn the language, slang, and other behaviors, sometimes inappropriate, to fit in. Arredondo (one of the authors) recalls a high school student refugee from the Soviet Union who arrived with some fluency with English. Vlad decided that to be cool, he would skip classes, which did not go over well with his parents as they had high expectations for their son. Peer pressure and bullying are also real. Immigrants stand out because of their visible appearance, including color, clothes, and accents.

While children may learn U.S. culture in school, adults tend to learn primarily through lived experiences, such as in their neighborhoods and workplace (Noe-Bustamante et al., 2022; Rumbaut, 2001; van Tonder & Soontiens, 2014). If they are in positions in which English is not necessary for performance, they will not feel compelled to learn to speak English. This is a disadvantage over time because they may need to depend on their children to be their interpreters in different settings (Rothe et al., 2010). Parents who migrate with their adult children are generally the least likely to acculturate. If they are homebound, with limited access to social engagement where English is spoken, they will experience isolation and be limited in their familiarity with the new culture (Wijekoon et al., 2023). Television and radio may be their easiest contact with the outside world where they receive some cultural comforts through programs in their primary language.

Acculturative Stress

The dissonance between beliefs, behaviors, values, and attitudes can lead to long-term strain marked by negative psychological and physical outcomes, also known as acculturative stress (Berry, 2006). Berry (1992) stated that the stress emanates from individuals' attempts to negotiate their culture of origin and the host culture. Previous studies have found that acculturative stress is strongly associated with detrimental effects to immigrants' physical and mental health (e.g., Bernal et al., 2022; Gonzalez-Guarda et al., 2021; Ponciano et al., 2022). For example, increased acculturative stress in Spanish-speaking immigrant populations leads to greater mental health concerns, such as depression, anxiety, and psychological stress (Miller De Rutté & Rubenstein, 2021). Another study that focused on Somali refugees identified similar themes with participants' narratives indicating that psychological distress (e.g., depression, posttraumatic stress disorder [PTSD]) is pervasive with shame and acculturative stress, heightening their mental health concerns (Alemi et al., 2022). Findings have consistently shown that acculturative stress is positively associated with sleep, including insomnia symptoms, sleepiness symptoms, sleep quality, and time to sleep among both adults and children (Marchante-Hoffman, 2018). For example, a recent literature review found that immigrants in the United States have poor sleep health and that acculturative stress may be the major influencing factor among immigrants (Chapagai & Martyn-Nemeth, 2022).

The strain from the premigration to the postmigration phase is cumulative. Challenges and barriers in the United States, along with unforeseen events such as the COVID-19 pandemic, do not allow much respite for immigrants with high aspirations. In line with MSJCC practices, counselors should provide open conversations related to internal locus of control and how taking charge of one's decision is not always feasible because of external barriers. As newcomers, immigrants and refugees may find themselves marginalized—an issue that can be introduced in counseling when clients feel frustrated about what they cannot "make happen."

Notably, acculturation takes its hardest toll on older immigrants (Cheung et al., 2011; Liu et al., 2020). Grandparents brought by their adult children have little flexibility to go out and about freely as they may have done so in their home country. If their children work outside of the home, they may stay by themselves most of the day, perhaps busying themselves with home tasks, calling someone in their home country, and watching television. Immigrants with professional careers often describe this challenge. As their parent ages, they need more support and care. Another acculturation challenge relates to health care. Older immigrants may have health issues previously treated or untreated, but finding appropriate medical care by a culturally and linguistically competent provider requires time, insurance coverage, and physical access to network providers.

Children are inherently more cognitively flexible than adults and are able to adapt to new cultural norms more easily. Still, they too may struggle because the environment and surroundings have changed. In fact, research has shown that this adjustment process becomes progressively more difficult after age 15 (Cheung et al., 2011; deSouza et al., 2023). It is not uncommon for immigrant children who come to the United States with an intact cultural identity to experience emotional turmoil because they now feel like outsiders, struggling with English-language textbooks, teachers, and unfriendly peers (Guerra et al., 2019).

To be culturally responsive, counselors need to keep in mind that acculturation is not an individual experience but involves significant others. Children are embedded within a family system with parents playing a crucial role during this time of transition. A study investigated how Chinese and Korean immigrant children's and their parents' acculturation levels impacted the child's acculturation experience. Findings suggest that when adolescents sense a lack of support from their family, they are more likely to experience depressive symptoms and an increased sense of helplessness (Kim et al., 2009). Similarly, another study found that Middle Eastern immigrant youth's agency significantly affects the well-being of their parents (Millau et al., 2018). Another example of familial influence involves a recent study that found that parents helped to reduce psychological stress for African immigrant youth as they acculturated, adapted, and integrated into their new school environments (Kumi-Yeboah et al., 2020). Parental support offered youth the opportunity to learn how to socialize and adopt multidirectional ways of coping in the acculturative process.

Counselors can partner with the family and facilitate these conversations to create understanding and hear different points of view about the transition. The postmigration stage also introduces intergenerational acculturation gaps, such as loss of family capital for parents as they attempt to lead and shelter their children in the difficult acculturation process. It is easy to lose objectivity with demands from multiple systems that immigrants must rely upon. In this process of change, counselors can support clients in identifying and cultivating protective factors (e.g., going to church or other religious services, having family meals, engaging in a social activity together) that support family coherence while still letting young people integrate, such as parental use of children's knowledge of the host country to navigate the new environment (Renzaho et al., 2017). Parents represent a crucial and powerful agent in children's adjustment to a new country, all while simultaneously going through their own acculturation process.

Identity Crises and Changes

In the postmigration phase, individuals will come to recognize how they are culturally different in terms of appearance, language, clothing, color, and preferred foods. Additionally, they will be confronted with values conflicts. Immigrants and refugees arrive with their cultural values, norms, and traditions. Differences in raising children, limiting adolescents' social life, and maintaining a closed family may be at odds with the practices of nonimmigrant parents. As newcomers, immigrants and refugees may feel that they do not fit in with the mainstream, majority White, U.S. cultural identity, regardless of their country of origin or age.

This awareness about fitting in or not leads to a process of identity confusion and exploration. Immigrants are faced with exploring the numerous identities associated with their country of origin, their new home, and their new ethnic minoritized status (e.g., Amini et al., 2022; Bobowik et al., 2022). In their homeland, they were just like everyone else culturally; in the United States, they may be visibly different and ascribed an identity of "minority group" that is totally unfamiliar. The identity exploration process could lead to maintaining (or "committing") to an identity or to greater identification with one's racial/ethnic identities.

Often, however, the identity questioning process leads to identity confusion and loss, which could have negative effects on one's psychosocial functioning. For example, Meca et al. (2017) found that Latinx immigrant adolescents with higher identity confusion presented with lower self-esteem and optimism, and higher depressive symptoms, rule-breaking behaviors, unprotected sex, and cigarette use. In work with Ghanaian and Nigerian first- and second-generation immigrant women (Keene, 2022), the participants disclosed that stereotype threat and emotional tax negatively affected their experiences at work. They were acutely aware of how they presented themselves in the workplace, which exacerbated their identity conflict and sense of difference.

Over the past 40 years, Arredondo has continued to learn about identity challenges for adult men. In her research with immigrant families in a Habitat for Humanity community in Phoenix, Arizona, before the 2008 recession in the United States, she heard accounts from men about their willingness and need to work two jobs to fulfill their role as family providers. They felt proud of the employment they had and how they could now afford their own home. Counselors working from a multicultural and social justice framework should apply critical consciousness to examine societal norms, values about employment, work ethic, and how these factors may influence clients' well-being and their ability to adapt to their new country.

These experiences of emotional and cognitive dissonance may manifest in the concept of dual consciousness. Du Bois (1903) referred to double consciousness as a sense of always looking at oneself through the eyes of others. For example, a White undocumented immigrant may quickly find social acceptance in a new group, yet the same individual could go through the dual consciousness of seeming to be American without legal documentation. Double consciousness adds a layer of complexity to the adjustment period because it can be difficult for immigrants to adapt to a new environment while grappling with a multifaceted sense of self; they are constantly viewing themselves from two cultural perspectives (i.e., home country and new home).

Consequently, immigrants and refugees must have bicognitive skills or cognitive flexibility. Bicognition refers to the ability to function comfortably and competently in one's preferred and "nonpreferred" or unfamiliar cognitive style (Ramirez et al., 1974). Ramirez et al. (1974) described the development of bilingual capabilities as an expression of bicognitive skills, an advantage to individuals negotiating two or more cultural contexts. Most bilingual individuals have the ability to "code-switch" mentally. Gloria Anzaldúa (2022), a Chicana, feminist author, referred to this as walking the borderlands—that is, the minoritized individual is on a metaphorical border line between two countries, having to mentally process cultural, linguistic, and value differences. Moreover, the uncertain and often hostile political climate in the United States, in addition to immigration policies and laws and macrosystem barriers, affects immigrants' sense of acceptance by U.S. society despite their efforts to acculturate (Aranda et al., 2015).

Financial Stress

Financial strain is a significant postmigration stressor related to daily living and sometimes survival in the new country. Financial stress encompasses material and economic hardships that may threaten the integrity, independence, dignity, and well-being of immigrant families. Although immigrants may have received financial assistance from family and friends to leave, there is still a level of financial distress that comes from various situations, such as paying back potential debts related to crossing to the United States or sending remittances to family back home and losing one's entire savings. In addition to resettling in a new country, finding housing, and securing employment, immigrants and refugees must learn how to navigate unfamiliar systems, at times with limited English proficiency.

Researchers have identified financial strain as a key stressor in the postmigration stage, leading to lower levels of positive mental health outcomes (Alexander et al., 2021; Sengoelge et al., 2022). A study investigating financial stress among U.S. immigrants during the COVID-19 pandemic reported dire situations (Solheim et al., 2022). Job loss in families that were already struggling financially, housing and food insecurity, and limited access to resources (e.g., lack of documentation, language barriers, lack of technology skills) left long-lasting negative effects on immigrants' well-being. To respond effectively, the MSJCC (Ratts et al., 2015) set the expectation that counselors take the time to familiarize themselves with the sociocultural systems that affect their clients' sense of well-being and address the corresponding issues appropriately with feasible recommendations. By becoming familiar with programs, resources, and supports available to immigrants and refugees, counselors can help reduce some of the financial stress experienced by their clients.

The list of financial stressors is extensive. Factors such as low income, limited English language proficiency, residential segregation, cultural differences, and lack of experience with banks and other financial institutions may hinder immigrants' and refugees' access to financial services. Financial support for refugees is possible, however. Individuals who meet the U.S. Refugee Admissions Program Access Categories have been granted refugee status (e.g., Russia, Bosnia, Haiti). A "second wave" of Russians is increasingly fleeing President Vladimir Putin's regime as his war in Ukraine rages on (Gilchrist, 2022). The United States forecasted the highest U.S. refugee ceiling since the early 1990s, resettling up to 125,000 refugees in 2022. These efforts were meant to give particular attention to resettling Central Americans fleeing violence, LGBTQ+ refugees, Afghans who worked for U.S.-based organizations, at-risk Uyghurs in China, Hong Kong dissidents, and refugees from Myanmar (Montoya-Galvez, 2021).

Once in the United States, refugee adults are given $325, and children are given $200 for 3 months. All refugees are entitled to 8 months of Refugee Cash Assistance from the date of their U.S. arrival. Moreover, Supplemental Security Income benefits (i.e., $674 per month) are offered to refugee elders over 65 years of age. Despite such assistance, financial hardships remain a significant stressor for many immigrants and refugees. According to a report from the Migration Policy Institute, national origin, rather than settlement location, was more highly correlated with how refugees fare (Fix et al., 2017). The report also highlighted how despite the variety of public welfare programs, all programs vary by state. Placement of refugees in a particular state or local community will influence service availability and the level of care migrants receive. The MSJCC (Ratts et al., 2015) encourage counselors to become aware of their clients' contexts, which means learning about local and state public assistance programs. A small community, for example, may have less experience hosting refugees and thus lack the skills or resources to provide the unique support refugees need to address their trauma. Consequently, it is the responsibility of the privileged counselor to gather relevant information and share it with refugee clients to help alleviate their financial stress.

Accounts of immigrant adaptation in the postmigration phase also come from narratives of women who may arrive as homemakers, service industry workers, or child caretakers. A community-based agency in San Jose, California, called Jobs to Grow, prepares women with skills to start their own small business. The immigrant women from Mexico and Vietnam participate in workshops where they learn about negotiating the practical side of getting a business permit and setting up a business bank account to assess the benefit of their proposed plans. The women in the program focus primarily on food businesses, such as small restaurants or food trucks, and childcare centers.

In a study in Chicago with women who had arrived primarily from Mexico, Solis-Cortes (2018) learned how the women who had arrived on their own, although perhaps mothers of children left behind, had become emancipated as soon as they could. Upon arrival, some lived with relatives but found employment immediately so that they could pay their hosts, send money home, and become self-supporting. They were determined to meet their goals and endeavored to engage with networks that could support their efforts. These women also became connected to women-centered agencies in Chicago that had programs to empower single women with goals to succeed financially and otherwise.

Negotiation of Racism/Discrimination

The entire migration experience is a difficult and arduous endeavor that affects immigrants across biopsychosocial domains and leads to both internalized and externalized consequences. As has been discussed, migrants and refugees are exposed to multiple stressors that affect their mental health and physical well-being before and during their migration journey, and when they arrive during the settlement and adjustment periods. Immigrants find themselves trying to cope with new rules, new expectations, and unfamiliar surroundings. Amid these adjustments come additional experiences of humiliation and degradation; the absence of peace and security; and, at times, human rights violations.

Perceived discrimination, the behavioral component of racism, refers to the behavioral manifestation of negative attitudes, judgments, or unfair treatments based on a person's identities, such as race, ethnicity, language, appearance, and documentation status (Contrada & Ashmore, 1999). Prejudice and racial/ethnic discrimination are relatively common experiences for immigrants and refugees living in the United States. Xenophobia, the fear of foreigners, fuels negative and hostile attitudes and behaviors toward perceived outsiders in the United States. Examples include the use of racial slurs in social settings or at work and racial profiling (e.g., a security guard targeting a shopper in a department store based on their race, ethnicity, religion, or national origin). Although the politics surrounding immigration have always been complicated, immigration may be even more politicized in today's society, in part because of a 24-hour news cycle and social media.

Research findings consistently point to an association between prejudicial attitudes, discriminatory behaviors, and detrimental health outcomes among immigrants (Benner et al., 2018; Szaflarski & Bauldry, 2019). Health behaviors associated with perceived discrimination include smoking, alcohol/drug use, obesity, hypertension, breast cancer, depression, anxiety, psychological distress, and self-reported health concerns across ethnoracial groups. A prevalent scenario during the President Trump era involved Latinx children, who, although born in the United States, were told "to go back home." Another example is the increased racism, discrimination, and violence against Asians, who were singled out because of their appearance during the COVID-19 pandemic (Croucher et al., 2020). Asian Americans reported an increase in racial slurs, wrongful workplace termination, physical violence, and extreme physical distancing as media and government officials increasingly stigmatized and blamed Asians for the spread of the virus.

The pervasive fear and toxic stress affect immigrants' daily life, health, and well-being. Unfortunately, the consequences from racism and prejudicial practices do not discriminate against age groups. Research shows that 70% of urban youth of color reported some form of racial discrimination, with over 40% of those experiences identified as at least "somewhat disturbing" (Tobler et al., 2013). Another report revealed that Latinx youth who perceived racial/ethnic discrimination were more likely to report PTSD symptoms, exhibiting avoidant behaviors, reexperiencing events, and hypervigilance (Brabeck et al., 2022). The prevalence of common mental health disorders, such as depression, anxiety, and PTSD, tends to be higher among migrants exposed to adversity than among host populations (World Health Organization, 2021).

Systemically, racism and discrimination emerge in insidious ways. For instance, residential segregation, inequities around job access, lack of quality schools, unsafe neighborhoods, and limited health care access often target individuals based on their foreign-born status, race, or ethnicity (Ayón, 2015). For example, Donald Trump kicked off his 2016 presidential campaign by referring to Mexican immigrants as "criminals" and "rapists." He also stated that noncitizens from countries such as Haiti and El Salvador should not remain in the United States. Structural racism and discrimination were further exposed during the COVID-19 pandemic. It was widely reported that severe outcomes, including hospitalizations, intensive care admissions, and deaths, disproportionately affected communities of color (Centers for Disease Control and Prevention, 2022). These inequities were reflected in who could stay home and who was required to work in person, who lost their jobs and who kept them, who had the resources to weather job or income losses, and who faced more hardship. Immigration status was among the fault lines of these divides. Reports exposed the limited access to quality health care for these populations (Acosta et al., 2021).

In addition to systemic barriers, perceived racial discrimination has negative effects on job satisfaction (Tabor & Dalton, 2021). Perceived workplace discrimination increases stress and lowers levels of self-reported mental health (Boulet et al., 2023). Negative attitudes and behaviors toward immigrants are key determinants of immigrants' health, yet they also influence immigrants' economic and sociocultural adjustment experiences (Esses, 2021). Counselors might explore, through societal lenses, the mental duress immigrants face when they do not feel that their workplace is equitable and inclusive or where they feel disrespected and invalidated. Taking the time to explore with clients microaggressions and societal perceptions about immigrants, and sharing the realities of the current U.S. sociopolitical climate, can put into perspective for the immigrant what they are experiencing. Simultaneously, counselors can collaborate with clients to identify ways one can support their progress and wellness.

The aforementioned stressors and events are only a few examples of distressing realities that can increase the risk of compromised mental and physical health among immigrants. Although migration is typically perceived as a risk factor, research suggests that perceived negative experiences around immigration and the acculturation process are the real stressors that ultimately lead to negative outcomes (Cardoso & Thompson, 2010). Immigrants cope with crises with hope; they recover from adversities and manifest resilience despite numerous stressors before, during, and after migration (Salcido, 2022). The adversity and protective factors intertwine in the postmigration period (Arredondo, 2018). Protective factors (e.g., employment, access to services, social support, host country language proficiency, family reunification) offer the possibility of buffering the negative impact that stems from migration stressors. The following case of Ahmed and Amar illustrates how counselors who apply the MSJCC (Ratts et al., 2015) can inform and support immigrants' perception of their own strengths and capabilities by collaborating with clients and using culturally appropriate, empowerment-based frameworks and techniques. Helping clients to express their feelings of anger or despair is also appropriate. The following example shows how counselors can promote resilience and strength.

CASE STUDY

Ahmed and Amar were brothers who escaped Bosnia as refugees with their parents. They lost family members and friends to the horrors of ethnic cleansing and other abuses. Through the assistance of a refugee settlement agency, they entered a high school while their parents found work in local factories that made cheese and ice cream. Ahmed was 14, and Amar was 16. Although the boys appeared to fit into their classrooms because they were White with blond hair in this predominantly White school, they were not fluent in English and were ashamed to speak up. Sadly, their teachers did not seem to notice their struggles nor did they reach out to them. Their names were different from those of U.S.-born students and hard to pronounce, making communication more challenging.

As Amar began to fail two of his classes, he was advised to seek academic support. He shared with his adviser that he was struggling to keep up not only because of the language differences but also because he was sad about losing his grandparents and favorite uncle in the war. He could not concentrate. The adviser introduced him to a clinical mental health counselor at the local counseling center so that he could begin to talk about his feelings. Meanwhile, he was provided academic support. Ahmed seemed to cope better. His English comprehension and speech were stronger, and he seemed to be more socially oriented and started to make friends, particularly with girls.

The parents had been science teachers in Bosnia and were struggling on multiple levels. Through the resettlement center, they were able to meet counselors accustomed to working with refugees. Several points of advice they received from these social justice–oriented counselors were that (a) they should not blame themselves for leaving, (b) holding on to their family values was necessary in the acculturation period, (c) they could bring in their sons for a family talk once a month for at least 1 year, and (d) they were courageous and intelligent people who would achieve their goals over time.

Reflection Questions

1. Would you consider Ahmed and Amar privileged? If so, why or why not?
2. If you were the mental health counselor assigned to Amar, how would you build a counseling relationship?
3. What values conflict might Amar be experiencing?
4. Although Ahmed and Amar may look visibly like the White majority, what identity conflicts might they experience?

Endurance, Strengths, and Protective Factors

In a study with immigrants and refugees from Southeast Asia, Mexico, and Central America, researchers learned of the multiple adaptations and changes immigrants make to reach their final destination (Cigrand et al., 2022). Perseverance, patience, and endurance were prominent attributes in negotiating uncertainty. Spirituality and religious beliefs were protective factors, as were family relationships. The immigrants and refugees found that if there were trustworthy bonds, the tough going could be a little less daunting and painful. In Figure 3.1, these behaviors are captured, illustrating a conceptualization of the interdependence of ongoing events, decisions, and emotions throughout the migration process. These attributes are outlined in the three stages of migration discussion. Traumatic experiences during the three migration stages can prevent migrants from flourishing in their new country of residence. Migration-related trauma affects immigrants in many capacities, to the point that it could impede them from living to their full potential (Erazo, 2018). Migration is growing in scope, complexity, and diversity. It is imperative that mental health systems and providers in the United States assess services, sensitivities, and interventions for the ever-growing number of immigrants who are in need and underserved. The phases of the migration process are complex (see Figure 3.1).

Many conditions exist in the country of origin that are out of the control of immigrants and refugees, but they are not rendered helpless. As studies and contemporary news stories indicate, immigrants are intent on arriving in the United States through a range of means, generally not easy, quick, or guaranteed. They display great endurance, patience, and determination. The postmigration phase is a journey with not only uncertainties but also hopes and persistence. Counselors must take into account these strengths, given that they will have the opportunity to support immigrants' mental well-being in the postmigration and acculturation phase. Counselors working from a social justice framework will also recognize the need to advocate for equity of services on behalf of their clients because they have contended with inequities and other forms of marginalization all their lives. Expanding the counseling role beyond a traditional therapeutic relationship and into a role of advocacy and social action creates room for growth on the part of counselors and their delivery models and systems. Consequently, at times it may require personal risk to one's job security when taking such actions.

The following case of Tuyan and Yolanda exemplifies how recognizing people's strengths and embracing an advocacy role as clinicians may lead to better working relationships and positive outcomes.

CASE STUDY

Tuyan and Yolanda met in a parents' group at their children's middle school. Although neither spoke English fluently, they found a sense of connection because of their migration histories. Tuyan was from Cambodia and had been in the United States for 6 months, and Yolanda was from Guatemala and had been in the United States for 1 month. Both women were single mothers to adolescents who fled with them through treacherous conditions. They still thought about the difficult journey and felt guilty about making their daughters leave their hometowns. The counselor facilitating the group, Sarah, was a White cisgender therapist fairly new to her position. Sarah wondered how she might get the women to feel a sense of belonging in the group and to speak up. The counselor also wondered how she could encourage them to communicate with other parents, who were primarily White and African American.

Given the majority nonimmigrant composition of the group, power dynamics may unintentionally affect the interactions and perceptions among group members. Language was only the initial barrier between group members, and she wondered if there were nonverbal means to engage all the parents. She also wondered about cultural assets participants could share and how to spark this conversation without putting Tuyan and Yolanda in an uncomfortable position. Recognizing the importance of inclusion and community building, Sarah was determined to create a safe and welcoming space that embraced and celebrated the diversity of the group. She decided to move things forward with the introduction of a genogram exercise. This activity invited all individuals to share their family tree.

Reflection Questions

1. How might Tuyan's and Yolanda's ongoing acculturation processes affect their experience in the group?
2. What behaviors might you apply to build a cohesive group with a wide range of identities?

3. How might the differences in the acculturation process for Tuyan, Yolanda, and their children influence their participation and comfort level in the group and with the counselor?
4. As you reflect on stressors and goals that push people from their countries, how would you support Tuyan and Yolanda?
5. How might you navigate assumptions others may hold about Tuyan's and Yolanda's immigrant status and situation?
6. What frameworks may be helpful in identifying inequities Tuyan and Yolanda may be facing?

Summary

In this chapter, the three stages of the migration process have been discussed in depth, detailing the cognitive, emotional, and behavioral/action processes that immigrants and refugees go through. Although this is not a linear process, the push and pull factors are motivators that often align with aspirations and hopes to be achieved in the long term. Migration is people centered; however, there are systems that impinge upon plans, decisions taken, and successes and setbacks in advancing one's plans. Bronfenbrenner's (1977) ecological model introduces the chronosystem, exosystem, macrosystem, mesosystem, and microsystem, which all affect the immigrant as the locus or center. This schema can facilitate a counselor's knowledge about challenges immigrants need to manage simultaneously, often with frustrations and enormous patience. As marginalized individuals, immigrants cannot readily confront systems they need to rely upon during their settlement in the United States.

Considerable discussion was given to the postmigration stage where the greatest acculturation stressors and transitions occur for individuals and their families. The range of stressors that need to be managed over time was introduced. These may be individual and family-centered stressors, in particular those of an emotional nature. Because adults have to push through the myriad systems and processes they encounter in the United States, they may not be able to address their sadness, frustration, losses, and anxiety. Again, counselors can be guided by the MSJCC (Ratts et al., 2015) to assess how and when to intervene and inquire about a client's emotions—losses, guilt, frustrations, and anger—because the client may not have the words to describe how they are feeling.

The context that surrounds immigrants and refugees must also be recognized by counselors. Xenophobia is a constant dynamic, and many immigrant and refugee children and adults will be exposed to racism and a range of other microaggressions on the school playground, in the workplace, and so on. The migration journey will be unique to each parent and child as well; thus, inquiry, genuine curiosity, empathy, and patience will benefit counselors who aim to be culturally responsive. The case studies in this chapter illustrate the complexity of circumstances encountered by immigrants, refugees, and their families and the conceptualization, actions, and advocacy that can be taken by counselors. In short, there are many opportunities for counselors to draw upon the MSJCC (Ratts et al., 2015) to apply a culturally responsive framework to their engagement with immigrants across the life span.

References

Alchin, L. (2018). *Push and pull factors of immigration.* https://www.emigration.link/

Alemi, Q., Mefom, E., Montgomery, S., Koga, P. M., Stempel, C., & Reimann, J. O. F. (2022). Acculturative stress, stigma, and mental health challenges: Emic perspectives from Somali young adults in San Diego County's 'Little Mogadishu.' *Ethnicity & Health, 27*(7), 1501–1517. https://doi.org/10.1080/13557858.2021.1910930

Alessi, E. J., Kahn, S., Chatterji, S., & Manning, D. (2019). A qualitative exploration of the child abuse experiences of sexual and gender minority refugees and asylees in the United States and Canada. In A. Güler, M. Shevtsova, & D. Venturi (Eds.), *LGBTI asylum seekers and refugees from a legal and political perspective: Persecution, asylum and integration* (pp. 31–47). https://doi.org/10.1007/978-3-319-91905-8_3

Alexander, N., Mathilde, S., & Øivind, S. (2021). Post-migration stressors and subjective well-being in adult Syrian refugees resettled in Sweden: A gender perspective. *Frontiers in Public Health, 9*, Article 717353. https://doi.org/10.3389/fpubh.2021.717353

American Immigration Council. (2023). *Temporary protected status: An overview* [Fact sheet]. https://www.americanimmigrationcouncil.org/research/temporary-protected-status-overview

Amini, B., Raheel, O., Exum, A., & Fazzino, T. L. (2022). Mental health of Iranian immigrants and their descendants: A review. *Professional Psychology: Research and Practice, 53*(2), 192–204. https://doi.org/10.1037/pro0000434

Anzaldúa, G. (2022). *The borderlands/la frontera: The new mestiza* (5th ed.). Aunt Lute Books.

Aranda, E., Vaquera, E., & Sousa-Rodriguez, I. (2015). Personal and cultural trauma and the ambivalent national identities of undocumented young adults in the USA. *Journal of Intercultural Studies, 36*(5), 600–619. https://doi.org/10.1080/07256868.2015.1072906

Armstrong, M. (2022, January 6). Migration destinations and origins. *The Statista Infographics Newsletter*. https://www.statista.com/chart/26424/top-destination-and-origin-countries-of-international-migrants/

Arredondo, P. (1986). Immigration as an historical moment leading to an identity crisis. *Journal of Counseling and Human Services, 1*, 79–87.

Arredondo, P. (2018). Latinx immigrants set the stage for 2050. In P. Arredondo (Ed.), *Latinx immigrants: Transcending acculturation and xenophobia* (pp. 1–13). Springer. https://doi.org/10.1007/978-3-319-95738-8_1

Arredondo-Dowd, P. M. (1981a). Personal loss and grief as a result of immigration. *Personnel and Guidance Journal, 59*(6), 376–378. https://doi.org/10.1002/j.2164-4918.1981.tb00573.x

Arredondo-Dowd, P. M. (1981b). The psychological development and education of immigrant adolescents: A baseline study. *Adolescence, 16*(61), 175–186.

Arredondo-Dowd, P. (1984). Identity themes for immigrant young adults. *Adolescence, 19*(76), 977–993.

Ayón, C. (2015). *Economic, social, and health effects of discrimination on Latino immigrant families.* Migration Policy Institute.

Brabeck, K. M., Cardoso, J. B., Chen, T., Bjugstad, A., Capps, R., Capoverde, E., & Trull, A. (2022). Discrimination and PTSD among Latinx immigrant youth: The moderating effects of gender. *Psychological Trauma: Theory, Research, Practice, and Policy, 14*(1), 11–19. https://doi.org/10.1037/tra0001126

Benner, A. D., Wang, Y., Shen, Y., Boyle, A. E., Polk, R., & Cheng, Y. P. (2018). Racial/ethnic discrimination and well-being during adolescence: A meta-analytic review. *American Psychologist, 73*(7), 855–883. https://doi.org/10.1037/amp0000204

Bernal, D. R., Misiaszek, K. H., Ayala, J., & Kenley, N. (2022). Second-class citizens? Subjective social status, acculturative stress, and immigrant well-being. *SN Social Sciences, 2*, Article 96. https://doi.org/10.1007/s43545-022-00371-2

Berry, J. W. (1992). Acculturation and adaptation in a new society. *International Migration, 30*(1), 69–85. https://doi.org/10.1111/j.1468-2435.1992.tb00776.x

Berry, J. W. (2006). Acculturation: A conceptual overview. In M. H. Bornstein & L. R Cote (Eds.), *Acculturation and parent-child relationships: Measurement and development* (pp. 13–30). Erlbaum. https://doi.org/10.4324/9780415963589-2

Bhugra, D., & Becker, M. (2005). Migration, cultural bereavement and cultural identity. *World Psychiatry, 4*(1), 18–24.

Bhugra, D., & Jones, P. (2001). Migration and mental illness. *Advances in Psychiatric Treatment, 7*(3), 216–222. https://doi.org/10.1192/apt.7.3.216

Bobowik, M., Benet-Martínez, V., & Repke, L. (2022). Ethnocultural diversity of immigrants' personal social networks, bicultural identity integration and global identification. *International Journal of Psychology, 57*(4), 491–500. https://doi.org/10.1002/ijop.12814

Boulet, M., Lachapelle, M., & Keiff, S. (2023). Demographic diversity, perceived workplace discrimination and workers' well-being: context matters. *Evidence-Based HRM*, 11(1), 35–51. https://doi.org/10.1108/EBHRM-08-2021-0179

Bronfenbrenner, U. (1977). Toward an experimental ecology of human development. *American Psychologist, 32*(7), 513–531. https://doi.org/10.1037/0003-066X.32.7.513

Byrow, Y., Pajak, R., Specker, P., & Nickerson, A. (2020). Perceptions of mental health and perceived barriers to mental health help-seeking amongst refugees: A systematic review. *Clinical Psychology Review, 75*, Article 101812. https://doi.org/10.1016/j.cpr.2019.101812

Cardoso, J. B., & Thompson, S. J. (2010). Common themes of resilience among Latino immigrant families: A systematic review of the literature. *Families in Society, 91*(3), 257–265. https://doi.org/10.1606/1044-3894.4003

Centers for Disease Control and Prevention. (2022, September 15). *Risk for COVID-19 infection, hospitalization, and death by race/ethnicity.* https://stacks.cdc.gov/view/cdc/121338

Chapagai, S., & Martyn-Nemeth, P. (2022). Sleep health, acculturation, and acculturative stress in immigrants in the United States: A scoping review. *Journal of Transcultural Nursing, 33*(3), 398–415. https://doi.org/10.1177/10436596211072884

Cheung, B. Y., Chudek, M., & Heine, S. J. (2011). Evidence for a sensitive period for acculturation: Younger immigrants report acculturating at a faster rate. *Psychological Science, 22*(2), 147–152. https://doi.org/10.1177/0956797610394661

Ciaramella, M., Monacelli, N., & Cocimano, L.C. E. (2022). Promotion of resilience in migrants: A systematic review of study and psychosocial intervention. *Journal of Immigrant and Minority Health, 24*(5), 1328–1344. https://doi.org/10.1007/s10903-021-01247-y

Cigrand, D. L., Fawcett, M., Miyakuni, R., Arredondo, P., & Onderak, G. (2022). A phenomenological study of perseverance and resilience through the migration journey. *Journal of Counseling & Development, 100*(2), 157–170. https://doi.org/10.1002/jcad.12413

Cohodes, E. M., Kribakaran, S., Odriozola, P., Bakirci, S., McCauley, S., Hodges, H. R., Sisk, L. M., Zacharek, S. J., & Gee, D. G. (2021). Migration-related trauma and mental health among migrant children emigrating from Mexico and Central America to the United States: Effects on developmental neurobiology and implications for policy. *Developmental Psychobiology, 63*(6), Article e22158. https://doi.org/10.1002/dev.22158

Contrada, R. J., & Ashmore, R. D. (Eds.). (1999). *Self, social identity, and physical health: Interdisciplinary explorations.* Oxford University Press.

Croucher, S. M., Nguyen, T., & Rahmani, D. (2020). Prejudice toward Asian Americans in the Covid-19 pandemic: The effects of social media use in the United States. *Frontiers in Communication, 5*, Article 39. https://doi.org/10.3389/fcomm.2020.00039

Crowley, C. (2009). The mental health needs of refugee children: A review of literature and implications for nurse practitioners. *Journal of the American Academy of Nurse Practitioners, 21*(6), 322–331. https://doi.org/10.1111/j.1745-7599.2009.00413.x

DeLuca, L. A., McEwen, M. M., & Keim, S. M. (2008). United States–Mexico border crossing: Experiences and risk perceptions of undocumented male immigrants. *Journal of Immigrant and Minority Health, 12*(1), 113–123. https://doi.org/10.1007/s10903-008-9197-4

Desai, D. H. (2023). Impact on mental health of immigrants: When will the world stop? *Journal of Educational & Psychological Research, 5*(2), 644–645. https://doi.org/10.33140/JEPR

deSouza, D. K., Lin, H., & Cox, R. B. (2023). Immigrant parents and children navigating two languages: A scoping review. *Journal of Family Theory & Review, 15*(1), 133–161. https://doi.org/10.1111/jftr.12484

Devereaux, R. (2018, January 8). Ignoring violence in El Salvador, Trump ends years of special protective status for immigrants. *The Intercept.* https://theintercept.com/2018/01/08/el-salvador-immigration-tps-trump/

Djelantik, A. A. A. M. J., de Heus, A., Kuiper, D., Kleber, R. J., Boelen, P. A., & Smid, G. E. (2020). Post-migration stressors and their association with symptom reduction and non-completion during treatment for traumatic grief in refugees. *Frontiers in Psychiatry, 11*, Article 407. https://doi.org/10.3389/fpsyt.2020.00407

Du Bois, W. B. (1903). *The souls of Black folk.* Longmans, Green.

Eberhart, C. (2023, April 1). *Border agents find 58 migrants crammed in Penske truck in alleged human smuggling.* Fox News. https://www.foxnews.com/us/border-agents-find-58-migrants-crammed-penske-truck-alleged-human-smuggling

Ellis, B. H., Murray, K., & Barrett, C. (2014). Understanding the mental health of refugees: Trauma, stress, and the cultural context. In R. Parekh (Ed.), *The Massachusetts General Hospital textbook on diversity and cultural sensitivity in mental health* (pp. 165–187). Humana Press. https://doi.org/10.1007/978-1-4614-8918-4_7

Erazo, T. (2018). Migration-related trauma and the UN's response. *Psychology International, 29*(7).

Esses, V. M. (2021). Prejudice and discrimination toward immigrants. *Annual Review of Psychology, 72*, 503–531. https://doi.org/10.1146/annurev-psych-080520-102803

Fix, M., Hooper, K., & Zong, J. (2017). *How are refugees faring? Integration at U.S. and state levels.* Migration Policy Institute. https://www.migrationpolicy.org/sites/default/files/publications/TCM-Asylum-USRefugeeIntegration-FINAL.pdf

Furnham, A. (2019). Culture shock: A review of the literature for practitioners. *Psychology, 10*(13), 1832–1855. https://doi.org/10.4236/psych.2019.1013119

Garcia, M. F., & Birman, D. (2022). Understanding the migration experience of unaccompanied youth: A review of the literature. *American Journal of Orthopsychiatry, 92*(1), 79–102. https://doi.org/10.1037/ort0000588

Gilchrist, K. (2022, July 14). *A second wave of Russians is fleeing Putin's regime.* CNBC. https://www.cnbc.com/2022/07/14/russians-flee-putins-regime-after-ukraine-war-in-second-wave-of-migration.html

Gonzalez-Guarda, R. M., Stafford, A. M., Nagy, G. A., Befus, D. R., & Conklin, J. L. (2021). A systematic review of physical health consequences and acculturation stress among Latinx individuals in the United States. *Biological Research for Nursing, 23*(3), 362–374. https://doi.org/10.1177/1099800420968889

Guerra, R., Rodrigues, R. B., Aguiar, C., Carmona, M., Alexandre, J., & Lopes, R. C. (2019). School achievement and well-being of immigrant children: The role of acculturation orientations and perceived discrimination. *Journal of School Psychology, 75*, 104–118. https://doi.org/10.1016/j.jsp.2019.07.004

Hagan, J., & Ebaugh, H. R. (2003). Calling upon the sacred: Migrants' use of religion in the migration process. *International Migration Review, 37*(4), 1145–1162. https://doi.org/10.1111/j.1747-7379.2003.tb00173.x

Hagan, J. M., & Straut-Eppsteiner, H. (2019). Religion on the move: The place of religion in different stages of the migration experience. In S. J. Gold & S. J. Nawyn (Eds.), *Routledge international handbook of migration studies* (2nd ed., pp. 282–293). Routledge.

Hahn, E., Richter, D., Schupp, J., & Back, M. D. (2019). Predictors of refugee adjustment: The importance of cognitive skills and personality. *Collabra: Psychology, 5*(1), Article 23. https://doi.org/10.1525/collabra.212

Hansen, T., & Robles Robles, M. E. (Eds.). (2021). *Voices of the border: Testimonios of migration, deportation, and asylum* (D. Hill & S. Honey, Trans.). Georgetown University Press.

Harris, D. L. (Ed.). (2019). *Non-death loss and grief: Context and clinical implications.* Routledge.

Harris, K. M., & Chen, P. (2023). The acculturation gap of parent–child relationships in immigrant families: A national study. *Family Relations, 72*(4), 1748–1772. https://doi.org/10.1111/fare.12760

Hernandez, A., Miroff, N., & Sacchetti, M. (2022, June 27). 46 migrants found dead in Texas inside sweltering tractor-trailer. *The Washington Post.* https://www.washingtonpost.com/nation/2022/06/27/migrants-dead-texas/

Institute for Immigration Research. (2023). *El Salvador: Salvadoran population in the Washington, DC and Baltimore, MD Metro areas.* https://iir.gmu.edu/immigrant-stories-dc-baltimore/el-salvador/el-salvador-salvadoran-population-in-the-washington-dc-and-baltimore-md-metro-areas

International Rescue Committee. (2023, September 12). *Is it legal to cross the U.S. border to seek asylum?* https://www.rescue.org/article/it-legal-cross-us-border-seek-asylum

Isacson, A. (2022, November 23). *Migration, country by country, at the U.S.-Mexico border.* Washington Office on Latin America. https://www.wola.org/2022/11/migration-country-by-country-at-the-u-s-mexico-border/

Janetsky, M., & Stunt, V. (2020, April 14). *Migrants take out huge loans to pay coyotes. Coronavirus could cause them to default.* VICE News. https://www.vice.com/en/article/pke5nb/migrants-take-out-huge-loans-to-pay-coyotes-coronavirus-could-cause-them-to-default

Jones, L. (2020). Grief and loss in displaced and refugee families. In S. J. Song & P. Ventevogel (Eds.), *Child, adolescent and family refugee mental health: A global perspective* (pp. 123–149). Springer.

Justice for Immigrants. (2016). *Root causes of migration.* https://justiceforimmigrants.org/wp-content/uploads/2016/11/Root-Causes.pdf

Keene, Y. A. (2022). *A multi-generational workplace perspective: The phenomenon of the millennial African immigrant woman in corporate America.* ResearchGate. https://www.researchgate.net/publication/363172688_A_Multi-Generational_Workplace_Perspective_The_Phenomenon_of_the_Millennial_African_Immigrant_Woman_in_Corporate_America

Kim, S. Y., Chen, Q., Li, J., Huang, X., & Moon, U. J. (2009). Parent–child acculturation, parenting, and adolescent depressive symptoms in Chinese immigrant families. *Journal of Family Psychology, 23*(3), 426–437. https://doi.org/10.1037/a0016019

Kübler-Ross, E., Wessler, S., & Avioli, L. V. (1972). On death and dying. *JAMA, 221*(2), 174–179. https://doi.org/10.1001/jama.1972.03200150040010

Kumi-Yeboah, A., Brobbey, G., & Smith, P. (2020). Exploring factors that facilitate acculturation strategies and academic success of West African immigrant youth in urban schools. *Education and Urban Society, 52*(1), 21–50. https://doi.org/10.1177/0013124519846279

Li, S. S. Y., Liddell, B. J., & Nickerson, A. (2016). The relationship between post-migration stress and psychological disorders in refugees and asylum seekers. *Current Psychiatry Reports, 18*(9), Article 82. https://doi.org/10.1007/s11920-016-0723-0

Liu, S., Dane, S., Gallois, C., Haslam, C., & Tran, T. L. N. (2020). The dynamics of acculturation among older immigrants in Australia. *Journal of Cross-Cultural Psychology, 51*(6), 424–441. https://doi.org/10.1177/0022022120927461

Lutheran Immigration and Refugee Service. (2021, July 14). *Why do people immigrate? The different causes of immigration.* https://www.lirs.org/causes-of-immigration/

Marchante-Hoffman, A. N. (2018). *Giving voice to underserved, foreign-born Latino youth: Trauma, stress, and health in the primary care setting* [Doctoral dissertation, University of Miami]. Scholarship@Miami. https://scholarship.miami.edu/esploro/outputs/doctoral/Giving-Voice-to-Underserved-Foreign-Born-Latino/991031447755602976

McGuire, J. (2022, June 9). Migration to the US is on the rise again—but it's unlikely to be fully addressed during the Summit of the Americas, or anytime soon. *FIU News.* https://news.fiu.edu/2022/migration-to-the-us-is-on-the-rise-again-but-its-unlikely-to-be-fully-addressed-during-the-summit-of-the-americas,-or-anytimesoon

Meca, A., Sabet, R. F., Farrelly, C. M., Benitez, C. G., Schwartz, S. J., Gonzales-Backen, M., Lorenzo-Blanco, E. I., Unger, J. B., Zamboanga, B. L., Baezconde-Garbanati, L., Picariello, S., Des Rosiers, S. E., Soto, D. W., Pattarroyo, M., Villamar, J. A., & Lizzi, K. M. (2017). Personal and cultural identity development in recently immigrated Hispanic adolescents: Links with psychosocial functioning. *Cultural Diversity and Ethnic Minority Psychology, 23*(3), 348–361. https://doi.org/10.1037/cdp0000129

Millau, M., Rivard, M., & Mello, C. (2018). Immigrant families' perception of the causes, first manifestations, and treatment of autism spectrum disorder. *Journal of Child and Family Studies, 27*(11), 3468–3481. https://doi.org/10.1007/s10826-018-1180-7

Miller De Rutté, A. M., & Rubenstein, B. P. (2021). Acculturative stress and the effects on health and health behaviors in Hispanic immigrants: A systematic review. *Hispanic Journal of Behavioral Sciences, 43*(4), 433–455. https://doi.org/10.1177/07399863211044897

Mitra, R., & Hodes, M. (2019). Prevention of psychological distress and promotion of resilience amongst unaccompanied refugee minors in resettlement countries. *Child: Care, Health and Development, 45*(2), 198–215. https://doi.org/10.1111/cch.12640

Montoya-Galvez, C. (2021, September 20). *U.S. to raise refugee cap to 125,000 spots in 2022.* CBS News. https://www.cbsnews.com/news/immigration-us-refugee-cap-125000-in-2022/

Morales, F. R., Hawkins, K., Gonzalez, D., Garcia, A., Patel, S. G., & Mercado, A. (2023). Strengths and resilience among Central American parents seeking asylum in the United States. *Journal of Cross-Cultural Psychology, 54*(4), 457–474. https://doi.org/10.1177/00220221231171083

Muruthi, B. A., Thompson Cañas, R. E., Zárate, J., Lahoti, A., Romero, L., & Stafford McRell, A. (2023). Policies during COVID-19 and their impact on immigrant families' psychological well-being: A critically engaged practice. *Families, Systems, & Health, 41*(2), 265–273. https://doi.org/10.1037/fsh0000808

National Immigration Forum. (2019, July 23). *Push or pull factors: What drives Central American migrants to the U.S.?* https://immigrationforum.org/article/push-or-pull-factors-what-drives-central-american-migrants-to-the-u-s/

Nava, G. (Director). (1983). *El norte* [Film]. American Playhouse; Independent Film Productions.

Noe-Bustamante, L., Mora, L., & Ruiz, N. (2022). *In their own words: Asian immigrants' experiences navigating language barriers in the United States*. Pew Research Center. https://www.pewresearch.org/race-ethnicity/2022/12/19/in-their-own-words-asian-immigrants-experiences-navigating-language-barriers-in-the-united-states/

Oberg, K. (1960). Cultural shock: Adjustment to new cultural environments. *Practical Anthropology*, 7(4), 177–182. https://doi.org/10.1177/009182966000700405

Ornelas, I. J., & Perreira, K. M. (2011). The role of migration in the development of depressive symptoms among Latino immigrant parents in the USA. *Social Science & Medicine, 73*(8), 1169–1177. https://doi.org/10.1016/j.socscimed.2011.07.002

Ponciano, C., Wang, C. D. C., & Jin, L. (2022). Attachment, acculturative stress, and mental health of Mexican immigrants. *Counselling Psychology Quarterly, 35*(2), 381–396. https://doi.org/10.1080/09515070.2020.1813688

Ramirez, M., III, Castaneda, A., & Herold, P. L. (1974). The relationship of acculturation to cognitive style among Mexican Americans. *Journal of Cross-Cultural Psychology, 5*(4), 424–433. https://doi.org/10.1177/002202217400500404

Ratts, M. J., Singh, A. A., Nassar-McMillan, S., Butler, S. K., & McCullough, J. R. (2015). *Multicultural and social justice counseling competencies*. Association for Multicultural Counseling and Development. https://www.counseling.org/docs/default-source/competencies/multicultural-and-social-justice-counseling-competencies.pdf?sfvrsn=20

Ratts, M. J., Singh, A. A., Nassar-McMillan, S., Butler, S. K., & McCullough, J. R. (2016). Multicultural and social justice counseling competencies: Guidelines for the counseling profession. *Journal of Multicultural Counseling and Development, 44*(1), 28–48. https://doi.org/10.1002/jmcd.12035

Ray, J., & Esipova, N. (2018, March 20). *Are migrants happier after they move?* Gallup. https://news.gallup.com/opinion/gallup/230639/migrants-happier-move.aspx

Renzaho, A. M. N., Dhingra, N., & Georgeou, N. (2017). Youth as contested sites of culture: The intergenerational acculturation gap amongst new migrant communities—Parental and young adult perspectives. *PLoS ONE, 12*(2), Article e0170700. https://doi.org/10.1371/journal.pone.0170700

Revens, K. E., Caro, L., Alvarez, D., Ordonez, S., Benitez, C., Garcia, P., Price, A., & Price, R. (2023). *The migrant experience: A journey of hope*. Camino. https://camino.org/wp-content/uploads/2023/06/Migrant-Journey-Report-ENG-1.pdf

Rogers, Z. (2022, July 26). *Cartels making $13 billion a year smuggling migrants across border, report says*. The National Desk. https://thenationaldesk.com/news/americas-news-now/cartels-making-13-billion-a-year-off-smuggling-migrants-through-border-nyt-report-says-mexio-immigrants-coyote-texas

Rothe, E. M., Tzuang, D., & Pumariega, A. J. (2010). Acculturation, development, and adaptation. *Child and Adolescent Psychiatric Clinics, 19*(4), 681–696. https://doi.org/10.1016/j.chc.2010.07.002

Rumbaut, R. G. (2001). Assimilation of immigrants. In N. J. Smelser & P. B. Baltes (Eds.), *International encyclopedia of the social & behavioral sciences* (pp. 845–849). Pergamon. https://doi.org/10.1016/B0-08-043076-7/02188-4

Salcido, V. V. (2022). *Ethnic-racial socialization, proactive coping with discrimination, and Latinx youth's psychological well-being*. The University of North Carolina at Greensboro. https://libres.uncg.edu/ir/uncg/f/Salcido_uncg_0154M_13607.pdf

Sangalang, C. C., Becerra, D., Mitchell, F. M., Lechuga-Peña, S., Lopez, K., & Kim, I. (2019). Trauma, post-migration stress, and mental health: A comparative analysis of refugees and immigrants in the United States. *Journal of Immigrant and Minority Health, 21*(5), 909–919. https://doi.org/10.1007/s10903-018-0826-2

Sengoelge, M., Nissen, A., & Solberg, Ø. (2022). Post-migration stressors and health-related quality of life in refugees from Syria resettled in Sweden. *International Journal of Environmental Research and Public Health, 19*(5), Article 2509. https://doi.org/10.3390/ijerph19052509

Sims, T., & Hinton, D. (2022). *How does trauma experienced during immigration affect mental health?* DigitalCommons@Kennesaw State University. https://digitalcommons.kennesaw.edu/cgi/viewcontent.cgi?article=1003&context=immigrationscholarship

Solheim, C. A., Ballard, J., Fatiha, N., Dini, Z., Buchanan, G., & Song, S. (2022). Immigrant family financial and relationship stress from the COVID-19 pandemic. *Journal of Family and Economic Issues, 43*(2), 282–295. https://doi.org/10.1007/s10834-022-09819-2

Solis-Cortes, L. (2018). *The lived experiences of undocumented Mexican immigrant women: Reflections of pre-migration factors and settlement in the Chicagoland area* (Publication No. 10973837) [Doctoral dissertation, The Chicago School of Professional Psychology]. ProQuest Dissertations and Theses Global.

Szaflarski, M., & Bauldry, S. (2019). The effects of perceived discrimination on immigrant and refugee physical and mental health. *Advances in Medical Sociology, 19*, 173–204. https://doi.org/10.1108/S1057-629020190000019009

Tabor, F., & Dalton, P. (2021). Perception of racial discrimination in the workplace and its impact on job satisfaction and job security. *Journal of Graduate Education Research, 2*(1), Article 9. https://scholarworks.harding.edu/jger/vol2/iss1/9

Thomas, A. A. (2022, August 5). Over 100 migrants found in packed truck at Mexican border. *Newsweek*. https://www.newsweek.com/over-hundred-migrants-found-packed-truck-mexican-border-1731182

Titzmann, P. F., & Lee, R. M. (2022). New temporal concepts of acculturation in immigrant youth. *Child Development Perspectives, 16*(3), 165–172. https://doi.org/10.1111/cdep.12458

Tobler, A. L., Maldonado-Molina, M. M., Staras, S. A., O'Mara, R. J., Livingston, M. D., & Komro, K. A. (2013). Perceived racial/ethnic discrimination, problem behaviors, and mental health among minority urban youth. *Ethnicity & Health, 18*(4), 337–349. https://doi.org/10.1080/13557858.2012.730609

Toro, R. I., & Nieri, T. (2018). Parent-child acculturation and cultural values differences: Associations with children's self-esteem and aggression. *International Journal of Intercultural Relations, 66*, 1–11. https://doi.org/10.1016/j.ijintrel.2018.05.004

Transactional Records Access Clearinghouse. (2022). *New data sheds light on what happens to people found inadmissible at U.S. ports of entry*. https://trac.syr.edu/immigration/reports/692/

U.S. Census Bureau. (n.d.). *U.S. population estimates*. https://www.census.gov/quickfacts/fact/table/US/PST045221

U.S. Customs and Border Protection. (2023, September 22). *Southwest land border encounters*. https://www.cbp.gov/newsroom/stats/southwest-land-border-encounters

van Tonder, C. L., & Soontiens, W. (2014). Migrant acculturation and the workplace. *Procedia – Social and Behavioral Sciences, 143*, 1041–1047. https://doi.org/10.1016/j.sbspro.2014.07.550

Ward, C., & Styles, I. (2012). Guilt as a consequence of migration. *International Journal of Applied Psychoanalytic Studies, 9*(4), 330–343. https://doi.org/10.1002/aps.321

Ward, C., & Szabó, Á. (2019). Affect, behavior, cognition, and development: Adding to the alphabet of acculturation. In D. Matsumoto & H. C. Hwang (Eds.), *The handbook of culture and psychology* (2nd ed., pp. 640–692). Oxford University Press. https://doi.org/10.1093/oso/9780190679743.003.0020

Wijekoon, S., Rudman, D. L., Hand, C., & Polgar, J. (2023). Late-life immigrants' place integration through occupation. *Journal of Occupational Science, 30*(1), 37–53. https://doi.org/10.1080/14427591.2021.1960589

World Health Organization. (2021, August). *Mental health and forced displacement*. https://www.who.int/news-room/fact-sheets/detail/mental-health-and-forced-displacement

Yoon, E., Cabirou, L., Liu, H., Kim, D., Chung, H., & Chang, Y. J. (2023). A content analysis of immigrant and refugee research: A 31-year review. *The Counseling Psychologist, 51*(4), 470–499. https://doi.org/10.1177/00110000231158291

Zhan, C., Nagy, G. A., Wu, J. Q., McCabe, B., Stafford, A. M., & Gonzalez-Guarda, R. M. (2022). Acculturation stress, age at immigration, and employment status as predictors of sleep among Latinx immigrants. *Journal of Immigrant and Minority Health, 24*(6), 1408–1420. https://doi.org/10.1007/s10903-022-01342-8

Chapter 4

Immigrant and Refugee Identity and Experiences Across the Life Span

Data from multiple sources such as the Migration Policy Institute, the Pew Research Center, and the U.S. Census Community Survey provide information on immigration patterns, populations, and statistics. Literature reviews and research summaries teach us about immigrant biographies and personal stories. Through these data and biographies, we obtain a better understanding of the genders, ages, family unit numbers and sizes, and other demographics of the 47 million immigrants and refugees in the United States (Center for Immigrant Studies, 2022). In each developmental period, immigrants, refugees, and their families encounter various identity challenges as they try to reconcile the past and the current acculturation processes.

To better recognize the life span challenges, counselors need to learn more about cross-cultural worldviews about development tasks. Development and learning expectations for children from India and Brazil are likely different from those of U.S. children. Tasks for adult men and women from Cuba and Ukraine will also be culture bound and will not necessarily align with what is expected in the United States. With respect to dating in various cultures, Muslim young adults are allowed to select their own partners today but adhere to culture-bound expectations about sexual and intimate practices reserved for marriage (Rashid, 2017), whereas American dating practices include premarital sex, which is practiced with significant partners or in casual relationships (Brown, 2020). In occupational settings, older employees are respected in Japan and China; however, ageism exists in the United States and Western cultures, where older workers are often devalued and deemed difficult to work with (Shortland, 2018).

This chapter discusses life span theory and key concepts for individualistic and collectivistic cultures, explores intersectionalities in identity development related to life span events, and provides case examples and biographies of immigrants and refugees to illustrate chapter content. The Multicultural and Social Justice Counseling Competencies (MSJCC) developed by Ratts et al. (2015) are also an emphasis in this chapter whereby the reader can make meaning of the chapter topics.

Learning Objectives

- Identify challenges related to life span events of immigrant identities and their respective life scenarios.
- Develop client- and family-centered perspectives based on an understanding of racial/ethnic/cultural intersectional identities related to life span experiences.
- Link cultural identity to life span experiences, immigration status, and intersectionality.
- Recognize immigrant and refugee identities and experiences related to cultural life span expectations from the family.
- Reference the MSJCC when necessary.

The following section introduces a self-assessment to gauge your existing knowledge of culturally responsive counseling frameworks designed to address inequities and marginalization, ethical considerations in working with immigrant and refugee populations, and the MSJCC (Ratts et al., 2015) needed to do so. This brief assessment aims to explore your current understanding of key concepts and provide a foundation for further learning. Answering the following questions will equip you to engage with the content.

Self-assessment: Please respond to the following statements by rating yourself on the following Likert scale: *strongly agree, agree, disagree, strongly disagree,* or *unsure.*

1. I feel confident in understanding life span tasks as they apply to identity development.
2. I can recognize challenges related to identity development through the transition and resettlement process related to life span experiences for immigrants and refugees.
3. I know how to assess the impact of career/family/spiritual life span development on the cultural identity development of my clients.

Theoretical Perspectives on Life Span Development

Socialization and life span development across cultures have received very little attention in research and the behavioral health field. The Western view of life span development has dominated literature, but in the last 25 years, other viewpoints have emerged. Examining individualistic and collectivistic cultures is key in learning the nuances of family traditions, values and expectations for growth and development, and gender-related roles. Of note is Arnett's (1995) theory of broad and narrow socialization, which considers the meaning behind the development of socialization practices by various cultures. Seven sources of life span socialization are family, peers, school/work, community, the media, the legal system, and one's cultural belief system (Arnett, 1995). Cultures described as broad encompass those that allow for independence, individuality, and self-expression; cultures described as narrow are those that value obedience and conformity (Arnett, 1995). Regarding the adult development milestones of marriage, parenthood, and employment, those experiencing a broad socialization will see more variability and flexibility in achieving success, whereas those experiencing a narrow socialization will see more conformity in terms of specific ages where success is evident (Arnett, 1995).

Of course, this is one person's theoretical perspective. Understanding the socialization practices of immigrants is necessary in shared exploration, between immigrant and counselor, of the meaning of life span tasks and timeliness of expectations by one's culture and family. The MSJCC (Ratts et al., 2015) that focus on client worldview and the counseling relationship—"counselors are aware, knowledgeable, skilled, and action-oriented in understanding clients' worldview" (p. 7) and "counselors are aware, knowledgeable, skilled, and action-oriented in understanding how client and counselor privileged and marginalized statuses influence the counseling relationship" (p. 9)—are critical for counselors to be competent and knowledgeable about life span development and cultural differences and similarities.

Psychological theory in life span development encompasses frameworks that focus on the impact of culture on one's developmental milestones. All theories are useful in conceptualizing life span tasks, but some are stage-oriented whereas others are more culture-oriented. Eurocentric theories of life span development include those of universal stage theorists such as Erik Erikson and Jean Piaget (see Maier, 1965), and these theorists have assessed the impact of culture on learning. However, culture-oriented theorists have integrated the influence of culture on social and cognitive development in more comprehensive and meaningful ways (see Kurt, 2020). Lev Vygotsky's theory focuses on how development is heavily impacted by social experiences (see Mecacci, 2021); Wilhelm Wundt studied the effect of culture on human behavior (see Albert & Trommsdorff, 2014); Urie Bronfenbrenner studied the effects of multiple environments or ecological systems on development (Bronfenbrenner, 1979); and Paul Baltes believed that development does not end at the beginning of adulthood but continues until death because developmental growth is not only a biological process but also a cultural process (see Staudinger, 2007).

The study of the ontogenesis process is more comprehensive in these cultural theories that expand stage theory and provide a more holistic perspective of development from a systems perspective. When discussing specific and different age-related responsibilities affected by the culture in which one lives, counselors will find that it makes more sense to apply one of these cultural theories to gain the most accurate comprehensive perspective possible. These approaches are in alignment with the MSJCC developed by Ratts et al. (2015). Specifically, counselors are encouraged to understand the influence of different sociocultural contexts on individuals' well-being.

Vygotsky's Social Development Theory

Vygotsky's sociocultural theory presents cognitive development as a direct result of social interactions and communication within a cultural group (Sigelman & Rider, 2015). Two relevant concepts specific to Vygotsky's theory are the zone of proximal development (Cole et al., 1978) and scaffolding (Wood et al., 1976). The *zone of proximal development* refers to the environment of learning whereby a young person develops cognitive growth by communicating with others and being exposed to the process of learning, and *scaffolding* refers to having a supportive teacher or other individual (e.g., peer, aide, parent) who guides them along their way in decreasing support as they grow and learn until they master a skill or fully understand a concept (Kurt, 2020). In terms of development and working in a zone of proximal development within one's family, children learn skills, beliefs, and practices relevant to their culture from parents, grandparents, older siblings, and extended family members, and then may pass along their knowledge and skill to younger family members and relatives. The key for parents in working within a zone of proximal development and being a scaffolding person is to focus on what their children already know and build on that knowledge to increase skills and awareness while decreasing instruction or overbearing monitoring as their child becomes proficient in their developmental task and cultural development (Cleare, n.d.).

Wundt's Totems and Cultural Psychology Research

Wundt introduced us to the study of culture and human behavior using experimentation and scientific study. He was also a pioneer in cultural psychology and taught the importance of researching the understanding of consciousness and mental states (Mcloud, 2023). In one specific research area of Wundt's studies of cultures, the topic of totems is introduced, which are symbols or representations used within human affiliations (Y.-T. Lee et al., 2018). Totems include tribal/group, gender, and individual aspects (Wundt, 1916). For example, preindustrial communities had totems associated with religion and spirits, while early European totems existed as coats of arms (Moahi, 2022). In South Africa, totem animals are used to protect the tribe by keeping the tribe in bonds of unity and dignity (Moahi, 2022). Among the Nor-Papua of New Guinea, the fish is a well-known totem; in northeast Deccan (India), the Birhor are organized into patrilineal totem groups whereby 12 are based on animals, 10 on plants, eight on Hindu localities, and the rest on objects; in Liberia, Kpelle totems include animals, plants, and natural phenomena (Haekel, n.d.).

Some ethnic groups bring the concept of a totem to their new life in the United States, thus adhering to the cultural values of their homeland. Totems can be important concepts to help counselors learn more about immigrants' life span development and family and the use of important symbolism to illustrate one's key concepts in their cultural identity. Although not necessarily referred to as totems, prayer books, bibles, and other religious artifacts such as rosary beads and medals may also take on cultural and religious meaning.

Bronfenbrenner's Ecological Systems Theory

Bronfenbrenner developed his theory based on how individuals develop in terms of five environmental systems: microsystem (a proximal level in which one is directly impacted by the settings with which one interacts), mesosystem (a level that involves multiple microsystems, such as family, school, or work), exosystem (a level that indirectly affects an individual's development), macrosystem (a level that includes beliefs, values, and norms as reflected by one's cultural, religious, and socioeconomic aspects of one's life), and chronosystem (a level in which an individual's development is shaped by time; Ettekal & Mahoney, 2017). In an example provided by Ettekal and Mahoney (2017), we see the first four systems in organized sports activities as follows: The microsystem is the specific organized sports activity, the mesosystem is the parent-coach relationship, the exosystem is the school district policy on sports as an extracurricular activity, and the macrosystem is the societal views of sports. Another example is the topic of sexual activities among adolescents. Depending on the culture and associated beliefs of sexual activity, an adolescent navigates their concept of their sexuality and gender identity development (microsystem), a sexual partner or partners (mesosystem), parents' attitudes about sex education and family values (exosystem), and societal views on adolescent sexual development (macrosystem). One can apply any number of events and topics to life span development as it applies through Bronfenbrenner's ecological systems theory, and it becomes helpful in giving a counselor a holistic perspective of the impact of culture on an individual's life span development. In the case of the aforementioned examples, counselors would need to keep in mind the cultural norms, values, and expectations as they relate to sexual activity and even gender role and sports expectations for immigrant and refugee young adults.

Baltes's Life Span Perspective of Development

Baltes's work was important because he was the first developmentalist to consider development beyond early adulthood. He took Erikson's stage model and the focus on generativity in particular (the eighth stage) and studied the ways in which people contribute to their families and communities as they age, such as by imparting the knowledge and wisdom they gained throughout their lives to others (Staudinger, 2007). In a discussion about the architecture of life span theory, Baltes et al. (1999) described the increased need for culture as we age and the decreased need for efficacy of culture (protective effects of culture manifest; Gonzales et al., 2002) as we age. The more one is culturally engaged, the more confident one is about cultural roles and purpose and seeking advice of others (Gonzales et al., 2002). Older adults, including immigrants, often have primarily positive memories of special people in their lives. It is not about living in the past but having fond associations for early cultural experiences and relationships.

Baltes was also the first to focus on biocultural development and defined it as follows: "factors associated with age related biological and socialization processes account for regularities and differences in human development" (Baltes et al., 1980, pp. 70–71). Furthermore, Baltes et al. (1980) discussed developmental behaviors associated with cultural transmission and intergenerational dynamics related to the development of socialization/cultural goals. *Normative influences* are known as biological and environmental factors that associate with a specific historical era (Neugarten, 1973) and historical contexts (Baltes et al., 1980). *Nonnormative influences* are those events that are not typical but affect development, such as trauma, divorce, illness, and other challenges to development (Baltes et al., 1979). The migration process may be considered a nonnormative influence on development given the impact of this type of change in one's life and the effects on one's development. The immigration process in itself is a developmental experience that impacts the process of development during the emerging adult maturation stage (Walsh et al., 2005). Indeed, the dimensions of personal identity model previously discussed (Arredondo & Glauner, 1992) posits that immigration is a historical moment setting in motion multiple life changes for adults and their children alike.

Baltes et al. (1980) also emphasized social behaviors developed in childhood leading to maintenance, transformation, or extinction of behaviors in late adulthood depending on their usefulness. Exploring essential behaviors and behaviors that have been extinguished with immigrant and refugee clients can help counselors understand cultural influences. For example, refugee adults may find that their skills in the agricultural world may not be transferable because they are living in an urban area; thus, they will seek out readily available employment opportunities and learn new skills in those positions. Another important concept to life span development in a cultural context is the *selective optimization with compensation model* introduced by Paul and Margaret Baltes, which explores how aging adults compensate some of their losses by increasing focus on other abilities still available to them (Feldman, 2018). This discussion supports the value of researching social behaviors of individuals and how they associate with one's cultural identity.

A counselor's attitude, beliefs, knowledge, skills, and action orientation about applying life span models in their work with immigrants and refugees are reflected in the MSJCC (Ratts, et al., 2015). Understanding our role in counseling is emphasized by these MSJCC. The examples that emanate from these different theoretical frameworks that respect culture remind counselors how much cultural perspectives need to be considered when working with immigrants and refugees.

Culture-Specific Development Over the Life Span

Life span development of various personality traits, behaviors, cultural beliefs, and socialization has been studied in a variety of ways and includes foci on cultural differences as well as similarities. Specific life span tasks that are culture oriented are not well researched and need to be a topic of study in the future. We will touch briefly on the topic based on what is available in the literature.

Albert and Trommsdorff (2014) studied culture-specific developmental trends and activities through an interpersonal relations approach and found important distinctions in our understanding and expectations of childhood, adolescence, adulthood, and old age. For example, childhood in many cultures is considered a stage that leads directly into adulthood (without an adolescent stage) when reproduction occurs as soon as physical development allows for it (Greenfield, 2010). When adolescence is viewed as a life stage, it is a period that, depending on the cultural definition of this stage, may involve gender-specific rituals, various stages of separation from family, and identity development (Albert & Trommsdorff, 2014). Adulthood is a stage in many cultures whereby we establish a family, become vocationally engaged, and continue to parent our children and take care of our parents as they age. Old age is a time in life when we are either taken care of by our family members (in collectivistic cultures) or expected to remain independent (in individualistic societies) until we need social services to provide for our needs (Albert & Trommsdorff, 2014). There are differences in levels to which people and families engage in these behaviors depending on the family orientation and cultural expectations.

Parenting is central to life span development as children and adolescents develop independent or collectivistic values within the family cultural identity. Bornstein et al. (2011) stated that parents "successfully transmit the prevailing culture across generations" (p. 214). Parents set the tone for specific characteristics and tasks for children and adolescents to complete and provide expectations for timing in which children meet specific developmental tasks (Albert & Trommsdorff, 2014). Parents encourage their children's development of characteristics and beliefs needed to contribute successfully to society (Albert & Trommsdorff, 2014). Some differences in parenting involve the attitude with which parents tolerate or do not tolerate behaviors of young children between the ages of 3 and 5 years that lead to independence (an individualistic trait) or reliance on the family or community (a collectivistic trait).

For example, Mayan mothers of infants keep their child physically close as much of the time as is possible, whereas some American mothers of infants put their child down to cry themselves to sleep (Feldman, 2018). Another example is young children in the Canadian Arctic who are tolerated and treated with understanding and acceptance by their Inuit parents, whereas young children in the Pacific Island of Tonga are treated with harsh discipline, physical punishment, and high expectations for behavior (Montgomery, 2022). In the United Kingdom, strict child labor laws prohibit a child under the age of 14 to care for younger siblings unsupervised, whereas the Fulani of West Africa have 4-year-old girls caring for younger siblings and 6-year-old girls contributing to the family economy by processing milk and butter and assisting their mothers in selling their goods at the local market (Montgomery, 2022). These and the following examples illustrate the many differences in parenting styles in the world.

Al-Hassan et al. (2021) found a direct relationship between Jordanian mothers' parenting and their children's development of collectivistic values. Qualities of children that Jordanian mothers encourage relate to collectivistic characteristics, including proper demeanor, decency, lovingness, and self-maximization. Proper demeanor has to do with politeness; decency is related to honesty and social responsibility; lovingness involves respecting others and developing harmony in relationships; and self-maximization is related to work ethic and independence (Al-Hassan et al., 2021). Compared with Jordanian mothers, mothers in the United States tend to encourage independence, confidence, self-reliance, and individuality, but overt selfishness is seen as counterproductive to a healthy family and community, and children and adolescents are taught to balance independence and consideration of others (Carteret, 2013).

Most collectivistic parents encourage a "we" attitude and promote dependence on the family and community. Negotiating cooperation is a value that collectivistic groups hold dear (Carteret, 2013). Rejection in collectivistic cultures promotes feelings of isolation, whereas isolation and independence are nurtured in individualistic cultures. Carteret (2013) gave the example of the lone cowboy in the Western world as a symbol of independence. Both collectivistic and individualistic cultures have many ways in which parenting contributes to the overall development of dependence or independence, and understanding these values helps counselors to work with a variety of immigrants and refugees from many types of cultures. Exploring parenting practices and childhood experiences assists counselors in engaging in dialogue with clients to understand how parenting is taught and practiced in various cultures. These examples will likely be exhibited by immigrant and refugee parents.

Child, adult, and older adult development can also be understood by a process known as age-grading, whereby people are classified by distinctions based on age and rules of behavior that are different for each age-grade (Ornstein, n.d.). An age-grade is a group of people approximately the same age who have responsibilities and privileges that are similar to each other in division of tribe or society (Baltes et al., 1980; Merriam-Webster, n.d.). These age-grades are known as young, grown up, and aged (Ornstein, n.d.). A study conducted by Kitayama et al. (2020) focused on age-grading in adults and older adults and measured personality traits, comparing aging Americans and Asians in how they balance approaching the reality of aging and cultural expectations associated with their groundedness in individualism or collectivism. American adults and Asian adults showed a high number of positive emotions as they aged, but these two groups differed when measuring extraversion, conscientiousness, personal growth, and purpose in life, which markedly declined for American adults but not for Asian adults. The authors summarized their findings in terms of American adult views of aging, which can be negative considering the individualistic view of independence (even in one's old age), and the Asian perspective on collectivism, which is positive given the way aging Asians are taken care of by family (Kitayama et al., 2020).

Personal Identity and Intersectionalities as Related to Life Span Development

Layers of cultural identity stem from developmental tasks specific to one's family and culture. Specific dimensions of personal identity and intersectionality as developed by Arredondo and Glauner (1992) encompass categories and layers of identity related to age, culture, ethnicity, gender identities, language, ability status, race, sexual orientation, and social class (Dimension A); educational background, geographic location, hobbies/recreational interests, military experience, relationship status, religion/spirituality, political orientation, work experience, and health care practices/beliefs (Dimension B); and historical movements/eras, sociopolitical climate, and ecological forces (Dimension C). Understanding immigrant identities as complex systems that affect development, beliefs, attitudes, behaviors, fears, hopes, and life dreams is important for counselors working with this population. Each dimension of identity has a different meaning for individuals across the life span. For example, immigrant men with a professional identity will aspire to such an identity status in the United States, whereas men with a laborer identity will seek employment that is familiar to them. Both seek affirmation of their work identity.

Immigrants may share similar migration experiences but differ in a multitude of ways in terms of intersectional identities and life experiences based on their cultural identity related to developmental tasks and behaviors. Migration itself becomes a developmental task for many immigrants and refugees. Depending on the time they entered the United States (whether during the 19th, 20th, or 21st century), age, whether as the result of a crisis or long-term planning, and whether they had family waiting for them to arrive, immigrants have unique experiences in their identity development/acculturation through the lens of the many layers of intersectionality and life span activities.

The employment dimension of intersectionality is important to consider when working with immigrants to understand the developmental task of becoming employed and making a living. More than 44.9 million immigrants lived in the United States in 2019, 13.75% of the total population compared with the record high of 14.8% in 1890 (Ward & Batalova, 2023). A stereotypical (and contradictory) view of an immigrant in the United States is that they are undocumented and are here to take jobs away from U.S. citizens (Chomsky, 2018). Although many Americans believe that most immigrants are undocumented, the majority of immigrants enter host countries legally (Kaushal, 2019). In 2017, the U.S. workforce was made up of 29 million immigrants, with 21.2 million documented workers and 7.6 million undocumented workers (Budiman, 2020). In 2020, documented immigrants worked in the following industries: food production, processing, distribution, retail (14%), agriculture (15%), construction (13%), personal/other services (15%), leisure/hospitality (12%), and manufacturing (14%). In contrast, undocumented workers were employed in food production, processing, distribution, retail (9%), agriculture (14%), construction (12%), personal/other services (7%), leisure/hospitality (8%), and manufacturing (6%; Bennett, 2020).

The topic of immigrant entrepreneurship is described in the literature and is an opportunity to understand this career development aspect of identity and life span development. For example, Anderson (2018) found that more than half of U.S. billion-dollar companies were developed by immigrants. Additionally, 40% of Fortune 500 companies were created by first- or second-generation immigrants (Partnership for a New American Economy, 2011). Brettell and Alstatt (2007) found that respondents in their study on immigrant entrepreneurship exhibited individual effort, the use of personal resources versus bank loans, and the ability to seize opportunities as personal qualities.

Racial/Ethnic Socialization

Parenting involves racial/ethnic socialization (RES) that affects all children and their cultural identity development. RES is the process through which parents contribute to their children's learning about their culture and their relationships with others outside their ethnic group (Kuang & Nishikawa, 2021). Parents are the main influence of ethnic socialization, along with peers (Rivas-Drake et al., 2009). RES is also known as the maintenance of one's heritage culture, awareness of discrimination and out-group threat, and creation of equal rights (Hughes et al., 2006; Kim et al., 2023). Furthermore, Hughes et al. (2006) identified four key aspects of family RES that have emerged in the literature: cultural socialization (i.e., passing down of cultural values, customs, traditions, and history), preparation for racism (i.e., preparing youth for potential discrimination and developing coping skills), promotion of mistrust (i.e., passing along the need for distrust of other racial/ethnic groups), and egalitarianism (i.e., communicating equality among racial/ethnic groups). All these aspects affect life span development and interrupt the natural progression of developing one's identity along with life tasks. Being able to work with immigrants on these aspects allows clients to explore their own RES and the meaning behind such socialization.

Studies about RES measure developmental features related to cultural identity development. Kuang and Nishikawa (2009) assessed the impact of ethnic socialization on Chinese Mulao adolescents' ethnic identity and self-esteem and found that the more students perceived messages of harmony from their parents, the stronger their ethnic identity and self-esteem. Kim et al. (2023) examined discrimination, racism, and RES of Asian American parents and found that RES may be connected to internalized racism (discrimination perpetuated by the majority culture). This is an important finding that relates to how we must study more about the impact of racism on ethnic socialization of immigrants and refugees, especially during times of increased discrimination such as during COVID-19 when the bulk of the blame for the pandemic was placed on Asian Americans. In their review of 10 years of RES literature involving 259 articles, Umaña-Taylor and Hill (2020) discovered four themes: cultural socialization, preparation for racism, promotion of mistrust, and egalitarianism. One of the more salient findings in reviewing the literature is that most likely all youth receive socialization about race and ethnicity in some way (Hughes et al., 2006).

The factors that appear in Appendix 4A are important for counselors to be aware of in terms of helping immigrant and refugee individuals and families navigate their developmental milestones in child-rearing, family, peer relationships, school/work, community, and the development of one's cultural belief system. These developmental milestones are very much connected to RES.

Specific life span development tasks related to family, child-rearing, employment, and aging need to be examined and discussed in the literature for counselors to understand the cultural differences in RES. Exploring one's RES in counseling is an excellent way to understand immigrant and refugee values that have been passed down from generation to generation.

Impact of Immigration on the Development of Immigrants and Refugees

Immigration is seen as its own developmental stage as immigrants and refugees are confronted with change, uncertainty, and culture shock as they transition into their new home. According to Pedersen (1995), culture shock consists of five stages: honeymoon, disintegration, reintegration, autonomy, and interdependence. Helping immigrants and refugees navigate these stages allows counselors to engage in their MSJCC competency development while assisting clients through challenging chapters in their lives. Understanding the stages of culture shock can enable counselors in helping immigrants and refugees cope and examine their needs at each stage as they settle into their new lives.

Perhaps one of the most critical phases of development that immigration impacts is that of emerging adulthood, whereby the immigration experience requires an extensive exploration of one's self-concept and self-narrative (Akhtar, 1999). In their study of emerging adult experiences, Walsh et al. (2005) found that immigrant emerging adults may have a more disorganized sense of self during migration, but they also had high levels of autonomy and relatedness with their parents. Immigrants' relatedness had meaning in closeness, caring, and identification with parents, and closeness in both social and intimate relationships. Walsh et al. compared findings with nonimmigrant emerging adults who reported "autonomy seeking" with more independent decision-making, emotional independence, and assertiveness in the relationship with parents. The differences between relatedness and independence can be seen from the perspective of collectivistic versus individualistic cultures. Knowledge of the differences between immigrants and nonimmigrants helps counselors understand the developmental stages of their clients.

As more information is needed about how immigration impacts immigrant and refugee developmental processes, researchers should focus on studying various age groups and specific developmental tasks not currently discussed in the literature. The aforementioned studies by Akhtar (1999) and Walsh et al. (2005) are excellent examples of the quality of attention to immigration and life span development that are needed in today's literature reviews.

We now turn to specific biographies to understand the concepts of life span development of identity through the transition of immigration. These biographies and personal stories are described through a lens of intersectionality and life span development tasks to facilitate a better understanding of immigrants, refugees, minors, and family units. The immigration demographics emphasize the life span development and constellation of immigrants and immigrant families in the United States and their intersecting identities.

Immigrant and Refugee Biographies

Nina Barragan

An immigrant from Argentina, Nina Barragan (2000) moved to the United States with her parents when she was 19 months old. Her grandparents had immigrated to Argentina from Europe when her parents were young. Life span tasks for this family included parents' immigration to the United States because of dissatisfaction with their home country of Argentina. Her parents believed that there was a better life waiting for them in the United States with a more stable society, better employment options, and a safe environment in which to raise their children (life span tasks included assimilation, parenting, employment, community building, and marriage fulfillment).

Barragan's (2000) father immigrated to the United States, leaving behind stressful family scenarios and a country in turmoil. He was determined to start over. Barragan's mother immigrated to the United States with plans to move back to Argentina at some point and realized after settling into a home in Iowa with her husband and six children that she would never return to Argentina because of her husband's unenthusiastic attitude toward their home country. Barragan watched her mother struggle with her own resistance toward assimilation because she continued to feel a tie to Argentina late into her life. Assimilation for this family was a considerable life span task with which Barragan's father struggled very little and her mother struggled very much.

Barragan's (2000) description of her process of "becoming American" shows us how she explored her intersectionality through the challenges of feeling isolated from extended family because her parents taught her the American ideal of individualism, or self-reliance, a life span task in the United States. They did not intentionally teach individualism as an American trait; they simply resisted assimilation, making sure they remained Argentine by speaking Spanish and practicing cultural rituals/values. But her father respected American ways in many ways, including being able to build things without being a professional, and he enjoyed doing carpentry work while remodeling their summer home. Her parents modeled for her how to be in the world of America, but not of it. Life span tasks included the development of an individualistic value and identity.

Extended family was a foreign concept to Barragan (2000). It was not until later in life when she returned to Argentina that she developed a sense of identity that included a family history. She has lived in Europe and Canada but returned to Iowa where she feels at home and lives with her husband and children. Her cultural intersectional identity developed through her transitional experiences of living in different parts of the world and finding herself when she returned to the most familiar place, Iowa. Life span tasks included making adult decisions about a preferred location of home.

Barragan (2000) wanted to assimilate to the degree that she could while always feeling like a "foreigner." A key factor in her difficulty in assimilating was her name: Rocío Aitana Lasansky. She intentionally changed her public name to Nina Barragan ("Nina" being a family nickname; "Barragan" being her mother's maiden name) after tiring of people mispronouncing her given name of "Rocío." She sees assimilation as a continual process and appreciates her American home and enjoys her national connection to America. Life span tasks included exploration of a name through identity development and a decision to change her name based on individual and family values.

Judith Ortiz Cofer

This story is about an immigrant whose life span development included lifelong self-identity development through the art of writing. Judith Ortiz Cofer (2000) describes having "enough space between my selves for my investigation to proceed" (p. 30) as an experience in exploring her intersectional identities. Being born in Puerto Rico and moving to the United States when her father took a position in New Jersey, Ortiz Cofer experienced loneliness for her homeland and curiosity about how to process life in the United States. She wrote from a young age in a journal, writing a few paragraphs daily to express her thoughts, feelings, and insights. It is not a surprise that she is an accomplished and well-known Latina writer.

Ortiz Cofer (2000) describes conflict between her mother and father about returning to their homeland of Puerto Rico. Her parents had arguments about her father's desire to succeed in the United States in his Navy career and instill the value of education in his children. Her mother struggled with loneliness and despair in missing her *familia* (family) and found solace in her religious practice and relentless reading of romance novels. Ortiz Cofer was responsible for purchasing books for her mother at the local market and found that reading them with her mother was a special way of sharing the Spanish language and the love of reading. Ortiz Cofer's mother was experiencing life span challenges of parenting and finding a place in a world she did not connect to. Reading romance novels provided her with an activity that satisfied her need to connect culturally with her daughter.

Ortiz Cofer (2000) watched her mother return to Puerto Rico after her father died, but she remained in the United States to continue her education, develop her career in teaching and writing, and marry and have a family of her own, all important life span milestones. In exploring her identities, she describes herself as a writer as being "always in the new territory of Myself Alone" (Ortiz Cofer, 2000, pp. 37–38).

Alex

Work experience is an intersectional identity factor in Arredondo and Glauner's (1992) intersectionality model that is important to note in terms of immigrant experiences, and vocational employment is an adult life span task. In the case of Alex (Brettell & Alstaff, 2007), there was initially a struggle to find his place in the workplace in the United States, but he eventually found value in being an entrepreneur. Alex came to the United States at the age of 24 years from Nigeria to attend college and complete his banking and finance degree. He worked in business before he decided to attend pharmacy school. He graduated with his pharmacy degree and worked at several hospitals during evening shifts, making very little money. He heard about selling insurance as a career and began working in insurance while continuing to work as a pharmacist. His interest in selling insurance was born out of a desire to have his own business and have more control over his time with family. He found that starting up his own insurance business was easy, and he had saved enough money as an investment for his company.

Alex currently utilizes support from his family and hopes to hire more staff in the future, particularly Spanish-speaking salespersons to attend to Hispanic customers. Barriers typical to immigrant entrepreneurs are language and finances for start-up costs (Brettell & Alstaff, 2007). Alex had a strong command of English when he arrived in the United States and was able to save up the start-up costs over a 10-year period. Exploring career identity is an important part of immigrants' intersectional development, and Alex's case illustrates the struggle in achieving occupational success. Adult life span tasks often involve career and job changes that allow for vocational goals to be met.

Dinesh

This immigrant example is about adult life tasks, such as saving money, taking on various worker roles to find the right fit, and finding motivation to make career decisions that matter, no matter the risk involved. Dinesh arrived in the United States from India with his wife and 5-year-old child and was sponsored by his brother-in-law (Brettell & Alstaff, 2007). He worked in mechanical engineering for several years as he moved from state to state to find better paying jobs. After a few layoffs and saving enough for start-up costs for his own company, Dinesh pursued a lifelong dream. He learned about the motel business by working with a friend in their business, and then bought his first motel with his savings and a loan. He and his family lived in their motel to save money and then bought their house after 2 years.

The biggest drawbacks to the motel business for Dinesh were managing employees and working long hours. He looks forward to retiring and selling his business and saying goodbye to 12-hour workdays. Sources of support for his business include ethnic resources in his Indian community and his own finances and motivation to succeed. Internal qualities of discipline in saving money, being motivated to work hard, managing other people, and balancing family and work contribute to his identity development and intersectionalities (Brettell & Alstaff, 2007).

Jose Antonio Vargas

This is a description of an immigrant who struggled with adolescent life span issues, including cultural identity development, vocational decisions, community building, communication style, and self-image development. Jose Antonio Vargas (2018) immigrated to the United States from the Philippines when he was 14 years old, and he struggled to understand his racial identity as Asian amid the confusion of a different language and a variety of persons of colors and races in his homeland and in the United States. He describes his Filipino grandparents (who were naturalized citizens) as having immigrated to the United States 10 years before his arrival, and they supported his transition when he arrived in California, helping him understand the racial divisions and diversity of his community. Other identities such as "Latino" or "Hispanic" were confusing to him, and he did not understand why some races were capitalized (such as Hispanic), but "white" and "black" were not. He did not understand his undocumented status until he applied for a learner's permit and was denied because his green card was fake, which surprised him and led to a series of questions for his grandparents about his status as an immigrant.

Impacting Vargas's (2018) confusion about his racial identity was his speech accent and appearance. Other students told him he didn't "look" or "seem" Filipino, but they had trouble identifying him as being of another race or ethnicity. Vargas had a teacher who once told him he was neither White nor Black, and, for that, he was fortunate. This statement led to more confusion and made him aware that there were privileges to being White.

Vargas (2018) learned that racial identity was as much about behavior as anything else. He describes hearing peers at school tell each other not to be "too" White, Black, and so on. Vargas's confusion about being Filipino is described in his autobiography *Dear America*, where he states that "we are the invisibles of the invisible" (p. 21). He ultimately spent time in his late teens and early 20s trying to "pass" as White, and this required more exploration of how he could fit into his place in life.

Videos, films, music, authors of color, and TV shows (e.g., *Ellen*) helped Vargas (2018) navigate his development and understanding of his racial and sexual identities. Celebrity immigrants inspired him and affirmed his experiences; Black authors gave him "permission to question America" (Vargas, 2018, p. 77). In trying to understand how to fit into American culture as an "illegal," he derived much of his perception from realizing that all Americans were immigrants.

Vargas's (2018) career trajectory started when he became interested in journalism in high school, where he was inspired by a mentor. His vocational identity took root and allowed him to take pride in his work and created excitement about his future. Adult mentors helped him identify a scholarship (Mountain View Los Altos [MVLA]) that helps low-income and first-generation college students attend college. This opportunity came in handy given his undocumented status. He has since become involved in MLVA and currently serves on the scholarship's advisory board.

Vargas (2018) is an inspirational writer who writes about his confusing intersectional identity development, the complicated immigration process, and what it is like to live "outside the law" and be vulnerable as a noncitizen. His autobiography is an excellent example of how one navigates one's intersectionalities and life span development.

John

This immigration example is about a refugee who struggled with developmental issues, such as cultural identity development, military identity, marriage and family, and acculturation once he was settled in the United States. John (pseudonym) was a refugee from Laos and had been connected to the Vietnam War with the agreement that the United States made with the Hmong at the time to help with the American agenda (personal communication, October 9, 2019). After the war ended and the communists took over John's village in Vietnam, he escaped to a refugee camp in Thailand. He spent 10 years in the crowded, unsanitary refugee camp until he was able to come to the United States as a refugee. He was assisted by the United Nations and was sponsored by his brother, who was already in the United States.

In terms of identity, John identified as a soldier in the Vietnam War, as a son to his mother whom he cared for, as a husband, as a father to three young children, and as a brother (to one he shared living quarters within the camp and to another who had already immigrated to the United States). During the 10-year period in the refugee camp while he and his family were waiting to be transferred to the United States, his wife, mother, and brother died. When he finally was able to come to the United States, he brought his three young children, lived with his brother, and acclimated to life in the United States. He was the main caretaker of his children (his brother who sponsored him from the United States also helped with childcare), worker, and homemaker. He struggled with language, shopping, finding work with his limited English in the beginning, and parenting (John, personal communication, October 9, 2019).

John's experiences are not unique to those who immigrated to the United States after the Vietnam War. Years spent in overcrowded refugee camps were challenging in terms of unsanitary sleeping quarters (e.g., maggots were present), scarcity of bathrooms, lack of work, abundance of worry about when they would be released to the United States, grief from losing so many family members due to living in a refugee camp, and loneliness in being away from family who stayed in communist Vietnam. Life span issues were addressed over the years as John was able to resolve much of the trauma of the refugee camp and explored gender roles in his family (John, personal communication, October 9, 2019).

Maria

Maria (pseudonym) was inspired to migrate when members of her family moved to the United States and found employment and safe living options. Her life span tasks included parenting, navigating family roles, finding employment, and developing her cultural identity.

Maria came to the United States from Mexico at the age of 26 after her husband and brothers moved here (personal communication, October 30, 2019). She waited for 2 years for her husband (who was sending money home at first) to call for her, but in time, he was struggling with keeping a job and struggling with an alcohol addiction. Maria's husband was unable to assist her in her journey or in settling down once she arrived in the United States. So, Maria's brothers sent her money and helped her prepare for the journey and arranged for the "courier." She had two young children at the time, and her brothers told her she could only bring one. She chose to bring her younger son, who was 3 years old at the time, and left her 5-year-old daughter with her parents until she could arrange for her daughter to join her later. The decision to leave a child behind was heart-wrenching.

The initial cost of a courier was $1,200, but she ended up paying more after many attempts to enter the United States (Maria, personal communication, October 30, 2019). During the journey, Maria had to dress like a man to avoid sexual assault and harassment. She and her son were separated at the border. Maria's brother's girlfriend stayed with her son, whom she had to leave in a hotel room with a man she did not know for 2 days. When her brother's girlfriend went back for him, he was alone, happily playing. Her son got to the destination of her brother's home a month before Maria was able to arrive. She was held up in her journey with long walks through the hot dry desert, hours spent in a crowded truck, and twice being arrested and sent back to Mexico. Finally, Maria was able to cross the border via a different route with a different courier.

Once Maria arrived in California, she was able to find orchard work (two different jobs) and reunite with her son and brothers (personal communication, October 30, 2019). She was able to send money to her parents to help them out. She has been doing orchard work in many states as the seasons demand workers. Both of her children live with her now, and she is settled in the United States but constantly worries about deportation of the family.

Maria's identity as a mother is her most important role. She would do anything for her family to have a good life, and she is happy to be working in the United States with her family. Life span challenges involved her cultural identity, parent identity, vocational identity, and family roles.

Reflection Questions

1. What do you understand about intersections of identity and life span issues and how to use this understanding in working with any of the immigrants in this chapter?
2. How would you work with the immigrants in this chapter to explore their identities and developmental challenges as they relate to their life stories?
3. How do you understand stages of development and how immigrants' migration experiences can be seen as their own developmental stage as they apply to immigrants in this chapter?
4. How can you work on your MSJCC development in self-awareness of attitudes and beliefs about immigrants and their culture?

Summary

The literature review in this chapter explores subjects, theory, and research related to life span development in a cultural context, parenting styles, and RES. RES is important for counselors to explore with immigrants and refugees to understand parenting styles and values taught to children and adolescents. We also discussed personality theory and intersectionalities in relation to the life span development of immigrants and refugees. Understanding intersectionalities of clients helps counselors explore the layers of cultural identity, along with life experiences. The descriptions of immigrants and refugees in this chapter address biographies and personal stories through a lens of intersectionality and life span development tasks. Through these data and biographies, readers gain a better understanding about immigrant men, women, minors, and family units. These immigration demographics emphasize the life span development and constellation of immigrants and immigrant families in the United States and their intersecting identities.

References

Abudabbeh, N. (2005). Arab families. In M. McGoldrick, J. Giordano, & N. G. Preto (Eds.), *Ethnicity and family therapy* (3rd ed., pp. 423–436). Guilford Press.

Akhtar, S. (1999). *Immigration and identity: Turmoil, treatment, and transformation.* Jason Aronson.

Albert, I., & Trommsdorff, G. (2014). The role of culture in social development over the lifespan: An interpersonal relations approach. *Online Readings in Psychology and Culture*, *6*(2), Article 1. https://doi.org/10.9707/2307-0919.1057

Al-Hassan, O. M., De Baz, T., Ihmeideh, F., & Jumiaan, I. (2021). Collectivism and individualism: Jordanian mothers' child-rearing values. *International Journal of Early Years Education*, *29*(2), 199–210. https://doi.org/10.1080/09669760.2020.1814216

Almeida, R. (2005). Asian Indian families. In M. McGoldrick, J. Giordano, & N. G. Preto (Eds.), *Ethnicity and family therapy* (3rd ed., pp. 377–394). Guilford Press.

Anderson, S. (2018). *Immigrants and billion-dollar companies* [Policy brief]. National Foundation for American Policy. https://nfap.com/wp-content/uploads/2019/01/2018-BILLION-DOLLAR-STARTUPS.NFAP-Policy-Brief.2018-1.pdf

Arnett, J. J. (1995). Broad and narrow socialization: The family in the context of a cultural theory. *Journal of Marriage and Family*, *57*(3), 617–628. https://doi.org/10.2307/353917

Arredondo, P., & Glauner, T. (1992). *Personal dimensions of identity model.* Empowerment Workshops.

Baltes, P. B., Cornelius, S. W., & Nesselroade, J. R. (1979). Cohort effects in developmental psychology. In J. R. Nesselroade & P. B. Baltes (Eds.), *Longitudinal research in the study of behavior and development* (pp. 61–87). Academic Press.

Baltes, P. B., Reese, H. W., & Lipsitt, L. P. (1980). Life-span developmental psychology. *Annual Review of Psychology, 31*, 65–110. https://doi.org/10.1146/annurev.ps.31.020180.000433

Baltes, P. B., Staudinger, U. M., & Lindenberger, U. (1999). Lifespan psychology: Theory and application to intellectual functioning. *Annual Review of Psychology, 50*, 471–507. https://doi.org/10.1146/annurev.psych.50.1.471

Barragan, N. (2000). Doing archaeology in my America. In M. N.-A. Danquah (Ed.), *Becoming American: Personal essays by first generation immigrant women* (pp. 1–11). Hyperion.

Bennett, J. (2020, February 24). *The share of immigrant workers in high-skill jobs is rising in the U.S.* Pew Research Center. https://www.pewresearch.org/short-reads/2020/02/24/the-share-of-immigrant-workers-in-high-skill-jobs-is-rising-in-the-u-s/

Berry, J. W., Phinney, J. S., Sam, D. L., & Vedder, P. (Eds.). (2006). *Immigrant youth in cultural transition: Acculturation, identity, and adaptation across national contexts.* Erlbaum. https://doi.org/10.4324/9780415963619

Bornstein, M. H., Putnick, D. L., & Lansford, J. E. (2011). Parenting attributions and attitudes in cross-cultural perspective. *Parenting: Science and Practice, 11*(2–3), 214–237. https://doi.org/10.1080/15295192.2011.585568

Brettell, C. B., & Alstatt, K. E. (2007). The agency of immigrant entrepreneurs: Biographies of the self-employed in ethnic and occupational niches of the urban labor market. *Journal of Anthropological Research, 63*(3), 383–397. http://www.jstor.org/stable/20479430

Bronfenbrenner, U. (1979). *The ecology of human development: Experiments by nature and design.* Harvard University Press.

Brown, A. (2020). *Nearly half of U.S. adults say dating has gotten harder for most people in the last 10 years.* Pew Research Center. https://www.pewresearch.org/social-trends/2020/08/20/nearly-half-of-u-s-adults-say-dating-has-gotten-harder-for-most-people-in-the-last-10-years/

Budiman, A. (2020, August 20). *Key findings about U.S. immigrants.* Pew Research Center. https://www.pewresearch.org/fact-tank/2020/08/20/key-findings-about-u-s-immigrants/

Carteret, M. (2013, September 30). *Culturally-based differences in child rearing practices.* Dimensions of Culture. https://www.dimensionsofculture.com/2013/09/how-individualism-and-collectivism-manifest-in-child-rearing-practices/

Center for Immigrant Studies. (2022). *Foreign-born population hits nearly 48 million in September 2022.* https://cis.org/Report/ForeignBorn-Population-Hits-Nearly-48-Million-September-2022

Chomsky, A. (2018). *"They take our jobs!" and 20 other myths about immigration* (Expanded ed.). Beacon Press.

Cleare, A. (n.d.). *Parents and the zone of proximal development (ZPD).* Positive Parenting Project. https://anitacleare.co.uk/parents-and-the-zone-of-proximal-development-zpd/

Cole, M., John-Steiner, V., Scribner, S., & Souberman, E. (Eds.). (1978). *Mind in society: The development of higher psychological processes.* Harvard University Press.

Commonwealth of Puerto Rico. (2014). *Commonwealth of Puerto Rico quarterly report dated July 17, 2014.* https://hacienda.pr.gov/sites/default/files/commonwealthquarterlyreport71714.pdf

Doerfler, B. (2014). *Puerto Rico: Language characteristics.* https://sites.psu.edu/intercommpuertorico/category/cultural-values/

Ettekal, A. V., & Mahoney, J. L. (2017). Ecological systems theory. In K. Peppler (Ed.), *The Sage encyclopedia of out-of-school learning* (pp. 239–241). Sage Publications.

Feldman, R. S. (2018). *Development across the life span.* Pearson.

Garcia-Preto, N. (2005). Latino families. In M. McGoldrick, J. Giordano, & N. G. Preto (Eds.), *Ethnicity and family therapy* (3rd ed., pp. 153–165). Guilford Press.

Genao, G. (2023). *Dominican Republic culture & traditions: Everything you need to know + a quick history.* Dominican Abroad. https://www.dominicanabroad.com/dominican-republic-culture-traditions/

Gonzales, N. A., Knight, G. P., Morgan-Lopez, A., Saenz, D., & Sirolli, A (2002). Acculturation and the mental health of Latino youths: An integration and critique of the literature. In J. M. Contreras, K. A. Kerns, & A. M. Neal-Barnett (Eds.), *Latino children and families in the United States: Current research and future directions* (pp. 45–74). Praeger.

Greenfield, P. M. (2010). Particular forms of independence and interdependence are adapted to particular kinds of sociodemographic environment: Commentary on "Independence and interdependence in children's developmental experiences." *Child Development Perspectives, 4*(1), 37–39. https://doi.org/10.1111/j.1750-8606.2009.00114.x

Haekel, J. (n.d.). Totemism. In *Britannica*. Retrieved July 30, 2023, from https://www.britannica.com/topic/totemism-religion

Hernandez, M. (2005). Central American families. In M. McGoldrick, J. Giordano, & N. G. Preto (Eds.), *Ethnicity and family therapy* (3rd ed., pp. 178–191). Guilford Press.

Hughes, D., Rodriguez, J., Smith, E. P., Johnson, D. J., Stevenson, H. C., & Spicer, P. (2006). Parents' ethnic-racial socialization practices: A review of research and directions for future study. *Developmental Psychology, 42*(5), 747–770. https://doi.org/10.1037/0012-1649.42.5.747

Jalali, B. (2005). Iranian families. In M. McGoldrick, J. Giordano, & N. G. Preto (Eds.), *Ethnicity and family therapy* (3rd ed., pp. 451–467). Guilford Press.

Kamya, H. (2005). African immigrant families. In M. McGoldrick, J. Giordano, & N. G. Preto (Eds.), *Ethnicity and family therapy* (3rd ed., pp. 101–116). Guilford Press.

Kaushal, N. (2019). *Blaming immigrants: Nationalism and the economics of global movement*. Columbia University Press. https://doi.org/10.7312/kaus18144

Killian, K. D., & Agathangelou, A. M. (2005). Greek families. In M. McGoldrick, J. Giordano, & N. G. Preto (Eds.), *Ethnicity and family therapy* (3rd ed., pp. 573–585). Guilford Press.

Kim, S. E., Hunt, E., Tsai, W., & Huang, C. Y. (2023). Examining racial discrimination, internalized racism, and racial–ethnic socialization among Asian American parents. *Asian American Journal of Psychology*. Advance online publication. https://doi.org/10.1037/aap0000321

Kitayama, S., Berg, M. K., & Chopik, W. J. (2020). Culture and well-being in late adulthood: Theory and evidence. *American Psychologist, 75*(4), 567–576. https://doi.org/10.1037/amp0000614

Knight, G. P., Gonzales, N. A., Saenz, D. S., Bonds, D. D., Germán, M., Deardorff, J., Roosav, M. W., & Updegraff, K. A. (2010). The Mexican American Cultural Values Scale for adolescents and adults. *The Journal of Early Adolescence, 30*(3), 444–481. https://doi.org/10.1177/0272431609338178

Kuang, L., & Nishikawa, S. (2021). Ethnic socialization, ethnic identity, and self-esteem in Chinese Mulao adolescents. *Frontiers in Psychology, 12*, Article 730478. https://doi.org/10.3389/fpsyg.2021.730478

Kurt, S. (2020, August 18). *Vygotsky's zone of proximal development and scaffolding*. Educational Technology. https://educationaltechnology.net/vygotskys-zone-of-proximal-development-and-scaffolding/

Lee, E., & Mock, M. R. (2005). Chinese families. In M. McGoldrick, J. Giordano, & N. G. Preto (Eds.), *Ethnicity and family therapy* (3rd ed., pp. 302–318). Guilford Press.

Lee, Y.-T., Chen, X., Zhao, Y., & Chen, W. (2018). The quest for today's totemic psychology: A new look at Wundt, Freud and other scientists. *Journal of Pacific Rim Psychology, 12*, Article e24. https://doi.org/10.1017/prp.2018.13

Maier, K. (1965). *Three theories of child development: The contributions of Erik H. Erikson, Jean Piaget, and Robert R. Sears, and their applications*. Harper & Row.

Mecacci, L. (2021). Vygotsky and psychology as normative science. *Integrative Physiological and Behavioral Science, 55*(4), 728–734. https://doi.org/10.1007/s12124-021-09638-4

Merriam-Webster. (n.d.). Age-grade. In *Merriam-Webster.com dictionary*. Retrieved July 1, 2023, from https://www.merriam-webster.com/dictionary/age-grade

Moahi, V. (2022, November 20). *How totems are used to establish kinship in African culture*. Africa Rebirth. https://www.africarebirth.com/how-totems-are-used-to-establish-kinship-in-african-culture/

Mcloud, S. (2023, February 15). *Wilhelm Wundt: Father of psychology*. Simply Psychology. https://www.simplypsychology.org/wundt.html

Montgomery, H. (2022, May 1). *Different cultures, different childhoods*. The Open University. https://www.open.edu/openlearn/history-the-arts/history/different-cultures-different-childhoods

Mukhopadhyay, S. (2023, January 15). *Indians are highest-earning ethnic group in the USA: Harsh Goenke explains why*. Mint. https://www.livemint.com/news/india/indians-are-highest-earning-ethnic-group-in-usa-harsh-goenka-explains-why-11673748104413.html

Neugarten, B. L. (1973). Personality change in late life: A developmental perspective. In C. Eisdorfer & M. P. Lawton (Eds.), *The psychology of adult development and aging* (pp. 311–335). American Psychological Association. https://doi.org/10.1037/10044-012

Ornstein, S. (n.d.). *Age-grading and aging*. American College of Health Care Administrators. https://www.achca.org/index.php?option=com_dailyplanetblog&view=entry&year=2020&month=01&day=07&id=57:age-grading-and-aging

Ortiz Cofer, J. (2000). Rituals: A prayer, a candle, and a notebook. In M. N.-A. Danquah (Ed.), *Becoming American: Personal essays by first generation immigrant women* (pp. 29–38). Hyperion.

Padilla, A. M. (2006). Bicultural social development. *Hispanic Journal of Behavioral Sciences, 28*(4), 467–497. https://doi.org/10.1177/0739986306294255

Partnership for a New American Economy. (2011). *The "new American" Fortune 500.* https://www.newamericaneconomy.org/sites/all/themes/pnae/img/new-american-fortune-500-june-2011.pdf

Pedersen, P. (1995). *The five stages of culture shock.* Greenwood Press.

Piercy, F. P., Soekandar, A., Limansubroto, C. D. M., & Davic, S. D. (2005). Indonesian families. In M. McGoldrick, J. Giordano, & N. G. Preto (Eds.), *Ethnicity and family therapy* (3rd ed., pp. 332–338). Guilford Press.

Rashid, N. (2017, April 20). *How young Muslims define "halal dating" for themselves.* National Public Radio. https://www.npr.org/sections/codeswitch/2017/04/20/502461218/how-young-muslims-define-halal-dating-for-themselves

Ratts, M. J., Singh, A. A., Nassar-McMillan, S., Butler, S. K., & McCullough, J. R. (2015). *Multicultural and social justice counseling competencies.* Association for Multicultural Counseling and Development. https://www.counseling.org/docs/default-source/competencies/multicultural-and-social-justice-counseling-competencies.pdf?sfvrsn=20

Rivas-Drake, D., Hughes, D., & Way, N. (2009). A preliminary analysis of associations among ethnic-racial socialization, ethnic discrimination, and ethnic identity among urban sixth graders. *Journal of Research on Adolescence, 19*(3), 558–584. https://doi.org/10.1111/j.1532-7795.2009.00607.x

Rojano, R., & Duncan-Rojano, J. (2005). Colombian families. In M. McGoldrick, J. Giordano, & N. G. Preto (Eds.), *Ethnicity and family therapy* (3rd ed., pp. 192–201). Guilford Press.

Schibusawa, T. (2005). Japanese families. In M. McGoldrick, J. Giordano, & N. G. Preto (Eds.), *Ethnicity and family therapy* (3rd ed., pp. 339–348). Guilford Press.

Shortland, S. (2018, January 4). *The implications of age diversity in multicultural team working.* Relocate Global. https://www.relocatemagazine.com/leadership-management-the-implications-of-age-diversity-in-multicultural-team-working-sshortland

Sigelman, C. K., & Rider, E. A. (2015). *Life-span development* (8th ed.). Cengage Learning.

Staudinger, U. (2007). Paul B. Baltes. *European Psychologist, 12*(1), 72–74. https://doi.org/10.1027/1016-9040.12.1.72

Torres, A. (2002). Puerto Ricans in the continental United States. In C. R. Ember, M. Ember, & I. Skoggard (Eds.), *Encyclopedia of world cultures* (pp. 280–284). Macmillan.

Umaña-Taylor, A. J., & Hill, N. E. (2020). Ethnic–racial socialization in the family: A decade's advance on precursors and outcomes. *Journal of Marriage and Family, 82*(1), 244–271. https://doi.org/10.1111/jomf.12622

Vargas, J. A. (2018). *Dear America: Notes of an undocumented citizen.* HarperCollins.

Walsh, S., Shulman, S., Feldman, B., & Maurer, O. (2005). The impact of immigration on the internal processes and developmental tasks of emerging adulthood. *Journal of Youth and Adolescence, 34*(5), 413–426. https://doi.org/10.1007/s10964-005-7259-7

Ward, N., & Batalova, J. (2023). Frequently requested statistics on immigrants and immigration in the United States. *Migration Information Source.* https://www.migrationpolicy.org/article/frequently-requested-statistics-immigrants-and-immigration-united-states

Wood, D., Bruner, J. S., & Ross, G. (1976). The role of tutoring in problem solving. *The Journal of Child Psychology and Psychiatry, 17*(2), 89–100. https://doi.org/10.1111/j.1469-7610.1976.tb00381.x

Wundt, W. (1916). *Elements of folk psychology: Outlines of a psychological history of the development of mankind* (E. L. Schaub, Trans.). Macmillan.

Appendix 4A

Characteristics of Immigrant Groups

African immigrants

Adaptation to American culture can be very stressful because immigrants and refugees are likely to feel a sense of deep loss of their tribe and culture.

Common language may be lost between parents and children, and this pains parents of African heritage.

Values are developed within a family and passed down from generation to generation through proverbs and stories.

Traditional religious beliefs are a comfort to many Africans, who believe in both natural and spirit worlds, and each of the thousand tribes in Africa has its own religious system.

Religion is practiced through mystical power, magic, and sorcery; objects in nature are revered, such as the sun and the stars; African immigrants feel a deep spiritual connection to those who have passed on.

Tribes have distinct languages, a shared history, and social/political organizations.

African immigrants who come to the United States are in lower numbers than other ethnic groups because of the narrow view of "family" that Americans have in contrast to the size of a "clanship" of an African family and the difficulty in bringing clan members to the United States.

Hospitality is extremely important.

Men are the heads of families, while mothers are caregivers to children and to older adults in their community; postmigration brings opportunities to women in employment, and any role changes need to be carefully explored to protect the male status.

Public displays of affection are rare in African culture.

Elaborate rituals are celebrated at life events such as birth, naming, marriage, and death. (Kamya, 2005)

Arab immigrants

Islam or Christianity is practiced.

Extended family is important, although nuclear family formation exists today.

Patriarchy is valued.

Arranged marriages may be practiced, although more and more marriages are based on romance and love.

Children are expected to follow and promote the customs and traditions of the family.

Unconditional love toward children is common (especially sons); discipline is practiced with mild punishment at times and fear at other times depending on the behavior issue.

Privacy is significant.

Elders are expected to be taken care of by other family members.

Sexuality is a taboo topic; homosexuality is not tolerated. (Abudabbeh, 2005)

Asian Indian immigrants

Male domination of women varies between and within groups.

Muslims believe in nonviolence.

Islamic beliefs range from fundamentalism to conservatism to progressive ideology.

Acculturation in the United States varies.

Asian Indians are the highest earning ethnic group in the United States, and they credit it to good education, being frugal, being smart, and working in high-paying jobs in engineering and medicine (Mukhopadhyay, 2023).

Asian Indian adolescents struggle with conflict between tradition of their culture and the values in the United States.

Although LGBTQ+ identity is not sanctioned, there exists a third gender or *hijra*, and individuals who identify as hijra bring good karma to events and celebrations.

Developmental transitions are challenging when individuals are trying to adhere to the karmic values of passivity, obedience, and sacrifice.

Life's challenges are accepted with expectations for reward in the next life. (Almeida, 2005)

Central American immigrants

Central America includes the countries of Belize, Guatemala, El Salvador, Honduras, Nicaragua, Costa Rica, and Panama.

Each country has its own cultural landscape, but many people share similar histories and values from these countries.

Central Americans have suffered similar colonization historical trauma passed down from generation to generation.

Central Americans deal with volcano eruptions and hurricanes, which are considered acts of God.

Many Central Americans are Catholic.

Values include allegiance to family, valuing of elders.
Mixed race and class backgrounds are common.
Indigenous heritage is important.
Children and adolescents have many distinct role models that are conflictual: hip-hop culture, macho or Latin sex symbol, gang member, or successful professional (which is a rare choice because of the associated pressure to not conform to the White world). (Hernandez, 2005)

Chinese immigrants

The family is central and valued over the individual.
A one-child system is favored over large families.
Male children are favored over female children.
Younger generations are rejecting conservatism and traditionalism.
Chinese immigrant writers emphasize contemporary racism, current experiences with discrimination, the search for a cultural identity, consumerism, political stress, and a focus on baby boomers and Gen X.
A nuclear family is valued over traditional extended family.
Parents now share decisions and power.
The husband-wife relationship has become more important than the traditional view that the child is most important.
Daughters are now sharing similar desirability as sons; daughters now have access to education and careers and help take care of aging parents.
Marriages are based on romantic love rather than arranged.
Children leave home now versus the tradition of living with their parents indefinitely.
Successful parenting is measured by children's success in education and career achievement.
Income is shared by adult family members instead of relying on the father to solely support the family. (E. Lee & Mock, 2005)

Colombian immigrants

Many Colombian immigrants are dual citizens and go back to Colombia a few times a year, maintaining contact with family members.
Traditional gender roles are important; however, more women are in the workforce and society in general.
Colombians are a very entrepreneurial people, often starting their own business postmigration.
Rebuscarse (the intent to reseek something) is fundamental for survival and coping.
Colombians have strengths in endurance and sacrifice, leadership and altruism, festive spirit, education, language, and diplomacy. (Rojano & Duncan-Rojano, 2005)

Cuban immigrants

Cubans value traditional gender roles with men as providers who use *respeto* as a way to maintain dominant power over women and children.
Women are allowed to work outside the home in certain gendered settings within family and business.
Machismo is strong; family cohesion and loyalty are present.
In some areas (e.g., South Beach, Florida), Cuban women are more acculturated and emphasize body image, beauty, and sexuality; alternative sexual orientations are accepted.
Intergenerational conflict occurs when older Cuban parents and grandparents hold nostalgic visions of their home country and younger Cuban individuals become adults in a new environment.
Organizations that focus on religious, social, health, political, and neighborhood support are common in community goings-on. (Garcia-Preto, 2005)

Dominican Republic immigrants

History is important: the Dominican Republic was the first location invaded and colonized by Columbus, and it is the birthplace of the "Latino" identity, of which Dominican folks are proud.
Most individuals from the Dominican Republic are of mixed race with mixed populations from the early slave trade from West Africa, Spanish, and Taino people.
Spaniard influence is part of Dominican families with generational trauma histories of colonization.
Spanish is the language, and Catholicism is the religion.
There are conflictual relationships with the United States because of two invasions by the United

States, the second one introducing baseball, which many Dominican individuals value as a unifying sport for young men today.
Traditions are musical and religious in nature; the merengue is the main dance; dancing is intrinsic to the Dominican life.
Community and family are the most beloved values; hospitality is important; many generations of one family will share a home.
Extravertedness is valued; introvertedness may seem rude.
Much of Dominican life is celebrated with food. (Genao, 2023)

Greek immigrants

History is important, and "larger than life" past personalities and achievements are celebrated.
Of particular pride is the legacy of greatness of Ancient Greece being the cradle of democracy, the location of the first Olympics, and the source of strong philosophers and conquerors.
Greek traditions (for birth, marriage, etc.) are important and still practiced by many immigrants postmigration.
Divorce is stigmatized, and postmigration Greek couples are required to meet with a Greek Orthodox bishop to get approval; as many as 75% of legal divorces are still observed as marriages in the Greek Orthodox church.
Church fills spiritual as well as social needs.
Greek women are expected to look after the home, care for older adults, and honor the dead.
Greek women are becoming more educated and professional postmigration.
Culture is patriarchal with power moving from father to eldest son and down the line to all male children.
Children may struggle with conflict in Greek and American values as they are drawn toward independence and other cultural values of the United States.
Fidelity in marriage is expected of women; men's "nature" requires that they engage in extramarital affairs.
LGBTQ+ identity is not supported in Greek culture. (Killian & Agathangelou, 2005)

Indonesian immigrants

Indonesians value artistic, religious, and cultural diversity.
Family closeness, loyalty, respect, and obligation are valued.
All family members preserve the family honor.
Parents approve the children's marital choice.
Children live with their parents and extended family long after educational pursuits are met and until they marry.
Extended family loyalties with in-laws can create tension in a family in the United States.
Gender roles are still observed, although women are taking on more variation in work and in the community.
Directness in conversation is difficult.
Shame about family misbehavior is evident throughout Indonesian families.
Individuals seem to be shy when around higher status people.
There are cultural sanctions against LGBTQ+ individuals, so gay and queer people marry into a heterosexual marriage and seek out same-gender sex in secret. (Piercy et al., 2005)

Iranian immigrants

Patriarchy has been traditional, and some families still adhere to respecting the father as the head of the family, although current Western influences (industrialism and urbanization) and migration impact the degree to which young individuals struggle with their tendency toward independence and loyalty to their father.
Male children tend to be more spoiled than female children, although expectations for all children about appropriate behavior are clear, with admonishments toward children to be obedient and to behave like adults.
Attitudes toward women are conservative; premarital sex is rare but has been found to be more common postmigration.
More women are educated and have begun to work outside the home, causing strife in the family.

Partial breakdown of extended family has been caused by families becoming more inclined toward the nuclear family.
Families and individuals strive for achievement and wealth.
A father may struggle with his children not adhering to his authority and may have uncertain feelings toward his professional wife.
Postmigration divorce rates are higher than in the homeland. (Jalali, 2005)

Japanese immigrants

Culture has been impacted by both traditional cultural values and the social and political environment of the United States.
Self-determination and self-sufficiency are emphasized.
Children are expected to develop independence while adhering to group norms and social expectations.
Adolescents can struggle with interdependence in family relationships.
Children are taught not to brag or "show off."
Tolerance of adversity is high, stemming from the Buddhist concept of fatalism.
Shikataganai is the acceptance of things one cannot change.
Gaman is known as a strength of character and the capacity to endure life's difficulties.
Inference in communication is important as nonverbal communication is valued over verbal communication.
Affection toward one's spouse in front of the children is not likely, and affection toward children is rare. (Schibusawa, 2005)

Mexican immigrants

Familismo is extremely important, and duty to one's parents overrides almost all other relationships (Garcia-Preto, 2005).
Youth may struggle with conflicting pressures of keeping to ethnic standards at home while adhering to mainstream values in the community and at school (Padilla, 2006).
Mexican adolescents often adopt a bicultural identity (Berry et al., 2006) and may be more successful in navigating conflicting pressures between home and school (Gonzales et al., 2002).
Traditional values include respect, religion, and traditional gender roles (Garcia-Preto, 2005).
Immigrant status is associated with ethnic cultural values (Knight et al., 2010).
Immigrant mothers and fathers tend to value familism, traditional gender roles, material success, independence, self-reliance, and personal achievement (Knight et al., 2010).

Puerto Rican immigrants

Values include family, respect, education, language, religion, and pride in their nationality (Doerfler, 2014).
Puerto Ricans are a sensitive people with a relaxed sense of time and empathetic attitudes toward others (Commonwealth of Puerto Rico, 2014).
Puerto Ricans admire intelligence, hard work, and dedication (Commonwealth of Puerto Rico, 2014).
Puerto Ricans view criticism, greed, and aggression as rude (Commonwealth of Puerto Rico, 2014).
Puerto Ricans are very prideful of their nation and region (Commonwealth of Puerto Rico, 2014).
Children are raised with affection and openness to learning; children are expected to learn Spanish to connect and maintain relationships with family members.
Gender roles are clear: Dad provides for the family, Mom cares for the family, and extended family members and godparents are very important (Torres, 2002).

Chapter 5

Disputing Biases and Assumptions Regarding Immigrants and Refugees

Historically, immigrants have been a source of cheap labor. In effect, their wages tend to be low because of the nature of their employment in industries such as agriculture, dairy, meatpacking, fisheries, and restaurants, among others. These jobs typically do not pay benefits, Social Security, or retirement, leaving long-term employees at a deficit when they retire or need disability services. Immigrants are often portrayed negatively in the media and by policy makers. The prevailing perception is that immigrants are unskilled and therefore cannot do more than manual labor. They are regularly viewed as uneducated. Another misperception about immigrants is that they are criminals and belong to gangs or drug cartels. Many Americans also regard immigrants as threats to their jobs.

In this chapter, we focus on immigration statistics and common misperceptions of immigrants. We examine whether immigrants take away jobs from Americans and how immigrants contribute to the U.S. economy. We also explore how counselors and employers can advocate for immigrants. References to the Multicultural and Social Justice Counseling Competencies (MSJCC; Ratts et al., 2015) are made where appropriate.

Learning Objectives

- Learn current data of immigration.
- Discover employer preferences in hiring immigrants.
- Understand the myths of immigration.
- Learn about the impact of U.S. policies, laws, and the economy on immigrants.

The following section introduces a self-assessment to gauge your existing knowledge of culturally responsive counseling frameworks designed to address inequities and marginalization, ethical considerations in working with immigrant and refugee populations, and the MSJCC (Ratts et al., 2015) needed to do so. This brief assessment aims to explore your current understanding of key concepts and provide a foundation for further learning. Answering the following questions will better equip you to engage with the content.

Self-assessment: Please respond to the following statements by rating yourself on the following Likert scale: *strongly agree, agree, disagree, strongly disagree, unsure*, or *not applicable.*

1. I feel confident about working with immigrants from all economic levels, in every documented status, and from any country.
2. I understand why people believe that immigrants take jobs away from American workers.
3. I know the data about arrests and legal issues with respect to immigrants.
4. I understand U.S. farmers can be advocates and support immigrant workers.

To view the influence of immigration and develop MSJCC competency, counselors need to understand how the number of immigrants in any given country or society impacts social issues, government policies, population, and economic gain. With this knowledge, counselors can better understand their immigrant and refugee clients, their worldview and journeys, and how their perspectives of migration affect their employment/career, family, quality of life, and physical and mental health.

Contextualizing Immigration Statistics

There are more immigrants in the United States than in any other nation in the world (Budiman, 2020). According to a study conducted in 2020, there are more than 40 million people living in the United States who were born in another country, accounting for approximately one fifth of the world's immigrants (Budiman, 2020). Although immigrants make up approximately 15% of the U.S. total population of 331.4 million (World Population Review, 2023), they account for a very low proportion in comparison with other countries. In fact, the United States is outside of the top 20 countries with the highest proportion of immigrants (Routley, 2022), falling behind nine Middle Eastern countries, including the United Arab Emirates, which has 8.7 million immigrants who compose approximately 88% of the country's total population (World Population Review, 2023). The United Arab Emirates has become a popular destination for immigrants who are seeking employment opportunities and higher standards of living (Malit & Youha, 2013).

Other countries, such as Australia (30%), Switzerland (29%), Canada (21%), Austria (19%), and Germany (19%), also have higher proportions of immigrants than the United States (Routley, 2022). Following the Middle Eastern countries, Australia has the next highest proportion of immigrants. Its immigration program consists of two separate plans: the Migration Program and the Humanitarian Program (Love & Spinks, n.d.). The Migration Program provides permanent visas for skilled and family migrants; it is designed to help decrease the workforce shortages where Australians cannot yet keep pace with industry demand (Love & Spinks, n.d.). As of September 2022, the Migration Program had a cap of 195,000 skilled and family visas (Australian Government Department of Home Affairs, 2023). Australia also provides permanent visas for refugees and other immigrant families in need through their Humanitarian Program. Thus, immigration has driven economic and social development in Australia for more than 2 centuries (Inglis, 2018).

As can be seen, although the United States takes in the highest number of immigrants, it does not have the highest proportion of immigrants in relation to its total population. For many Americans, this distinction is often overlooked.

Currently, it is estimated that nearly 258 million people (or 3.4% of the global population) reside outside their own country of origin (Kaushal, 2019; United Nations, 2017). The high rate of mobility is due to significant economic opportunity, accessible transportation, political issues influencing decisions to relocate, violence in a home country, and human trafficking (Koser, & Laczko, 2010). The cost of immigration travel and postmigration long-distance communication, as well as travel time, have all decreased significantly over recent years, allowing for more immigration (Kaushal, 2019).

In 2016, it was estimated that the total number of refugees and asylum seekers in the world was 25.9 million, with Turkey hosting the largest number of refugees (3.1 million) and the United States hosting the most international immigrants at 49.8 million (United Nations, 2017). International migrants come to the United States from the following countries (with the respective percentages of the global population of migrants in parentheses): Asia (28%), Mexico (25%), the Caribbean (10%), Central America (8%), South America (7%), China (6%), India (6%), the Middle East and North Africa (4%), sub-Saharan Africa (5%), the Philippines (4%), and El Salvador (3%; Budiman, 2020). Attention to the needs of immigrants begins with understanding where they are from and if they return to their homeland at any point for short or long visits.

Immigrant Movement and Jobs

Although concerns about undocumented workers abound internationally, most immigrants enter host countries legally (Kaushal, 2019). Immigration is not solely caused by political or economic policies or crises; immigration occurs because globally low costs are associated with international travel, and host countries have liberalized their immigration policies (Kaushal, 2019). U.S. citizens can get short-term visa-free or visa entry in 116 countries, and the United States allows visa-free entry to citizens of 38 countries; 26 European countries allow passport-free travel; many Latin American, African, and three South Asian countries are visa-free; and the United States, India, the United Kingdom, and China provide long-term visas to foreigners from many countries (Kaushal, 2019).

It is widely believed that employers prefer to hire temporary or undocumented migrant workers over equally qualified citizens because immigrants accept employment requiring longer hours and less pay (Fellini et al., 2007; Kuhn & Shen, 2015) and there is a need for migrant workers to fill jobs that citizens refuse (Fellini et al., 2007). Counterarguments focus on the practice of employers discriminating against migrants to protect citizens; however, very few studies exist that explore hiring practices of employers when choices are between citizens and migrant workers (Kuhn & Shen, 2015).

One such study was conducted using Chinese internal national data on jobs offered to native (to the province) citizens and to nonnative citizens who travel outside their birth province and are migrants (Kuhn & Shen, 2015). Kuhn and Shen (2015) analyzed data of employers' choices during the largest migration in human history (Chan, 2013) involving 221,135 applications made by 78,031 workers to 3,489 ads placed by 1,551 firms. Findings indicated that workers from other provinces were 19% more likely to receive an employer contact over native workers, and this preference is limited to situations in which companies were seeking less skilled and lower paid employees (Kuhn & Shen, 2015). Factors that may have impacted preferences for workers from other provinces included payroll savings on immigrant workers and productivity advantage that workers from other provinces have over native workers; however, none of these factors were found to be conclusively definitive and need to be examined in future research (Kuhn & Shen, 2015). Counselors exploring their biases and beliefs about this topic can examine their level of MSJCC competency in self-awareness and knowledge.

Americans largely agree that undocumented and documented immigrants work in jobs in the United States that citizens do not want. About 77% of adults believe that undocumented immigrants fill jobs that U.S. citizens would rather not do (Krogstad et al., 2020). In 2017, for example, 2.3 million undocumented immigrants worked in the service sector and 1.3 million worked in the construction sector (Krogstad et al., 2020).

Additionally, documented immigrants are more likely than U.S. citizens to start a new business, small or large (Azoulay et al., 2020).

In the service industry, U.S. employers often find it difficult to hire American workers as illustrated by a recent interview with an anonymous restaurant employer: "You cannot hire an American here that will show up to work. They will not be committed to their job. In America . . . restaurant work is not a serious profession" (Burnett, 2019, para. 15). Stout (2008) found that employers risk fines and raids because immigrants are much easier to work with and more dependable than American employees.

Labor force demographics impact the availability of American workers in the United States. The labor force participation rate in the United States peaked at 67.3% in early 2000 and has declined, reaching a near 40-year low of 62.4% in September 2015 (Krueger, 2017). In 2020, during the COVID-19 pandemic, rates dropped to 60%, and in 2023, labor force participation regained momentum and was reported at 62% (U.S. Bureau of Labor Statistics, n.d.). Furthermore, an increase in school enrollment has largely offset declining labor force participation for young workers since the 1990s (Krueger, 2017). Labor force rates have been declining for prime-aged men (between 25 and 54 years old) for the past several decades (Richwine, 2016). The labor force participation rate has stopped rising for cohorts of women born after 1960 (Krueger, 2017).

Cohen (2017) found that some employers have a difficult time finding Americans who will work for a particular income, even when it is well above minimum wage (as set by current wage recommendations at the U.S. Department of Labor) and turn to hiring guest workers who are qualified via an H-2B visa and who are satisfied to receive the salaries offered. Latinx immigrants can make six times higher salary in the United States than in Mexico (Pérez, 2017; J. Rosenow, personal communication, March 4, 2021). Employers are required to advertise on a state website of job listings and at least twice in a local newspaper before they can hire immigrant workers (Cohen, 2017). Employers should post their job on a state workforce agency website and wait 30 days before considering hiring an immigrant (VisaNation, n.d.).

The United States has attracted low-skilled immigrants to jobs even as low-skilled Americans have worked less. This does not suggest that immigrants push out Americans from the workforce, but it does mean that immigrants replace Americans who do not want to do the work that immigrants are willing to accept. Employers find immigrants reliable, hard-working, and willing to take seasonal employment (Hopkins, 2007; Jan, 2017).

Often, when a choice is offered, many employers discriminate against Black workers and hire Hispanic employees because they believe that U.S. workers are "lazy and unreliable" (Richwine, 2019, para. 28). Hiring practices also impact who gets hired. Giuliano et al. (2009) found that Latinx managers hire more Latinx employees and fewer Whites. Black employees are hired at a higher rate than White workers by Black employers (Bates, 1994; Stoll et al., 2004; Turner, 1997). Across the board, for young male employees in the United States, employers are more likely to hire employees who match their racial identity (Fadlon, 2015).

As Americans leave the workforce, whether because of competition from immigrants, inadequate wages, distaste for manual labor, or some other reason, employers turn increasingly to immigrants (Richwine, 2016). This is problematic because instead of searching for ways to motivate Americans to get back to work, through higher wages or less access to welfare, government leaders and employers have chosen to hire immigrants. According to Richwine (2016), limiting immigration would not solve all the problems facing low-skilled Americans, but it may be one way in which to provide an incentive to return to work.

Richwine (2019) also found numerous settlement cases suggesting that discrimination against American workers is widespread. According to Richwine, U.S.-born workers compete directly with immigrants and can encounter fewer employment opportunities, lower wages, and terrible work conditions. The source of the cases Richwine illuminated is the Equal Employment Opportunity Commission (EEOC). The EEOC has uncovered evidence that U.S. companies have been actively seeking to replace low-skilled American workers with immigrants for about 20 years. Richwine presented several examples of these EEOC cases in which low-skilled American workers, mostly Black but sometimes White as well, are consistently passed over for manual labor jobs in favor of Hispanics. In addition to potentially creating tension between Black and Brown individuals vying for the same job, from a larger perspective, this practice can be considered one of many results of White settler colonialism.

In short, the literature presents mixed evidence for job competition between immigrants and U.S. citizens. Whereas some researchers have found that immigrants do not take away jobs from Americans, others have demonstrated that immigrants are often chosen over U.S.-born workers for low-skilled jobs. This paradox is evidenced by employers' frustration in finding Americans who want to work in low-skilled jobs and employers who believe that immigrant workers are more reliable employees than U.S.-born workers. More research is still needed to understand the complexities of employment in the United States and how immigration reform can enhance employment opportunities for everyone while prioritizing highly motivated American workers.

Advocacy For and With Immigrants

A nonprofit organization called Puentes/Bridges exists in southeastern Wisconsin. This organization is led by dairy farmers who employ Mexican workers and who advocate for immigration reform so that their workers can work under the H-2A visa currently unavailable to dairy farms. One of the members of Puentes/Bridges is John Rosenow, who has a 600-cow dairy farm in rural Wisconsin and has employed Mexican workers since 1998 (J. Rosenow, personal communication, March 4, 2021). Mr. Rosenow employs 11 Mexicans, and he visits many of their families in Mexico on an annual basis so that he can better connect with and understand his employees. "I want to be a good employer," Mr. Rosenow states, and by this, he means that he wants to advocate for Mexican workers' rights, understand their family and culture, and provide them with meaningful employment (J. Rosenow, personal communication, March 4, 2021). Mr. Rosenow hires Mexican workers because they are "wonderful workers," an "ideal workforce" (J. Rosenow, personal communication, March 4, 2021). According to Mr. Rosenow, the Mexicans he employs find farming meaningful, love working with animals, don't mind dirty work, love the weather changes, and are extremely reliable (J. Rosenow, personal communication, March 4, 2021). By contrast, Mr. Rosenow has found the labor supply in America to be unreliable in farm work (J. Rosenow, personal communication, March 4, 2021). For more information about Puentes/Bridges, readers can check out this link: https://www.puentesbridges.org.

Immigrants and Their Contribution to the U.S. Economy

Many believe that undocumented immigrants use resources without paying taxes that fund those services. In fact, immigrants pay more into the public sector for services than they use (Chomsky, 2018). Additionally, undocumented immigrants work in the U.S. formal economy where they experience tax deductions in their paychecks that do not benefit them. When immigrants present false Social Security numbers to obtain jobs, they contribute to the Social Security system and receive no benefits themselves, although they may pay into this system for years (Chomsky, 2018). In fact, as of 2005, undocumented immigrants using fake Social Security cards paid $7 billion a year; thus, immigrants are subsidizing the Social Security system (Chomsky, 2018). By becoming knowledgeable of research such as Chomsky's (2018), counselors can develop their MSJCC competency and engage in advocacy when they share this information with policy makers, community members, and the public.

Immigrants With Disabilities

When it comes to lack of access to benefits, immigrants and refugees living with one or more disabilities experience challenges in obtaining health care and accommodations at school or work. Echave and Gonzalez (2022) found that 5.6% of immigrants ages 18–64 years live with a disability and 2.3% experience multiple disabilities (e.g., difficulties in ambulatory functioning, cognitive processing, independent living, vision, hearing, self-care). Nevertheless, approximately one in five immigrants with disabilities are uninsured, accounting for close to 19% of this population (Echave & Gonzalez, 2022). Although the uninsured rate among naturalized citizens (9.5%) is similar to that of U.S.-born adult citizens with disabilities (10.4%), undocumented immigrants are three times more likely to be uninsured (30.3%; Echave & Gonzalez, 2022). Consequently, a small portion of adult immigrants in the United States have access to the care and benefits that they require.

U.S. Citizenship and Immigration Services (USCIS) has policies and procedures that allow immigrants to apply for naturalization without meeting the English language and civics requirements due to a physical developmental disability or mental impairment (USCIS, n.d.). Under the Trump administration, the N-648 application was modified to make it more difficult for immigrants to apply for citizenship by doubling the length of the disability waiver application and creating redundant and useless items to complete (Kim, 2022). After much frustration on behalf of the public and under recent administration, the N-648 application process has been revised to undo the efforts by former President Trump and make the process more concise and supportive of immigrants (Kim, 2022). The process to apply for naturalization is less cumbersome, and many useless parts of the process have been removed, including asking applicants how they are treated by medical staff or requiring applicants to complete a new form from the beginning if they missed an item on an existing application (Kim, 2022). The new changes will create a smoother application process for immigrants with disabilities.

One of the most common challenges reported by immigrants with disabilities is finding reputable health care information (Bogenschutz, 2014). Finding information about insurance, whether private or public, is particularly difficult. Another challenge is finding accurate instruction regarding disability-specific information, including health care providers who can assist with those disabilities. These difficulties are commonly exacerbated because of language barriers and interpretation challenges (Bogenschutz, 2014). Roughly one in three immigrants with disabilities have limited English proficiency (Echave & Gonzalez, 2022). As a result, equitable access to health care services is easily hindered. Providers typically do not allow extra time for communication, do not make communication accommodations, and do not assist people with disabilities in understanding medical terminology (Bogenschutz, 2014). Additionally, because of a limited number of bilingual staff, immigrant clients usually wait longer to be seen or choose to rely on family members for interpretation services (Pereira et al., 2012). The lack of access to information and language barriers that immigrants with disabilities encounter can frequently result in this population not receiving the care that they require.

Furthermore, immigrants with disabilities face socioeconomic disadvantages that often result in poor working conditions and benefits. In fact, immigrant adults with disabilities are more likely to be employed in comparison with U.S.-born adults who are dealing with the same or similar disabilities (Xiang et al., 2010). In 2007, 40.8% of immigrants with disabilities were employed compared with only 34.9% of U.S.-born citizens (Xiang et al., 2010). Research has also shown that the top occupations for immigrants with disabilities include intense physical exertion (Echave & Gonzalez, 2022). These jobs are commonly low-paying and are unlikely to offer flexibility for immigrants with disabilities, including paid time off and health insurance (Echave & Gonzalez, 2022). Working these jobs leads to more restrictions, and together, these factors place immigrants with disabilities at a higher risk for worsening their existing conditions. Potential methods for supporting immigrant workers with disabilities include increasing the availability of paid sick leave, providing greater access to health insurance through employers, and offering extended workforce development programs for immigrants with disabilities (Echave & Gonzalez, 2022). It is important for counselors to advocate for immigrants with disabilities by campaigning for the improvement of workforce development programs and employment barriers. In doing so, counselors develop their MSJCC competency.

Likewise, immigrants with disabilities are at a socioeconomic disadvantage compared with U.S. citizens. Approximately 49.3% of adult immigrants with disabilities report having incomes under 200% of the federal poverty level (Echave & Gonzalez, 2022). The U.S. federal government supports individuals with the Supplemental Security Income (SSI) program. SSI is a welfare program for individuals with low income, fewer overall resources, and commonly no or a limited work history (American Psychological Association, 2010). Despite SSI and other programs of assistance, individuals with disabilities in the United States are more likely to be unemployed and live in poverty (American Psychological Association, 2010).

Beyond the general requirements to receive SSI benefits, immigrants with disabilities must meet additional criteria (Echave & Gonzalez, 2022). An example of these criteria includes having been lawfully admitted for permanent residence with 40 qualifying quarters of earnings or on active duty in the U.S. armed forces (Echave & Gonzalez, 2022). A survey conducted from 2015 to 2019 found that one in eight adult immigrants with disabilities (12.7%) reported receiving SSI compared with 16% of U.S.-born citizens (Echave & Gonzalez, 2022). All in all, socioeconomic constraints and barriers to access of government public services can decrease the well-being of and equal opportunities for immigrants with disabilities.

Additionally, chronic stress arising from disabilities is positively correlated to depression and anxiety (Jarama et al., 1998). Immigrants with disabilities face a variety of stressors, including financial burdens, disparities in access to health care, social barriers, difficulties adapting to a new culture, and stressors due to limitations of their disability. Research has shown that having a disability is a stressor that can lead to unfavorable mental health outcomes (Jarama et al., 1998). Stressors among immigrants may also be magnified because of their minority and ethnic status. Therefore, immigrants with disabilities are at high risk for mental health disorders, such as depression and anxiety (Jarama et al., 1998).

One factor that contributes to a successful lifestyle for individuals with disabilities is social support. *Social support* is commonly defined as reciprocal, accessible, and reliable social relationships that provide resources and assistance with stressors (Miyawaki et al., 2022). Social relationships include emotional closeness, tangible support, appraisal support, esteem support, and companionship (Jarama et al., 1998). In a study examining 200 Korean immigrants, social supports were found to moderate the harmful effects of stressors and positively impact mental health (Lee et al., 1996). Thus, increasing access to social and emotional supports for immigrants with disabilities should result in a decrease of mental health disorders, which is important advocacy work according to the MSJCC framework (Ratts et al., 2015).

Immigrants with disabilities face many barriers that negatively affect their well-being. These barriers include but are not limited to discrimination, socioeconomic disadvantages, employment barriers, and finding reputable health care information and practitioners without insurance (Echave & Gonzalez, 2022). Clinicians and social advocates can improve the mental and physical health of immigrants with disabilities through different approaches, such as increasing access to government public services, helping develop and promote disability inclusion, advocating for inclusive health care, and advocating for improvements of job access and quality. Finally, as advocates, it is important for counselors to support immigrants with disabilities by educating themselves and others on the disadvantages this population and their families face, while helping create new pathways and resources.

Immigrants and Crime Rates

A common current belief is that immigrants are "drug dealers, criminals and rapists" as stated by Donald Trump during his 2016 presidential campaign (BBC News, 2016). In a study conducted by Light et al. (2020) in Texas, however, it was found that undocumented immigrants commit felony offenses considerably less frequently than U.S.-born citizens. U.S.-born citizens are also more than twice as likely to be arrested for violent crimes and drug crimes and more than four times as likely to commit property crimes (Light et al., 2020). Smith and Buchman (2022) reported that U.S. citizens are twice as likely to be arrested for a violent offense than an undocumented immigrant and that the only crime most likely to be committed by legal immigrants is a traffic violation. Orrenius and Zavodny (2019) noted the lack of evidence indicating that immigrants, documented and undocumented, are responsible for crimes that threaten U.S. public safety. They stated that research studies overwhelmingly find that geographic areas with more immigrants have a similar or reduced rate of violent crimes than communities with a fewer number of immigrants. These and similar studies point to generally law-abiding immigrants, both undocumented and documented, and how much they contribute to the safety of communities.

Immigrants and Education

U.S. media and policy makers often promote immigrants as undesirable, criminally inclined, and uneducated. In her study of news coverage about immigrants from September 1, 2017, to August 31, 2018, Han (2019) found that the following news outlets (with the number of times they disparaged immigrants using derogatory, misleading, or racist terms in parentheses) were guilty of describing immigrants in a negative light: *New York Post* (N = 545), *The Washington Post* (N = 6,847), *The New York Times* (N = 5,780), *Chicago Sun-Times* (N = 669), *USA Today* (N = 362), *Los Angeles Times* (N = 1,420), and *The Denver Post* (N = 510). It is imperative that counselors understand that U.S. policy makers and the media portray immigrants and immigration in a particular way that promotes racist and discriminatory attitudes among U.S. citizens. With this knowledge, counselors can strengthen their MSJCC competency.

In reality, immigrants often bring education accolades with them when they migrate and are highly motivated to pursue educational aspirations to accomplish their career and financial goals once they arrive in the United States. Immigrants globally are more educated because of increased educational opportunities in their home countries (Krogstad & Radford, 2018). For example, in 2016, 30% of U.S. immigrants ages 25 and older held at least a bachelor's degree compared with 31.6% of U.S.-born citizens (Krogstad & Radford, 2018).

As previously discussed, one of the reasons immigrants come to the United States is to obtain an education and seek opportunities in succeeding in their goals of financial success and stability. Part of their desire to become educated and succeed in a financially secure career is the belief that the American dream is real for citizens and immigrants alike. The American dream is often described as equal access to upward mobility and economic self-sufficiency through hard work (Churchwell, 2021). Immigrants who pursue the American dream realize they will likely encounter racism and discrimination and know they will have to work harder than U.S. citizens to succeed (Knight et al., 2016). Nevertheless, immigrants continue to come to the United States in search of education and better vocational opportunities than they had in their homeland.

The United States has long been and continues to be regarded as a location of preference for immigrants who want to obtain a higher education in highly acclaimed colleges and research facilities and who want opportunities for employment (Olsen-Medina & Batalova, 2020). Research shows that 32% of adult immigrants in the United States have at least a bachelor's degree compared with 33% of U.S.-born adults (Olsen-Medina & Batalova, 2020). Additionally, educational attainment for immigrants has increased dramatically in some areas of the United States. The proportion of immigrant college graduates of working age (25–64 years) was 52% in 2019 compared with 22% in 1990 (Johnson et al., 2021). In contrast, the proportion of U.S.-born college graduates of working age was 38% in 2019 compared with 27% in 1990 (Johnson et al., 2021).

High school dropout rates have improved for all groups ages 16–24 since 2010 with the following statistics (2023 rates vs. 2010 rates): Hispanic students dropped out of high school at the rate of 7.8% compared with 16.7%; American Indian/Alaskan Native students dropped out at the rate of 10.2% compared with 15.4%; Black students dropped out at the rate of 5.9% compared with 10.3%; White students dropped out at the rate of 4.1% compared with 5.3%; and Asian students dropped out at the rate of 2.1% compared with 2.8% (National Center for Education Statistics, 2023). Educational attainment is rising for immigrants and citizens alike as individuals become more inclined to solidify their goals and dreams for a secure future.

CASE STUDY

This case is illustrative of Jorge, an immigrant who had a choice between illegal work in Mexico or legal work as an undocumented immigrant in the United States. He chose to come to the United States based on recommendations from family who had already immigrated to the Midwest.

> Jorge described his situation in Mexico: "So, I brought everything with me, my clothes, I mean the situation that was going on, I was going to get killed or I was going to keep working in the streets." As Jorge notes, poverty and violence were rampant in his hometown; his choices were either to be in constant danger from the local gangs or to deal drugs in the street for survival. His hope in coming to the United States was to survive and to engage in work that was safe and honorable—a life he was unable to create for himself in Mexico. When Jorge came to the United States, jobs were abundant and he felt safe. After bringing only what he could on his back during his migration, he settled in the Midwest with relatives who had come before him and created the life he wanted, working jobs where employers appreciated him. Jorge liked the setting of his job, the kindness of his employers, and the stability of his life.

Reflection Questions

1. How do you make sense of U.S. assumptions about immigrants that are not reflective of their experiences, such as in Jorge's case?
2. In what ways could you help Jorge gain perspective on his life in terms of vocational choices he made regarding legal versus illegal work?
3. In what ways do you believe that you can help immigrants like Jorge in developing decision-making skills?

Summary

Immigrants historically have contributed to great successes in the United States (e.g., the construction of the railroad) through the various employment opportunities available to them. Typically, immigrant jobs do not pay benefits, Social Security, or retirement. This can leave immigrant and refugee employees at a disadvantage when they retire or need disability benefits. Immigrants are often regarded as unskilled and unable to do more than manual labor. Another common misperception about immigrants is that they are criminals. However, as shown in this chapter, U.S. citizens commit more crimes than immigrants overall. We addressed these and other misconceptions about immigrants and focused on work patterns and related employment issues. Counselors need to be aware of community attitudes toward their immigrant and refugee clients to better serve their needs.

References

American Psychological Association. (2010). *Disability & socioeconomic status.* https://www.apa.org/pi/ses/resources/publications/disability

Australian Government Department of Home Affairs. (2023, August 24). *Migration program planning levels.* https://immi.homeaffairs.gov.au/what-we-do/migration-program-planning-levels

Azoulay, P., Jones, B. F., Kim, J. D., & Miranda, J. (2020, October 5). *Immigrants to the U.S. create more jobs than they take.* Kellogg Insight. https://insight.kellogg.northwestern.edu/article/immigrants-to-the-u-s-create-more-jobs-than-they-take

Bates, T. (1994). Utilization of minority employees in small business: A comparison of nonminority and Black-owned urban enterprises. *The Review of Black Political Economy, 23*(1), 113–121. https://doi.org/10.1007/BF02895743

BBC News. (2016, August 31). *'Drug dealers, criminals, rapists': What Trump thinks of Mexicans.* https://www.bbc.com/news/av/world-us-canada-37230916

Bogenschutz, M. (2014). "We find a way": Challenges and facilitators for health care access among immigrants and refugees with intellectual and developmental disabilities. *Medical Care, 52*(10, Suppl. 3), S64–S70. https://doi.org/10.1097/mlr.0000000000000140

Budiman, A. (2020, August 20). *Key findings about U.S. immigrants.* Pew Research Center. https://www.pewresearch.org/fact-tank/2020/08/20/key-findings-about-u-s-immigrants/

Burnett, J. (2019, August 21). *Employers struggle with hiring undocumented workers: 'You cannot hire American here.'* National Public Radio. https://www.npr.org/2019/08/21/752336132/employers-struggle-with-hiring-undocumented-workers-you-cannot-hire-american-her

Chan, K. W. (2013). China: Internal migration. In I. Ness (Ed.), *The encyclopedia of global human migration.* John Wiley & Sons. https://doi.org/10.1002/9781444351071.wbeghm124

Chomsky, A. (2018). *"They take our jobs!" and 20 other myths about immigration* (Expanded ed.). Beacon Press.

Churchwell, S. (2021, Winter). A brief history of the American dream. *The Catalyst.* https://www.bushcenter.org/catalyst/state-of-the-american-dream/churchwell-history-of-the-american-dream

Cohen, P. (2017, July 13). Q. and A.: If workers are scarce, is it the work or the wages? *The New York Times.* https://www.nytimes.com/2017/07/13/business/economy/labor-market-wages.html

Echave, P., & Gonzalez, D. (2022). *Being an immigrant with disabilities.* Urban Institute. https://www.urban.org/sites/default/files/2022-04/Being%20an%20Immigrant%20with%20Disabilities.pdf

Fadlon, Y. D. (2015). Statistical discrimination and implication of employer-employee racial matches. *Journal of Labor Research, 36*(2), 232–248. https://doi.org/10.1007/s12122-015-9203-2

Fellini, I., Ferro, A., & Fullin, G. (2007). Recruitment processes and labour mobility: The construction industry in Europe. *Work, Employment and Society, 21*(2), 277–298. https://doi.org/10.1177/0950017007076635

Giuliano, L., Levine, D. I., & Leonard, J. (2009). Manager race and the race of new hires. *Journal of Labor Economics, 27*(4), 589–631. https://doi.org/10.1086/605946

Han, S. (2019, February 28). *How news coverage perpetuates harmful language about immigration.* Berkeley Media Studies Group. https://www.bmsg.org/blog/how-news-coverage-perpetuates-harmful-language-about-immigration/

Hopkins, A. (2007, February 25). *Hispanics do jobs others in U.S. "won't stand for."* Reuters. https://www.reuters.com/article/us-usa-immigration-hispanics-general-fea/hispanics-do-jos-others-in-u-s-wont-stand-for-idUSN1649636320070226

Inglis, C. (2018). Australia: A welcoming destination for some. *Migration Information Source*. https://www.migrationpolicy.org/article/australiawelcomingdestination-some

Jan, T. (2017, October 5). A landscaper's 'hire American' plan ended with bringing in Mexican workers to finish the job. *The Washington Post*. https://www.washingtonpost.com/business/economy/a-landscapers-hire-american-plan-ended-with-bringing-in-mexican-workers-to-finish-the-job/2017/10/05/f4656234-9743-11e7-b569-3360011663b4_story.html

Jarama, S. L., Reyst, H., Rodriguez, M., Belgrave, F. Z., & Zea, M. C. (1998). Psychosocial adjustment among Central American immigrants with disabilities: An exploratory study. *Cultural Diversity and Mental Health, 4*(2), 115–125. https://doi.org/10.1037/1099-9809.4.2.115

Johnson, H., Perez, C. A., & Cuellar Mejia, M. (2021). *Immigrants and education in California* [Fact sheet]. Public Policy Institute of California. https://www.ppic.org/publication/immigrants-and-education-in-california/#:~:text=Educational%20attainment%20among%20recent%20immigrants,31%20percentage%20points%20since%201990

Kaushal, N. (2019). *Blaming immigrants: Nationalism and the economics of global movement*. Columbia University Press. https://doi.org/10.7312/kaus18144

Kim, J. (2022, October 25). *U.S. removes Trump-era barriers to citizenship-test waivers for disabled immigrants*. National Public Radio. https://www.npr.org/2022/10/25/1131203371/biden-immigrants-disabilities-citizenship-english-civics-test-trump

Knight, M. G., Roegman, R., & Edstrom, L. (2016). My American dream: The interplay between structure and agency in West African immigrants' educational experiences in the United States. *Education and Urban Society, 48*(9), 827–851. https://doi.org/10.1177/0013124515589596

Koser, K., & Laczko, F. (2010). *World migration report 2010: The future of migration: Building capacities for change*. International Organization for Migration. https://publications.iom.int/system/files/pdf/wmr_2010_english.pdf

Krogstad, J. M., Lopez, M. H., & Passel, J. S. (2020, June 10). *A majority of Americans say immigrants mostly fill jobs U.S. citizens do not want*. Pew Research Center. https://www.pewresearch.org/fact-tank/2020/06/10/a-majority-of-americans-say-immigrants-mostly-fill-jobs-u-s-citizens-do-not-want/

Krogstad, J. M., & Radford, J. (2018, September 14). *Educational levels of U.S. immigrants are on the rise*. Pew Research Center. https://www.pewresearch.org/short-reads/2018/09/14/education-levels-of-u-s-immigrants-are-on-the-rise/

Krueger, A. B. (2017). Where have all the workers gone? An inquiry into the decline of the U.S. labor force participation rate. *Brookings Papers on Economic Activity, 2017*(2), 1–87. https://doi.org/10.1353/eca.2017.0012

Kuhn, P., & Shen, K. (2015). Do employers prefer migrant workers? Evidence from a Chinese job board. *IZA Journal of Labor Economics, 4*(1), Article 22. https://doi.org/10.1186/s40172-015-0038-0

Lee, M. S., Crittenden, K. S., & Yu, E. (1996). Social support and depression among elderly Korean immigrants in the United States. *The International Journal of Aging and Human Development, 42*(4), 313–327. https://doi.org/10.2190/2vhh-jlxy-ebvg-y8jb

Light, M. T., He, J., & Robey, J. P. (2020). Comparing crime rates between undocumented immigrants, legal immigrants, and native-born US citizens in Texas. *The Proceedings of the National Academy of Sciences, 117*(51), 32340–32347. https://doi.org/10.1073/pnas.2014704117

Love, S., & Spinks, H. (n.d.). *Immigration*. Parliament of Australia. https://www.aph.gov.au/About_Parliament/Parliamentary_Departments/Parliamentary_Library/pubs/rp/BudgetReview202021/Immigration

Malit, F. T., Jr., & Youha, A. A. (2013). Labor migration in the United Arab Emirates: Challenges and responses. *Migration Information Source*. https://www.migrationpolicy.org/article/labor-migration-united-arab-emirates-challenges-and-responses

Miyawaki, C. E., Liu, M., Park, V. T., Tran, M. T., & Markides, K. S. (2022). Social support as a moderator of physical disability and mental health in older Vietnamese immigrants in the U.S.: Results from the Vietnamese Aging and Care Survey (VACS). *Geriatric Nursing, 44*, 151–158. https://doi.org/10.1016/j.gerinurse.2022.01.012

National Center for Education Statistics. (2023). *Status dropout rates.* U.S. Department of Education. https://nces.ed.gov/programs/coe/indicator/coj

Olsen-Medina, K., & Batalova, J. (2020). College-educated immigrants in the United States. *Migration Information Source.* https://www.migrationpolicy.org/article/college-educated-immigrants-united-states

Orrenius, P., & Zavodny, M. (2019). *Do immigrants threaten U.S. public safety?* (Working Paper No. 1905). Federal Reserve Bank of Dallas. https://doi.org/10.24149/wp1905

Pérez, D. M. (2017, February 1). Mexicans working in the United States earn six times more than at home. *El País.* https://english.elpais.com/elpais/2017/02/01/inenglish/1485948570_616168.html

Ratts, M. J., Singh, A. A., Nassar-McMillan, S., Butler, S. K., & McCullough, J. R. (2015). *Multicultural and social justice counseling competencies.* Association for Multicultural Counseling and Development. https://www.counseling.org/docs/default-source/competencies/multicultural-and-social-justice-counseling-competencies.pdf?sfvrsn=20

Richwine, J. (2016, September 28). *Immigrants replace low-skill natives in the workforce.* Center for Immigration Studies. https://cis.org/Immigrants-Replace-LowSkill-Natives-Workforce

Richwine, J. (2019, October 24). *No Americans need apply: EEOC lawsuits reveal how employers are eager to replace low-skill native workers with immigrants.* Center for Immigration Studies. https://cis.org/Report/No-Americans-Need-Apply

Routley, N. (2022, November 22). *Countries with the highest (and lowest) proportion of immigrants.* Visual Capitalist. https://www.visualcapitalist.com/countries-with-the-highest-proportion-of-immigrants/

Smith, N., & Buchman, C. (2022). *U.S. citizens most likely to be arrested for violent crime.* News Nation. https://www.newsnationnow.com/us-news/immigration/u-s-citizens-most-likely-to-commit-crimes-than-immigrants/

Stoll, M. A., Raphael, S., & Holzer, H. J. (2004). Black job applicants and the hiring officer's race. *Industrial and Labor Relations Review, 57*(2), 267–287. https://doi.org/10.1177/001979390405700206

Stout, R. J. (2008). *Why immigrants come to America: Braceros, indocumentados and the migra.* Praeger.

Turner, S. C. (1997). Barriers to a better break: Employer discrimination and spatial mismatch in metropolitan Detroit. *Journal of Urban Affairs, 19*(2), 123–141. https://doi.org/10.1111/j.1467-9906.1997.tb00400.x

United Nations, Department of Economic and Social Affairs, Population Division. (2017). *International migration report 2017: Highlights* (ST/ESA/SER.A/404). https://www.un.org/en/development/desa/population/migration/publications/migrationreport/docs/MigrationReport2017_Highlights.pdf

U.S. Bureau of Labor Statistics. (n.d.). *Civilian labor force participation rate.* https://www.bls.gov/charts/employment-situation/civilian-labor-force-participation-rate.htm

U.S. Citizenship and Immigration Services. (n.d.). *N-648, medical certification for disability exceptions.* https://www.uscis.gov/n-648

VisaNation. (n.d.). *PERM advertising process.* https://www.immi-usa.com/perm/perm-advertising-requirements/

World Population Review. (2023). *Immigration by country 2023.* https://worldpopulationreview.com/country-rankings/immigration-by-country

Xiang, H., Shi, J., Wheeler, K., & Wilkins, J. R., III. (2010). Disability and employment among U.S. working-age immigrants. *American Journal of Industrial Medicine, 53*(4), 425–434. https://doi.org/10.1002/ajim.20802

Chapter 6

Mental Health Needs of Immigrants and Refugees

In the previous chapters, there has been discussion about life circumstances, contexts, legislation and policies, and other structures and systems that affect the aspirations and dreams of immigrants and refugees as they navigate uncharted territory for a better life. The premigration and migration-specific phases in their journeys leave imprints that do not readily disappear. Thus, it is in the postmigration years that mental and physical health issues will likely emerge for individuals across the life span. The acculturation process previously discussed has differential effects on family members not only because of developmental differences but also because of other experiences, including witnessing violence and death. Among the most prevalent mental health issues reported are depression, loss and grief, trauma and posttraumatic stress, isolation, and anxiety. Somatization or psychosomatic symptoms are also prevalent. Within these large categories are a range of presenting issues, symptoms, and diagnoses. Of course, there are contextual considerations because migration does not happen in isolation. The focus on families is primary because of the intergenerational situations that generally arise.

In the subsequent chapters (7–10), we will provide more specific examples of presenting concerns for immigrants across the life span—children, adolescents, and adults. There are multiple physical and mental consequences of migration that may emerge many years after individuals are seemingly settled. In this chapter, we will describe multiple factors affecting immigrant mental well-being. These include emotional, physical, and ecological factors and their manifestation in different situations. To this end, the biopsychosocial model will be introduced to guide counselors as they assess narratives and presenting issues they hear. Identity variables and how these apply in understanding individuals' experiences will also be reviewed. There will be a section describing theories relevant for gathering insights about immigrants' well-being.

Overall, the chapter broadens the conversation about the complex factors and conditions that affect immigrants' and refugees' mental health. Readers will also be reminded about the frameworks introduced in Chapter 1 that are relevant to conceptualizing and formulating treatment plans. For counselors, the Multicultural and Social Justice Counseling

Competencies (MSJCC; Ratts et al., 2015) will be an excellent resource to conceptualize and assess what they may hear as presenting issues. Although there may be tendencies to take action to "fix" something that is a concern to the immigrant and refugee clients with whom they meet, counselors have to apply their listening skills, ask questions, and discern underlying emotional distress. Counselors need to be prepared to unpack the different narratives to provide culturally responsive care.

Learning Objectives

- Apply a biopsychosocial framework to understand symptoms and presenting issues.
- Identify the strengths and resilience that contribute to individuals' accomplishments during times of distress.
- View mental, physical, and spiritual health from non-Western perspectives.
- Identify theories and models that would be most appropriate for culturally responsive, situational responses.
- Apply the MSJCC with case scenarios.

The following section introduces a self-assessment designed to gauge your knowledge on the topic of holistic and culturally sensitive approaches to mental health services for immigrants and refugees. This brief assessment aims to explore your existing understanding of key concepts and provide a foundation for further learning. Answering the following questions will better equip you to engage with the material in the chapter.

Self-assessment: Please respond to the following statements by rating yourself on the following Likert scale: *strongly agree, agree, disagree, strongly disagree, unsure*, or *not applicable.*

1. When I think of the postmigration phase, I often consider this the easiest time for immigrants and refugees because they have arrived where they want to be.
2. I need to learn more about the spiritual and religious belief systems of immigrants and refugees from different countries.
3. I appreciate the intersection of mental and physical well-being considering the stressors during the premigration, migration-specific, and postmigration phases.
4. I am aware of sociopolitical conditions that make immigrants targets of hate crimes and, in turn, affect their sense of psychological safety for themselves and their children.
5. I need to learn more about culture-specific diagnoses and how they differ from the Eurocentric assessment and diagnosis process.

A Comprehensive Approach to Address Immigrants' and Refugees' Mental Health Needs

Immigration is a historical moment in the lives of individuals and their families. The decision to migrate sets in motion multiple unknown scenarios. Migration involves many dangerous physical and mentally arduous behaviors and tests of self-determination. It is in the postmigration years that cumulative stress, new stressors, and their consequences emerge, affecting mental and physical well-being. For example, refugee displacement and resettlement cannot be anticipated; thus, refugees and their families bear the brunt of what may seem to be poorly planned and executed physical relocations based on new governmental policies or what may seem like power struggles between resettlement agencies and host countries. Refugees who flee their country because of civil war or a natural disaster experience constant mental and physical anxiety. Their body must respond to real challenges to move away from danger.

Counseling professionals will learn about immigrants and refugees through different narratives, research data, and other information that may shed light on their mental and physical well-being. Accordingly, counselors need to attend to the range of postmigration presentations and situations and how these contribute to the interdependent nature or the nexus of immigrants' mental and physical issues. Counselors should approach counseling with both a holistic and a microlevel mindset simultaneously that is truly immigrant and refugee centered.

Mental health issues do not emerge in isolation (Carrasco-Sanz et al., 2018; Jorgenson & Nilsson, 2021; Maung et al., 2021); context and other conditions intervene, leading to a range of consequences. Not to be overlooked are the migrants' preexisting physical and mental health conditions that may have been treated or untreated in their country of origin. For example, refugees from some African countries, particularly girls, have been kidnapped from their schools (The Guardian, 2014). Another condition is malnutrition; extreme poverty leads to a lack of access to basic food staples and has been associated with poor youth development that may last a lifetime. Malnutrition can lead to adverse cognitive, mental health, and brain consequences in early childhood (Galler et al., 2021). In addition, symptoms of somatization are often precursors to manifestations of psychological distress (García-Sierra et al., 2020). Symptoms for children, adolescents, and adults have different implications. For children, there may be developmental delays, and for adolescents, there may be identity confusion that manifests through a range of emotional expressions, including self-isolation, suicidal ideation, and other self-harming behaviors.

Arredondo, one of the authors, found in her home visits with immigrant families, primarily from Jamaica and Haiti in the Boston area, that sleep disorders were common. Children had nightmares leading to bed-wetting at ages 5 and 6. For parents who had to work outside of the home, their absence created great anxiety for their children, although in a couple of instances, the grandmother was in the home to care for them. Dislocation led to fears and a desire to hold on to the parents. Family visits by counselors were pivotal in providing more context and history about what could have been misconstrued as an isolated situation of a child's nightmares and bed-wetting. The visits also allowed for resources to be shared with the parents that they could not access on their own because of work commitments. Taking the time to understand rather than making assumptions leads to culturally responsive support and interventions.

Predictors of Emotional, Physical, and Sociocultural Stress

The biopsychosocial model (see Figure 6.1) provides a comprehensive overview of biological, psychological, and social and environmental factors that may be in play simultaneously. According to this model (Engel, 1980), interactions between people's genetic makeup (biology), mental health (psychology), and sociocultural environment (social world) contribute to their experience of overall well-being. These discrete factors may manifest as symptoms such as irritability and sadness, or invisible conditions such as genetic vulnerability and metabolic disorders and/or issues of diet. For a counseling assessment, counselors may hear the client's emotions, learn about reasons for their grief, and gain some understanding about their coping strengths. However, counselors need to learn more in the intake process. The in-depth information may lead to referrals for medical examinations, psychological testing, or other types of assessments. Of course, these assessments must be culturally appropriate to provide a more fitting treatment plan. The biopsychosocial model can readily be applied throughout a counselor's engagement with immigrant and refugee clients.

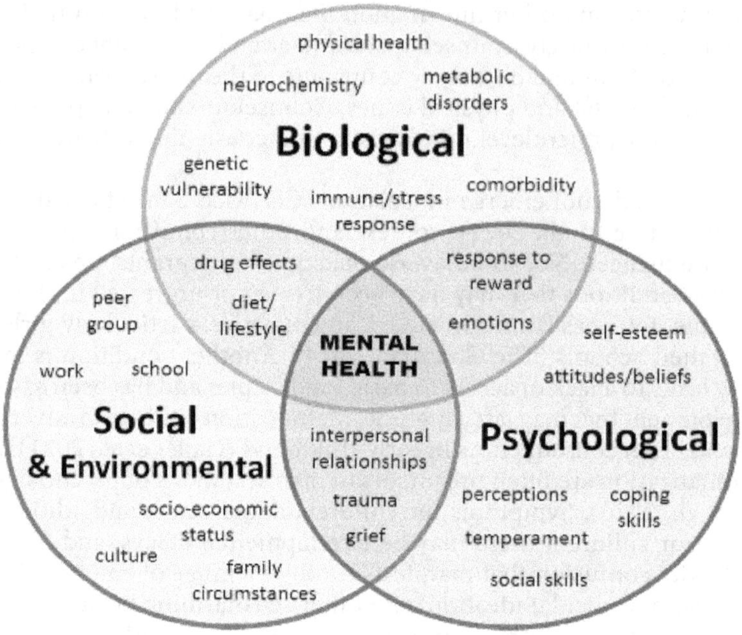

FIGURE 6.1
The Biopsychosocial Model

Note. From "The Biopsychosocial Model of Mental Health: Revisited." Copyright 2023 by The Open University. Reprinted with permission.

Experiences of acculturative stress occurring in the postmigration phase often reflect intertwining multiple factors and precursor situations from the premigration and migration-specific phases to the here and now of the migrants' circumstances. Some examples of the factors clinicians can tease out include trauma history (cumulative), posttraumatic stress, violence in many manifestations, polyvictimization, persecution, separation from family, and family conflict, all migration-related experiences. Counselors may develop an inventory of what to check for with a given client's or the family's presenting situation by using predictors. What might they need to know more about in terms of the migration-specific journey that could illuminate areas for client support? Is there a sense of vulnerability or are there symptoms of agoraphobia symptomatic of past experiences? The biopsychosocial model can be an excellent resource in the assessment process with clients.

Emotional/Psychological Stressors

Among the most prevalent emotional stressors are cumulative stress, posttraumatic stress, loss and grief, and guilt. These are of an intrapersonal nature and not readily visible to a counselor. Although there is an overlap with other stressors and life circumstances, specific naming of emotional stressors, not always easily described by clients, provides counselors with insights about what they may be seeing and hearing in the counseling process. Therefore, counselors need to apply their best attending skills to notice what is said or not said, and how to inquire if a client does not share experiences that happen to others in the migration journey. For instance, if there is a situation in which an immigrant adolescent states that he was separated from his brother when they arrived in El Paso, Texas, it is fair to ask, "Do you have any idea where he may be?" or "I imagine not knowing where he is makes you anxious and responsible for what happens to him." Attentiveness to clients' lived experiences and making connections will advance the therapeutic alliance and add understanding to the clients' overall situation.

Physical/Health Stressors

The migration process requires physical and mental endurance (Sangalang et al., 2019). However, in the premigration phase, individuals may have experienced torture and violence. This inhumane practice of force often requires victims to report on others, with threats of harm or death to family members, often with the oppression of gangs. The torture can have lifelong physical effects while also contributing to psychological health issues (Zimbrean & Dahal, 2020). Additionally, in the postmigration phase, refugees may have mobility and strength-related problems because of their confinement. Refugees who have been caged for extended periods of time lose strength in their limbs and may suffer from intestinal issues. Immigrants who trekked across Mexico and crossed the border may have been injured and not had broken bones properly set, or they may have back injuries from carrying heavy objects or other migrants. These are all unique considerations clinicians need to keep in mind.

Refugee adults present with higher odds of having a chronic disease compared with nonrefugee immigrant adults and an increased risk for diabetes compared with U.S.-born controls. The most commonly reported chronic diseases among Iraqi, Somali, and Bhutanese refugee adults include diabetes and hypertension (Kumar et al., 2021). Working in factories or the service industry may require heavy lifting, and toiling in agricultural fields is backbreaking. Collecting immigrants' and refugees' health history prior to arrival, in addition to conditions from their experiences at refugee camps or the migration journey, will add critical information to an individual's presenting physical health status.

In terms of health, children and adolescents are differentially affected because they are still in physical growth states. If they experienced malnutrition in their country of origin, have child diabetes or asthma, or lack immunizations, these health-related disparities will predispose them to illness in the postmigration phase (Jensen et al., 2019; Scharpf et al., 2021). Unaccompanied minors often engage in risky behavior during their journey. Many have taken "la bestia," a train that accelerated their travel from Central American countries through Mexico, but there are many accounts of boys falling off the top of the train and losing a limb. Regardless, they find a way to continue. In her book *Enrique's Journey*, Nazario (2006) described the brutal journey and the desperateness to ride the train, despite the danger inherent in falling off or being pushed off. Size matters, and generally smaller statured children and adolescents are bullied, injured, or left behind. All these risky behaviors contribute to health, physical, and psychological stressors later.

McLaurin and Liebman (2012) reported the following health issues among migrants, particularly those working in the agricultural industry: cancer, diabetes, hepatitis, HIV/AIDS, hypertension, immunizations, oral health issues, and tuberculosis. Specific to children's health, the report indicated that children of farmworkers have unique challenges and risks because of their proximity to unhealthy conditions in agriculture.

Health issues for children as a result of the migration process have been documented, and several essential findings are relevant for counselors. In one multinational study, it was found that migrant children had higher risks for malnutrition, obesity/overweight problems, and iron deficiency (Dondi et al., 2020). In an international study examining the effects of migration on children's health, pediatricians perceived chronic diseases as the most frequent health problem, with migrant children presenting with worse health than nonmigrant children (Carrasco-Sanz et al., 2018). Proper oral health care was cited as a concern by 86% of the respondents. Additionally, the European primary care physicians indicated that the most frequent barriers to care (90%) were cultural and language barriers.

When counselors anticipate and deconstruct the types of stressors immigrants typically report or do not mention, they may engage clients in more meaningful discussions, rather than asking a long list of questions and seeming surprised by the responses or not asking questions related to physical well-being. Counselors informed by the MSJCC (Ratts et al., 2015) will prepare themselves for counseling with immigrants and refugees by learning about the two stages of the migration process that precede the postmigration phase. This approach will heighten counselors' preparedness and knowledge about multiple conditions, as embodied in the biopsychosocial model, that may explain how immigrants, refugees, or their families present.

Sociocultural Stressors

Context matters—geography, the sociopolitical climate in the United States, neighborhoods, xenophobia, and other social determinants contribute to mental and physical well-being. The ecological systems framework of Bronfenbrenner (1977; see also Bronfenbrenner & Morris, 1998) introduced in Chapters 3 and 4 outlines five systems that affect immigrants in the postmigration phase. To recap, these systems are the microsystem, mesosystem, exosystem, macrosystem, and the chronosystem. The microsystem is shaped by individuals through the relationships with whom they engage, mainly by choice. For migrants, these generally are family members and individuals from their country of origin who previously emigrated. This is the most proximate system and can also include people in their new neighborhoods and workplace. These are individuals upon whom they may rely on the most.

The mesosystem serves a connecting function. For example, immigrants and refugees with deep connections to their religious and spiritual belief system may begin to make connections to churches, temples, and other services that also provide social support. One of the authors (Arredondo) was part of a team of counselors and psychologists who met with women after mass at their local Catholic church. They met in the church rectory to learn more about how to navigate services for their children, particularly medical appointments. In these gatherings, delivered in Spanish, the mothers came to realize that they had similar concerns and priorities and began to form friendship networks.

The exosystem is more external and may offer connections to social and health care agencies and educational institutions once the immigrants know how to access these, although counselors and school officials can be helpful to these processes. The previous example applies here.

The macrosystem imposes on individuals and families because it includes the overarching, intrusive, and controlling governmental and legislative bodies that invent laws and policies that often complicate the lives of immigrants and refugees. For example, in Oregon, Washington, and other states, undocumented immigrants were not able to obtain a driver's license until legislation was passed to make this possible. In the summer of 2023, the state of Florida passed legislation that prohibited the issuance of a driver's license for undocumented immigrants even if they have a valid license from another state (Vicks, 2023). Immigrants expressed great distress and fear, and those interviewed reported that they were moving out of Florida because they no longer felt safe.

The chronosystem is described as a "space" where the relationship between time, events, and conditions (outside of one's control) affects one's development and plans. For example, the executive order of President Obama known as Deferred Action for Childhood Arrivals, signed in 2012, allowed many undocumented individuals under age 30 and who met criteria to enroll in higher education or to start their own businesses. This historical event stands in contrast to policies instituted during the Trump administration to delay entry processes for those from Middle Eastern countries. The pandemic that began in 2020 can also be viewed through the chronosystem lens. Migration and resettlement plans ceased when borders closed due to concerns related to COVID-19.

By applying the socioecological framework, counselors can also identify the many possible ecological factors out of an individual's control that affect their mental and physical well-being. The next section outlines some ecological factors and how they may affect immigrants and refugees.

Ecological Factors

Laws and the legal system in the United States. In Chapter 2, historical and contemporary legislations that function as gatekeeping and classify immigrants and refugees were discussed. Because of immigration policies and the uncertainty that comes with indefinite and undocumented status, family separations and stays in detention camps can span years, leaving people in limbo. They are neither accepted to enter the United States nor able to return to their country of origin. These situations weigh on individuals' mental well-being. Legal status was also discussed in Chapter 2 with different statuses contributing to an array of emotions. Individuals with undocumented status are likely to carry more mental and physical distress than others when considering their circumstances. Hiding, avoiding being caught, exposing their family to harm, and being unable to achieve economic goals often lead to unhealthy responses such as alcohol use, domestic violence, depression, and physical maladies. Although individuals with refugee status have some legal protective factors, many are still in recovery from long internments where their overall health was compromised (Byrow et al., 2022).

U.S. Immigration and Customs Enforcement practices. U.S. Immigration and Customs Enforcement (ICE) practices can engender fear and traumatize individuals and families. In Spanish, the term *la migra* refers to ICE, the body that chases down individuals in the United States to remove them, sometimes unlawfully. The term can also refer to the Border Patrol and other immigration enforcement agencies. As clinicians, it is important to consider that although ICE does not pursue those who are documented, bearing witness to the loss of a loved one can lead to outcomes that influence an individual's mental health. Images of ICE agents taking away parents leave lasting impressions on children and others left behind. Going through these experiences may increase a person's anxiety, fear of federal agents and police officers, and hypervigilance when engaging in everyday activities. ICE raids in California, for example, have torn away working adults in low-wage employment, and now their families have even less (Foster LLP, n.d.; Pinkerton, 2014). It is critical that counselors take these events and their impact into consideration when determining treatment plans and find resources for workers, communities, and employers who may be affected by raids.

Separation of children from parents. Separation of children from parents in any phase of the migration journey contributes to long-lasting psychological distress. The Migration Policy Institute (see Capps et al., 2015) reported on the effects of parental detention or deportation on a child's well-being and examined the consequences on children. Among the effects were increased economic and social instability, residential instability, and even family dissolution. Without the breadwinners, families must rely on public benefits and suffer other material losses. Witnessing and/or being the survivor of a parent's detention or deportation provokes psychological trauma and, among boys, increased aggression.

Another report focused on the needs of U.S. citizen children with a parent who had been detained or deported and their involvement with health and social services agencies (McLeigh, 2010). The study took place in California, Florida, Illinois, South Carolina, and Texas. The findings corroborate those in the first report with respect to material and economic hardship. Two additional findings were reported: (a) The families faced multiple barriers when trying to access health and social services, and (b) the children's trauma was heightened because they were unable to communicate with the detained parent(s). Spouses and partners of detainees also experienced depression, aloneness, and isolation. According to the researcher, the effects on the remaining parent had a trickle-down effect on the children, putting them at risk of a decrease in cognition, emotional expression, and appropriate behaviors. Children become collateral damage (McLeigh, 2010).

Capps et al. (2020) addressed the effects of immigration enforcement on the mental health of Latino students. The study, carried out in Texas and Rhode Island, found that more than 50% of the students reported symptoms such as anxiety, posttraumatic stress, and depression that warranted treatment. Although immigration enforcement is higher in Texas, adolescents in Rhode Island also feared the worst.

Refugees face similar experiences, with the children and families affected in unique ways. For example, the United Nations Higher Commission for Refugees (UNHCR, 2013) reported that more than 70,000 Syrian refugee families live without fathers, and thousands of refugee children are unaccompanied or separated from both their parents. This separation may lead to breakdown in family structures with emotional and economic impacts. Many children endure injuries and physical trauma, illness due to interrupted preventive health care, and psychological trauma. Among the global trends for refugees reported by the UNHCR in 2022 was the forced displacement of 108.4 million people. The primary reasons were persecution, violence, conflict, human rights violations, and other seriously disturbing events.

Counselors have a duty to inquire about these traumatic experiences and offer services that are developmentally, psychologically, and culturally appropriate. As previously mentioned, counselors need to be knowledgeable about contextual conditions in migrants' home countries that affect their physical and mental well-being in the United States.

Access to quality health services. A lack of access to quality health services is a prevalent issue for migrants (World Health Organization [WHO], 2022). This manifests itself in several ways. First is the lack of health care insurance. The majority of immigrants do not have employer-sponsored health care insurance, often because they are employed fewer than 40 hours a week. Employers avoid providing coverage, and immigrants may work 40 or more hours but in different settings. This disadvantages entire families. The WHO (2022) recognized that immigrants and refugees, particularly in irregular situations, are often excluded from national programs for health promotion, disease prevention, and treatment and care. Higher user fees, lower levels of health literacy, poor cultural competency among health providers, stigma, and inadequate interpreting services are also common.

A second example is the location and availability of services. Most migrants typically visit the emergency room for all symptoms because they are familiar with the location of hospitals, there are no clinics in their neighborhoods, and/or they do not have a primary care physician. In their research on the benefits of the Affordable Care Act, Joseph and Marrow (2017) found differential effects for immigrants. Their findings indicated that there was an improvement in coverage through the Affordable Care Act for low-income and racial/ethnic minoritized groups, particularly African Americans and Asian Americans (Adams, 2015; National Academies of Sciences, Engineering, and Medicine, 2015). However, this shift in coverage rendered many immigrants as outsiders and not beneficiaries of the Affordable Care Act. As Joseph and Marrow (2017) and Adams (2015) pointed out, they have a demographic profile (i.e., low income, racial/ethnic minorities, and citizenship status) but did not have access to the benefits. This is generally not well known, and quite often the opposite narrative is promulgated, suggesting that immigrants receive free services they are not entitled to receive.

Finding culturally and linguistically appropriate health education resources and care is difficult, and making an appointment at a local clinic is no assurance that the provider is prepared to work with immigrants and refugees (Office of Refugee Resettlement, n.d.). All tasks, including a comprehensive culture-centered intake, the use of culturally and linguistically appropriate assessments, and building a counseling relationship cannot be guaranteed. As a result, an immigrant, refugee, or their family may leave without relief of their distress or the resources that can be of benefit medically and mentally. In short, cultural malpractice (Arredondo et al., 2008) occurs far too often.

Xenophobia and hate crimes. Xenophobia and hate crimes also contribute to immigrant mental distress. A 2020 report on hate crime statistics showed that 62% of victims were targeted because of the offenders' bias toward race/ethnicity/ancestry, which continues to be the largest bias motivation category (Smith, 2021). Bullying in the workplace and in school has vastly increased. For example, U.S.-born ethnic minority children and adults were threatened by White peers, being told they are foreigners and to leave, "to go back to their country" (Romero, 2022; Wang, 2022).

Xenophobia is not a new behavior in the United States (see Chapter 2), but the focus on immigrants of color has reached new levels. Immigrants know that they are targeted and that images in the press and social media cast them in a negative light, making them want to hide. Consequently, immigrants experience increased hypervigilance, become mistrustful of others, and feel unsafe. Colorism and anti-LGBTQ+ messages are not lost on the victims; rather, they absorb and internalize these, contributing to anxiety, fears, and isolation.

MSJCC-oriented counselors cannot minimize the psychological harm of racist threats. Both privileged and marginalized counselors must take actions and engage in advocacy when physical harm is threatened and their immigrant clients fear speaking with law enforcement. It is their responsibility as counselors to step in and speak up.

Language interpretation. Language brokering has effects on family relationships, youth self-efficacy, and pressures. In a meta-analysis of studies addressing language brokering by immigrant youth, Shen et al. (2022) reported findings on emotions and how these contributed to well-being and family relationships. Their primary finding was that youth are not equally affected. Some youth experience satisfaction, enjoyment, and a source of pride in translating for their parents whereas other youth do not. It was found that youth with positive feelings were better adjusted, had a greater sense of ethnic identity, and had lower levels of substance use. Conversely, individuals who reported negative feelings about brokering tended to have poorer family relationships and depressive symptoms (Kam & Lazarevic, 2014; Shen et al., 2017).

Manifestation of Stressors

The consequences of emotional and physical stressors are behavioral and psychological, as outlined in the biopsychosocial model, where self-esteem, temperament, attitudes, and beliefs may affect the self and relationships. Quite often, clinicians jump to make a diagnosis, categorizing a person as depressed, anxious, or traumatized using assessments or initial interviews. Although this is normative practice, the predictors or precursors may not be sufficiently unpacked. In most studies of immigrants' and refugees' mental health, the focus is on depression, trauma, and psychopathology, not fully contextualizing the rationale for a given diagnosis (Anderson & Edwards, 2020; Betancourt et al., 2012; Bouza et al., 2018; Fazel, 2012). For example, displacement, family separation, witnessing violence, and illness may contribute to a diagnosis, but they must be understood through narratives and other forms of engagement beyond an assessment with culture-bound norms. Additionally, while making assessments, counselors must also attend to the client's social and coping skills and learn about their interpersonal relationships. Are these factors causing more stress?

In studies, both qualitative and quantitative, respondents cite a range of consequences of stressors. These include examples of somatization such as poor sleeping and eating habits, bed-wetting, headaches, backaches, difficulty breathing, and other symptoms without an easy explanation. In one of the author's (Arredondo) work with immigrant women, physicians often referred their patients who did not have a physical diagnosis, but the physicians knew that something was contributing to a patient's headaches, lethargy, and so on. In these instances, gathering as much contextual and relational information as possible through narratives often offered clarity to the way clients were presenting. Referring to the socioecological model will support clinicians in reflecting on clients' concerns more contextually and will help determine whether strategies and interventions for health promotion need to happen for individuals and/or the family system.

CASE STUDY

Stress may manifest as physical symptoms (Salari et al., 2020), especially when stressors begin to accrue. The following case study about Jaime and Lorena exemplifies the insidious ways in which stressors may arise.

> Jaime and Lorena were alarmed when the school principal called for a meeting. There they learned that their 7-year-old son Carlitos had wet his pants on the playground. Apparently, this had happened before but had not been reported to the parents. Lorena admitted to Jaime that Carlitos had been bed-wetting for the past month. She did not want to make a big deal about it and did not share it with the family because she felt responsible. Her father had died in Guatemala, and, given her undocumented status, she was unable to go to the funeral. She expressed her sentiments of loss at home freely, prompting her son to comment, "Are you going to die too?" Lorena explained that Jaime worked long hours, and she did not want to bother him about Carlitos. Embarrassed and anxious, Lorena asked her oldest daughter to accompany them to the school meeting; she did not consider their English to be strong and felt anxious about the school visit. She became alarmed about the possibilities that her son might be kept out of school and questioned whether she was a bad parent.

Reflection Questions

1. How would you assess Lorena's behavior? Was it protecting Carlitos or her spouse?
2. From a social justice perspective, how can you explain Lorena's initial behavior?
3. If you were the school counselor, what intervention might you recommend for Carlitos?

This case shows the underlying factors that may contribute to stressors for individuals in the same family. Lorena wants to be responsible for everyone but cannot make it all work. Therapists should be ready to connect with Lorena and identify ways they can support her. She appears to be trying to manage for everyone but does not know how to let go or do less.

Even prior to a formal intake with immigrant and refugee clients, there is a predisposed assumption that immigrants and refugees are "naturally" depressed, anxious, and sad based on their journeys. Although this may be so, given all the experiences in the premigration and migration-specific phases, it is still necessary to assess what is "normal" given an individual's circumstances for arriving in the United States. For example, if a family in a refugee resettlement camp lost parents and others to a disease, consider whether their anxiety about drinking only bottled water or washing their bedsheets daily is appropriate. Examples in previous chapters described the push factors for migration—fear and sadness because of others' violent deaths or not being able to be at a grandparent's funeral because of safety concerns. Immigrants and refugees may still be carrying unresolved loss and sadness. Friendships form during the migration journey, and perhaps a new friend was left behind. Inviting explanations for sadness and anger is necessary to make sense of feelings and the relevance and depth of incidents to the expressed feelings. Empathic inquiries matter.

Another manifestation of stress, loss, and sadness is a loss of hope. This is an expression of "giving up," despair because one cannot change the situation, and/or resignation to accept only the negatives in life. A loss of hope can be associated with deep depression, suicidal thoughts, and perhaps other forms of self-harm. (Refer to the Kübler-Ross model of loss and grief in Chapter 3.) The definition of hope can guide a conversation. Hope can convey optimism, looking ahead for something to happen, and a desire for something good to occur. Perhaps a question that can be posed is, "You have been through a lot. What makes you hopeful? When you wake up in the morning, what do you wish for the day?" If the person cannot express the sentiment in English, ask them to express themselves in their primary language and to draw an image of hope. Perhaps the counselor can begin by drawing a heart.

Refugee-Specific Circumstances

It has been stated that immigrants and refugees do not have the same premigration-to-postmigration experiences, although they may have similar physical and emotional stressors that they must manage in the acculturation process. A few examples of ecological factors affecting refugees will be discussed in this section. The topics covered include living in war zones, forced migration and displacement, natural disasters, and civil wars and ethnic cleansing. Many refugees from countries affected possess a collectivistic worldview, which means that counselors need to recognize that interdependence and relationships are priorities.

Surviving in Areas of Conflict

Living in war zones precipitates a set of unpredictable factors. The world witnessed the assault on Ukraine in February 2022 and the dire consequences for families both in Ukraine and in other Eastern European regions. Dreams were shattered and lives were lost; psychological, physical, and spiritual emotions manifested. In qualitative research with refugees from Myanmar (formerly Burma; Maung, 2021), Somalia (Jorgenson & Nilsson, 2021), and Syria (Atari-Khan et al., 2021), specific challenges were identified in the transition and settlement phase in the United States. These included language barriers, employment, discrimination against color and appearance, "different" or non-Western clothing, a focus for disparagement, and marginalization. Finding social support is not easy, and the uncertainty of personal and familial well-being weighs emotionally in the form of survivor guilt.

Forced Migration and Displacement

Resettlement is associated with more psychological problems. Individuals who are relocated do not have control of their next moves, and although it is not always the case, helplessness and an externalized locus of control are typical (e.g., Magwaza & Bhana, 1991; Masoom, 2018). This is in contrast to immigrants from Central America, for example, who seemingly take charge of their migration process and all its uncertainties. Although they do not have full control of arriving to the United States, they have plans for the migration journey.

As a result of the war in Syria, innocent people fled to avoid warfare but had to live in war zones and were subject to arrest, torture, and death; families were systematically killed (Atari-Khan et al., 2021). This terror reigned throughout the country. At the same time, many fled their homes to unknown locations within their country and in Europe where they believed a safer lifestyle was possible. The situation has not ended as of this writing.

Moving in Response to Adverse Effects From Environmental Factors

Natural disasters also create migrants. This involuntary, unplanned migration precipitates emotional experiences of confusion, loss, physical and emotional pain, anxiety, and insecurity. In their discussion of Latinos experiencing disaster situations such as earthquakes, Arredondo et al. (2008) discussed the effects on the lives of survivors, from physical to emotional disruptions. Physically, there were migration journeys to safer locations or to relatives within the country; displacement within the country or to another country; and physical loss of homes, businesses, and loved ones. For families who live off the land, fishing, or other industries that are also controlled by nature, they may be losing decades of family economic investments. When Hurricane Katrina devastated New Orleans in 2005, refugees from Vietnam who had set up small fishing businesses lost everything (Assefa, 2015). People were forced to move, and hard-earned dreams were dashed. Emotional stressors that manifested include anxiety, depression, loss and grief, and trauma. Survivors may fear that a disaster could happen again.

Moving to Escape Conflict, Persecution, and Terrorism

Civil wars and ethnic cleansing continue in countries fraught with a need for superiority and disparagement of others' lives because of their ethnicity, religion, and political affiliations. As discussed in the case study in Chapter 3, the civil war in Bosnia in the 1990s led to deaths because of one's ethnicity, although both the persecuted and the oppressors shared similar cultural backgrounds. In 2023, Peru, Haiti, some African countries, and Afghanistan fought civil wars. The United States continues to live through what are dimensions of civil unrest, where many undocumented immigrants and refugees now feel unsafe. Additionally, marginalization based on political party affiliations affects economic and psychological well-being. Illicit businesses such as smuggling of drugs and guns and kidnapping put many more "regular" citizens at risk through extortion and fear that family members will be harmed. Sadly, immigrants often fall victim to the cruelties and crimes of others.

Variables Among Immigrants and Refugees

Thus far in the book, we have discussed identity and developmental factors that influence different experiences throughout the migration process. These similar and differential experiences are highlighted for counselors as they consider engagement with immigrants, refugees, and their families while addressing their mental health needs. These factors include age and developmental status, unaccompanied minor status, country of origin, gender, LGBTQ+ identity, documented or undocumented status, parent(s) with children or without children, color and language, colorism, religious beliefs and practices, and other identity factors highlighted in the dimensions of personal identity model (Arredondo & Glauner, 1992). Clinicians should consider the differential experiences as they conceptualize trauma-informed care, while also focusing on the whole person and the variables that intertwine and contribute to the present lives of their immigrant clients. Below, we address some of these variables among immigrants and refugees.

Age

Research findings point to age during migration as a risk factor for psychotic disorders and other forms of psychological trauma. In a meta-analysis of five studies, Anderson and Edwards (2020) found that (a) for individuals who migrate as young adults (ages 19–29), there is a similar risk of a psychotic disorder as compared with the host population, and (b) individuals who migrate prior to age 18 had nearly twice the risk of a psychotic disorder as compared with the host population. The researchers concluded that migrant status is a well-established risk factor for psychotic disorders, but the underlying etiology is not well understood. It is possible to speculate that those under 18 arrive with deep trauma, having witnessed horrific violence in their country of origin; that refugees are surrounded by fear and death; and that unaccompanied minors are exposed to bullying, assaults, and other physical violence, even torture. The study does not differentiate between females and males, a relevant factor for explanations and treatment.

Refugee children between the ages of 5 and 13 tend to struggle with emotional regulation during resettlement, particularly with sadness and anger (Elsayed et al., 2019). Long after reaching the host country in the postmigration stage, refugee, migrant, and asylum-seeking youth continue to face adversities in various forms, and this becomes even more complex when considering intersecting variables. For example, unaccompanied refugee migrant children under the age of 18 have higher prevalence of mental health disorders than accompanied refugee peers (Khan et al., 2020). And although it is not as common for older adults to leave their home country, it is likely that some do; in 2017, older migrants comprised 12% of the international migrants (Dugarova, 2017). These older adult refugees also present with higher risk for poor mental health (Bogic et al., 2015; Porter & Haslam, 2005).

Gender

The literature consistently reports that many female refugees present with high levels of trauma. For instance, Sudhinaraset et al. (2019) found that one in three refugee women had experienced a traumatic event prior to migration: 17% physical assault, 11.7% captivity, 10.5% sexual assault, and 17.4% weapon assault. Researchers have examined the effects of acculturative stress, age, and gender on mental and physical well-being. In her dissertation study of adult women of Mexican origin living in the United States, Mendoza Griego (2022) found that perceived discrimination had a statistically significant negative effect on women's anxiety, depressive symptoms, and role.

The health of refugee and immigrant females after settlement in a new country can be adversely or positively affected by individual, interpersonal, community, and organizational factors. A study that held focus groups with immigrant women found that the migration process had an adverse impact on their emotional health and limited their social ties (Rios Casas et al., 2020). The women also reported negative impacts based on U.S. immigration policies that put them at risk for detention and deportation. These policies contributed to their fear of being separated from their families and made it difficult to plan a future in the United States.

Moreover, transgender immigrants often face great hardship in attaining legal status in the United States. Data have shown that transgender people are killed every 3 days, with the majority of these murders happening in Latin America (Maderazo, 2009). The fear and hope for a safer and better quality of life affect these individuals' mental health as well. Participants in a study who identified as Latina transgender women reported increased stress and anxiety due to threats of violence because of their gender identity, a situation that was further complicated by their immigration status (Cerezo et al., 2014).

Religious Beliefs and Practices

Spirituality and religious beliefs can be buffers and sources of support in the face of loss and grief, trauma, and uncertainty. Praying to one's higher power can be a means of coping. For Catholics, praying the rosary at home with family provides a sense of connectedness and cohesion. Praying to certain saints like the Saint of Lost Causes and particularly the Virgin of Guadalupe can make a difference. Faith embodies hope and resilience (Arredondo et al., 2014). A psychosocial framework was applied in a qualitative study with Latinx immigrants to understand their sense of well-being, and the cultural themes that emerged included responsibility to family and a relationship with God and faith (Rojas-Perez et al., 2022).

In a study with Middle Eastern Muslim men, it was found that their stronger religiosity is associated with better mental health following trauma exposure (El-Awad et al., 2022). Similarly, Wu et al.'s (2021) study of refugees in Utica, New York, showed that the refugees' perceived ability to practice their religion is strongly related to happiness and well-being in their community. In another study (Menjivar, 2003) of Catholic and Evangelical Guatemalans and Salvadorans in San Francisco who have precarious legal status, it was found that these individuals relied on both Catholic and Protestant churches for support. In fact, some went to multiple churches to seek support (Menjivar, 2003). However, there were different experiences for religious refugee adolescents and their religious immigrant peers. Religious refugee adolescents experienced more separation and internalized symptoms than their religious immigrant peers. The researchers all believed that differences in the acculturation process affect religious immigrants and refugees differently.

In studies addressing resilience among Burmese and Syrian women, it was found that religious beliefs bolstered hope and a positive outlook (Atari-Khan et al., 2021; Maung et al., 2021). Personal faith provided a sense of hope and of not being alone because a higher being was looking out for them. For Burmese refugee women in the United States, participants described religious beliefs and practices and spirituality as bedrocks for coping (Maung et al., 2021). Another study was carried out with Syrian mothers in refugee camps in Turkey and Syria who were displaced because of civil wars (El-Khani et al., 2017). The women in the study had many relational coping strategies, particularly with other mothers. These women, all Muslim, expressed that trust in God was a form of comfort, instilling a sense of hope for the future (El-Khani et al., 2017).

For counselors, a valuable resource is the book, *Intersections of Religion and Migration* (Saunders et al., 2016). The chapters on different immigrant and refugee populations provide descriptions of how religious and faith-based institutions provide safe spaces for immigrants to get through their challenges and to have their cultural heritage and ethnic identities affirmed. Faith is a powerful force, providing hope and optimism in the worst of times.

Theories to Reference in Mental Health Treatment

Attachment Theory

Attachment theory has long been heralded as relevant to understanding the ability to build healthy and sustainable relationships. John Bowlby, a British psychologist, articulated several premises: (a) Children come into the world predisposed to form attachments; (b) attachment to a primary figure needs to occur by age 2.5 with a sensitive period being up to age 5; and (c) continual disruption in the relationship or contact with the primary caregiver sets up the child for eventual cognitive, emotional, and social relationship issues (Mcleod, 2023). All these perspectives need to be questioned because of the realities faced by immigrants and their children. Parents prioritize their children's safety amid uncertainties. In collectivistic cultures, attachments and interdependence are commonplace.

In the premigration phase, parents often make momentous decisions about which child they can take with them. In one author's (Arredondo) community service with migrants in Phoenix in 2016, she saw a couple with a 7-year-old child. The parents related that it was easier to travel with an older child. However, this is not always the case. During the migration process, mothers have been separated from infants and children under 5 years old at the border. There are terrifying images of Border Patrol agents separating mothers and babies or little children. There are also images of children of different ages, but not yet teens, separated from parents and taken to a Homeland Security system that is arbitrary and not humane.

Researchers have applied attachment theory to understand how migrant and refugee youth adapt, demonstrate resilience, and develop relationships. In their study, Juang et al. (2018) learned that youth could experience better outcomes by maintaining close connections to people and places that provide them with a sense of safety, comfort, and encouragement as they manage challenging life transitions and by finding ways to create connections and a sense of belonging with people, place, and social networks in their new neighborhood. Close bonds bolster youth social and emotional development through healthy attachments.

Also related to the discussion about attachment is the concept of separation and individuation developed by Mahler et al. (1975). The emphasis is on separation by age 3, with the implication of the effects on an individual later in their life. A limitation of this culture-bound mindset is that most immigrant families live within collectivistic socialization patterns. There is no value or encouragement placed on moving away from one's parents' home. Understanding the cultural norms about staying together as a family and allowing the immigrant adolescents and young adults to move out at appropriate ages will benefit the counselor.

Models of Grief and Loss

Models of grief and loss are of relevance to supporting migrants in the acculturation and settlement process. It has been theorized that the migration process parallels that of losing a loved one who has died insomuch as migrants are grieving the loss of their homes, separation from family members, and at times loss of their loved ones—among other factors—before, during, and after the migration process. As discussed in Chapter 3, loss and grief as a result of immigration was outlined by Arredondo-Dowd (1981) as a four-step process, adapted from Bowlby's (1961) attachment and loss model and Kübler-Ross's (1969) five stages of death and dying. Counselors can use this model to familiarize themselves with the context and potential grief migrants go through. Generally, the reactions of children and adolescents differ from those of the parents, who are clear about their goal to be in the United States. Adolescents, in particular, are often reluctant migrants. Homesickness may set in, no matter how awful the experiences in the premigration phase, because of family and friends left behind. With acculturative stress increasing for all family members, anger may be displaced on others and conflict may increase.

Another model includes Cascado et al.'s (2010) description of migratory loss. Cascado and colleagues defined migratory loss as a process of personal and identity loss, affecting the mental health of Latino students. Similarly, Arredondo (1986) described the identity challenges for male immigrants and refugees, especially those who had a profession previously, were self-employed, or had not worked in a setting where no one spoke their first language. The men had identity crises because they were challenged about completing their obligations as breadwinners and their sense of self-efficacy was being eroded. Immigration and exile, according to Lijtmaer (2022), are social traumas involving mourning and bereavement. These are associated with a loss of security, familiarity, and historical continuity, all with psychological implications.

The concepts of bereavement and anticipatory grief were discussed for immigrants dealing with transnational deaths. In a qualitative study with middle-aged and older immigrants, it was found that geographic distance complicated the grieving process, caregiving, and participating in burial rituals (Nesteruk, 2018). When immigrants leave their families, they often experience survivor's guilt and other emotions related to losing a loved one at a distance. This is an emotional burden for all immigrants, but it is more acute for undocumented immigrants. As previously stated in the case scenario of Lorena, returning to her father's funeral in Guatemala was not possible because she was undocumented.

Locus of Control and Locus of Responsibility

As has been discussed, immigrants and refugees are purposeful and responsible, trying to take charge whenever and wherever possible throughout the migration and acculturation processes. At the same time, the ecological factors are ones over which they do not have control but affect their sense of personal power. Internal locus of control has often been presented as an ideal psychological state, particularly in an individualistic culture (Rotter, 1954), and external locus of control is described as an indicator of passivity, lack of initiative, and helplessness. In counseling discussions, it is often heard that racial/ethnic minorities do not assume control for their actions and their issues are due to their own lack of responsibility.

A multicultural scholar, Derald Wing Sue, conceptualized a model with four quadrants: internal locus of control, internal locus of responsibility, external locus of control, and external locus of responsibility and ecological factors that affect individuals' abilities to take control (Sue, 1978). This model is relevant to recognizing how and why immigrants make the decisions they make. In brief, it can be stated that immigrants (a) exert internal locus of control when they decide to leave their home county; (b) assume internal responsibility for the well-being of their family members who leave with them and those they leave behind; (c) manifest external locus of control by paying a smuggler to transport them by bus, boat, or another means to cross the border; and (d) externalize their locus of responsibility to governmental agencies, which set policies in place (given that immigrants do not make the laws that grant them citizenship status). This is an opportunity for the counselor to speak up on behalf of the client and to engage in dialogues about past decisions and how the immigrant client took charge then. Affirmations about how the client made purposeful decisions go a long way.

For counselors, perspective-taking about the locus of control model is necessary when a client expresses frustrations about not being able to take control of their own affairs, for example, opening a bank account or waiting for a month for a medical appointment for their child. A counselor may think that the immigrant is not being persistent, but this may not be a fair assessment. Immigrants who speak with an accent may encounter biases, or immigrants may face cumbersome systems, such as those that are accessed only digitally, that make them feel helpless and powerless. Counselors need to listen with empathy and provide encouragement.

Resilience and Perseverance

Interviews with immigrants and refugees reported in multiple studies highlight the resilience and perseverance of immigrants and refugees throughout their lives (Cigrand et al., 2022). Resilience can be described as "the ability to adapt and cope successfully despite threatening and challenging situations" (Agaibi & Wilson, 2005, p. 198). In the resilience and coping literature, this is a person-centered approach with descriptions of how individuals manage to transcend challenges. Resilience requires cognitive and emotional skills, proactive planning, and goals to get to their destination. One notable difference in the definition of resilience is how it manifests differently from Western approaches, with communities as a key factor to mental well-being.

In a review of refugee behaviors managing death-defying circumstances, Hassan et al. (2016) reported that most refugees are highly resilient. In their study, they described resilience as a holistic, interdependent approach that includes multiple relationships and external and internal conditions. Among these are strong family and social networks, coping strategies that are communal and individual, religion, beliefs systems, and worldviews, as well as individual qualities. Accordingly, these factors contribute to more positive mental health outcomes for refugees (Siriwardhana et al., 2014). A concept introduced in qualitative research with Burmese refugee women was posttraumatic growth (Maung et al., 2021). This concept signals the women's capabilities to face and manage adversities, with outcomes being (a) greater appreciation of life, (b) recognition of strengths and personal limitations, (c) religious and spiritual development, and (d) interpersonal development. Immigrants recognize the adversity they face and apply strengths-based approaches to manage them (Yakushko & Morgan-Consoli, 2014).

The following case study offers the opportunity to apply the concepts from this chapter into practice. The case of Mei is not uncommon in that her migration process may be influencing how she presents herself. Consider Mei's context and situation, then answer the reflection questions to gauge your learning.

CASE STUDY

I (Arredondo) met Mei when she enrolled in counseling graduate program at a public university in Boston. Originally from Taiwan, Mei left her parents and siblings behind to "gain her independence," she stated. She wanted to control her life, contrary to her traditional Chinese upbringing. Because she intended to overstay her tourist visa, she found that by being accepted into a university, she would qualify for a student visa. She arrived in the United States alone and found a rooming house near the university, not ideal for a single 26-year-old woman, but this was what she could afford. Mei endeavored to meet her basic needs by finding resources in the local Chinatown community. Physically, she was slender, about 5'4", with tenseness in her face and body that I noticed, and apprehension about speaking with me. I invited her to tell me what was on her mind at the end of class. Mei's greatest struggles were with the English language, understanding and being understood, fears about her safety in an unfamiliar city and on public transportation, running out of money, staying healthy, guilt about leaving her family, and anxiety about her studies. It was not a smooth journey, but her concerns were "normal" considering her context.

In class, Mei was often marginalized by her professors, who were impatient with her accent and would move on rather than wait for her to complete her statement. In small groups, peers often talked around her. Although her feelings were hurt, Mei persisted. She graduated with a master's degree in counseling in 2 years, a goal she had set. She struggled with imposter syndrome and felt nervous about the future. Mei remained conflicted about her new life and the thought that perhaps she should go back to Taiwan to be with her family. She also felt guilty about the educational advancement she had accomplished while her family's situation stayed the same as when she left Taiwan. She told me she was seeking support in making her next professional and personal move.

Reflection Questions

1. What cultural insights do you have about Mei based on her intersecting identities?
2. What emotions are you experiencing as you think about her situation?
3. What are the connecting points for you and Mei?
4. What models may be helpful in supporting Mei during her personal and professional crossroads?
5. Consider Mei's identities. How might you move forward with a culturally aware lens?

Summary

The postmigration stage often entails a confusing, lonesome, and difficult adjustment. Immigrants and refugees may arrive at their destination with the hope of gaining independence and more opportunities, but navigating unfamiliar spaces comes with challenges and stressors that affect their wellness. There is a clear intersection between mental and physical health, so taking the initiative as a counselor to explore clients' needs and offer culturally relevant interventions and resources could lead to a better transition as clients adjust to their new life. Listening with empathy and with awareness of sociopolitical conditions could open a space where clients feel comfortable and safe, setting them up with tools for success. It is critical to view mental, physical, and spiritual health from a non-Western perspective. Counselors must familiarize themselves with theories and models that are culturally and situationally responsive. Applying the biopsychosocial model can facilitate conceptualization of the biological, psychological, social, and environment factors that affect the mental health and mental well-being of immigrants and refugees.

References

Adams, C. J. (2015). Structure and agency: Africana immigrants in China. *The Journal of Pan African Studies, 7*(10), 85–108. http://jpanafrican.org/docs/vol7no10/Bodomo-6-Adams.pdf

Agaibi, C. E., & Wilson, J. P. (2005). Trauma, PTSD, and resilience: A review of the literature. *Trauma, Violence and Abuse, 6*(3), 195–216. https://doi.org/10.1177/1524838005277438

Anderson, K. K., & Edwards, J. (2020). Age at migration and the risk of psychotic disorders: A systematic review and meta-analysis. *Acta Psychiatrica Scandinavica, 141*(5), 410–420. https://doi.org/10.1111/acps.13147

Arredondo, P. (1986). Immigration as an historical moment leading to an identity crisis. *Journal of Counseling & Human Services, 1*, 79–87.

Arredondo, P., Bordes, V., & Paniagua, F. (2008). Special considerations with Latinos in disaster circumstances. In A. J. Marsella, J. L. Johnson, P. Watson, & J. Gryczynski (Eds.), *Ethnocultural perspectives on disaster and trauma* (pp. 299–320). Springer.

Arredondo, P., Gallardo-Cooper, M., Delgado-Romero, E. A., & Zapata, A. L. (2014). *Culturally responsive counseling with Latinas/os.* American Counseling Association.

Arredondo, P., & Glauner, T. (1992). *Dimensions of personal identity model.* Empowerment Workshops.

Arredondo, P., Toporek, R., Brown, S. P., Jones, J., Locke, D. C., Sanchez, J., & Stadler, H. (1996). Operationalization of the multicultural counseling competencies. *Journal of Multicultural Counseling and Development, 24*(1), 42–78. https://doi.org/10.1002/j.2161-1912.1996.tb00288.x

Arredondo, P., Tovar-Blank, Z. G., & Parham, T. A. (2008). Challenges and promises of becoming a culturally competent counselor in a sociopolitical era of change and empowerment. *Journal of Counseling & Development, 86*(3), 261–268. https://doi.org/10.1002/j.1556-6678.2008.tb00508.x

Arredondo-Dowd, P. (1981). Personal loss and grief as a result of immigration. *The Personnel and Guidance Journal, 59*(6), 376–378. https://doi.org/10.1002/j.2164-4918.1981.tb00573.x

Assefa, H. (2015, August 26). *How Louisiana's Vietnamese community started over—twice.* CNN. https://www.cnn.com/2015/08/19/us/vietnamese-community-louisiana-katrina-anniversary/index.html

Atari-Khan, R., Covington, A. H., Gerstein, L. H., al Herz, H., Varner, B. R., Brasfield, C., Shurigar, B., Hinnenkamp, S. F., Devia, M., Barrera, S., & Deogracias-Schleich, A. (2021). Concepts of resilience among trauma-exposed Syrian refugees. *The Counseling Psychologist, 49*(2), 233–268. https://doi.org/10.1177/0011000020970522

Betancourt, T. S., Newnham, E. A., Layne, C. M., Kim, S., Steinberg, A. M., Ellis, H., & Birman, D. (2012). Trauma history and psychopathology in war-affected refugee children referred for trauma-related mental health services in the United States. *Journal of Traumatic Stress, 25*(6), 682–690. https://doi.org/10.1002/jts.21749

Bogic, M., Njoku, A., & Priebe, S. (2015). Long-term mental health of war-refugees: A systematic literature review. *BMC International Health and Human Rights, 15*, Article 29. https://doi.org/10.1186/s12914-015-0064-9

Bouza, J., Camacho-Thompson, D. E., Carlo, G., Franco, X., García Coll, C., Halgunseth, L. C., Marks, A., Stein, G. L., Suárez-Orozco, C., & White, R. M. B. (2018). *The science is clear: Separating families has long-term damaging psychological and health consequences for children, families, and communities.* Society for Research in Child Development. https://www.srcd.org/briefs-fact-sheets/the-science-is-clear

Bowlby, J. (1961). Processes of mourning. *The International Journal of Psycho-Analysis, 42*, 317–340.

Bronfenbrenner, U. (1977). Toward an experimental ecology of human development. *American Psychologist, 32*(7), 513–531. https://doi.org/10.1037/0003-066X.32.7.513

Bronfenbrenner, U., & Morris, P. A. (1998). The ecology of developmental processes. In W. Damon & R. M. Lerner (Eds.), *Handbook of child psychology: Theoretical models of human development* (pp. 993–1028). John Wiley & Sons.

Byrow, Y., Liddell, B., O'Donnell, M., Mau, V., McMahon, T., Bryant, R., Benson, G., & Nickerson, A. (2022). Profiles of post-migration stressors and mental health in refugees: A latent class analysis. *Psychiatry Research, 311*, Article 114494. https://doi.org/10.1016/j.psychres.2022.114494

Capps, R., Cardoso Berger, J., Brabeck, K., Fix, M., & Ruiz Soto, A. G. (2020). *Immigration enforcement and the mental health of Latino high school students.* Migration Policy Institute. https://www.migrationpolicy.org/research/immigration-enforcement-mental-health-latino-students

Capps, R., Koball, H., Campetella, A., Perreira, K., Hooker, S., & Pedroza, J. M. (2015). *Implications of immigration enforcement activities for the well-being of children in immigrant families: A review of the literature.* Migration Policy Institute. https://www.migrationpolicy.org/research/implications-immigration-enforcement-activities-well-being-children-immigrant-families

Carrasco-Sanz, A., Leiva-Gea, I., Martin-Alvarez, L., del Torso, S., van Esso, D., Hadjipanayis, A. K., Ruiz-Canela, J., Perez-Gonzalez, O., & Grossman, Z. (2018). Migrant children's health problems, care needs, and inequalities: European primary care paediatricians' perspective. *Child: Care, Health and Development, 44*(2), 183–187. https://doi.org/10.1111/cch.12538

Cascado, B. L., Hong, M., & Harrington, D. (2010). Measuring migratory grief and loss associated with the experience of immigration. *Research on Social Work Practice, 20*(3), 611–620. https://doi.org/10.1177/1049731509360840

Cerezo, A., Morales, A., Quintero, D., & Rothman, S. (2014). Trans migrations: Exploring life at the intersection of transgender identity and immigration. *Psychology of Sexual Orientation and Gender Diversity, 1*(2), 170–180. https://doi.org/10.1037/sgd0000031

Cigrand, D. L., Fawcett, M., Miyakuni, R., Arredondo, P., & Onderak, G. (2022). A phenomenological study of perseverance and resilience through the migration journey. *Journal of Counseling & Development, 100*(2), 157–170. https://doi.org/10.1002/jcad.12413

Dondi, A., Piccinno, V., Morigi, F., Gori, D. & Lanari, M. (2020). Food insecurity and major diet-related morbidities in migrating children: A systematic review. *Nutrients, 12*(2), 379. https://doi.org/10.3390/nu12020379

Dugarova, E. (2017). *Ageing, older persons and the 2030 Agenda for Sustainable Development.* United Nations Development Programme. https://www.undp.org/publications/ageing-older-persons-and-2030-agenda-sustainable-development

El-Awad, U., Atefeh, F., Lohaus, A., Petermann, F., & Reinelt, T. (2022). Different relations of religion and mental health. *European Journal of Healthy Psychology, 29*(1), 26–37. https://doi.org/10.1027/2512-8442/a000100

El-Khani, A., Uph, F., Peters, S., & Calam, R. (2017). Syria: Coping mechanisms utilised by displaced refugee parents caring for their children in pre-resettlement contexts. *Intervention, 15*(1), 34–50. https://doi.org/10.1097/WTF.0000000000000136

Elsayed, D., Song, J.-H., Myatt, E., Colasante, T., & Malti, T. (2019). Anger and sadness regulation in refugee children: The roles of pre- and post-migratory factors. *Child Psychiatry & Human Development, 50*(5), 846–855. https://doi.org/10.1007/s10578-019-00887-4

Engel, G. L. (1980). The clinical application of the biopsychosocial model. *The American Journal of Psychiatry, 137*(5), 535–544. https://doi.org/10.1176/ajp.137.5.535

Fazel, M., Reed, R. V., Panter-Brick, C., & Stein, A. (2012). Mental health of displaced and refugee children resettled in high-income countries: Risk and protective factors. *The Lancet, 379*(9812), 266–282. https://doi.org/10.1016/S0140-6736(11)60051-2

Foster LLP. (n.d.). *ICE arrests more than 200 people in 4-day California raid.* https://www.fosterglobal.com/blog/ice-arrests-more-than-200-people-in-4-day-california-raid/

Galler, J. R., Bringas-Vega, M. L., Tang, Q., Rabinowitz, A. G., Musa, K. I., Chai, W. J., Omar, H., Abdul Rahman, M. R., Abd Hamid, A. I., Abdullah, J. M., & Valdés-Sosa, P. A. (2021). Neurodevelopmental effects of childhood malnutrition: A neuroimaging perspective. *NeuroImage, 231*, Article 117828. https://doi.org/10.1016/j.neuroimage.2021.117828

García-Sierra, R., Fernández-Cano, M. I., Manresa-Domínguez, J. M., Feijoo-Cid, M., Moreno Gabriel, E., Arreciado Marañón, A., Ramos-Roure, F., Segura-Bernal, J., & Torán-Monserrat, P. (2020). Psychological distress and somatization in immigrants in primary health care practices. *Healthcare, 8*(4), Article 557. https://doi.org/10.3390/healthcare8040557

The Guardian. (2014, April 18). *88 Nigerian schoolgirls abducted by Islamic extremists still missing.* https://www.theguardian.com/world/2014/apr/19/88-nigerian-schoolgirls-abducted-by-islamic-extremists-still-missing

Hassan, G., Kirmayer, L. J., Mekki-Barrada, A., Quosh, C., el Chammay, R., Deville-Stoetzel, J. B., Youssef, A., Jefee-Bahloul, H., Barkeel-Oteo, A., Coutts, A., Song, S., & Ventevogel, P. (2015). *Culture, context and the mental health and psychosocial wellbeing of Syrians: A review for mental health and psychosocial support staff working with Syrians affected by armed conflict.* United Nations High Commissioner for Refugees. https://www.unhcr.org/media/culture-context-and-mental-health-and-psychosocial-wellbeing-syrians-review-mental-health-and

Jensen, T. K., Skar, A. S., Andersson, E. S., & Birkeland, M. S. (2019). Long-term mental health in unaccompanied refugee minors: Pre- and post-flight predictors. *European Child & Adolescent Psychiatry, 28*(12), 1671–1682. https://doi.org/10.1007/s00787-019-01340-6

Jorgenson, K. C., & Nilsson, J. E. (2021). The relationship among trauma, acculturation, and mental health symptoms in Somali refugees. *The Counseling Psychologist, 49*(2), 196–232. https://doi.org/10.1177/0011000020968548

Joseph, T. D., & Marrow, H. B. (2017). Health care, immigrants, and minorities: Lessons from the Affordable Care Act in the U.S. *Journal of Ethnic and Migration Studies, 43*(12), 1965–1984. https://doi.org/10.1080/1369183X.2017.1323446

Juang, L. P., Simpson, J. A., Lee, R. M., Rothman, A. J., Titzmann, P. F., Schachner, M. K., Korn, L., Heinemeier, D., & Betsch, C. (2018). Using attachment and relational perspectives to understand adaptation and resilience among immigrant and refugee youth. *American Psychologist, 73*(6), 797 –811. https://doi.org/10.1037/amp0000286

Kam, J. A., & Lazarevic, V. (2014). The stressful (and not so stressful) nature of language brokering: Identifying when brokering functions as a cultural stressor for Latino immigrant children in early adolescence. *Journal of Youth and Adolescence, 43*(12), 1994–2011. https://doi.org/10.1007/s10964-013-0061-z

Khan, F., Eskander, N., Limbana, T., Salman, Z., Siddiqui, P. A., & Hussaini, S. (2020). Refugee and migrant children's mental healthcare: Serving the voiceless, invisible, and vulnerable global citizens. *Cureus, 12*(8), Article e9944. https://doi.org/10.7759/cureus.9944

Kübler-Ross, E. (1969). *On death and dying.* Macmillan.

Kumar, G. S., Beeler, J. A., Seagle, E. E., & Jentes, E. S. (2021). Long-term physical health outcomes of resettled refugee populations in the United States: A scoping review. *Journal of Immigrant and Minority Health, 23*(4), 813–823. https://doi.org/10.1007/s10903-021-01146-2

Lijtmaer, R. (2022). Social trauma, nostalgia and mourning in the immigration experience. *The American Journal of Psychoanalysis, 82*(2), 305–319. https://doi.org/10.1057/s11231-022-09357-8

Maderazo, J. W. (2009). *A transgender person is murdered every 3 days in the world . . . mostly in Latin America.* Vivir Latino.

Magwaza, A. S., & Bhana, K. (1991). Stress, locus of control, and psychological status in Black South African migrants. *The Journal of Social Psychology, 131*(2), 157–164. https://doi.org/10.1080/00224545.1991.9713838

Mahler, M., Pine, F., & Bergman, A. (1975). *The psychological birth of the human infant: Symbiosis and individuation.* Basic Books.

Masoom, M. R. (2018). The control of externality among the street children and marginalized people of Dhaka City: A key indicator to ensure sustainable livelihood. *Asian Journal of Humanity, Art and Literature, 5*(2), 109–116.

Maung, J., Nilsson, J. E., Jeevanba, S. B., Molitoris, A., Raziuddin, A., & Soheilian, S. S. (2021). Burmese refugee women in the Midwest: Narratives of resilience and posttraumatic growth. *The Counseling Psychologist, 49*(2), 269–304. https://doi.org/10.1177/0011000020971635

McLaurin, J. A., & Liebman, A. K. (2012). Unique agricultural safety and health issues of migrant and immigrant children. *Journal of Agromedicine, 17*(2), 186–196. https://doi.org/10.1080/1059924X.2012.658010

McLeigh, J. D. (2010). How do Immigration and Customs Enforcement (ICE) practices affect the mental health of children? *American Journal of Orthopsychiatry, 80*(1), 96–100. https://doi.org/10.1111/j.1939-0025.2010.01011.x

Mcleod, S. (2023). *Bowlby's attachment theory.* SimplyPsychology. https://www.simplypsychology.org/bowlby.html

Mendoza Griego, M. D. C. (2022). *The effects of acculturative stress on the physical/mental health of immigrant Mexican women* [Doctoral dissertation, Walden University]. Walden University ScholarWorks. https://scholarworks.waldenu.edu/cgi/viewcontent.cgi?article=14850&context=dissertations

Menjivar, C. (2003). Religion and immigration in comparative perspective: Catholic and evangelical Salvadorans in San Francisco, Washington, DC and Phoenix. *Sociology of Religion, 64*(1), 21–45. https://doi.org/10.2307/3712267

National Academies of Sciences, Engineering, and Medicine. (2015). *The integration of immigrants into American society.* National Academies Press. https://doi.org/10.17226/21746

Nazario, S. (2006). *Enrique's journey.* Random House.

Nesteruk, O. (2018). Immigrants coping with transnational deaths and bereavement: The influence of migratory loss and anticipatory grief. *Family Process, 57*(4), 1012–1028. https://doi.org/10.1111/famp.12336

Office of Refugee Resettlement. (n.d.). *Refugee health overview.* https://www.acf.hhs.gov/orr/programs/refugees/refugee-health

The Open University. (2023). *The biopsychosocial model of mental health: Revisited.* https://www.open.edu/openlearn/science-maths-technology/exploring-the-relationship-between-anxiety-and-depression/content-section-2

Pinkerton, J. (2014, January 30). Chinatown raid targets exploitation of illegal workers. *Chron.* https://www.chron.com/news/houston-texas/houston/article/Chinatown-raid-targets-exploitation-of-illegal-5188938.php

Porter, M., & Haslam, N. (2005). Predisplacement and postdisplacement factors associated with mental health of refugees and internally displaced persons: A meta-analysis. *JAMA, 294*(5), 602–612. https://doi.org/10.1001/jama.294.5.602

Ratts, M. J., Singh, A. A., Nassar-McMillan, S., Butler, S. K., & McCullough, J. R. (2015). *Multicultural and social justice counseling competencies.* Association for Multicultural Counseling and Development. https://www.counseling.org/docs/default-source/competencies/multicultural-and-social-justice-counseling-competencies.pdf?sfvrsn=20

Rios Casas, F., Ryan, D., Perez, G., Maurer, S., Tran, A. N., Rao, D., & Ornelas, I. J. (2020). "Se vale llorar y se vale reír": Latina immigrants' coping strategies for maintaining mental health in the face of immigration-related stressors. *Journal of Racial and Ethnic Health Disparities, 7*(5), 937–948. https://doi.org/10.1007%2Fs40615-020-00717-7

Rojas-Perez-O., Heppner, P. P., & Flores, L. Y. (2022). Tu bienestar es mi bienestar: A qualitative study of Latinx well-being through a qualitative lens. *Journal of Latinx Psychology*, 10(2), 140–155. https://doi.org/10.1037/lat0000175

Romero, L. A. (2022). Unsacred children: The portrayal of unaccompanied immigrant minors as racialized threats. *American Behavioral Scientist*, *66*(12), 1669–1687. https://doi.org/10.1177/00027642221083529
Rotter, J. B. (1954). *Social learning and clinical psychology*. Prentice Hall.
Salari, N., Hosseinian-Far, A., Jalali, R., Vaisi-Raygani, A., Rasoulpoor, S., Mohammadi, M., Rasoulpoor, S., & Khaledi-Paveh, B. (2020). Prevalence of stress, anxiety, depression among the general population during the COVID-19 pandemic: A systematic review and meta-analysis. *Globalization and Health*, *16*(1), Article 57. https://doi.org/10.1186/s12992-020-00589-w
Sangalang, C. C., Becerra, D., Mitchell, F. M., Lechuga-Peña, S., Lopez, K., & Kim, I. (2019). Trauma, post-migration stress, and mental health: A comparative analysis of refugees and immigrants in the United States. *Journal of Immigrant and Minority Health*, *21*(5), 909–919. https://doi.org/10.1007/s10903-018-0826-2
Saunders, J. B., Fiddian-Qasmiyeh, E., & Snyder, S. (Eds.). (2016). *Intersections of religion and migration: Issues at the global crossroads*. Palgrave Macmillan.
Scharpf, F., Kaltenbach, E., Nickerson, A., & Hecker, T. (2021). A systematic review of socio-ecological factors contributing to risk and protection of the mental health of refugee children and adolescents. *Clinical Psychology Review*, *83*, Article 101930. https://doi.org/10.1016/j.cpr.2020.101930
Shen, Y., Seo, E., Jiles, A. I., Zheng, Y., & Wang, Y. (2022). Language brokering and immigrant-origin youth's well-being: A meta-analytic review. *American Psychologist*, *77*(8), 921–939. https://doi.org/10.1037/amp0001035
Shen, Y., Tilton, K. E., & Kim, S. Y. (2017). Outcomes of language brokering, mediators, and moderators: A systematic review. In R. S. Weisskirch (Ed.), *Language brokering in immigrant families: Theories and contexts* (pp. 47–71). Routledge. https://doi.org/10.4324/9781315644714-4
Siriwardhana, C., Sheik Ali, S., Roberts, B., & Steward, R. (2014). A systematic review of resilience and mental health outcomes of conflict-driven adult forced migrants. *Conflict and Health*, *8*, Article 13. https://doi.org/10.1186/1752-1505-8-13
Smith, E. L. (2021). *Hate crime recorded by law enforcement, 2010-2019* (NCJ 301554). U.S. Department of Justice, Office of Justice Programs, Bureau of Justice Statistics. https://bjs.ojp.gov/library/publications/hate-crime-recorded-law-enforcement-2010-2019
Sudhinaraset, M., Cabanting, N., & Ramos, M. (2019). The health profile of newly-arrived refugee women and girls and the role of region of origin: Using a population-based dataset in California between 2013 and 2017. *International Journal for Equity in Health*, *18*(1), Article 158. https://doi.org/10.1186/s12939-019-1066-3
Sue, D. W. (1978). Eliminating cultural oppression in counseling: Toward a general theory. *Journal of Counseling Psychology*, *25*(5), 419–428. https://doi.org/10.1037/0022-0167.25.5.419
United Nations Higher Commission for Refugees. (2013). *Child recruitment, child labour, discrimination and loneliness—The crisis of Syria's refugee children*. https://www.unhcr.org/neu/733-child-recruitment-child-labour-discrimination-and-loneliness-the-crisis-of-syrias-refugee-children.html
United Nations Higher Commission for Refugees. (2022). *Global trends: Forced displacement in 2022*. https://www.unhcr.org/global-trends-report-2022
Vick, D. C. (2023, June 7). New Florida law invalidates out-of-state licenses for 'undocumented immigrants.' *Route Fifty*. https://www.route-fifty.com/management/2023/06/new-florida-law-invalidates-out-state-licenses-undocumented-immigrants/387265/
Wang, S. C., & Santos, B. M. C. (2022). "Go back to China with your (expletive) virus": A revelatory case study of anti-Asian racism during COVID-19. *Asian American Journal of Psychology*, *13*(3), 220–233. https://doi.org/10.1037/aap0000287
World Health Organization. (2022). *Refugee and migrant health*. https://www.who.int/news-room/fact-sheets/detail/refugee-and-migrant-health
Wu, S., Ellingson, S., Hagstrom, P., & Kucinskas, J. (2021). Religion and refugee well-being: The importance of community. *Journal for the Scientific Study of Religion*, *60*(2), 291–308. https://doi.org/10.1111/jssr.12702
Yakushko, O., & Morgan-Consoli, M. L. (2014). Gendered stories of adaptation and resistance: A feminist multiple case study of immigrant women. *International Journal for the Advancement of Counseling*, *36*(1), 70–83. https://doi.org/10.1007/s10447-013-9191-y
Zimbrean, P. C., & Dahal, R. (2020). Risk factors and prevalence of mental illness. In A. Annamalai (Ed.), *Refugee health care* (pp. 195–214). Springer. https://doi.org/10.1007/978-3-030-47668-7_13

Part II

Counseling With Immigrants, Refugees, and Their Families From Generational and Developmental Perspectives

Chapter 7

Counseling With Immigrant, Refugee, and Birthright Children

According to demographic data, children born in the United States of immigrant parents are fast becoming the generation to make their mark in different ways. As noted in Chapter 1, they are called "birthright" children because, by birth, they have the rights of every person born in the United States and its territories. In addition, immigrant children are brought and/or sent by their parents or other family members to the United States. Other children, who may have come with their parents but were separated at the border, as was the practice between 2016 and 2020, may have arrived in the United States as unaccompanied minors. The majority likely came to the United States as adolescents or arrived with their parents through primarily undocumented means. Refugee children are another population who have distinct needs and status based on their experiences in moving from one culture to another to escape persecution and violence in their country of origin (United Nations, n.d.).

Because of the stressors newcomer families face, immigrant children are also experiencing adversity in their homes and communities. According to research on adverse childhood experiences (ACEs), although immigrant parents report fewer ACEs than their U.S.-born counterparts (Martin et al., 2018), immigrant children are more likely to face poverty (30%), unsafe neighborhoods (20%), and emotional neglect (18%). Birthright, immigrant, and refugee children go to schools, playgrounds, and other settings where children may be taken to or convene. There are many unknowns about the mental health issues of these children, but it can be surmised that although they may not verbalize their distress of being different, marginalized, or excluded from activities, they have experienced it. Counselors working with birthright, immigrant, and refugee children and their families must be well informed about the myriad factors influencing their mental health, as well as the role the Multicultural and Social Justice Counseling Competencies (MSJCC; Ratts et al., 2015) play in highlighting their nonprivileged but marginalized status.

Learning Objectives

- Identify developmental needs of immigrant and refugee children from birth to 12 years old.
- Differentiate the mental health needs of these groups: birthright children, second- and third-generation children, and refugee children.
- Describe how school counselors and other health and mental health providers can support immigrant and refugee children.
- Consider how counselors can support immigrant child development directly with clients and systemically within their families, schools, communities, and settings where services are supposed to be provided.
- Discern how federal and state immigration policies affect immigrant children's developmental experiences.

The following section introduces a self-assessment to gauge your existing knowledge of culturally responsive counseling frameworks designed to address inequities and marginalization, ethical considerations in working with immigrant and refugee populations, and the MSJCC (Ratts et al., 2015) needed to do so. This brief assessment aims to explore your current understanding of key concepts and provide a foundation for further learning.

Self-assessment: Please respond to the following statements by rating yourself on the following Likert scale: *strongly agree, agree, disagree, strongly disagree, unsure*, or *not applicable.*

1. I understand the unique needs of refugee and immigrant child clients, especially the differences among immigrant and refugee children, unaccompanied minors, and birthright children.
2. I am competent in gaining insight into child development issues as they apply to my clients of minor standing who are refugees and immigrants.
3. I feel I can effectively collaborate with families of children who are immigrants and refugees to proactively support the child as the client.
4. I can implement strategies in school, agencies, and community systems (e.g., courts) to systemically support immigrant children and their families.

When people in the United States discuss immigrants, they are most often referring to adults. Yet, about 250,000 babies were born to undocumented immigrant parents in the United States in 2016 (Pew Research Center, 2018). Children and youth ages 5–17 years account for 5% of immigrants and 18% of the U.S.-born population (Ward & Batalova, 2023). Mathema (2017) reported that an estimated 6 million children in the United States live with one or more undocumented family members. Data from the U.S. Census Bureau (2019) suggest that 18.2 children, or 25% of the U.S. population, live in immigrant families. Therefore, counselors need to be prepared to work with immigrant and refugee children, recognizing this context in culturally responsive ways.

Developmental Considerations for Immigrant Children

To work with immigrant and refugee children, counselors need to consider their developmental histories. The World Health Organization (WHO, 2021) created standards for health care professionals, including those providing mental health services, which communicate this person-centered perspective. Competency Standard 1.1 states, "Adapts practice to the needs of the person in view of their migration and displacement experiences, taking into consideration the impact of these experiences on access to health care, including barriers to access" (WHO, 2021, p. 6). For example, a significant number of children born to immigrants are born premature (Bediako et al., 2018), which can result in higher incidences of disabilities. When developmental concerns arise, counselors must assert the need for early intervention programs, such as universal screenings and quality day care and preschool options, which promote prevention and provide interventions when needed to support prosocial behavior, cognitive development, and school readiness in children (Donoghue et al., 2017). Ideally, these services and settings would also be bilingual and provide culturally responsive services.

Premature Births

A child is considered premature when born 3 or more weeks before the expected due date (Mayo Clinic, 2023). Premature babies have increased risk for a wide variety of medical issues, including breathing, heart, and brain problems. In the 2011–2012 National Survey of Children's Health, preterm children with at least one immigrant parent made up 11.3% (n = 8,871) of the sample (Bediako et al., 2018). Within this sample of preterm children of immigrants, 11.86% (n = 1,241) were first- or second-generation children, and 79.71% (n = 7,630) were third-generation children (Bediako et al., 2018). Chronic developmental issues, including developmental delays, cerebral palsy, and hearing problems, were more prevalent in the third-generation children than in the first- or second-generation children who were relatively similar in socioeconomic status.

These data corroborate a concept known as the *immigrant paradox* (García Coll & Marks, 2012). As described by Marks et al. (2014), "the immigrant paradox in childhood and adolescence is a population-level phenomenon wherein U.S.-born youth (or more highly acculturated immigrants) have less optimal developmental outcomes than newcomer immigrant youth" (p. 59). While there is enough evidence across studies to suggest the idea of the immigrant paradox, the concept is still being studied in earnest, as there appears to be high variability based on factors such as acculturation, race, and academic and behavioral outcomes measured (Marks et al., 2014).

Early Intervention

For good reason, immigrants, especially undocumented ones, may be leery of seeking out professional resources for themselves or their children (Dickerson, 2021). While disparities are evident in quality of and access to health care for immigrant families and their children (Calvo & Hawkins, 2015), counseling professionals who work with immigrant families must underscore the need for early intervention for all infants and toddlers, especially those born premature. Medical professionals should also be consulted. If parents agree to screenings, helping professionals should practice cultural sensitivity when conducting comprehensive screenings in consideration of contextual variations such as exposure to trauma, unsafe environmental circumstances, limited access to food, and insufficient health care and childcare options (Bhayana & Bhayana, 2018).

Counselors must first accurately identify children who have behavioral or mental health concerns. While use of universal screenings is still being debated (Wallace, 2018), universal screening should be considered a best practice to improve the likelihood that immigrant families receive early intervention for their children who need it. In planning for universal screenings, counselors must also select screening tools most appropriate for the cultures represented or ones that are culturally adaptable (Bhayana & Bhayana, 2018; Lewis, 2021). It is important for mental health care providers and physicians to take into account cultural differences in development and the child's history, which may include nutritional differences and deficits, traumatic events, gaps in education, and language changes in the home, among others. Since children born outside of the United States (Valicenti-McDermott et al., 2010) or those who come from racial/ethnic minority backgrounds receive diagnoses of autism spectrum disorders later than White children (Mandell et al., 2006, 2009) and have triple the number of office visits related to developmental delays or mental health issues to receive a diagnosis (Mandell et al., 2002), universal screenings can benefit immigrants and refugees and increase the likelihood that disabilities or other concerns are identified earlier.

The alternative, which is developmental monitoring and screening, seems to fall short in early identification of children with disabilities or mental health needs (Martin-Herz et al., 2012). Developmental monitoring and screening methods rely on parental knowledge of U.S. developmental milestones, and expectations must be congruent with these developmental markers. This is unlikely since immigrant and refugee families may view child development based on cultural practices (Morrier et al., 2008) or what is normative in their cultural upbringings and previously contentious life circumstances. Cultural differences in parenting were discussed in Chapter 4 and is a valuable reference point. Furthermore, recurring physician visits are necessary to assess development, although immigrant families have likely had little to no access to screenings or immunizations in their country of origin (American Academy of Pediatrics, n.d.) and may be less likely to consistently access medical resources than others (Javier et al., 2009), especially specialty care (American Academy of Pediatrics, n.d.), due to lack of knowledge about U.S. health care systems and lower access to insurance options.

Nonetheless, this disparity in identification suggests much work is needed for all health care and mental health care providers to connect with the immigrant community, provide psychoeducation about child development and the need for well-child checks, and become more responsive to families who are seeking services for their children. One alternative, a home-based "Visiting Moms" outreach intervention for high-risk immigrant and refugee mothers, not only creates opportunities for assessment of mothers and their children, but also provides social, emotional, and practical support, education, and role modeling to reduce isolation of newcomer mothers in their homes (Paris & Bronson, 2006). When mothers across cultures initiate play with their children, children's play is more sophisticated, leading to positive developmental outcomes (Cote & Bornstein, 2009). Outreach interventions such as the Visiting Moms program—which counselors can initiate—may have a secondary effect in development of immigrant parents' trust in community support programs, which can improve early development of immigrant and refugee children. Finally, advocacy for programs and adequate public policies that ensure access to health care, including funding to support mental health and outreach initiatives, and other community resources for children of undocumented parents and refugees, is paramount to supporting development of immigrant children. Early intervention, as a protective factor, improves outcomes and decreases the need for interventions across the life span.

Risk of Abuse or Neglect

For parents who work outside of the home, access to childcare is critical for the development of children, including immigrant children. Mothers of immigrant children typically prefer childcare options that are safe and trustworthy, provide learning and appropriate developmental growth opportunities, and are aligned to familial needs (Vesely et al., 2021). Even so, barriers exist. For example, day care access for immigrant families typically involves required immunizations for public day care facilities, which is problematic because of lack of access to insurance for health care (Vesely et al., 2021). Additionally, transportation issues and hours required by employers that do not align to day care options (Vesely et al., 2021) create more stressors for parents or circumstances that are not ideal for children.

Lack of reliable childcare options leaves immigrant parents, especially those who are undocumented, in precarious situations in which they are more likely to seek family, friend, and neighbor (FFN) care (Park & Peña, 2021). While this type of care is accessible, flexible, and affordable, FFN caregivers may be untrained or inattentive to children and their development or have fewer resources, so developmental gaps may emerge. Worse yet, neglectful and potentially abusive situations may occur when acquaintances are asked to provide day care (Vesely et al., 2021). For example, 34% of FFN providers were experiencing food insecurity in 2021 and 2022 (Stanford University Rapid Survey Project, 2021, 2022). Thus, counselors working in schools and communities may be able to work with families and/or FFN childcare providers to access state-funded initiatives such as the Center for Inclusive Childcare Video and Resource library. These resources for FFN providers have versions for Hmong, Somali, and Spanish-speaking populations (Center for Inclusive Childcare, n.d.).

Some research indicates that immigrant and refugee children are also at greater risk for abusive and neglectful situations in their homes because of the stress parents face in navigating multiple issues (Grumi et al., 2017; Yoo, 2019). For example, increased deportation rates have led to distrust and disuse of federal programs such as Medicaid and the Special Supplemental Nutrition Program for Women, Infants, and Children among noncitizens, lessening the ability of parents to provide for their children. Furthermore, research has shown that "family members (mostly mothers and children) left behind after parental detainments and deportations experience increased economic hardship, psychological distress, externalizing behavioral problems such as aggression, internalizing behavioral problems such as anxiety and depression, and loss of educational aspirations" (Perreira & Pedroza, 2019, p. 154).

However, access to immigrant support services is associated with lower incidence of child maltreatment (Seon & Klein, 2021). Counselors who work with immigrant children experiencing anxiety, depression, or other mental health concerns should consider parental anxiety and stress and refer them accordingly for their own support. Counselors must also advocate for safe childcare options, work with chambers of commerce or other employer groups to allow parents to transport their children during work hours (e.g., from school to after-school programs), collaborate with immigrant support service agencies, and connect with local immigrant communities to provide prevention programs, as well as utilize developmental screenings to identify abuse, neglect, or disorders in children.

Counselors should also be aware that immigration status has been found to be a protective factor for Latino children (Loria & Caughy, 2018). Specifically, in a study to investigate the ACEs of children, of which 29% (n = 6,483) were Latino with 9% (n = 612) identifying as first generation, 57% (n = 3,842) as second generation, and 30% (n = 2,029) as third or higher generation, Latino immigrant children had a lower prevalence of exposure to two or more ACEs compared with nonimmigrant Latino children. Similarly, LaBrenz et al. (2019) found that foreign-born Spanish-speaking immigrant caregivers reported lower traditional ACE scores than U.S.-born Spanish-speaking caregivers. The foreign-born caregivers reported fewer mental health issues; however, they did have higher rates of substance use. These studies endorse the concept of the immigrant paradox discussed earlier in this chapter.

Differences Associated With Childhood Experiences of Immigrants and Refugees

Because of the differences noted in the research literature for immigrant populations such as birthright children, unaccompanied children, children who have immigrated (second- and third-generation children), and refugee children, the following discussion differentiates the protective and risk factors for each of these groups, with corresponding recommendations for counseling practitioners. It is important for counselors working with children to recognize these differences and determine whether they apply to the minors with whom they work.

Birthright Children

Children who are born to undocumented immigrants in the United States are protected by the Fourteenth Amendment of the U.S. Constitution and are known as birthright citizens (Harrington, 2018). Birthright children tend to have parents or family members who are undocumented. Also noteworthy is that birthright children do not afford their parents a pathway to citizenship; thus, the term “anchor baby” is a myth (Suárez-Orozco et al., 2011). From 2013 to 2018, for example, U.S. Immigration and Customs Enforcement (ICE) deported more than 231,000 people who had reported having at least one U.S. citizen child (American Immigration Council, 2021). Furthermore, ICE deported 27,980 people with birthright children in 2019.

Birthright children are more likely to have at least one parent who is undocumented. As previously mentioned, children living with undocumented parents may experience negative effects of parental stress due to fear of deportation (Grumi et al., 2017; Yoshikawa & Kalil, 2011). Suárez-Orozco et al. (2011) discussed how this leaves children and families in “interminable liminality” (p. 444) and with a sense of ambiguity about their future, often leading to anxiety and insecurity. When parents have conversations with their children about their documentation status, the risks they take as an undocumented person, and the restrictions they have (e.g., cannot drive legally), the children may experience increased anxiety. Even so, immigrants in one study felt that these conversations were necessary to protect and prepare their children for contingency plans (Cross et al., 2021). Counselors and others who work with immigrant children should recognize that this anxiety may be present in children of undocumented parents and help the parents identify their social support networks. Grumi et al. (2017) found that supportive community and social networks mitigated stress associated with the fear of deportation and other stressors such as economic ones. Counselors can encourage and create opportunities for networking among immigrant families and other families in communities.

D’Alonzo and Greene (2020) recommended specific strategies to establish trust with the immigrant community: (a) view trust as being built over time dynamically rather than dichotomously (trust vs. mistrust); (b) recognize the scope and impact of stressors faced by immigrants; (c) separate fact from fiction by dispelling rumors or clarifying roles of professionals providing service; (d) work to understand how deportation stress may affect families; (e) manage mistrust by listening to concerns and being open to criticism and change; (f) build bridges by connecting to others who are trusted within the community; and (g) establish a positive presence by engaging informally with the immigrant community (e.g., attending cultural events). Immigrants may not know one another, and if they are undocumented, there may be mistrust about someone reporting them.

Because undocumented parents of birthright children may face financial stressors such as lower paying jobs (Grumi et al., 2017), remittances to family in the home country, and monetary obligations to smugglers (Yoshikawa & Kalil, 2011), helping professionals can also recommend public support assistance options for which immigrants and their children may qualify. According to Broder and Lessard (2023), “qualified immigrants” include the following:

- Lawful permanent residents, or LPRs (people with green cards)
- Refugees, people granted asylum or withholding of deportation/removal, and conditional entrants
- People granted parole by the U.S. Department of Homeland Security (DHS) for a period of at least one year
- Cuban and Haitian entrants

- Certain abused immigrants, their children, and/or their parents
- Certain survivors of trafficking
- Individuals residing in the United States pursuant to a Compact of Free Association (COFA; for Medicaid purposes only). (pp. 2–3)

Additionally, Iraqis and Afghans who have been granted special immigrant visas, and as of 2022, Ukrainians who were paroled into the United States are benefit-eligible similar to refugees. Counselors should also know the laws in their states, as some states (e.g., California, Connecticut, Illinois, Maine, Minnesota, Washington) provide state-funded nutrition assistance to some or all immigrants who are rendered ineligible for the federal Supplemental Nutrition Assistance Program.

Birthright children may not have memories of the country from which their family immigrated, yet they are likely to be experiencing development within two or more cultures. Many birthright children will learn to speak English and the language of their parents and families at the same time. This opportunity to learn two languages during childhood can be a benefit, but well-intending educators in the United States may suggest to parents to speak only English at home to develop their children's English language proficiency. Some research, however, counters this notion, suggesting that reducing opportunities to learn one's heritage language not only impedes children's language development in the home but also hinders relationships with their family members (Place & Hoff, 2011). While more research is needed, children's development of both their heritage language and the English language in the United States seems to have positive benefits for cognitive development, especially executive functioning (Adesope et al., 2010). Thus, counselors should encourage families and other professionals to support bilingual opportunities for children in homes, schools, and the community. One further note is that parents whose second language is English may not be the best English-speaking models for their children because of insufficient experiences with pronunciation and relevant vocabulary.

The involvement of ICE with undocumented adults and their children is a viable reality. From 2013 to 2018, 231,000 immigrants who were deported disclosed that they had at least one child who was a U.S. citizen (Preston, 2020). Quite likely a higher number of children experienced the deportation of a parent. In addition to deportation, ICE enforcement can lead to other stressors in the homes of undocumented immigrants, such as arrests, long-term ankle-monitoring, and high costs of bonds for release (Capps et al., 2007). The evidence that family separation adversely affects mental health is well documented (Benuto et al., 2018; Bouza et al., 2018; Patel et al., 2021).

School counselors play a central role in the lives of parents and children regardless of their immigration status. Goh at al. (2007) encouraged counselors to build cultural and language bridges to children and their families to best support children's bicultural development through (a) creation of a climate of cultural acceptance in schools; (b) development of programs that create space for students to showcase their cultures (without asking them to speak for their culture); (c) engagement with parents in formal and informal spaces both at school and in the community; and (d) contracting with certified interpreters to ensure clear communication with parents in their preferred language. When establishing relationships with immigrant families, school support services personnel can use genograms, ecomaps, and timelines to understand the family system of a student and identify resources they have or need as a part of a family-focused interview (Eppler & Weir, 2009).

Unaccompanied Children

In addition to children who are separated from their immigrating families, some children enter the United States unaccompanied. From 2012 to 2021, 11%–21% of the unaccompanied children were between the ages of 0 and 12 years. Most of the unaccompanied children come to the United States from Guatemala (47%), Honduras (32%), and El Salvador (13%). Unaccompanied children from Mexico (1%) and other countries (7%) make up a much smaller representation of this population. The length of time unaccompanied children are placed with the Office of Refugee Resettlement (ORR) varies (see Table 7.1). The ORR attempts to place unaccompanied children with families who meet specific background checks and commit to providing food, shelter, and medical care. While waiting for placement or when placement is not possible, the ORR (2022) provides “a continuum of care for the children in a shelter facility, foster care or group home (which may be therapeutic), staff-secure or secure care facility, a residential treatment center, or special needs care facility” (para. 8).

TABLE 7.1

Office of Refugee Resettlement Average Length of Time Children Are in Detention Centers

Year	Days
2021	37.00
2020	102.00
2019	62.00
2018	60.00
2017	48.00
2016	38.00
2015	34.00
Cumulative average	54.43

For many unaccompanied children as young as 7 years of age, such as those from Central America, immigration to the United States is an issue of survival to avoid gang, domestic, and sexual violence, including homicide and other life-threatening conditions, and these children face innumerable traumatic events during the migration journey (United Nations High Commissioner for Refugees, 2014). They experience both physical and emotional pain and a sense of helplessness when witnessing traumatic events (e.g., sexual assault, death) of same-age travel companions on the migration journey (Tello et al., 2017). In the United States, unaccompanied youth remain vulnerable as they labor to gain precarious access to shelter, food, and education without the support of significant caregivers. Thus, their physical and mental health and development are likely to be negatively impacted from their experiences in each stage of their migration journey (Silva et al., 2023). Based on a review of research studies, Demazure et al. (2017) recommended cognitive behavior therapy (CBT) approaches such as trauma-focused CBT and systemic and multimodal interventions in individual or group formats to reduce symptoms in mental health disorders such as posttraumatic stress disorder (PTSD), anxiety, and depression in unaccompanied youth. Treatment focused on strengthening coping, self-esteem, emotional regulation, resilience, and social connectedness was also endorsed (Demazure et al., 2017), as were school-based interventions using the practice model and CBITS (cognitive behavioral intervention for trauma in Schools; Franco, 2018).

Children Who Have Immigrated

Many children who have immigrated experienced various forms of trauma premigration. Often, these children were part of a family system that left their country of origin due to economic necessity or dangerous conditions (e.g., war zones, areas hit by natural disasters, gang violence, police brutality; Jud et al., 2020). Trauma in their country of origin, along with the difficulties associated with the migration process, can lead to cumulative trauma and can cause acute mental health disorders such as PTSD (Perreira & Ornelas, 2013). One meta-analysis of studies of children who have immigrated before the age of 18 indicated that they are twice as likely as U.S.-born children to have psychotic disorders (Suárez-Orozco et al., 2011).

The process of migration can be harrowing for children. They may face violence within their family, within their community, or by strangers. Children are also regularly exposed to violence, abuse, and exploitation during their migration journeys (Jud et al., 2020). They may also be witness to others, including other children and family members, who die on their migration journey. In a study of immigrant and refugee children between the ages of 6 and 11, Mancini (2020) found several children exceeded clinical thresholds for depression and anxiety, and most had trauma symptoms or met the clinical threshold for PTSD, with at least 12 children's scores indicating psychological impairment on clinical assessments. The school-based intervention Mancini subsequently implemented, the Somatic Soothing and Emotional Regulation Skill Development program, showed an overall positive medium effect (.46) on the Pediatric Symptom Checklist. Specifically, clinically decreased anxiety and depression were noted, with teachers reporting improved coping, attendance, engagement, and problem-solving in the classroom. Psychological first aid is another evidence-based intervention recommended for children who have recently migrated and experienced traumatic incidents (Elmore Borbon et al., 2021). Counselors should also be aware that basic needs of recently migrated immigrants may be a priority over mental health initially (Cigrand et al., 2022).

For second- and third-generation children in the postmigration stage of the process, changes in culture and language can lead to acculturative stress or a sense of not knowing how to belong (van Ecke, 2005). Still, it is important to highlight the theme of resilience of immigrant families, including their children, in the migration process (Cigrand et al., 2022; Motti-Stefanidi, 2021; Roberto et al., 2016). For immigrant children, Motti-Stefanidi (2018) discussed promotive and protective factors, which include resources, assets, social supports, and adaptation or the ability to respond to adversity as they navigate developmental and acculturative tasks while maintaining psychological well-being. The process of adaptation may involve resolving or integrating value-based differences between collectivistic and individualistic cultures, with an emphasis on biculturalism over time (Nguyen & Benet-Martínez, 2013).

Positive adjustment is also linked to finding life satisfaction and sense of positive self-esteem (Nguyen & Benet-Martínez, 2013). Postmigration education and employment of children as they became adults were associated with improved psychosocial indicators, yet the researchers noted they were unsure if psychological health improved education and employment or if the data were affected by school dropout rates or employment failures because of the difficulties that immigrants with intense psychological problems battle with (Montgomery, 2010). Abramitzky and Boustan (2022) reported that immigrant children are more upwardly mobile as adults than U.S.-born children given that they ascend out of poverty-stricken countries and homes. Indeed, they have had to navigate multiple hardships and overcome them to land on their feet.

Inherent in the previous discussion of resilience is the expectation that immigrant children adapt to the host country. However, supporting immigrant children and their adjustment involves not only their resilience but also the acceptance of cultural multiplicity in society (Verkuyten et al., 2019). That is, it is necessary for receiving people, communities, institutions, and nations to also adapt to societal and cultural changes in response to immigrants' coalescence into host countries. In the United States, though, immigrants continue to experience trauma and discrimination postmigration due to lack of acceptance and ethnocentrism of the dominant White culture.

Children who are undocumented immigrants often express feelings of isolation and alienation because they are excluded due to their status (Verkuyten et al., 2019). In one study of American children's attitudes about what it means to be an American, White European American children "considered White Americans to be 'more American' than Black Americans, who were in turn 'more American' than Asian Americans, who were in turn 'more American' than Latino Americans" (Brown, 2011, p. 114). Even so, Brown (2011) also reported that most children felt that immigrants had a right to come to America to seek a better way of life but preferred they should do so legally, suggesting undocumented immigrants would be less likely to be accepted.

In a study on bullying of immigrants, (a) both Latinx and Asian immigrant students reported schools as unsafe, (b) they were victims of violence or property crime, and (c) Latinx third-generation students were more likely to be bullied than their first- or second-generation counterparts (Peguero, 2009). These students are not included or chose not to engage in extracurricular activities due to the uncertainty of their ability to commit to them in the long term, as many immigrant families move around and change schools to avoid issues with ICE (Peguero, 2009).

These studies suggest school counselors' psychoeducation in schools with all elementary students may be beneficial to mitigate xenophobic attitudes (e.g., my country is the best) and bullying and to foster understanding of their immigrant peers.

Refugee Children

From 2018 to 2020, 27,812 refugee children between the ages of 0 and 17 arrived in the United States, which is 43.3% of the refugee arrivals to the United States. Counselors must be aware of the prevalence of refugees and recognize them as distinctive from other types of immigrant children; however, the diversity within this population is also important to remember. The experience of refugee children varies somewhat in relation to their country of origin (see Lewis et al., 2021, for a summary of the literature). For example, refugees who come from high-income countries, defined by the World Bank as a nation with a gross national income per capita of $12,696 or more, typically do not lack basic material necessities; still, both their health and psychological well-being are at risk (Fazel et al., 2012). Nevertheless, resettlement agency staff note that a majority of refugee families are low-income (Im & Swan, 2021). Economic resources within families affected children positively, while low socioeconomic status produced a higher incidence of depression in refugee children. With regard to subsequent issues, academic problems and behavioral difficulties were prevalent in the low-socioeconomic status group, while it is important to note that criminal activity, alcohol/drug use, and self-harm were rarely a concern (all < 5.45%). Thus, counselors must be attentive to the identified needs of refugee families and avoid broad assumptions to best support them. The following discussion delineates some of the issues and differences within the population of refugee children to which counselors should attend.

In a systematic review of the literature, Fazel et al. (2012) identified the following key risk factors for refugee children. Sex designated at birth was noted in some studies as a risk factor; that is, some girls were more likely than boys to experience internalizing disorders postmigration. Children who endured displacement struggled with psychosocial adaptation and higher levels of anxiety and depression compared with nondisplaced children. Some refugee children were left alone or separated from people or family they knew in the migration process, so they had to rely on strangers for safety (Betancourt et al., 2012). The transit experience can also be a risk factor for mental health concerns. Most refugee children and their families experience significant stalls in their transit; that is, refugee families are often held in a "temporary" placement, sometimes for months or years, awaiting a more permanent placement in their host country (Fee, 2022). The length of time, the uncertainty of these transit experiences, and the helpless detachment of parents from their children may cause children to develop resignation syndrome, or the refusal of food or water (Doherty, 2018). Thus, understanding the premigration, transit, and postmigration experiences of children is necessary to fully assess and treat refugee children.

Displacement due to war/conflict contributed to more severe mental health symptoms for children than for those displaced due to natural disasters (Myles et al., 2018). In a study of 60 displaced refugee children, many exposed to war or violence, Betancourt et al. (2012) noted high rates of "probable posttraumatic stress disorder (30.4%), generalized anxiety (26.8%), somatization (26.8%), traumatic grief (21.4%), and general behavioral problems (21.4%)" (p. 682). These refugee children witnessed so much horror at young ages, including traumatic loss, bereavement, separation from family, and/or exposure to community and domestic violence.

Exposure to violence both in the premigration and migration stages of the refugee's journey also increases children's anxiety and sleep disturbances (Myles et al., 2018). Children who experienced violence before displacement tended to internalize these traumatic experiences, while those who experienced trauma during migration or postmigration were more withdrawn. For example, children whose parents were missing or tortured were strongly associated with mental health problems (Fazel et al., 2012). Children who experienced personal injury were more likely to manifest PTSD symptoms. Assessments for PTSD identify trauma experiences related to personal injury as life-threatening incidents, such as fire, flood, or other natural disaster; combat or war; rape or sexual molestation; and child abuse or neglect. Clinicians can respond to the mental health needs of child refugees diagnosed with PTSD, internalizing disorders, adjustment disorders, and/or attachment disorders by using CBT, play therapy and expressive arts interventions, and individualized multimodal interventions (Cowling & Anderson, 2021).

Researchers noted that polyvictimization (Betancourt et al., 2012) and cumulative stress (Myles et al., 2018) were present with a significant number of immigrant children, with the number of lifetime events or the duration of those situations being most predictive of long-term symptomatology. In responding to polyvictimization, Finkelhor et al. (2011) urged helping professionals to (a) assess for a broad range of types of victimization, (b) prioritize polyvictims by intervening (victimization is likely to persist without intervention), (c) avoid minimizing victims' histories, (d) provide treatments that do not only focus on one type of victimization (i.e., commonly sexual abuse), (e) focus prevention efforts on underlying risk factors across systems, (f) treat underlying vulnerabilities or skill deficits, and (g) advocate and work toward broader child protection.

Despite adversity, the refugee community tends to demonstrate resilience. Thus, resiliency and strengths-based approaches are recommended as a cornerstone of treatment (Lewis et al., 2021). Social support was a protective factor for refugee children during and after migration. Children who were accompanied to their host country, as opposed to those who were not, demonstrated fewer PTSD symptoms (Fazel et al., 2012). Similarly, children who knew relatives in their host country had lower levels of anxiety and depressive symptoms. Parental support and family cohesion led to more positive psychological outcomes in children, whereas family discord, difficulty with adaptation to the new culture by parents, and divorce negatively impacted refugee children. Mental health professionals working with refugee children note that trauma-informed care practices that emphasize the strengths of clients are essential for work with refugees in resettlement programs (Im & Swan, 2021). However, in doing so, professionals must not overlook the adversity these children faced, especially when using trauma screenings that may not be culturally valid (Im & Swan, 2021). In community counseling settings and schools, counselors should work to foster social support for refugee children. Acceptance by others, such as a perceived sense of safety and positive peer relationships, lowered depression, anxiety (Sujoldzić et al., 2006), and PTSD (Geltman et al., 2005) symptoms in refugee children.

The Effects of Detention Centers on Children

In 2018, the United States adopted a "zero-tolerance policy" requiring children to be separated from adults who were accompanying them for the purpose of prosecuting the adults (U.S. Department of Justice, 2018). The removal of children was sometimes abrupt (e.g., children taken from parents' arms, from their family as they slept, while seeking medical care; Habbach et al., 2020). At face value, this was traumatizing and inhumane behavior for unsuspecting immigrants. The children removed by the U.S. Customs and Border Protection (CBP) were then housed in CBP facilities, although some reports note that children were at times taken to hotels and other offsite accommodations (Edyburn & Meek, 2021). CBP was supposed to hold children for only 72 hours before placing them with ORR; however, researchers have reported that this time frame was not enforced (see Table 7.1; Edyburn & Meek, 2021) and conditions were inhumane (Carrasco, 2019).

There is evidence that detention centers in the United States have caused irreparable mental harm to immigrant children. First, many children have not been placed or returned to their families. For example, more than 600 children had not been returned to their families 2 years after a federal judge ordered the Trump administration to do so (Alvarez, 2020). Parental separation due to deportation or detention by ICE escalates the risk of children's mental health problems such as anxiety, behavior problems, depression, and symptoms of PTSD (Rojas-Flores et al., 2017; Zayas et al., 2015). Whereas child separation from parents negatively impacts children, maintenance of relationships within immigrant families is important to mental health. For example, in a study of displaced Croatian children, mothers who were less connected with their children, as perceived by the children, increased the likelihood of elevated levels of depression in children (Ajdukovic & Ajdukovic, 1998). However, children who had parental support were more likely to show lower depressive levels and reduced evidence of their traumatic histories in later years.

Exacerbating the issue, children raised in public care settings tend to be at higher risk for mental health problems (Vostanis, 2010). The development of attachment disorders is one of the primary concerns in immigrant and refugee children who are held in detention centers (van Ecke, 2005). According to the Office of Inspector General (2019), "care provider facilities reported that separation from parents and a hectic reunification process added to the trauma children had already experienced" (p. 13). Relationships that are suddenly ruptured can lead to feelings of insecurity and a lack of safety (Juang et al., 2018). Social isolation and distrust are common in this group (Ehntholt & Yule, 2006), as well as a higher risk of emotional and behavioral problems (Lu et al., 2020). Not only does separation from parents negatively affect children's socioemotional development, but it leads to poorer literacy achievement compared with children who immigrated with parents. Children tend to suffer from a lack of a stimulating environment and disrupted parenting, which, in general, impedes their learning and social development. Lu et al. (2020) noted such adjustment challenges when children are separated from or once they are reunited with their families, which go beyond the general acculturation difficulties all immigrant children face. The effects of attachment and separation and the impact on mental health were discussed in Chapter 6.

Vostanis (2010) stressed the importance of not only more programs but also quality multimodal programming to provide for children's safety, basic and emotional needs, and quality care by skilled care providers. Juang et al. (2018) asked practitioners to consider ways to help immigrants and refugees establish a "connection to place" such as safe havens or places where other immigrant children might be playing in order to provide some kind of secure attachment when caregivers are in precarious deportation situations. When war or violence displaces children, international collaborative efforts can also benefit this group (Vostanis, 2010).

Implications for Counselors

While researchers have narrowed their studies of immigrants to birthright children, unaccompanied children, second- and third-generation children, and refugee children, there are some common recommendations for practitioners across these groups. Research seems to point to interventions that support children and their development holistically. That is, programs that engage both parents and their children are supported in the literature. For example, child-parent centers that offer not only comprehensive education to children but also menu-based family services can be beneficial (Reynolds et al., 2017). Parents who learn formal child development knowledge tend to implement positive parenting practices and behaviors (Cabrera et al., 2017). Lui (2015) found that intergenerational cultural conflicts can have negative impacts on children's mental health and academic performance. Thus, counselors may need to work with families to navigate cultural adaptation, including value differences between grandparents, parents, and their children. (This topic will be discussed in more depth in Chapter 8.)

Working With the Family Unit

Migration is often one way that families intend to provide safety and a satisfactory lifestyle for their children. Even so, assimilation to a new country lasts a lifetime and may never be achieved because of xenophobia and prejudices against immigrants. Motti-Stefanidi and Masten (2017) argued that the biggest developmental task for immigrant children is to navigate between two or more cultures. It seems that parents must also determine how they will navigate two cultures and may respond by choosing differing ways of parenting as they acculturate to their host country. Although there are differences in reasons why individuals and families immigrate, and the resources they are able to access once they have moved to a new country, a growing body of research shows that fathers contribute to children's development over and above their mothers (Cabrera & Bradley, 2012; Cabrera et al., 2017; Updegraff, 2012; Valdez & Martinez, 2019). John and Montgomery (2012) found that while some first-generation Asian Indian parents established traditional socialization goals for their children focusing on obedience and family-centered Indian cultural practices, other Asian Indian parents encouraged a blended approach to socialization, which involved incorporating both traditional Indian and U.S. cultural values and practices.

Systemic support for families is important so that children have access to health care for physical and mental wellness, which should include early childhood screenings, access to culturally informed counselors in schools and clinical settings, and community-based programming that welcomes people from various cultural backgrounds. Working with families to identify their strengths can also be an effective way to support them (Eppler & Weir, 2009)

Support in Schools

A multitiered approach to supporting all students, including immigrants and refugees, is recommended for school counselors and other school-based mental health providers (Betters-Bubon et al., 2016; Edirmanasinghe et al., 2022). Attia et al. (2023) underscored the importance of advocacy in addition to provision of direct services such as bridging gaps in understanding of U.S. educational systems, teaching self-advocacy skills, and providing psychoeducation on available resources and social supports.

Immigrants' experiences in K–12 school settings are paramount. Abrego (2011) argued that child immigrants are fundamentally shaped by their school environment and are protected through educational law by being a student. The case of *Plyler v. Doe* (1982) determined that all children, including undocumented children, should be provided access to a public education. Schools cannot ask for documentation concerning a child's immigration status, and Social Security numbers cannot be used as a prerequisite for enrollment. Moreover, school personnel are forbidden to share information about a child's immigration status with any individual, institution, or government agency.

Educational specialists and researchers have recognized for decades that educational disparities exist for students in schools who are immigrants and refugees (Andon et al., 2014; Pivovarova & Powers, 2019). As previously mentioned, early screening and intervention for this population is highly recommended. Gagné et al. (2019) underscored the need for early intervention for first- and second-generation immigrant children and refugees before age 5. In a retrospective, longitudinal study of immigrant and refugee children ($N = 9{,}216$), Gagné and colleagues examined six academic trajectories, from consistently high to low declining achievement. Literacy and number proficiency scores as early as kindergarten were predictive of academic success in Grades 4–10. Lack of social-emotional competency in kindergarten was associated with declining academic scores in middle school and high school, whereas prosocial emotional competency was indicative of higher reading and math achievement. Thus, counselors should work with parents to access educational services as early as possible for the sake of their children's development. Advocacy to make these services available to immigrant families is also essential.

In addition to early screening, helping professionals must consider the probability of asynchronous development in immigrant children. Children who were separated from parents (e.g., detention centers, staged migration planning) were more likely to be trained in numeracy skills in their home countries (Lu et al., 2020). Furthermore, numeracy skills are more transferable across cultures and languages. Conversely, literacy skills are less transferable across countries; literacy tests reflect how well immigrant children successfully acquire a new language but must also take into account the age of children when these assessments take place. Children's social environment after immigration affects language development (Lu et al., 2020). A family environment facing high levels of turmoil may impede children's language acquisition.

Disrupted Education

Many immigrant children who come to the United States have come from low-income settings and may have had little to no access to education systems like urban public schools. Upon entering the United States, they are immediately immersed in education systems that they, and most likely their parents, have no experience in (Fazel et al., 2012). Thus, school counselors and other educators should consider the importance of supporting students in the transition into the school setting (Crosnoe & Ansari, 2016) as well as the academic and social-emotional needs of these students once they have started their K–12 school experience.

First, counselors and educators must engage with and respect parents and families of immigrant children. Starting a relationship with immigrant families should involve partnering with them to support cross-cultural understanding (Newcomer et al., 2021). In schools, when language barriers exist, counselors and other helping professionals can utilize interpreters (possibly through the Red Cross or other community agencies) or bilingual community volunteers who are willing to help make connections to families or to translate materials to ensure immigrants can access communications. Other programs, like the one developed by Lepore (2015) called Project Liberty, provide immigrant families with opportunities to connect with each other and with other families in their community via after-school and evening activities.

In addition to making connections to families, research points to the necessity of Tier 1 or class-wide interventions, which are delivered to all students to create a school-wide culture that not only accepts but also celebrates diversity. Furthermore, culturally responsive pedagogy explores the role of culture in development, which provides immigrant and refugee students the opportunity to adapt and blend various aspects of their identities (Newcomer et al., 2021). As a part of facilitating culturally responsive pedagogy, educational professionals found success when they opened up space for students to share their personal experiences (Newcomer et al., 2021). "Sharing stories" allows immigrant children to connect with other children on universal concepts (e.g., holidays) while giving all children the opportunity to learn about similarities and differences across cultures. In addition, both counselors and teachers can support immigrant students in learning new concepts by scaffolding instruction, especially through modeling, schema building, and contextualizing ideas or terms (Newcomer et al., 2021). Sharing around traditions, foods, and countries of origin using a map must be done with caution. It is necessary to recognize that some topics, though they seem benign (about grandparents or other family members), may trigger pain and trauma.

Mental Health

Immigrant and refugee students who have experienced resettlement stress and/or traumatic experiences while immigrating are at increased risk for mental health issues that may filter into the classroom. Classroom climate, attentive teachers and counselors, and positive peer interactions in schools are protective factors that can positively impact the mental health of immigrant and refugee children. For example, a creative art-based expression intervention program with refugee and nonrefugee immigrant children in elementary schools has shown promising results to improve the mental health and social relationships of these students (Kevers et al., 2022). In particular, the program not only slightly improved the classroom climate for all students but also seemed to have a positive effect on PTSD symptoms in the immigrant and refugee children. In working with children in individual counseling, Lewis et al. (2021) recommended strengths-based approaches that build on the resilience of immigrants and refugees. Counselors can also provide individual or group counseling to immigrant students to help them to develop coping strategies and social networks, and to provide psychoeducation about American culture so that immigrant students can more easily adapt to schools and their environment while parents may also be learning to adjust at the same time (Goh et al., 2007).

Group Counseling

Group counseling options for students from immigrant families may be helpful. Counselors can initiate community building with immigrant children, which can be beneficial to help students gain knowledge about their host culture; provide opportunities to ask questions in a safe space; normalize feelings of grief, loss, and acclimation to many changes they may be experiencing; and bring up incidents of discrimination (Chen et al., 2010). Group counseling that integrates cognitive behavior theory, especially the Teaching Recovery Techniques (TRT) program (Sarkadi et al., 2018; Smith et al., 1999), has been useful in school settings to decrease depressive symptoms of immigrant participants (Ooi et al., 2016). TRT is an intervention based on trauma-focused CBT that supports children and their parental figures. Children learn stress management techniques to manage emotions, learn cognitive and affective strategies to process thoughts and emotions, and experience gradual exposure to past trauma to reduce triggering events, along with self-regulation strategies. Simultaneously, counselors provide psychoeducation to parents to develop skills (e.g., communication to improve familial relationships or to process difficult memories; Sarkadi et al., 2018). Of course, the language for delivery of these interventions needs to be anticipated. Interpreters may be needed when presenting to parents.

Special Statuses

Once identified, immigrant and refugee children must be served appropriately in schools and other settings. Thus, counselors need to be prepared to work with families to intervene early to identify developmental delays and respond with counseling support to immigrant children with disabilities, including ensuring services provided to them are more than English as a Second Language services. When students are put into transitional bilingual programs, often designated as remedial, counselors must act as antiracist advocates to work toward appropriate education for students based on their abilities and reinforce the benefits of bilingual educational opportunities (Hill et al., 2008). Students with identified disabilities may need additional support, such as 504 plans and individualized education plans, for which all students are eligible according to the law (*Plyler v. Doe*, 1982). Immigrant and refugee students should also be considered for gifted programming (B. Harris et al., 2009; C. R. Harris, 1990).

The following case study of Azim, a Syrian refugee, is provided so that you can consider applications of some of the information provided in this chapter. In this scenario, it is important to recognize the importance of a plan that includes multidisciplinary collaboration to provide layers of support to Azim as he transitions to the U.S. education system and culture. For example, connecting with his mother and providing her ongoing support and resources may be one of the most important ways to positively impact Azim's development. Additionally, the team of mental health professionals must thoughtfully consider the assessments they use to accurately assess Azim, including formative, informal, and culturally responsive tools to limit bias in the results. Finally, interventions should range from individual counseling to address Azim's immediate needs to school-wide diversity initiatives to create a positive culture of acceptance for all students.

CASE STUDY

Azim is a 5-year-old Syrian refugee who entered the United States almost a year ago with his mother, Hana. Hana brought Azim to "Kindergarten Roundup," where he was assessed for readiness for school. The student services team, including the school psychologist, school counselor, school nurse, and school social worker, met before Kindergarten Roundup to develop a plan for how to assess Azim. The team reviewed the English Learner Toolkit provided by the U.S. Department of Education (2016). The school social worker offered to connect with Hana before the screening to complete the Home Language Survey and identify basic needs in the home such as food, clothing, employment, and childcare. She elicited the help of a certified interpreter to aid her in the process. At school, the school psychologist elected to use the Kindergarten ACCESS (WIDA Consortium, 2021) assessment tool specifically developed for English language learners (ELLs). In addition to ensuring that Azim was supported by the ELL teacher, the school counselor worked on creating an accepting school environment by developing classroom lessons focused on diversity and appreciation of individual differences. She also posted a bulletin board with a world map and asked students to put their name to show where they or their ancestors were from. At the first staff meeting of the year, a guest speaker and a principal led a discussion about how to support newcomers in classrooms using culturally sensitive pedagogy.

Once the school year started, Azim's classroom teacher noticed Azim would cry regularly in class. The school counselor met with Azim and used drawings and play-based activities to engage him so that he could express himself and share his concerns. They also made a memory book about Azim's father and brother. The school counselor connected with Azim's mother to find out more about his behavior at home and learned he was crying at home regularly too. The school counselor and the social worker worked with Hana to refer Azim and his mother to a clinical mental health counselor to assess Azim for depression and for further work on acculturation in the United States. The school social worker also started an open group for parents of newcomers one night a week to provide a safe space to ask questions, share resources, and develop social supports within this community.

Reflection Questions and Recommendations for Further Professional Development

1. If you were Azim's mental health counselor, what strategies would you use to engage him and his mother in counseling?
2. Read *Refugee and Migrant Health: Global Competency Standards for Health Workers* (WHO, 2021). Identify standards you still need to develop to work with the immigrant and refugee populations competently.
3. Identify the most valid and reliable assessment tools to assess the mental health of immigrant children by interviewing an expert in the field or by conducting a review of the research literature. Consider how you can develop competency to deliver them most effectively.

Summary

Children who are immigrants and refugees likely have had childhood experiences different from their same-age peers U.S.-born peers. These may include forced separation from family members, placement in various types of care facilities, a range of traumatic experiences from premigration through postmigration, and/or a disrupted education. Counselors, educators, and others who work with immigrant children must use multiple methods of assessment to conceptualize a holistic understanding of their needs, and then intervene early to provide a system of supports for the sake of the children's academic and social-emotional development, their mental health, and their overall well-being. Counselors are also reminded to refer to the MSJCC (Ratts et al., 2015) to assess their attitudes, awareness, knowledge, and skills when engaging with these children and their families. It may be easy to work from faulty assumptions that all refugee and immigrant children have experienced similar histories. As has been outlined in the chapter, there are many differences among birthright, first-, second-, and third-generation children.

References

Abramitzky, R., & Boustan, L. (2022). *Streets of gold: America's untold story of immigrant success.* PublicAffairs.

Abrego, L. J. (2011). Legal consciousness of undocumented Latinos: Fear and stigma as barriers to claims-making for first- and 1.5-generation immigrants. *Law & Society Review, 45*(2), 337–370. https://doi.org/10.1111/j.1540-5893.2011.00435.x

Adesope, O. O., Lavin, T., Thompson, T., & Ungerleider, C. (2010). A systematic review and meta-analysis of the cognitive correlates of bilingualism. *Review of Educational Research, 80*(2), 207–245. https://doi.org/10.3102/0034654310368803

Ajdukovic, M., & Ajdukovic, D. (1998). Impact of displacement on the psychological well-being of refugee children. *International Review of Psychiatry, 10*(3), 186–195. https://doi.org/10.1080/09540269874763

Alvarez, P. (2020, December 2). *Parents of 628 migrant children separated at border still have not been found, court filing says.* CNN. https://www.cnn.com/2020/12/02/politics/family-separation-us-border-children/index.html

American Academy of Pediatrics. (n.d.). *Immigrant child health toolkit.* https://downloads.aap.org/AAP/PDF/cocp_toolkit_full.pdf

American Immigration Council. (2021). *U.S. citizen children impacted by immigration enforcement.* https://www.americanimmigrationcouncil.org/research/us-citizen-children-impacted-immigration-enforcement

Andon, A., Thompson, C. G., & Becker, B. J. (2014). A quantitative synthesis of the immigrant achievement gap across OECD countries. *Large-Scale Assessments in Education, 2*(1), Article 7. https://doi.org/10.1186/s40536-014-0007-2

Attia, M., Staton, A. R., Evans, A., & Tang, S. (2023). Supporting immigrant students in schools: A qualitative investigation. *Journal of Child and Adolescent Counseling, 9*(1), 34–49. https://doi.org/10.1080/23727810.2023.2168361

Bediako, P. T., BeLue, R., & Hillemeier, M. M. (2018). Immigrant generational status and developmental problems among prematurely born children. *Journal of Immigrant and Minority Health, 20*(2), 422–430. https://doi.org/10.1007/s10903-017-0560-1

Benuto, L. T., Casas, J. B., Gonzalez, F. R., & Newlands, R. T. (2018). Being an undocumented child immigrant. *Children and Youth Services Review, 89*, 198–204. https://doi.org/10.1016/j.childyouth.2018.04.036

Betancourt, T. S., Newnham, E. A., Layne, C. M., Kim, S., Steinberg, A. M., Ellis, H., & Birman, D. (2012). Trauma history and psychopathology in war-affected refugee children referred for trauma-related mental health services in the United States. *Journal of Traumatic Stress, 25*(6), 682–690. https://doi.org/10.1002/jts.21749

Betters-Bubon, J., Brunner, T., & Kansteiner, A. (2016). Success for all? The role of the school counselor in creating and sustaining culturally responsive positive behavior interventions and supports programs. *Professional Counselor, 6*(3), 263–277. https://doi.org/10.15241/jbb.6.3.263

Bhayana, A., & Bhayana, B. (2018). Approach to developmental disabilities in newcomer families. *Canadian family physician/Le Médecin de famille canadien, 64*(8), 567–573.

Bouza, J., Camacho-Thompson, D. E., Carlo, G., Franco, X., García Coll, C., Halgunseth, L. C., Marks, A., Stein, G. L., Suárez-Orozco, C., & White, R. M. B. (2018). *The science is clear: Separating families has long-term damaging psychological and health consequences for children, families, and communities.* Society for Research in Child Development. https://www.srcd.org/briefs-fact-sheets/the-science-is-clear

Broder, T., & Lessard, G. (2023). *Overview of immigrant eligibility for federal programs.* National Immigration Law Center. https://www.nilc.org/issues/economic-support/overview-immeligfedprograms/

Brown, C. S. (2011). American elementary school children's attitudes about immigrants, immigration, and being an American. *Journal of Applied Developmental Psychology, 32*(3), 109–117. https://doi.org/10.1016/j.appdev.2011.01.001

Cabrera, N. J., & Bradley, R. H. (2012). Latino fathers and their children. *Child Development Perspectives, 6*(3), 232–238. https://doi.org/10.1111/j.1750-8606.2012.00249.x

Cabrera, N. J., Malin J. L., Kuhns, C., & West, J. (2017). The early home environment of Latinx boys and their peers: A developmental perspective. *Infant Mental Health Journal*, 38(1), 97–114.

Calvo, R., & Hawkins, S. S. (2015). Disparities in quality of healthcare of children from immigrant families in the US. *Maternal and Child Health Journal, 19*(10), 2223–2232. https://doi.org/10.1007/s10995-015-1740-z

Capps, A., Castañeda, R. M., Chaudry, A., & Santos, R. (2007). *Paying the price: The impact of immigration raids on America's children.* National Council of La Raza and The Urban Institute. https://www.urban.org/research/publication/paying-price-impact-immigration-raids-americas-children

Carrasco, L. F. (2019, September 20). Border detainees subject to food and sleep deprivation. *Arizona Daily Star.* https://tucson.com/news/report-border-detainees-subject-to-food-sleep-deprivation/article_9f89e2aa-bed7-53e7-9d6c-9d1c7c435f55.html

Center for Inclusive Childcare. (n.d.). *Parents, grandparents, and caregivers.* https://www.inclusivechildcare.org/parents-grandparents-and-caregivers

Chen, E. C., Budianto, L., & Wong, K. (2010). Professional school counselors as social justice advocates for undocumented immigrant students in group work. *The Journal for Specialists in Group Work, 35*(3), 255–261. https://doi.org/10.1080/01933922.2010.492897

Cigrand, D. L., Fawcett, M., Miyakuni, R., Arredondo, P., & Onderak, G. (2022). A phenomenological study of perseverance and resilience through the migration journey. *Journal of Counseling & Development, 100*(2), 157–170. https://doi.org/10.1002/jcad.12413

Cote, L. R., & Bornstein, M. H. (2009). Child and mother play in three U.S. cultural groups: Comparisons and associations. *Journal of Family Psychology, 23*(3), 355–363. https://doi.org/10.1037/a0015399

Cowling, M. M., & Anderson, J. R. (2023). The effectiveness of therapeutic interventions on psychological distress in refugee children: A systematic review. *Journal of Clinical Psychology, 79*(8), 1857–1874. https://doi-org/10.1002/jclp.23479

Crosnoe, R., & Ansari, A. (2016). Family socioeconomic status, immigration, and children's transitions into school. *Family Relations, 65*(1), 73–84. https://doi.org/10.1111/fare.12171

Cross, F. L., Martinez, S. B., & Rivas-Drake, D. (2021). Documentation status socialization among Latinx immigrant parents. *New Directions for Child and Adolescent Development, 2021*(177), 31–49. https://doi.org/10.1002/cad.20420

D'Alonzo, K. T., & Greene, L. (2020). Strategies to establish and maintain trust when working in immigrant communities. *Public Health Nursing, 37*(5), 764–768. https://doi.org/10.1111/phn.12764

Demazure, G., Gaultier, S., & Pinsault, N. (2018). Dealing with difference: A scoping review of psychotherapeutic interventions with unaccompanied refugee minors. *European Child Adolescent Psychiatry, 27*(4), 447–466. https://doi.org/10.1007/s00787-017-1083-y

Dickerson, C. (2021, July 9). Undocumented and pregnant: Why women are afraid to get prenatal care. *The New York Times*. https://www.nytimes.com/2020/11/22/us/undocumented-immigrants-pregnant-prenatal.html

Doherty B. (2018). "Begging to die": Succession of critically ill children moved off Nauru. *The Guardian (Australian Edition)*. https://www.theguardian.com/australia-news/2018/aug/25/begging-to-die-succession-of-critically-ill-children-moved-off-nauru

Donoghue, E. A., Council on Early Childhood, Lieser, D., DelConte, B., Donoghue, E., Earls, M., Glassy, D., Mendelsohn, A., McFadden, T., Scholer, S., Takagishi, J., Vanderbilt, D., & Williams, P. G. (2017). Quality early education and child care from birth to kindergarten. *Pediatrics, 140*(2), Article e20171488. https://doi.org/10.1542/peds.2017-1488

Edirmanasinghe, N. A., Attia, M., Brant-Rajahn, S., & Staton, A. R. (2022). Working with immigrant children in schools: Applying a multi-tiered approach. *Journal of Child and Adolescent Counseling, 8*(2), 59–71. https://doi.org/10.1080/23727810.2022.2074771

Edyburn, K. L., & Meek, S. (2021). Seeking safety and humanity in the harshest immigration climate in a generation: A review of the literature on the effects of separation and detention on migrant and asylum-seeking children and families in the United States during the Trump administration. *Social Policy Report, 34*(1), 1–46. https://doi.org/10.1002/sop2.12

Ehntholt, K. A., & Yule, W. (2006). Practitioner review: Assessment and treatment of refugee children and adolescents who have experienced war-related trauma. *The Journal of Child Psychology and Psychiatry, 47*(12), 1197–1210. https://doi.org/10.1111/j.1469-7610.2006.01638.x

Elmore Borbon, D., Tant, E., & Rosado, J. (2021). *Children, youth, and families who experience migration-related trauma and family separation* [Policy brief]. National Center for Child Traumatic Stress. https://www.nctsn.org/sites/default/files/resources/fact-sheet/children_youth_and_families_who_experience_migration_related_trauma_and_family_separation.pdf

Eppler, C., & Weir, S. (2009). Family assessment in K–12 settings: Understanding family systems to provide effective, collaborative services. *Psychology in the Schools, 46*(6), 501–514. https://doi.org/10.1002/pits.20393

Fazel, M., Reed, R. V., Panter-Brick, C., & Stein, A. (2012). Mental health of displaced and refugee children resettled in high-income countries: Risk and protective factors. *The Lancet, 379*(9812), 266–282. https://doi.org/10.1016/S0140-6736(11)60051-2

Fee, M. (2022) Lives stalled: The costs of waiting for refugee resettlement. *Journal of Ethnic and Migration Studies, 48*(11), 2659–2677. https://doi.org/10.1080/1369183X.2021.1876554

Finkelhor, D., Turner, H., Hamby, S. L., & Ormrod, R. (2011). *Polyvictimization: Children's exposure to multiple types of violence, crime, and abuse.* Office of Juvenile Justice and Delinquency Prevention. https://www.ojp.gov/pdffiles1/ojjdp/235504.pdf

Franco, D. (2018). Trauma without borders: The necessity for school-based interventions in treating unaccompanied refugee minors. *Child and Adolescent Social Work Journal, 35*(6), 551–565. https://doi.org/10.1007/s10560-018-0552-6

Gagné, M., Guhn, M., Emerson, S., Magee, C., Milbrath, C., & Gadermann, A. (2019). Thriving, catching up or falling behind: Immigrant and refugee children's kindergarten competencies and later academic achievement. *International Journal of Population Data Science, 4*(3). https://doi.org/10.23889/ijpds.v4i3.1222

García Coll, C., & Marks, A. K. (Eds.). (2012). *The immigrant paradox in children and adolescents: Is becoming American a developmental risk?* American Psychological Association. https://doi.org/10.1037/13094-000

Geltman, P. L., Grant-Knight, W., Mehta, S. D., Lloyd-Travaglini, C., Lustig, S., Landgraf, J. M., & Wise, P. H. (2005). The "Lost Boys of Sudan": Functional and behavioral health of unaccompanied refugee minors resettled in the United States. *Archives of Pediatrics & Adolescent Medicine, 159*(6), 585–591. https://doi.org/10.1001/archpedi.159.6.585

Goh, M., Wahl, K. H., McDonald, J. K., Brissett, A. A., & Yoon, E. (2007). Working with immigrant students in schools: The role of school counselors in building cross-cultural bridges. *Journal of Multicultural Counseling and Development, 35*(2), 66–79. https://doi.org/10.1002/j.2161-1912.2007.tb00050.x

Grumi, S., Milani, L., & Di Blasio, P. (2017). Risk assessment in a multicultural context: Risk and protective factors in the decision to place children in foster care. *Children and Youth Services Review, 77*, 69–75. https://doi.org/10.1016/j.childyouth.2017.04.009

Habbach, J., Hampton, K., & Mishori, R. (2020). *"You will never see your child again": The persistent psychological effects of family separation.* Physicians for Human Rights. https://phr.org/our-work/resources/you-will-never-see-your-child-again-the-persistent-psychological-effects-of-family-separation/

Harrington, B. (2018). The citizenship clause and "birthright citizenship": A brief legal overview. *Congressional Research Service.* https://crsreports.congress.gov/product/pdf/LSB/LSB10214

Harris, B., Plucker, J. A., Rapp, K. E., & Martinez, R. S. (2009). Identifying gifted and talented English language learners: A case study. *Journal for the Education of the Gifted, 32*(3), 368–393. https://doi.org/10.4219/jeg-2009-858

Harris, C. R. (1990). *Identifying and serving the gifted new immigrant/refugee: Problems, strategies, implications* (ED319209). ERIC. https://files.eric.ed.gov/fulltext/ED319209.pdf

Hill, S., Gomez, R., & Gomez, L. (2008). What a difference a year makes: A large urban school district's transformation from remedial to an enrichment dual language education. *Journal of Bilingual Education Research & Instruction, 10*(1), 168–192.

Im, H., & Swan, L. E. T. (2021). Working towards culturally responsive trauma-informed care in the refugee resettlement process: Qualitative inquiry with refugee-serving professionals in the United States. *Behavioral Sciences, 11*(11), Article 155. https://doi.org/10.3390/bs11110155

Javier, J. R., Huffman, L. C., Mendoza, F. S., & Wise, P. H. (2009). Children with special health care needs: How immigrant status is related to health care access, health care utilization, and health status. *Maternal and Child Health Journal, 14*(4), 567–579. https://doi.org/10.1007/s10995-009-0487-9

John, A., & Montgomery, D. (2012). Socialization goals of first-generation immigrant Indian parents: A Q-methodological study. *Asian American Journal of Psychology, 3*(4), 299–312. https://doi.org/10.1037/a0025556

Juang, L. P., Simpson, J. A., Lee, R. M., Rothman, A. J., Titzmann, P. F., Schachner, M. K., Korn, L., Heinemeier, D., & Betsch, C. (2018). Using attachment and relational perspectives to understand adaptation and resilience among immigrant and refugee youth. *American Psychologist, 73*(6), 797–811. https://doi.org/10.1037/amp0000286

Jud, A., Pfeiffer, E., & Jarczok, M. (2020). Epidemiology of violence against children in migration: A systematic literature review. *Child Abuse & Neglect, 108*, Article 104634. https://doi.org/10.1016/j.chiabu.2020.104634

Kevers, R., Spaas, C., Derluyn, I., de Smet, S., Van Den Noortgate, W., Colpin, H., & De Haene, L. (2022). The effect of a school-based creative expression program on immigrant and refugee children's mental health and classroom social relationships: A cluster randomized trial in elementary school. *American Journal of Orthopsychiatry, 92*(5), 599–615. https://doi.org/10.1037/ort0000628

LaBrenz, C. A., Panisch, L. S., Lawson, J., Borcyk, A. L., Gerlach, B., Tennant, P. S., Nulu, S., & Faulkner, M. (2019). Adverse childhood experiences and outcomes among at-risk Spanish-speaking Latino families. *Journal of Child and Family Studies, 29*(5), 1221–1235. https://doi.org/10.1007/s10826-019-01589-0

Lepore, M. F. (2015). Adventures in America: Easing the transition of refugees in school and community. *Making Connections, 16*(1), 11–24.

Lewis, F. J., Tor, S., Rappleyea, D., Didericksen, K. W., & Sira, N. (2021). Behavioral health and refugee youth in primary care: An ecological systems perspective of the complexities of care. *Children and Youth Services Review, 120*, Article 105599. https://doi.org/10.1016/j.childyouth.2020.105599

Loria, H., & Caughy, M. (2018). Prevalence of adverse childhood experiences in low-income Latino immigrant and nonimmigrant children. *The Journal of Pediatrics, 192*, 209–215. https://doi.org/10.1016/j.jpeds.2017.09.056

Lu, Y., He, Q., & Brooks-Gunn, J. (2020). Diverse experience of immigrant children: How do separation and reunification shape their development? *Child Development, 91*(1), e146–e163. https://doi.org/10.1111/cdev.13171

Lui, P. P. (2015). Intergenerational cultural conflict, mental health, and educational outcomes among Asian and Latino/a Americans: Qualitative and meta-analytic review. *Psychological Bulletin, 141*(2), 404–446. https://doi.org/10.1037/a0038449

Mancini, M. A. (2020). A pilot study evaluating a school-based, trauma-focused intervention for immigrant and refugee youth. *Child and Adolescent Social Work Journal, 37*(3), 287–300. https://doi.org/10.1007/s10560-019-00641-8

Mandell, D. S., Ittenbach, R. F., Levy, S. E., & Pinto-Martin, J. A. (2006). Disparities in diagnoses received prior to a diagnosis of autism spectrum disorder. *Journal of Autism and Developmental Disorders, 37*(9), 1795–1802. https://doi.org/10.1007/s10803-006-0314-8

Mandell, D. S., Listerud, J., Levy, S. E., & Pinto-Martin, J. A. (2002). Race differences in the age at diagnosis among Medicaid-eligible children with autism. *Journal of the American Academy of Child & Adolescent Psychiatry, 41*(12), 1447–1453. https://doi.org/10.1097/00004583-200212000-00016

Mandell, D. S., Wiggins, L. D., Carpenter, L. A., Daniels, J., DiGuiseppi, C., Durkin, M. S., Giarelli, E., Morrier, M. J., Nicholas, J. S., Pinto-Martin, J. A., Shattuck, P. T., Thomas, K. C., Yeargin-Allsopp, M., & Kirby, R. S. (2009). Racial/ethnic disparities in the identification of children with autism spectrum disorders. *American Journal of Public Health, 99*(3), 493–498. https://doi.org/10.2105/ajph.2007.131243

Marks, A. K., Ejesi, K., & García Coll, C. (2014). Understanding the U.S. immigrant paradox in childhood and adolescence. *Child Development Perspectives, 8*(2), 59–64. https://doi.org/10.1111/cdep.12071

Martin, K. J., Cowden, J. D., Williams, D. D., & Randell, K. A. (2018). Adverse childhood experiences among immigrants and their children. *Pediatrics, 142*(1), 753. https://doi.org/10.1542/peds.142.1MA8.753

Martin Herz, S. P., Kemper, T., Brownstein, M., & McLaughlin, J. F. (2012). *Developmental screening with recent immigrant and refugee children*. EthnoMed. https://ethnomed.org/resource/developmental-screening-with-recent-immigrant-and-refugee-children/

Mathema, S. (2017). *Keeping families together: Why all Americans should care about what happens to unauthorized immigrants*. Center for American Progress. https://www.americanprogress.org/article/keeping-families-together/

Mayo Clinic. (2023, February 25). *Premature birth*. https://www.mayoclinic.org/diseases-conditions/premature-birth/symptoms-causes/syc-20376730

Montgomery, E. (2010). Trauma and resilience in young refugees: A 9-year follow-up study. *Development and Psychopathology, 22*(2), 477–489. https://doi.org/10.1017/s0954579410000180

Morrier, M., Hess, K., & Heflin, L. (2008). Ethnic disproportionality in students with autism spectrum disorders. *Multicultural Education, 16*(1), 31–38.

Motti-Stefanidi, F. (2021). A multisystem perspective on immigrant children and youth risk and resilience: A commentary. *New Directions for Child and Adolescent Development, 177*, 219–227. https://doi.org/10.1002/cad.20428

Motti-Stefanidi, F., & Masten, A. S. (2017). A resilience perspective on immigrant youth adaptation and development. In N. J. Cabrera & B. Leyendecker (Eds.), *Handbook on positive development of minority children and youth* (pp. 19–34). Springer. https://doi.org/10.1007/978-3-319-43645-6_2

Motti-Stefanidi, F., Pavlopoulos, V., & Asendorpf, J. B. (2018). Immigrant youth acculturation and perceived discrimination: Longitudinal mediation by immigrant peers' acceptance/rejection. *Journal of Applied Developmental Psychology*, *59*, 36-45. https://doi.org/10.1016/j.appdev.2018.03.001

Myles, P., Swenshon, S., Haase, K., Szeles, T., Jung, C., Jacobi, F., & Rath, B. (2018). A comparative analysis of psychological trauma experienced by children and young adults in two scenarios: Evacuation after a natural disaster vs forced migration to escape armed conflict. *Public Health*, *158*, 163–175. https://doi.org/10.1016/j.puhe.2018.03.012

Newcomer, S. N., Ardasheva, Y., Morrison, J. A., Ernst-Slavit, G., Morrison, S. J., Carbonneau, K. J., & Lightner, L. K. (2021). "Whoa . . . Welcome to America!": Supporting refugee background students' socioemotional well-being, English language development, and content area learning. *Journal of Research in Childhood Education*, *35*(3), 417–437. https://doi.org/10.1080/02568543.2020.1734697

Nguyen, A.-M. D., & Benet-Martínez, V. (2013). Biculturalism and adjustment: A meta-analysis. *Journal of Cross-Cultural Psychology*, *44*(1), 122–159. https://doi.org/10.1177/0022022111435097

Office of Inspector General. (2019). *Care provider facilities described challenges addressing mental health needs of children in HHS custody*. https://s3.documentcloud.org/documents/6380666/Inspector-General-Report-from-HHSOIG.pdf

Office of Refugee Resettlement. (2022). *About the program*. https://www.acf.hhs.gov/orr/programs/ucs/about

Ooi, C. S., Rooney, R. M., Roberts, C., Kane, R. T., Wright, B., & Chatzisarantis, N. (2016). The efficacy of a group cognitive behavioral therapy for war-affected young migrants living in Australia: A cluster randomized controlled trial. *Frontiers in Psychology*, *7*, Article 1641. https://doi.org/10.3389/fpsyg.2016.01641

Paris, R., & Bronson, M. (2006). A home-based intervention for immigrant and refugee children trauma survivors: Paraprofessionals working with high-risk mothers and infants. *Zero to Three*, *27*(2), 37–45. https://www.zerotothree.org/resource/a-home-based-intervention-for-immigrant-and-refugee-trauma-survivors/

Park, M., & Peña, J. F. (2021). *The invisible work of family, friend, and neighbor caregivers and its importance for immigrant and dual language learner families* [Policy brief]. Migration Policy Institute. https://www.migrationpolicy.org/sites/default/files/publications/nciip-ffn-care-brief_final.pdf

Patel, S. G., Bouche, V., Martinez, W., Barajas, K., Garcia, A., Sztainer, M., & Hawkins, K. (2021). "Se extraña todo": Family separation and reunification experiences among unaccompanied adolescent migrants from Central America. *New Directions for Child and Adolescent Development*, *2021*(176), 227–244. https://doi.org/10.1002/cad.20404

Peguero, A. A. (2009). Victimizing the children of immigrants: Latino and Asian American student victimization. *Youth & Society*, *41*(2), 186–208. https://doi.org/10.1177/0044118X09333646

Perreira, K. M., & Ornelas, I. (2013). Painful passages: Traumatic experiences and post-traumatic stress among U.S. immigrant Latino adolescents and their primary caregivers. *International Migration Review*, *47*(4), 976–1005. https://doi.org/10.1111/imre.12050

Perreira, K. M., & Pedroza, J. M. (2019). Policies of exclusion: Implications for the health of immigrants and their children. *Annual Review of Public Health*, *40*(1), 147–166. https://doi.org/10.1146/annurev-publhealth-040218-044115

Pew Research Center. (2018). *Number of U.S.-born babies with unauthorized immigrant parents has fallen since 2007*. https://pewrsr.ch/2OiaqIr

Pivovarova, M., & Powers, J. M. (2019). Generational status, immigrant concentration and academic achievement: Comparing first and second-generation immigrants with third-plus generation students. *Large-Scale Assessments in Education*, *7*(1), Article 7. https://doi.org/10.1186/s40536-019-0075-4

Place, S., & Hoff, E. (2011). Properties of dual language exposure that influence 2-year-olds' bilingual proficiency. *Child Development*, *82*(6), 1834–1849. https://doi.org/10.1111/j.1467-8624.2011.01660.x

Plyler v. Doe, 457 U.S. 202 (1982). https://www.loc.gov/item/usrep457202/

Preston, J. (2020, June 18). *The true costs of deportation*. The Marshall Project. https://www.themarshallproject.org/2020/06/22/the-true-costs-of-deportation

Reynolds, A. J., Hayakawa, M., Ou, S.-R., Mondi, C. F., Englund, M. M., Candee, A. J., & Smerillo, N. E. (2017). Scaling and sustaining effective early childhood programs through school-family-university collaboration. *Child Development, 88*(5), 1453–1465. https://doi.org/10.1111/cdev.12901

Roberto, S., Moleiro, C., Ramos, N., & Freire, J. (2016). "The place I long to be": Resilience processes in migrants. *PSICOLOGIA, 30*(2), 47–60. https://doi.org/10.17575/rpsicol.v30i2.1111

Rojas-Flores, L., Clements, M. L., Hwang Koo, J., & London, J. (2017). Trauma and psychological distress in Latino citizen children following parental detention and deportation. *Psychological Trauma: Theory, Research, Practice, and Policy, 9*(3), 352–361. https://doi.org/10.1037/tra0000177

Sarkadi, A., Ådahl, K., Stenvall, E., Ssegonja, R., Batti, H., Gavra, P., Fängström, K., & Salari, R. (2017). Teaching recovery techniques: Evaluation of a group intervention for unaccompanied refugee minors with symptoms of PTSD in Sweden. *European Child & Adolescent Psychiatry, 27*(4), 467–479. https://doi.org/10.1007/s00787-017-1093-9

Seon, J., & Klein, S. (2021). Geographically accessible immigration support and parenting services and child maltreatment. *Journal of Public Child Welfare, 15*(2), 203–222. https://doi.org/10.1080/15548732.2019.1693476

Silva, M. A., McQuaid, J., Rojas Perez, O., & Paris, M. (2022). Unaccompanied migrant youth from Central America: Challenges and opportunities. *Current Opinion in Psychology, 47*, Article 101415. https://doi.org/10.1016/j.copsyc.2022.101415

Smith, P., Dyregrov, A., & Yule, W. (1999). *Children and war: Teaching recovery techniques.* Children and War Foundation.

Stanford University Rapid Survey Project. (2021). *Who is providing for child care providers?* [Fact sheet]. https://rapidsurveyproject.com/who-is-providing-for-child-care-providers

Stanford University Rapid Survey Project. (2022). *Households with young children and child care providers are still facing hunger* [Fact sheet]. https://rapidsurveyproject.com/our-research/households-with-young-children-still-facing-hunger

Suárez-Orozco, C., Yoshikawa, H., Teranishi, R., & Suárez-Orozco, M. (2011). Growing up in the shadows: The developmental implications of unauthorized status. *Harvard Educational Review, 81*(3), 438–473. https://doi.org/10.17763/haer.81.3.g23x203763783m75

Sujoldzić, A., Peternel, L., Kulenović, T., & Terzić, R. (2006). Social determinants of health—A comparative study of Bosnian adolescents in different cultural contexts. *Collegium Antropologicum, 30*(4), 703–711.

Tello, A. M., Castellon, N. E., Aguilar, A., & Sawyer, C. B. (2017). Unaccompanied refugee minors from Central America: Understanding their journey and implications for counselors. *The Professional Counselor, 7*(4), 360–374. https://doi.org/10.15241/amt.7.4.360

United Nations. (n.d.). *Refugees and migrants: Definitions.* https://refugeesmigrants.un.org/definitions

United Nations High Commissioner for Refugees. (2016). *Children on the run: Unaccompanied children leaving Central America and Mexico and the need for international protection.* https://www.unhcr.org/us/children-run

Updegraff, K. A., Umaña-Taylor, A. J., McHale, S. M., Wheeler, L. A., & Perez-Brena, N. J. (2012). Mexican-origin youth's cultural orientations and adjustment: Changes from early to late adolescence. *Child Development, 83*(5), 1655–1671. https://doi.org/10.1111/j.1467-8624.2012.01800.x

U.S. Census Bureau. (2019). *2002–2019 American Community Survey 3-year public use microdata samples* [SAS data file]. https://www.census.gov/programs-surveys/acs/microdata/access.html

U.S. Department of Education. (2016). Tools and resources for identifying all English learners. In *English learner toolkit.* https://www2.ed.gov/about/offices/list/oela/english-learner-toolkit/chap1.pdf

U.S. Department of Justice, Office of Public Affairs. (2018, April 6). *Attorney General announces zero-tolerance policy for criminal illegal entry* [Press release]. https://www.justice.gov/opa/pr/attorney-general-announces-zero-tolerance-policy-criminal-illegal-entry

Valdez, C. R., & Martinez, E. (2019). Mexican immigrant fathers' recognition of and coping with maternal depression: The influence of meaning-making on marital and co-parenting roles among men participating in a family intervention. *Journal of Latinx Psychology, 7*(4), 304–321. https://doi.org/10.1037/lat0000132

Valicenti-McDermott, M., Shulman, L., Hottinger, K., Burrows, B., Bernstein, L., & Seijo, R. (2010, May 1–4). *Effect of ethnicity, bilingualism and other demographic characteristics at age of diagnosis of autism spectrum disorder* [Paper presentation]. Pediatric Academic Societies Annual Meeting, Vancouver, British Columbia, Canada.

van Ecke, Y. (2005). Immigration from an attachment perspective. *Social Behavior and Personality, 33*(5), 467–476. https://doi.org/10.2224/sbp.2005.33.5.467

Verkuyten, M., Wiley, S., Deaux, K., & Fleischmann, F. (2019). To be both (and more): Immigration and identity multiplicity. *Journal of Social Issues, 75*(2), 390–413. https://doi.org/10.1111/josi.12324

Vesely, C. K., DeMulder, E. K., Sansbury, A. B., Davis, E. F., Letiecq, B. L., Willard, I., Goodman, R. D., & de la Comunidad, A. (2021). 'A place where my children could learn to read, write, and play': The search for early care and education among undocumented Central American immigrant mothers. *Early Childhood Research Quarterly, 56*, 306–319. https://doi.org/10.1016/j.ecresq.2021.03.016

Vostanis, P. (2010). Mental health services for children in public care and other vulnerable groups: Implications for international collaboration. *Clinical Child Psychology and Psychiatry, 15*(4), 555–571. https://doi.org/10.1177/1359104510377715

Wallace, I. F. (2018). *Universal screening of young children for developmental disorders: Unpacking the controversies* (Publication No. OP-0048-1802). RTI Press. https://doi.org/10.3768/rtipress.2018.op.0048.1802

Ward, N., & Batalova, J. (2023). *Frequently requested statistics on immigrants and immigration in the United States.* Migration Information Source. https://www.migrationpolicy.org/article/frequently-requested-statistics-immigrants-and-immigration-united-states

WIDA Consortium. (2021). *Test policy handbook.* Board of Regents of the University of Wisconsin System.

World Health Organization. (2021). *Refugee and migrant health: Global competency standards for health workers.* https://apps.who.int/iris/handle/10665/350533

Yoo, S.-Y. (2019). The impact of immigrant parental stress on the risk of child maltreatment among Korean immigrant parents. *Journal of Child & Adolescent Trauma, 12*(1), 49–59. https://doi.org/10.1007/s40653-017-0173-9

Yoshikawa, H., & Kalil, A. (2011). The effects of parental undocumented status on the developmental contexts of young children in immigrant families: Undocumented status in immigrant families. *Child Development Perspectives, 5*(4), 291–297. https://doi.org/10.1111/j.1750-8606.2011.00204.x

Zayas, L. H., Aquilar-Gaxiola, S., Yoon, H., & Rey, G. N. (2015). The distress of citizen-children with detained and deported parents. *Journal of Child and Family Studies, 24*(11), 3213–3223. https://doi.org/10.1007/s10826-015-0124-8

Chapter 8

Counseling With Immigrant, Refugee, and Birthright Adolescents

Adolescence, defined as the stage between 10 and 19 years of age by the World Health Organization (n.d.), has always been described as a significant developmental period. This chapter uses this definitional age range to refer to "adolescents" or "youth" unless otherwise specified in the research provided. Social relationships and identity development are recognized as essential in this period as both sexes evolve physically, cognitively, and emotionally. Erikson (1964) described identity development as the primary task of adolescence. Of course, we have come to recognize that identity is not fixed in adolescence but continues to evolve. For immigrant and birthright adolescents, there likely are different factors affecting how they see themselves. Academic and career development, including considerations for postsecondary options, is one important part of adolescence. Questions about appearance, such as standards of beauty that are culture bound, puberty, developing physical features, family responsibilities, social status, and academic and extracurricular demands at school may take a toll on mental well-being and impact an adolescent's sense of belonging. Family discord can occur as adolescents move toward adulthood, particularly if an adolescent is responsible for younger siblings or is the voice for the family, if the adolescent is in a family in which members are undocumented, and/or if the adolescent has unresolved feelings about leaving their family or friends in their home country.

Learning Objectives

- Delineate the developmental needs of immigrant and refugee adolescents 13–18 years old.
- Differentiate the mental health needs of adolescents who have immigrated from the mental health needs of first- and second-generation adolescents with immigrant parents.
- Describe how student support services personnel and other providers who work in schools can support youth who are immigrants and refugees.

- Identify the barriers immigrant and refugee adolescents must navigate to achieve their academic and career goals, as well as the assets they have to do so.
- Discern how familial and community expectations affect immigrant and refugee youth (IRY).

The following section introduces a self-assessment to gauge your existing knowledge of culturally responsive counseling frameworks designed to address inequities and marginalization, ethical considerations in working with immigrant and refugee populations, and the Multicultural and Social Justice Counseling Competencies (MSJCC; Ratts et al., 2015) needed to do so. This brief assessment aims to explore your current understanding of key concepts and provide a foundation for further learning.

Self-assessment: Please respond to the following statements by rating yourself on the following Likert scale: *strongly agree, agree, disagree, strongly disagree,* or *unsure.*

1. I understand the unique needs of refugee and immigrant adolescent clients, especially unaccompanied immigrant youth.
2. I have a basic understanding of the legal rights of IRY so that I can recognize situations when their rights are being exploited or ignored.
3. I feel I can effectively collaborate with families of IRY to support the mental health of the adolescent client.
4. I can implement strategies in school and community systems to systemically support immigrant adolescents for the sake of their academic, career, and social-emotional development.
5. I recognize how the process of acculturation may improve or impede IRY academic, career, and social-emotional outcomes.

Who Are IRY?

Youth who are foreign born or have lived with at least one foreign-born parent in 2015–2019 make up 22% (i.e., almost 10.4 million) of the 14–24-year-old demographic in the United States (Annie E. Casey Foundation, 2023). In 2019, foreign-born youth between 5 and 17 years of age made up 5% of the total U.S. population (Batlova et al., 2021). The highest percentage of this group were born in Latin America, followed by Asia. The population of IRY continues to grow in rural settings (Lichter & Johnson, 2020). In most states in the United States, immigrant children are more likely than U.S.-born children to have two parents in the home. As far as educational attainment, more than 5.3 million IRY had enrolled in higher education in 2018; of those, 1.7 million were first-generation and 3.6 million were second-generation immigrant students (Higher Ed Immigration Portal, n.d.).

Unaccompanied Immigrant Youth

In 2021, 147,000 unaccompanied immigrant youth arrived through the Mexican-U.S. border. Three fourths of these youth were between the ages of 15 and 17, and at least two thirds were males. Counseling professionals need to be aware of typical experiences detained unaccompanied adolescents have endured. First, it is typical for unaccompanied immigrant youth to have experienced dangerous conditions in their home country. For example, young women and girls are vulnerable to gender-based violence, especially femicide, or gender-related killings. According to a United Nations Office on Drugs and Crime (2022) report, femicide is an international issue, with Asia recording the largest number of female-related killings followed by Africa, the Americas (i.e., North, South, and Central America and the Caribbean), Europe, and Oceania. Femicide and other forms of violence are notoriously prevalent in Central America in an area known as the Northern

Triangle, inclusive of the countries of El Salvador, Guatemala, and Honduras (Bay, 2021; Wolfe, 2023). Such societal violence in Central America and other countries may compel parents and their children to leave their homes to seek safer conditions in other countries (Anastario et al., 2015; United Nations High Commissioner for Refugees, 2018).

As previously mentioned in other chapters in this book, the migration process is also often fraught with life-threatening situations in which migrant youth are at increased risk (e.g., sex trafficking; Leyva-Flores et al., 2019; Vogt, 2013). Once immigrants who are minors arrive in the United States, they may evade U.S. Immigration and Customs Enforcement (ICE) officials or be detained by them. If they enter federal custody, after officials have determined that they are unaccompanied, they are placed in one of three settings based on an assessment process: nonsecure shelter care, secure care, or transitional foster care (Anastario et al., 2015). If these officials can find a suitable sponsor, they are then transferred to those placements. Many of these placements include a parent or family member (Office of Refugee Resettlement, 2023a). Even though many immigrants and refugees have faced traumatic events, only around 10% who were detained receive post-release services despite the likelihood that they have been exposed to family separation, trauma before and during their migration to the United States, interrupted education, and other experiences that can cause psychological distress (Lichter & Johnson, 2020).

Legal Rights

Unaccompanied immigrant youth have a few legal options in the United States. These options include sponsorship, special status classification, and deportation.

Sponsorship. The number of unaccompanied youth placed with sponsors across the United States has risen almost every year since 2015 (Office of Refugee Resettlement, 2023a). In 2023, many of these youth (n = 113,495) were released to sponsors (Office of Refugee Resettlement, 2023b), who are usually family members willing to provide food, housing, and medical and mental health care to unaccompanied immigrant youth and have completed a background check and met other eligibility criteria to be granted placement. Home studies are conducted when unaccompanied immigrant youth have been identified as a victim of abuse, neglect, or sex trafficking or have a disability (William Wilberforce Trafficking Victims Protection Reauthorization Act, 2008), although these studies are not conducted as often as recommended. Unaccompanied immigrant youth who have been abused, neglected, or trafficked or who have a disability may be granted a T visa, or temporary legal status in the United States for up to 4 years under the Victims of Trafficking and Violence Protection Act (2000). This act allows persons who meet these criteria the ability to seek assistance from law enforcement and other social services to avoid further victimization and harm. If granted a T visa, immigrants are subsequently eligible to apply for lawful permanent residence (green card) after 3 years of lawful presence in the United States.

Special immigrant juvenile status. Unaccompanied immigrant youth are eligible to apply for special immigrant juvenile status (SIJS) when they are unable to reunite with their parents due to abuse, abandonment, or neglect and meet certain other criteria (e.g., unmarried). Mental health providers should be aware of SIJS and advocate for unaccompanied immigrant youth if the minors qualify for this protection. SIJS allows immigrant youth, who need protection from the state juvenile court, to obtain lawful permanent immigration status (U.S. Citizenship and Immigration Services [USCIS], 2023).

Deportation. Unaccompanied youth are also at risk for deportation, which is the action of forcing a noncitizen to leave a country where they currently reside, and they may face these legal proceedings without representation. Since immigrant court cases are deemed civil rather than criminal in classification, unaccompanied youth are not appointed lawyers in these venues. However, counselors should be aware that children who enter the

United States without legal documentation may access legal pro bono federal, state, and local governmental services, as well as those provided by nonprofit organizations. Legal representation matters: 12% of unaccompanied minors represented by an attorney were deported, whereas 80% of minors are deported when legal representation is not utilized (Goldberg, 2020).

Deferred Action for Childhood Arrivals

Twenty-five percent of children and adolescents in the United States are immigrants, and these include naturalized U.S. citizens, authorized immigrants, and undocumented immigrants (Annie E. Casey Foundation, 2023). Students who were not born in the United States but immigrated, live, and attend school in the United States are considered undocumented students (Enyioha, 2019). According to the National Immigration Law Center, an undocumented immigrant is someone who (a) entered the United States without inspection or with fraudulent documents or (b) entered legally as undocumented but then violated the terms of their status and remained in the United States without permission (Enyioha, 2019). A particularly critical aspect of this issue in the United States is the question of undocumented immigrants who were brought into this country as minors. These minor children, who become undocumented students, were youth when their parents or family members brought them to the United States. Therefore, in many cases, they have lived most of their lives in the United States and have grown up learning the English language and American customs (Enyioha, 2019). To protect these immigrant youth who arrived in the United States when they were children, USCIS created Deferred Action for Childhood Arrivals (DACA).

DACA is an administrative relief program that protects eligible immigrant youth from being deported (University of California at Berkeley, 2023). The secretary of the U.S. Department of Homeland Security (DHS) announced on June 15, 2012, that certain people who came to the United States as children and meet the required guidelines may request consideration of deferred action for a period of 2 years (DHS, 2021). This allows undocumented youth to be eligible for work authorization but does not provide lawful status (DHS, 2021). Even so, because of the uncertainty of their status, many DACA students face constant fear of their family members being deported while they are at school.

To become a DACA recipient, one must obtain an application. To meet DACA requirements, undocumented immigrants must have been physically present in the United States and under the age of 31 as of June 15, 2012, have arrived in the United States prior to their 16th birthday, and have continuously resided in the United States since June 15, 2007. Furthermore, at the time of making their request for consideration of deferred action with USCIS, applicants must have had no unlawful record on June 15, 2012, were enrolled in school or graduated or obtained a general equivalency diploma, were not convicted of a felony or significant misdemeanor or three or more other misdemeanors, and did not pose a threat to national security or public safety (DHS, 2021).

DACA provides undocumented beneficiaries with a Social Security number, temporary lawful presence, and better opportunities for the future (USCIS, 2023). DACA provides many students with the ability to live free from deportation and work legally in the United States (Gonzales, 2009). Although U.S federal law guarantees undocumented students a free public K–12 education, they face many more challenges than their citizen peers when pursuing higher education, including social, financial, and legal barriers. For instance, these students must overcome the obstacles of language barriers, separated families, fear of deportation, pressure to contribute to family income, eligibility rights, and the lack of information about postsecondary education (Gonzales, 2009). In fact, in November 2017, the Migration Policy Institute reported that out of 690,000 DACA recipients, only 18% were enrolled in higher education (Capps et al., 2017).

Although federal law does not deter DACA students from pursuing a postsecondary degree, it also does not override state statutes that can stand in the way of postsecondary pursuits. Because education of undocumented minors is not mentioned in the U.S. Constitution, federal statutes, or treaties, individual states must make their own determinations about undocumented minors. Not only are there restraints from state laws, but there are several federal laws and regulations in place that deter DACA students from obtaining higher education. For instance, the Illegal Immigration Reform and Immigrant Responsibility Act (1996) vastly changed the immigration laws of the United States. This act suggests that undocumented students cannot receive federal postsecondary benefits based on where they live and created a longer, more difficult process for undocumented immigrants to legalize their status (National Conference of State Legislatures, 2021).

Nationwide, all DACA students are ineligible for federal financial aid, including grants, work-study, and government loans (U.S. Department of Education, n.d.). Title IV of the Higher Education Act requires that all applicants for federal financial aid be U.S citizens or U.S. permanent residents (Enyioha, 2019). Similarly, the Personal Responsibility and Work Opportunity Responsibility Act prohibits undocumented students from receiving forms of government assistance, including federal financial aid (Ruge & Iza, 2005). Public postsecondary institutions receive funding from their state; therefore, they are obligated to abide by the laws of their state regarding postsecondary education for DACA students (Enyioha, 2019). Unlike public education systems, privately funded universities do not have to abide by the state laws and can determine their own regulations regarding DACA students (Gonzales, 2009). Nonetheless, private school tuition is often twice the cost of public in-state tuition, which can be cost-prohibitive without any financial assistance. Even though both public and private institutions may allow DACA students admission, unless their families are able to afford college expenses (e.g., tuition, fees, room, board, books, supplies), they are commonly not able to attend. Therefore, although these institutions may not directly deny undocumented students college access, they can indirectly impact their ability to attend by not offering them financial assistance.

DACA status does not provide undocumented students access to federal or state-based financial aid, although this varies by state. In response to disparity across states regarding whether to grant undocumented students' postsecondary enrollment, in 2008, DHS and ICE issued a letter indicating that states have the power to determine whether DACA students have access to higher education institutions (Billini, 2021). Thus, each state may decide how to regulate its public postsecondary education system and has the authority to prohibit, limit, or permit undocumented students the right to pursue higher education within the state (Enyioha, 2019). Unfortunately, in some states such as Georgia and Indiana, DACA students are banned from pursuing public higher education (Billini, 2021).

In the Arizona 2022 midterm elections, a referendum was approved to provide students access to in-state tuition (USCIS, 2023). Similarly, 23 other states provide in-state tuition privilege to DACA students, including California, Colorado, Connecticut, District of Columbia, Florida, Hawaii, Illinois, Kansas, Kentucky, Maryland, Minnesota, Nebraska, Nevada, New Jersey, New Mexico, New York, Oklahoma, Oregon, Rhode Island, Texas, Utah, Virginia, and Washington (Higher Ed Immigration Portal, n.d.). In addition, some states (California, Colorado, Connecticut, District of Columbia, Hawaii, Illinois, Maryland, Minnesota, Nevada, New Jersey, New Mexico, New York, Oregon, Rhode Island, Texas, Utah, Virginia, and Washington) do offer some state financial aid and access to scholarships (Higher Ed Immigration Portal, n.d.; Kovacs, 2022). Yet, most DACA students must rely on privately funded scholarships or their own financial resources, such as employment income and familial savings. The reality is that private scholarships have scarce funding, and most of them require U.S. citizenship or permanent legal residence (Gonzales, 2009). Therefore, even with DACA, undocumented students still face the challenge of locating financial assistance to help fund their education.

U.S. citizens have privileges that DACA students do not have with respect to higher education. They have access to employment, financial aid, and a legal status. Not only do DACA students not have these privileges, but they face discrimination and financial concerns and endure fear in relation to immigrant enforcement. Over the years, the DACA program has faced many threats such as lawsuits from across the country. In 2017, the Trump administration planned to phase out the DACA program in its entirety (Garcini et al., 2021). Although the Biden administration issued an executive order to protect this program, the existence of DACA continues to face uncertainty. As a result, there are heightened concerns among DACA recipients about their future and the possibility of stricter immigration enforcement. The uncertainty of their status and the uncertainty of what Congress may decide result in many recipients experiencing fear, anxiety, lowered self-esteem, depression, and marginalization (Billini, 2021). Furthermore, Kreisberg and Hsin (2020) believed that educational regression of undocumented college students (i.e., decreases in expected achievement of high-performing undocumented high school students as they pursue postsecondary degrees) relates to stressors associated with the lack of parity relative to "socio-legal structures at the national, state, and college level" (p. 3840).

In addition to challenges at the systemic or macrolevel, DACA students can experience microsystem- or mesosystem-level challenges such as discrimination, which is a type of stressor that can result in substantial mental health consequences (Velarde Pierce et al., 2021). Individuals experiencing discrimination have a higher predisposition to mental health distress such as anxiety and depressive symptoms, suicidal ideation, and psychological distress (Velarde Pierce et al., 2021). DACA students in the postsecondary education system may be more vulnerable to discrimination, as they are more likely to be associated with individuals from other racial/ethnic groups (Velarde Pierce et al., 2021). Furthermore, DACA students may face discrimination related to their immigrant status. This type of discrimination may show in the form of stigma, racist microaggressions, and institutional neglect (Velarde Pierce et al., 2021). In the college setting, Nienhusser et al. (2016) noted that microaggressions occur often in the college choice process; microaggressions described by Sue (2010) are "everyday verbal, nonverbal, and environmental slights, snubs, and insults, whether intentional or unintentional, that communicate hostile, derogatory, or negative messages to target people based solely upon their marginalized group membership" (p. 3). Despite facing the effects of microaggressions, undocumented college students were recognized to have positive attributes (Nienhusser & Romandia, 2022), including awareness of intersecting aspects of their identity and the ability to navigate barriers with resilience to attain academic, career, and personal success. Nevertheless, a study found that undocumented immigrant students, because of microaggressions, had academic self-doubt and feelings of inferiority, which ultimately impacted their college decision-making process (Nienhusser et al., 2016).

Compounding these challenges to mental health and achievement, DACA students often experience guilt and stress about their decision to pursue DACA status. When DACA students confirm their unlawful presence in the United States, they expose their undocumented family members to ICE (Billini, 2021). Therefore, many DACA recipients feel terrified with the anticipation and threat of a family member being deported or detained, which can lead to diminished academic achievement and increased mental health distress (Velarde Pierce et al., 2021). Because of fear and uncertainty, discrimination, and the threat of losing their families, DACA recipients predominantly experience emotions and states of stress, fear, and anxiety. As previously mentioned, the environmental stressors, including systemic oppression, policy changes, past and current trauma, and uncertainty about the future, can lead to an increase in mental health distress and concerns (Cadenas et al., 2020). Based on clinical research, the most reported and observable psychological stressors experienced by DACA recipients include grief and loss, depression, anxiety, PTSD, complex trauma, adjustment difficulties, and low self-esteem or self-worth (Cadenas et al., 2020).

Although the mental health of undocumented students may be compromised, DACA recipients may avoid seeking mental health services because they do not see the potential usefulness for addressing the underlying barriers associated with their legal vulnerability (Cadenas et al., 2020). In order to support DACA students and improve one's counseling practice, clinicians need to review existing models and recommendations for supporting this population. Commonalities among these frameworks include (a) being attentive to the way that immigrants' psychological experiences are shaped by social and contextual factors; (b) recognizing discrimination within the system; (c) assessing for multiple forms of trauma; and (d) appreciating challenges related to their experiences at the premigration, migration-specific, and postmigration stages (Cadenas et al., 2020). Mental health practice with immigrants is enriched by using intersectional, ecological, social justice, and critical frameworks (Cadenas et al., 2020). Not only is it crucial to review existing models, but when working with DACA students, counselors should call on their MSJCC skills as they listen to their stories, gain understanding about their cultural beliefs and acculturative status, learn about immigration policy and legal rights, stay apprised of fluctuating policy changes, identify one's own biases and misconceptions, and connect with community resources (Cadenas et al., 2020).

The term legally illegal connotes the limbo these individuals face, expressing in derogatory terms the idiosyncratic characteristics of DACA recipients in a society where they are allowed to be present but have no pathway to citizenship or residency (Sahay et al., 2016). The temporary and limiting nature of this status creates notable constraints, such as lack of access to opportunities, inability to plan, and constant preoccupation with sociopolitical stressors (Cadenas et al., 2020). Furthermore, the U.S. immigration policy affects DACA students' well-being via political posturing threatening deportation, limiting educational access, and disrupting social participation. College students who are undocumented must navigate university systems that directly and indirectly prevent their participation, while also dealing with a multitude of stressors generated by U.S. immigration policies. As helping professionals, we must advocate to provide DACA students with equitable access to postsecondary options and resources so that they can pursue their preferred career opportunities to succeed as adults.

Developmental Needs of IRY

Academic Development

Disparities related to educational outcomes of IRY are evident. Foreign-born immigrants are at higher risk for dropping out of middle school or high school (10.1%) than the 2020 national average of 5.3%, whereas only 5.1% of U.S.-born first-generation immigrants and 4.9% of second-generation (or higher) immigrants dropped out of high school (National Center for Education Statistics, 2023). Undocumented immigrants' educational attainment is significantly lower than that of U.S.-born IRY (Segal, 2018). Furthermore, racial/ethnic minorities and English language learners are disproportionately identified to receive special education services (Bevan-Brown, 2006; Estrem & Zhang, 2010; Gabel et al., 2009). This represents a tracking system that often is not reversible and affects placement in other higher level classes.

In supporting the academic development of IRY, counselors should recognize the layers of demographic diversity within this population to avoid making stereotypical assumptions about "all" immigrants. Contextual factors, such as home and school environments, have subsequent implications for the academic development, education, and achievement of

IRY (Gindling & Poggio, 2012; Pivovarova & Powers, 2019). Familial contextual factors that have a protective effect on academic outcomes include an IRY family's valuing of education, financial resources, educational attainment of parents, and English language proficiency in the home. Many immigrant families (e.g., Latinx) value education and see it as a way of providing financial stability (Arellanes et al., 2019). School counselors and other educational personnel can work with immigrant students and parents to help them understand the impact that academic preparation has on postsecondary education and careers (Watkinson & Hersi, 2014). Still other factors, such as socioeconomic status, affect academic outcomes (American Psychological Association, 2017; Crosnoe & López Turley, 2011). About 24% of immigrant youth in the United States live in low-income families, and 26% have no parent with a high school diploma (Crosnoe & López Turley, 2011); notably, these data challenge helping professionals to recognize that a large proportion of IRY live above the poverty line and in homes with parents who have at least a high school diploma. Furthermore, 53.2% of immigrants in the United States speak English very well.

Contextual factors in families that put IRY at academic risk include separation from their parents during their migration and interrupted schooling. IRY who had been separated from their parents during migration were much more likely to have an education gap than either immigrant children born in the United States or those who migrated with their parents (Arellanes et al., 2019). Foreign-born immigrants educated outside the United States were more likely to experience interrupted schooling (Potochnick, 2018).

Counselors and other school personnel need to recall Maslow's (1943) hierarchy of needs to recognize the basic physiological needs of IRY to be met before educational growth can be expected. Furthermore, all counselors, educators, and others who work with IRY must consider their MSJCC competency development to avoid acting on biased beliefs that may affect IRY outcomes. For example, school personnel tend to perpetuate the Asian model minority myth by engaging adolescents from immigrant groups that are believed to be more educationally successful, while simultaneously ascribing negative attitudes or behaviors toward Latinx students who tend to face socioeconomic barriers (Crosnoe & López Turley, 2011). Asian families also experience economic hardships. It is also important for educational personnel to consider that the purpose of school may vary for IRY (Drake, 2017). Some high school IRY, for instance, may see the school setting as a necessity to learn English to find employment or may simply attend school to comply with the law rather than having other educational priorities (Drake, 2017). This is juxtaposed with the fact that secondary school research provides data showing how immigrant youth are often more academically successful compared with children with U.S.-born parents (Crosnoe & López Turley, 2011). Thus, some IRY see K–12 schooling as a path to upward mobility and aspire toward college and other postsecondary options.

Of course, relationships with school personnel affect academic development of IRY (Suárez-Orozco et al., 2010). Teachers and student support personnel such as school counselors can impact immigrant and refugee students' sense of belonging in schools (Durand & Blackwell, 2022; Eckstein et al., 2021). Middle school immigrant students' perceived feelings of acceptance and respect in the school environment relate to feeling appreciated for their academic success and effort (Durand & Blackwell, 2022). Other examples of school-based interventions that educators can implement to support IRY academically focus on developing basic skills and an understanding of what is expected of them to succeed in the classrooms in their respective host country, engaging IRY in conversations about their cultural knowledge, initiating mentor programs, and offering in-school counseling groups (e.g., grief) for the sake of building connections and support among IRY around their lived experiences (Drake, 2017).

Career Development

Undocumented adolescents are among the most vulnerable of workers in the United States and they face a unique set of obstacles to obtain a sufficient education and career (Autin et al., 2018). Thus, counselors should be knowledgeable of the factors that contribute to academic and career development, including career decision-making, among this population. Perez et al. (2009) identified protective factors that support academic achievement for immigrant youth, such as parental valuing of education, participation in extracurricular and volunteer activities, and personal and environmental resources. For adolescents, working long hours is a risk factor for academic difficulty (Perez et al., 2009; Staff et al., 2020). For IRY, working long hours can also lead to feeling disconnected from peers in schools, less time for homework and participation in extracurricular activities, and increase in the likelihood of dropping out of high school. Still, counselors and educators must recognize that working adolescents may improve family circumstances such as living conditions (e.g., affording rent in a safer neighborhood, preventing homelessness) and food insecurity in their homes.

For many adolescent immigrants, the transition from adolescence to adulthood (and more specifically from high school to college or the workforce) can be a daunting experience. Some contextual factors such as family values, culture, and access to academic and financial resources contribute significantly to the academic success and career decision-making of immigrant adolescents (Bonifacio, 2016). In addition to barriers that may impede academic development, IRY face other impediments that affect their postsecondary and career attainment. For example, immigrant adolescents may not be able to rely their familial and social networks for support because they may not have knowledge or experience to navigate U.S. educational systems, the job market, or financial assistance applications needed to overcome barriers (Schuchart & Siebel, 2021). These issues are often known as information gaps (George-Jackson & Gast, 2015). Similarly, access gaps (Cook et al., 2015) can also impede IRY who do not have access to services and educational opportunities afforded to others; examples include broadband or Wi-Fi access in their homes, computer/technology hardware and software, caring adults who understand school curriculum and expectations, and career development opportunities to access the labor market (Organisation for Economic Co-operation and Development, 2020). It is also noteworthy that financial pressures may continue because of obligations to families in the home country.

To reduce these gaps and improve access to postsecondary options, Perez (2010) provided some practical recommendations, including sharing lists of scholarship/financial resources for particular racial/ethnic groups, engaging in outreach and recruitment of undocumented students, and organizing events involving panel discussions from current or past students so that undocumented students and their families can learn requirements as well as strategies to enroll and persist through college. Additionally, counselors can advocate for system-wide institutional assessments of higher education to understand the professional development and training needs of an institution so that undocumented students and refugees are adequately supported (Valenzuela, et al., 2015).

The career development process consists of exploring and deciding on a career, gaining knowledge and training to begin to pursue that career, and understanding the steps to take to find that first job or pursue graduate education (Storlie, 2011). For IRY, the career development process can be constrained by legal limitations that may impact many other aspects of their lives (Ortiz & Hinojosa, 2010). Adolescent immigrants face economic, structural, social, and psychological barriers when securing educational and career-related success. The most detrimental of barriers is related to potential economic barriers (Autin et al., 2018). High socioeconomic status individuals and families tend to have resources to cross the borders legally, whereas undocumented immigrants tend to belong to lower socioeconomic brackets (Autin et al., 2018). In addition, undocumented immigrants are more likely to obtain lower paying jobs and do not have access to social service benefits such as food stamps that could help offset their income (Autin et al., 2018). A research study conducted by the University of Florida reported that the primary barrier for adolescent immigrants and refugees trying to pursue their desired career paths was lack of economic resources (Autin et al., 2018), including paying out-of-state tuition for college courses, funding their housing, and lack of access to federal financial aid (Autin et al., 2018). Simply put, economic barriers may directly and indirectly impact immigrant adolescents' career decision-making and outcomes.

Another routine stage in adolescent career development is creating plans for postsecondary education or the workforce. Approximately 65,000 undocumented students graduate from high school annually (this number increases every year because there are more students enrolled) with career aspirations, yet many face multiple obstacles when determining their next steps (Cisneros, 2013). While immigrant and refugee students have reported a strong desire to develop careers, citizenship status is a potential obstacle when considering postsecondary education. Although many undocumented students have the ambition to attend college, they encounter legal or financial barriers that limit their access. As mentioned earlier in this chapter, in 1965, Title IV of the Higher Education Act mandated that all students be U.S. citizens or U.S. permanent residents to receive federal aid (Cisneros, 2013). Federal aid includes work-study opportunities or federal loans (Cisneros, 2013). Although this act did not take away college access to undocumented students, it did make affordability more difficult in both public and private institutions.

While obtaining a postsecondary education has been made difficult for immigrants and refugees, higher education can significantly increase individual earnings and lower unemployment rates (Pew Research Center, 2016). Individuals in the workforce without a college degree reported that their upward mobility in the job market was limited by their lack of educational credentials (Pew Research Center, 2016). Furthermore, the Pew Research Center (2016) found that Americans who lack a 4-year college degree declined to apply for a job they felt they were qualified for because the job in question required a bachelor's degree. Therefore, limiting college access for undocumented immigrant and refugee students can greatly hinder their career development and narrow the opportunities they have when creating postsecondary plans.

As a result of limitations on educational opportunities, undocumented students' sense of well-being, employment rates, income, and future socioeconomic status can be negatively affected (Groce & Johnson, 2021). Counselors working with immigrant and refugee students need to recognize that many of these students have high college aspirations but face barriers that can be detrimental when addressing the next stages in their career development. Counselors can support IRY by advocating and finding alternative solutions to help them achieve their postsecondary goals. This is where the MSJCC (Ratts et al., 2015) are an asset. Counselors must remember the lack of privilege and the marginalization of most immigrants and refugees and not "blame the victim."

Many facets of the ordinary career planning process conflict with or are not relevant to immigrant or refugee students. The career development of students who are interested in pursuing higher education is a key developmental milestone that can be significantly more complicated for immigrant and refugee students (Ortiz & Hinojosa, 2010). As part of their postsecondary journey, students must become aware of their interests, strengths, values, and abilities while exploring majors and career options. A key factor in career development is the assertion that making a career choice fundamentally relies on the match between the student's skills, values, and dispositions and the characteristics of the career or job setting (Ortiz & Hinojosa, 2010). For students, solidifying a career choice can rely on an individual's ability to envision themselves in a career and understand what role they can play in the workplace (Ortiz & Hinojosa, 2010).

This can be difficult when career assessment and self-assessment processes are not compatible with the lives of immigrant students. These types of assessments focus on individual skills and interests and commonly provide insight into career opportunities and suggestions. Some career assessments are available in multiple languages, but it still can be difficult to find career assessments written in an immigrant's preferred language or that have multicultural considerations (Rowland & Davis, 2014). Similar to standardized testing, career assessments are commonly based on the knowledge and values of majority groups, which can create bias against minority groups (Kim & Zabelina, 2015). Variables such as race, community status, language background, socioeconomic status, and culture can affect the outcomes of these assessments and, if not considered, make the results less valid or reliable (Kim & Zabelina, 2015). Individual culture and background may lead to the inaccuracy of assessments; therefore, the results can be misleading for IRY (Rowland & Davis, 2014). Thus, it is up to counselors to have extensive conversations with the immigrant and refugee adolescents to further explore their dreams, interests, and opportunities. Regardless of the dream, it is a starting place for planning.

There are many factors that are not typically considered in career development and decision-making that need to be integrated into the career counseling of adolescent immigrant students. For instance, Asian and African immigrant students are more likely to integrate their parents' opinions regarding their career choice and feel pressured to choose careers that bring status to the family (Ortiz & Hinojosa, 2010). For some cultures, certain career choices come with stigma, and immigrant youth may express poor self-concept and low self-efficacy regarding several career options (Wambu, 2018). Therefore, career development strategies designed for immigrant students must address the needs of immigrant populations, including parents, use career counseling techniques that attend to the unique experiences of immigrant students, and provide immigrant students with a social network to guide and support their career planning process (Watkinson & Hersi, 2014). Counselors can consider the following: become familiar with college access for immigrants, research funding resources for first-generation students, solicit support for outside resources, and develop trusting and therapeutic relationships with IRY and their families (Groce & Johnson, 2021).

In addition, IRY may not be able to always rely on the support of their parents and social networks. Some immigrants and refugees are unaccompanied minors; other parental figures do not possess the necessary knowledge to assist their adolescent in the career planning and preparation process (Schuchart & Siebel, 2021). Thus, another strategy that counselors can use to enhance the career development of immigrant adolescents is school-family partnerships (Watkinson & Hersi, 2014). These partnerships can provide immigrant students with the support they need in navigating career planning while also informing parents and family members about the career development process (Watkinson & Hersi, 2014). For example, counselors can refer immigrant adolescent students to job shadow opportunities, internships, tutoring programs, and enrichment programs that build basic skills and provide mentorship to support their engagement in career development and decision-making (Watkinson & Hersi, 2014). Furthermore, school-family partnerships help to eliminate the cultural disconnect that can occur between immigrant students and school culture (Watkinson & Hersi, 2014). At the same time, parents should be informed about the benefits for their children since these may be very different types of experiences.

For some IRY, economic, structural, social, and psychological barriers exist as well. It is our job as counselors to act as advocates and consider multicultural factors when engaging in career counseling while creating programs that provide sufficient resources for adolescent immigrants and refugees. While there are barriers that IRY face as they navigate their career development process, counselors can reduce information and access gaps so that first-generation students and others living in immigrant families can reach their post-secondary goals. Once again, counselors are encouraged to reference the MSJCC (Ratts et al., 2015), Bronfenbrenner's (1977) ecological model, and the family's migration process.

Social-Emotional Development

Adolescence is an extremely important time for social-emotional development when heightened sensitivity to social stimuli and the increased need for peer interaction emerge. Adolescence is also a time when mental health problems can manifest, with 50% of all lifetime mental illnesses beginning by age 14 and reaching 75% by age 24 (National Alliance on Mental Illness, 2023).

For adolescents, establishing self-identity and creating a sense of belonging are key developmental tasks that can be inhibited by discrimination and bullying, which can lead youth to choose antisocial types of behavior such as gang affiliation or juvenile delinquent activities to find that connection to others.

Discrimination

U.S. federal law prohibits discrimination based on national origin (U.S. Department of Health and Human Services, 2023). Yet, U.S. governmental policies have historically classified and limited rights of individuals based on race and country of origin, from the first national census in 1790 to the eugenics movement of the 1920s (Prewitt, 2005) to current immigration policy (Parker, 2022). Although federal policies have been discriminatory of people based on national origin for decades (Pincus, 1999/2018), discrimination toward students of color and immigrants, as well as fear of deportation within the IRY group, has increased since the Trump administration (Johnston et al., 2022). This phenomenon, known as the "Trump effect," uses political rhetoric to incite fear of immigrants among U.S. citizens, and it continues to permeate K–12 schools and harm students' mental health (Torres et al., 2022; Tummala-Narra, 2020). Ozdimir et al. (2018) found similar issues in Sweden, noting ethnic harassment was based on prejudiced beliefs about immigrants, referencing Coenders et al.'s (2004) ethnic group competition theory as one rationale for hurtful actions toward immigrant youth based on perceived threats of these ethnic groups. The process of *othering*, described by Curle (2020) as focusing on differences to dismantle connectedness between people because of political, sociocultural, and other motives, can lead to discrimination, bullying, and acculturation issues for immigrant adolescents.

The othering of adolescents with an immigrant background seems to be an international phenomenon with detrimental outcomes for mental and physical health, as well as academic and other developmental problems (Genç, 2022; Zeiders et al., 2020). Adolescents who reported experiencing high levels of discrimination combined with high levels of moral injury had poorer mental health (Tummala-Narra, 2020). For many IRY in the United States, discrimination is unrelenting. For Somali IRY, who are at increased risk for discrimination due to the intersecting marginalized identities many of these youth represent (e.g., Black, Muslim, immigrant), discrimination is reported as persistent in their lives (McEwen et al., 2022).

For example, Somali young adults identifying as immigrants or refugees reported that they had experienced high rates of discrimination in childhood and adolescence on a daily basis as well as additional critical incidents across their lifetime (Lincoln et al., 2021). Somali girls are at an additional risk to be marginalized due to the divergence of cultural expectations of their gender roles in the United States versus Somalia (Ellis, MacDonald, et al., 2010). For instance, more than 45% of girls in Somalia are married before the age of 18 (UNICEF, 2006). Also, many Somali girls wear the Muslim headscarf known as a hijab as a religious expectation, which is valued as a source of strength by Somali adolescent girls but is ridiculed by others (Leet-Otley, 2020). Lincoln et al. (2021) found the mental health of Somali youth was negatively impacted due to the discrimination they experienced.

Although adolescence is a difficult time for most individuals, and increasingly so for IRY due to the added layers of discrimination, bullying, and acculturation challenges, the school environment can be a welcoming and supportive space for the social-emotional development of IRY with intentional planning across the institution. Schools that focus on teacher training, curricular tasks, and classroom environments, aspects of the school as an organization, and district policies and practices can play an instrumental role in the intellectual and social-emotional development of immigrant and refugee adolescents (Eccles & Roeser, 2011). Gorski (2017) provided strategies for educators and other helping professionals to work toward equity for all students, including IRY, such as rejecting deficit ideologies and building coalitions with educators who are "different from me in terms of race, sexual orientation, gender, religion, home language, class, (dis)ability, and other identities" (p. 2).

Instilling cooperative classroom environments can make the IRY population feel supported in school by peers and adults from a variety of backgrounds (Miklikowska et al., 2021). Intercultural learning experiences coupled with learning about one's own heritage led to positive social outcomes for IRY in highly diverse schools (Aral et al., 2022). One model example within the University of Rochester (Rochester, Minnesota) is a refugee student alliance group, which connects refugee youth with mentors who provide college and career coaching, encourage IRY to engage in volunteer and leadership opportunities in their school and community, solicit donations for winter clothing and other IRY needs, and facilitate events such as film night to foster public discussions on topics such as the effect of climate change on migration (Refugee Student Alliance, n.d.).

Educators and community organizers must also consider how their actions can support or be considered adversarial to IRY. At a field placement site for interns under supervision of one of the authors (Cigrand), the following example was shared. Students with undocumented family members were not attending one class regularly. When the school counselor connected with the students, she learned that they felt uncomfortable going into a particular teacher's classroom because they feared ICE involvement (even though schools are not accessible to ICE) due to displays of Trump election merchandise in the classroom. Counselors can clarify legal rights with their students to dispel misconceptions. Furthermore, using the 2015 Professional Standards for Educational Leaders (National Policy Board for Educational Administration, 2015) as a guide, school administration can work with school personnel collaboratively to create culturally responsive schools through the implementation of policies and practices so that all students feel safe in schools (Pacheco, 2021).

Bullying

Marginalization and bullying of IRY is another pervasive issue in schools and other places where IRY engage with other youth. Notably, immigrant youth not only were more likely to be bullied than their peers but also were more likely to experience bullying related to religious or racial factors, which may be associated with discrimination, acculturation, and mental health among minoritized populations (Maynard et al., 2016). Bicultural acculturation and family support seem to be two factors that have the effect of decreasing the stress from discrimination (Haft et al., 2021). As immigrants acculturate to their host country, ethnic discrimination as perceived by immigrant adolescents reportedly decreases (Motti-Stefanidi et al., 2018). Vitoroulis and Georgiades (2017) found that ethnic congruence in schools, such as engaging with a peer group of other immigrant adolescents, seems to be a protective factor in decreasing bullying and discrimination and increasing peer relationships and social support networks. Motti-Stefanidi et al. (2018) recommended offering programming such as literacy programs to support IRY interactions with educators and peers. However, this recommendation is in a sense "blaming the victim" for the discrimination or bullying by putting the onus on the immigrant to change for the sake of assimilating with the host, or predominantly White, Americanized culture. Trying to assimilate does not lead to acceptance.

Other methods to decrease bullying and discrimination that focus on bullies or student and adult attitudes that may be oppressive should also be considered. Specific aspects of school environments can be beneficial or detrimental to the academic, career, and social-emotional development of immigrant students (Eckstein et al., 2021). One might imagine that moving from one country to another country, especially if multiple transitions occur during the migration journey to maintain the safety of the immigrant or refugee and their family members, may create a sense of insecurity or lack of belongingness. Therefore, IRY may benefit from school efforts to create a sense of social belongingness in adolescence (Albarello et al., 2021).

To create belongingness, American schools may find inspiration in the Japanese concept of *ibasho*. In Japan, private citizens came together to address a community issue in which students would not attend school because they did not feel accepted. So, citizens worked to create a refuge or a place of healing for these "truant" students by blending concepts of place, human relationships, and time. The emerging Japanese educational concept of ibasho, or a physical and psychological place where individuals feel a sense of acceptance, freedom, and security, is the type of space and climate schools should strive to achieve to support IYR (Kayama & Yamakawa, 2020). Tanaka (2021) provided a detailed discussion of the emergence of ibasho. In sum, refuge or "free schools" are provided to youth who have dropped out of traditional schools so that they have the opportunity to connect with other teens with similar passions and have a positive effect on society through mentor guidance, with the freedom to feel empowered to follow their interests rather than conform to rigid school systems. Safe spaces that encourage intercultural expression and connection to caring adults and like-minded peers seem to be an option that IRY could benefit from.

One bridge-building concept offered by Juang et al. (2018) focuses on creating "connections to people" between IRY and their peers and teachers, possibly through "connections to place" (p. 805), which could be applied to a school building or "school spirit" in a community. Finding social ties or spaces that IRY feel attached to not only may create a sense of security for them but also may foster relationships with others who feel attached to the same space, school, or community. To demonstrate and support immigrant students' safety and belongingness, some educators have practiced communicating affirmation, building shared knowledge and capacity, finding and mobilizing resources, and creating space for conversation (Lowenhaupt et al., 2021). Peer cooperation, when it is modeled and reinforced, can contribute to positive intergroup attitudes within classrooms for IRY (Miklikowska et al., 2021). The Joy Labs (Johnson, n.d.) is an example of cocreating a sense of belonging in community spaces. Johnson's work involves collaborating with community organizations, including immigrants and refugees, to paint murals and panels that are installed on community buildings. This intergenerational project meant community members ages 2–80 years helped to use art to provide welcoming messages to newcomers in the community. Additional groups and panels planned for this ongoing project focused on building community cohesion through storytelling and shared artistic creations.

The aforementioned project also aligns with Arora et al.'s (2021) recommendations about promoting family engagement of IRY; counselors and other helping professionals must be sensitive to the barriers that may prevent these families from participating in events and increase the training of adults working in schools and communities for the sake of developing positive relationships and diminishing discriminatory interactions. To build intercultural groups of support of IRY, D'Alonzo and Greene (2020) encouraged building trust within communities for the sake of empathizing with IRY and recognizing stressors, building bridges between individuals with common interests, separating fact from fiction in order to dispel myths, and engaging in positive, proactive damage reparation.

Gang Affiliation

According to the Federal Bureau of Investigation (FBI, n.d.), more than 33,000 prison gangs and street gangs are currently active in the United States. Of those, notorious transnational gangs, such as the Mara Salvatrucha (MS-13) and 18th Street gangs, continue to expand their influence in the United States and target adolescent-age recruits (FBI, n.d.). These gangs emerged in the 1980s in Los Angeles, California, and have expanded their networks to the Central American countries of El Salvador, Guatemala, and Honduras (FBI, n.d.). Other gangs, such as the Oriental Boys, have Vietnamese affiliations (Hong, 2010). Evidence of active gang violence can be found across the United States and around the world, with an ever-evolving list which can be found on the Gang Activity Map website (globalincidentmap.com).

While there is insignificant evidence to suggest immigration brings crime to communities (Scott, 2022), refugee youth are more likely than their U.S.-born peers to engage with gangs (FBI, 2023). Subsequent criminal behavior for youth who engage in gangs may include drug trafficking, firearms dealings, and related violent behaviors such as homicide. In a systematic review, Higginson et al. (2018) reported that gang affiliation is associated with increased alcohol and substance use, violent forms of delinquency, and increased sexual activity. Thus, prevention and intervention efforts are needed to reduce gang affiliation of IRY. Consideration of risk and protective factors may be helpful to do so.

Some risk factors for gang affiliation include being male, being between 12 and 20 years of age (when youth are at the highest risk for gang membership), having experiences with persistent racial discrimination, acculturation issues (Goodrum et al., 2015), and victimization (Higginson, et al., 2018). Additionally, Garduno and Brancale (2017) found that Hispanic youth were at higher risk for gang affiliation if they had low expectations of graduating from high school, experienced feelings of sadness and loneliness regularly, were recruited by a gang, or had siblings in gangs. Parenting practices can also be a risk factor; that is, harsh discipline, lack of parental monitoring, and poor parent-child relationships increase the risk for gang affiliation (Barnes et al, 2010; Goodrum et al., 2015; Kubik et al., 2019). At times, parents support gang engagement for the sake of supplementing income for the family (Ngo et al., 2013; M. J. Rossiter & Rossiter, 2009).

Parenting practices can also be a protective factor for IRY to avoid gang involvement, even in areas where gangs are prevalent (Cruz-Santiago & Ramirez-Garcia, 2011; Goodrum et al., 2015; Higginson et al., 2018). To support IRY, parents shared the importance of "(1) protecting adolescents from neighborhood violence, (2) building strong parent-adolescent relationships, and (3) addressing cultural divides between parents and adolescents" (Cruz-Santiago & Ramirez-Garcia, 2011, p. 100). Parental monitoring of IRY was associated with a reduction in gang involvement in several studies (Cruz-Santiago & Ramirez-Garcia, 2011; Higginson et al., 2018).

Another protective factor is peer support, especially when parents are overworked (Goodrum et al., 2015). However, Hong (2010) noted that conflict between teens from differing cultural groups, such as peer rejection and bullying, can increase the propensity for IRY gang involvement. Similarly, schools can also be a protective or risk factor, depending on the relationships and culture of the school and supports to reduce barriers to success (Hong, 2010). School-based and community-based programs that engage youth positively with adult mentors and role models, or in volunteer opportunities, recreational activities, church or faith communities, and civic engagement, can forestall criminal involvement and gang engagement of IRY (A. Rossiter et al., 2015). In addition to supporting prosocial activities, counselors can help to intervene by learning the signs and signals of gang members, using suppression strategies such as challenging efforts individually, and quelling student efforts to aggrandize gang activity rather than ignoring these forms of recruitment in schools (Paterson, 2010). Counseling leaders can provide psychoeducation to parents and communities such as regular gang awareness training in communities where gangs are prevalent (Office of Juvenile Justice and Delinquency Prevention [OJJDP], 2020). Programming such as safe-passage-to-school programs, consistent discipline practices, and conflict-resolution strategies in collaboration with schools, law enforcement, and community organizations are also recommended interventions (OJJDP, 2020).

Acculturation

As mentioned in previous chapters, the process of acculturation involves both cultural shedding, or losing some aspects of one culture, and cultural learning, or integrating aspects of another culture (Berry, 2015). This process can be beneficial developmentally but can bring about particularly difficult challenges for adolescents. To assess adolescents' levels of acculturation, counselors can administer the Acculturation, Habits, and Interests Multicultural Scale for Adolescents (Unger et al., 2002), which may provide both the counselor and client with insight about the adolescent's perspective on their acculturation process. At the same time, the onus of acculturation is not solely on the immigrant or refugee. Counselors can also advocate for newcomers by communicating to employers, school personnel, and others in the community, noting acceptance of cultural pluralism in society (e.g., through national policy that promotes cultural diversity), which can positively affect the process of acculturation for newcomers.

With regard to acculturation models, Berry's (1974, 1997) acculturation framework has two dimensions—cultural maintenance and cultural contact—and four acculturation strategies, which are widely recognized and researched. These strategies are integration, assimilation, separation, and marginalization. One extension of Berry's framework is the relative acculturation extended model (RAEM; Navas et al., 2007). The RAEM asserts that the complexity of acculturation can be affected by the preferences of the host and immigrant populations; that is, there are real and ideal perceptions by both groups regarding the acculturation process, which may be affected by political and governmental systems, economic and workforce needs, and social and familial beliefs and customs (Navas et al., 2007). In this model, conflict emerges when there is disparity between the ideal and the real preferences of host and immigrant groups. In reality, these disparities have always occurred for IRY.

The RAEM seems to align with Hillekens et al.'s (2019) findings indicating that ethnic majority and ethnic minority adolescents differ in how they view ethnic heritage and assimilation to mainstream culture. That is, ethnic majority (i.e., typically White) adolescents may immediately see cultural differences between cultures as conflicting, whereas ethnic minority adolescents may see them as compatible. Peers in school settings may reinforce these ideal versus real perspectives. Yet, both groups can be coached or guided to recognize similarities among cultures while also engaging in curious exploration and appreciation of differences.

Adolescent acculturation related to one's ethnic identity and mainstream acclimation (i.e., real) may depend on the degree of fit with expectations (i.e., ideal) of the majority population (Brown & Zagefka, 2011; Zagefka & Brown, 2002). That is, the concept of person-environment fit (Lewin, 1951), described formulaically as $B = f(P, E)$, has been used to explain group phenomena, where a member's personal characteristics (P) interact with the environmental factors (E) of the group, its members, and the situation to elicit behavior (B). The concept of degree of fit, or fit mismatch, can affect immigrant and refugee adolescents in two specific ways: (a) the degree to which they fit with peers and (b) the degree to which they fit with their family system.

For IRY, it is important to remember "fitting" in both systems will not ever be possible, as they likely differ considerably. Some families, though, feel the need to choose so that they and their children can "fit" in the mainstream population, which may mean giving up cultural beliefs such as religion. For example, in a qualitative interview as a part of a study conducted by Cigrand et al. (2022), one Hmong refugee shared that his family followed shamanism in Laos but now practice Christianity, saying, "We follow the rule in America . . . God is my God, and I am American."

Der Vang (2013) noted that Hmong adolescents sometimes give up more than religion to adapt to U.S. culture; loss of cultural identity may include less proficiency in using the written and verbal Hmong language, cultural identification as Asian instead of Hmong, and leaving behind cultural practices such as marriage and birth rituals. The crux of the issue for many immigrant adolescents, though, is while they become "Americanized," there is evidence that many of their nonimmigrant peers still see them as immigrants and different, leading to discriminatory behavior (Benner et al., 2015) and marginalization.

To work toward positive change, counselors who work with both host and newcomer populations can help peers recognize how thoughts, feelings, and behaviors may be more compatible than conflicting to augment person-environment fit in cross-cultural groups (Hillekens et al., 2019). In practice, counselors can engage in coconstruction of intercultural norms within neighborhoods, communities, schools, and other settings as an avenue to encourage groups to explore common ground when working with members from various cultures. Paralta (2010) demonstrated how this can be done through art and storytelling. Levy and Adjapong (2020) recommended cocreating spaces for social and emotional support of clients from various cultures. Facilitation of peer-to-peer or mentor programs, such as conversation clubs, is another method to develop language proficiency, as well as mutual understanding and a sense of connection between immigrant adolescents and adolescents from the host country (Pryce et al., 2018).

Language

While language can be a barrier to IRY, language proficiency is one of the strongest predictors of adaptation to a new culture (Wilson et al., 2013). Learning English as a part of adjusting to culture in the United States can relieve some pressure on adolescents (McCleary et al., 2020). Nonetheless, the effect of language acquisition of IRY on families is complex, as it affects relationship dynamics. If adolescence was not difficult enough for youth as they work developmentally toward adulthood, intergenerational conflicts can be exacerbated when adolescents exhibit language development and other cultural differences from their parental figures (e.g., change in values) as a part of their acculturation process. This familial disruption caused by asynchronous acculturative development between adolescents and their parents or other adult family members can be described as the acculturation gap-distress theory (Telzer, 2010) or intergenerational cultural conflict (Lui, 2015). While a slower pace of language adoption diffuses family hassles, a fast pace of language acquisition by IRY increases child disclosure to parents of their acculturation experiences (Aumann et al., 2022). Differences among first, second, and subsequent generations also impact language usage, communication, and familial relationships. For example, first-generation Hmong refugees are more likely to speak fluent Hmong, while subsequent generations are less likely to communicate via the Hmong language, are increasingly more Americanized, and use English primarily (Der Vang, 2013). Acculturation across generations often leads to changes in familial and community norms, along with the sense of connection within those systems.

Because children often speak English more fluently than the adults in their families, they sometimes act as language brokers. In addition, cultural brokering, which involves mediating a new culture for one's family, is another role IRY might undertake as adolescents (Jones & Trickett, 2005). In either role, IRY may become the holders of the power; that is, they are made responsible for speaking for their families, or they assume that role out of necessity (Partida, 1996). This responsibility occurs across cultures and in a variety of settings (e.g., banks, accountant offices, schools); it typically falls on the oldest child, yet the role is more likely to be designated to a female (Mier-Chairez et al., 2019). This process can be collaborative with parents or other family members. This can also lead to role confusion, as at times these adolescents are called upon to act like adults and other times they are expected to stay in their minor or "child" role (Antonini, 2022).

Whether the brokering process has positive or negative effects on adolescents seems to be contextual (Mier-Chairez et al., 2019). For example, the process of language brokering has been described by some adolescents as embarrassing and burdensome (Guan et al., 2015), but it has also led to positive outcomes such as trusting, respectful relationships with parents (Corona et al., 2012). At times, English-speaking adolescents feel a sense of shame regarding their parents' difficulties with English language acquisition or may feel stress when faced with brokering serious situations. Other researchers suggest that language brokering, especially by adolescents who live with their parents, may foster empathy for their parental experiences, as well as a sense of resilience in the adolescents when facing stressful events (Weisskirch et al., 2021). These divergent findings suggest that counselors and other helping professionals who work with immigrant families may need to discuss the brokering role with the adolescent before, during, and after brokering events to mitigate stress, advocate for developmentally appropriate responsibilities, consider alternatives if they are accessible, and reinforce positive aspects of this role and subsequent interchanges with all parties.

Mental Health of IRY

Person-Environment Fit

The concept of person-environment fit previously discussed can be applied to the ways in which an adolescent fits or does not fit within their school systems, communities, and their homes and seems to be a key factor related to the mental health of IRY (Eccles & Roeser, 2011). Especially for adolescents from African, Latinx, Middle Eastern, or Asian cultures that tend to be more collectivistic, the typical teenage developmental process can be intensified by differences in cultural expectations of family or cultural leaders and White cultural normativity. Specifically, Lui (2015) suggested intergenerational conflict significantly predicts internalizing problems and adaptive functioning development and, to a lesser extent, externalizing problems in IRY. The degree of intergenerational cultural conflict can also affect educational outcomes (Lui, 2015) and, particularly in Asian populations, help-seeking behaviors related to mental health services (Chang et al., 2013). Lui's findings point to intergenerational cultural conflict as an equally important cultural risk factor when compared with discrimination in impacting IRY's mental health outcomes.

Standards of Beauty

Another important aspect of acculturation for adolescents is finding ways to fit in regarding standards of beauty, dress, and body image. Often, standards of beauty are both idealistic and based on American (e.g., White, Western) culture (Marrinan, 2019). Researchers have noted immigrant adolescents maintain distorted body images of themselves (Kimber, Couturier, et al., 2015; Kimber, Georgiades, et al., 2015). In the United States, McCollough et al. (2022) reported that acculturative stress may create body image concerns for immigrant youth. They found that two groups of immigrant adolescents faced health risks based on cultural expectations regarding weight: (a) underweight adolescents who reported high assimilation with U.S. culture who were satisfied with their weight and (b) overweight adolescents who reported they were not assimilated to U.S. culture nor were they satisfied with their weight. Magtoto et al. (2013) found that both immigrant adolescent girls and boys reported more binge eating, more dieting, and lower body satisfaction when compared with North American–born peers of the same gender. In addition, immigrant adolescent boys were more likely to purge than North American–born boys. In one study of Latina mother-daughter communication about body satisfaction, mothers encouraged daughters to accept their bodies and appreciate aspects of their bodies when daughters criticized their own bodies (Romo & Mireles-Rios, 2016). While the relationship between beauty standards and body image has been established (Cash et al., 2004) and is a significant issue for developing adolescents, more research is needed on the relationship among self-acceptance, body image, and beauty standards in immigrant adolescents as it affects their mental health during the acculturation process.

Depression

In general, teens report depression and anxiety as the highest ranking problem among their peers (Horowitz & Graf, 2019). In one study of more than 4,000 youth, a large number (76%) of first- and second-generation adolescents from immigrant families reported depressive symptoms (Han, 2014). Depression in IRY has been associated with poverty, displacement, acculturative stress (Potochnick & Perreira, 2010), traumatic events, and discrimination (Metzner et al., 2022). Experiences with discrimination by adults in school settings have a significant effect on depressive symptomatology for both male and female adolescents (Tummala-Narra & Claudius, 2013). On the other hand, adults can have an ameliorating effect on depression, as Oppedal et al. (2020) noted that the cultural competence of IRY, acquired through connection with culturally competent role models, mentors, positive feedback from significant others, and knowledge of host country cultural practices, may reduce depressive symptoms in immigrant youth populations.

Although depression is a prevalent presenting mental health concern among immigrants and refugees, counselors should consider the concept of the immigrant paradox when working with IRY. As discussed in Chapter 6, the immigrant paradox, which has been supported in several studies, suggests that first-generation immigrants' developmental outcomes tend to be better than those of their same-age second- and third-generation peers; this finding includes depression (Harker, 2001). Even so, first-generation immigrant adolescents access mental health services less often than second- and third-generation immigrants and nonimmigrants. Thus, Georgiades et al. (2018) underscored the need to identify and address barriers to identification and treatment of mental disorders such as depression among IRY.

Regarding providing treatments and interventions, helping professionals must consider the need for outreach to identify and provide services to adolescents with depressive symptoms. Tummala-Narra (2015) found that over half of the participants (i.e., U.S.-born and foreign-born adolescents) in her study never sought help from adults at school (e.g., teachers, school counselor) and more than three quarters of the participants never sought help from mental health professionals when they experienced a difficult situation. In particular, females experience higher incidences of depression than their male peers, with more variability in their symptoms over time (Cobb & Martínez, 2023); thus, creating opportunities to connect with female IRY may be even more essential. Researchers (Mohammadifirouzeh et al., 2023; Tummala-Narra, 2015; Wang et al., 2019) seem to speculate that mental health stigma, financial or transportation barriers, and cultural help-seeking behaviors are main concerns; however, as mental health professionals, we must ask ourselves what we must do differently to connect with these adolescents despite the barriers mentioned in study after study. For individual clients, cognitive behavioral interventions focused on stress management, coping skill development, and positive self-talk strategies such as the Creating Opportunities for Patient Empowerment program for Syrian refugees (Doumit et al., 2020) have research support.

At the mesosystem level, counselors should consider engaging immigrant families through cultural organizations and places of worship for the sake of providing psychoeducation about the importance of positive parenting practices, including navigating communication and acculturation of teens, collaborative problem-solving, and stress-reduction techniques for parents and their children (Cobb & Martínez, 2015). Providing psychoeducation to help with recognition of mental health issues may also increase the likelihood that parents will refer their adolescents to counselors (Mohammadifirouzeh et al., 2023; Wang et al., 2019).

Suicide

The factors relating to suicidal ideation, attempts, and deaths of immigrant youth are complex; thus, it is not surprising current research raises more questions than answers. For example, results vary regarding suicidality among immigrants as compared with host country populations. Variation also exists when ethnic minority as a variable is examined (Han, 2014). Latino youth are the fastest growing population in the United States and have the highest rates of depression among minority groups yet are often untreated due to lack of access to mental health services (Basu et al., 2022). A significant number of this population identify as first-, second-, or third-generation immigrants. Latino adolescents have higher rates of depression and suicide attempts compared with non-White and African American youth (Guzmán et al., 2009). Research suggests that other IRY from a variety of ethnic groups are also at a particularly high risk for suicide, including Afghans (Morrow & Krishna, 2019); refugees from several countries in Central and South America, Europe, and Asia (Jin et al., 2021); and Middle Eastern and North African first-generation immigrant adolescents (Stark et al., 2022). Counselors working with Somali youth should be aware of the concept of *haram* (meaning *forbidden* in Islam) behaviors (Wolf et al., 2016); that is, consider how questions about suicidal ideation may be disparaging if reported by Somali youth. Some researchers adapt assessment tools to exclude questions about suicidal ideation and self-harm (Ellis, Lincoln, et al., 2010; Lincoln et al., 2016).

Developing protective factors and engaging IRY using evidence-based interventions can reduce depression and suicide in IRY. One salient factor seems to be a sense of belonging and connection with peers and role models. Adolescents who demonstrate resilience, as associated with feeling hopeful and a sense of belonging in schools, were less likely to report suicidal ideation (Stark et al., 2022). Stressful events, on the other hand, raised suicidal risk (Stark et al., 2022) in IRY. Safe neighborhoods with low crime rates can also reduce cultural stress of immigrant youth and their families (Lorenzo-Blanco et al., 2019).

Trauma

Although immigrants are less likely than their U.S.-born peers to experience anxiety, depression, or trauma-related disorders (Salas-Wright et al., 2018; Shekunov, 2017), it remains a significant issue with this adolescent population. Helping professionals must also recognize within-group differences of IRY; that is, variation in experiences across immigrant and refugee groups as related to trauma exposure should be expected. In an international study of migrant youth, Gatt et al. (2020) discussed how types of traumatic events vary among migrant groups. Some IRY have had exposure to life-threatening accidents or combat/war experience, whereas others have experienced the death of a family member or close friend. South African youth reported a higher average number of traumatic events in comparison with youth from five other countries that were studied (Gatt et al., 2020).

In an analysis of 60 war-affected refugee youth, clinical assessments from the National Child Traumatic Stress Network's core data set indicated "high rates of probable posttraumatic stress disorder (30.4%), generalized anxiety (26.8%), somatization (26.8%), traumatic grief (21.4%), and general behavioral problems (21.4%)" (Betancourt et al., 2012, p. 682). Many of these refugee youth who were exposed to war or political violence also had evidence of complex trauma; were more likely to experience multiple traumatic events, such as forced displacement, traumatic loss, bereavement, or separation; and were more likely to be exposed to violence in their community and/or in their homes. For these refugee youth, academic problems and behavioral difficulties were prevalent while criminal activity, alcohol/drug use, and self-harm were rare (Betancourt et al., 2012).

Furthermore, specific contextual factors affect the mental health of IRY. Moral injury exacerbates mental health disorders like PTSD and depression in this population (McEwen et al., 2022). Extreme poverty premigration is highly associated with traumatic experiences during the migration journey; for adolescents, this may mean separation from parents to enter the country or delayed migration, in which parents enter the country while their children wait a year or more to join them in the United States (Perreira & Ornelas, 2013). However, a low percentage of immigrant youth who experience trauma develop PTSD, which attests to their resilience (Perriera & Ornelas, 2013). In addition to resilience, there is some evidence that reunification of IRY with their families is another promotive factor that reduces incidence of PTSD, whereas living in foster care or with an American host family tends to worsen mental health unless IRY are ethnically or culturally matched in placement (O'Higgins et al., 2018). Furthermore, from a systematic review and meta-analysis of five studies of immigrants and refugees with trauma histories, Anderson and Edwards (2020) reported that people who migrated prior to age 18 had nearly twice the risk of psychotic disorder relative to the host population. However, it is important to note here that the studies examined by Anderson and Edwards did not include studies of immigrants in the United States.

Research on service pathways demonstrates a significant gap in identifying IRY who need referrals for mental health counseling; willingness to use mental health services offered was also an identified concern (Mitra & Hodes, 2019). Even so, providers of mental health services view IRY as having a marked propensity to develop connectedness (Forrest-Bank et al., 2019). These same providers recommend systemic interventions to support IRY, such as working with the adolescents' family or engaging in group counseling as preferred over individual counseling. In a review of interventions for IRY who had experienced trauma, narrative exposure therapy (especially KIDNET, or narrative exposure therapy for children) showed a large effect size in reducing symptoms associated with PTSD (Genç, 2022). Similarly, Lely et al. (2019) identified narrative exposure therapy as an effective treatment for IRY, such as North Korean refugee youth (Park et al., 2020). Eye-movement desensitization and reprocessing seemed to show efficacy in reducing trauma symptoms in a meta-analysis as well (Rafieifar & Macgowan, 2022).

Throughout this chapter, the evidence related to the complexity of supporting the development of IRY should be apparent. On top of the typical developmental needs of adolescents, IRY also face added layers of socioecological factors that affect them as individuals, as well as their family systems and school experience. Therefore, counselors and other helping professionals working with IRY must first get to know the adolescent, family, and the contextual factors contributing to their developmental needs in academic, career, social-emotional, and mental health domains. Once professionals working with IRY understand adolescents within the systems they encounter, it is more likely that they can proceed with interventions that help to support them and improve the systems imposing on IRY (Ellis et al., 2020).

The following case study of Hawi, an Ethiopian immigrant, is provided so that you can apply some of the information you read in this chapter. In this scenario, it is important to recognize that Hawi is a victim of harassment rather than "the problem." Thus, a collaborative approach to address the systemic issues at the school is warranted. Furthermore, mental health professionals can also support Hawi by prioritizing family communication to clarify school system policies, reinforce her strengths, listen to familial needs and concerns, and offer resources to them that may be beneficial.

CASE STUDY

Hawi is a 15-year-old Ethiopian immigrant who entered the United States when she was 9 years old with her father, mother, and younger brother. Both Hawi's uncle, who is now a U.S. citizen, and her parents live in Minnesota. Her parents are in the process of applying for citizenship as well. Hawi is a strong student at school, but according to teachers, she has become more withdrawn as the year has progressed and she recently elbowed a classmate in gym class. Her attendance at school used to be exceptional, but she has been missing school somewhat frequently in the last few months. She disclosed to her school counselor that a group of mostly male classmates, including the boy she elbowed, have used racial slurs and sexually inappropriate comments toward her and her social group, sometimes in front of school personnel, with little consequence. She shared that she is thinking of dropping out of school to take a job in a nursing home when she turns 16 years old. She also said her parents have been rather ashamed of her discipline referral, so they think taking a job is a good alternative to deal with the issues with boys at school. This plan would help support their low-income family and match Hawi with a husband.

In response, the school counselor invites the school social worker, physical education teacher, and a preferred teacher of Hawi to problem-solve Hawi's current school attendance and potential dropout risk. The social worker offers to reach out to the regional Diversity Council to connect with their Ethiopian community group to identify a liaison who may be willing, along with the social worker, to meet with Hawi's parents to explain the discipline referral, assess their concern about Hawi, and report Hawi's academic strengths as well as the school's attendance concerns. The school counselor and gym teacher work together to co-lead psychoeducational lessons on healthy dating relationships, safe sex, sexual harassment, dating violence, and area resources for youth in Hawi's gym class, with the intention to deliver them annually to all ninth-grade students in future years. The preferred teacher also volunteers to connect with Hawi to talk about possible after-school jobs that may align with her strengths and career interests. Finally, the team recommends to the school administrator that the district provide mandatory training to faculty and staff on bullying and harassment and strategies to respond and report them consistently.

Reflection Questions and Recommendations for Further Professional Development

1. Thinking of the MSJCC, consider how power and privilege dynamics could lead to imposition of your values on Hawi. What values do Hawi and her family prioritize that may be in conflict with your own values or societal norms? How will you work to avoid value imposition and support Hawi through this process of distress?
2. You are scheduled to meet with Hawi for individual counseling. What presenting issues would you prioritize in the first few sessions with Hawi? Why?
3. Read the following journal article while considering the systemic needs of the student: Meshesha, H. S., & Johnson, V. (2021). A systematic review of culturally responsive approaches to child and adolescent mental health care in Ethiopia. *Frontiers in Sociology*, *5*, Article 583864. https://doi.org/10.3389/fsoc.2020.583864

4. Based on the information in this article and the information you read in this chapter, how would you support Hawi within her family system? How would you support her family?
5. Would you apply the Indivisible Self model to this case? Why or why not?

Summary

Immigrant and refugee adolescents are likely to have unique developmental needs that are dependent on various factors, such as whether they are first-generation immigrants or refugees or are second- or third-generation adolescents with immigrant family members. Since identity development is an important aspect of adolescence, processes such as acculturation may affect how adolescents fit or align with norms within their peer groups and family units. Because of prospective difficulties in fitting in with family and/or peer groups, as well as past trauma histories, IRY who do not feel accepted or supported may experience depression and suicidal thoughts or turn to gangs for a sense of belonging. Counselors, educators, family members, and other adults can support the mental health and academic and career development of adolescent immigrants and refugees by engaging with them in schools and community settings; creating safe spaces for building connections with peers and caring adults; and providing affirmation of them, their interests, experiences, and cultural perspectives. "Seeing" immigrant and refugee adolescents, reducing educational access and information gaps, and increasing relationships and belonginess are essential for immigrants and refugees to succeed in this stage of development.

References

Albarello, F., Crocetti, E., & Rubini, M. (2021). Developing identification with humanity and social well-being through social identification with peer groups in adolescence. *Journal of Youth and Adolescence*, *50*(6), 1157–1172. https://doi.org/10.1007/s10964-020-01214-0

American Psychological Association. (2017). *Education and socioeconomic status*. https://www.apa.org/pi/ses/resources/publications/education

Anastario, M. P., Barrick, K., Gibbs, D., Pitts, W., Werth, R., & Lattimore, P. K. (2015). Factors driving Salvadoran youth migration: A formative assessment focused on Salvadoran repatriation facilities. *Children and Youth Services Review*, *59*, 97–104. https://doi.org/10.1016/j.childyouth.2015.10.019

Anderson, K. K., & Edwards, J. (2020). Age at migration and the risk of psychotic disorders: A systematic review and meta-analysis. *Acta Psychiatrica Scandinavica*, *141*(5), 410–420. https://doi.org/10.1111/acps.13147

Annie E. Casey Foundation. (2023, August 28). *Who are children in immigrant families?* https://www.aecf.org/blog/who-are-the-children-in-immigrant-families

Antonini, R. (2022). Children's narratives of the emotional impact of child language brokering. *MediAzioni*, *33*(1), D132–D154. https://doi.org/10.6092/issn.1974-4382/15269

Aral, T., Schachner, M. K., Juang, L., & Schwarzenthal, M. (2022). Cultural diversity approaches in schools and adolescents' willingness to support refugee youth. *British Journal of Educational Psychology*, *92*(2), 772–799. https://doi.org/10.1111/bjep.12458

Arellanes, J. A., Viramontez Anguaino, R. P., & Lohman, B. J. (2019). Bettering the educational attainment for Latino families: How families view the education of their children. *Journal of Latinos and Education*, *18*(4), 349–362. https://doi.org/10.1080/15348431.2018.1426465

Arora, P. G., Alvarez, K., Huang, C., & Wang, C. (2021). A three-tiered model for addressing the mental health needs of immigrant-origin youth in schools. *Journal of Immigrant and Minority Health*, *23*(1), 151–162. https://doi.org/10.1007/s10903-020-01048-9

Aumann, L., Titzmann, P. F., & Lee, R. M. (2022). Striking a new path to study the adaptation processes of immigrant adolescents: Changes in language use and family interactions. *Developmental Psychology*, *58*(6), 1163–1175. https://doi.org/10.1037/dev0001351

Autin, K. L., Duffy, R. D., Jacobson, C. J., Dosani, K. M., Barker, D., & Bott, E. M. (2018). Career development among undocumented immigrant young adults: A psychology of working perspective. *Journal of Counseling Psychology*, *65*(5), 605–617. https://doi.org/10.1037/cou0000280

Barnes, J. C., Beaver, K. M., & Miller, J. M. (2010). Estimating the effect of gang membership on nonviolent and violent delinquency: A counterfactual analysis. *Aggressive Behavior*, *36*(6), 437–451. https://doi.org/10.1002/ab.20359

Basu, A., Boland, A., Witt, K., & Robinson, J. (2022). Suicidal behaviour, including ideation and self-harm, in young migrants: A systematic review. *International Journal of Environmental Research and Public Health*, *19*(14), Article 8329. https://doi.org/10.3390/ijerph19148329

Batlova, J., Hanna, M., & Levesque, C. (2021). *Frequently requested statistics on immigrants and immigration in the United States*. Migration Policy Institute. https://www.migrationpolicy.org/print/16995

Bay, S. (2021). Criminalization is not the only way: Guatemala's law against femicide and other forms of violence against women and the rates of femicide in Guatemala. *Washington International Law Journal*, *30*(2). https://digitalcommons.law.uw.edu/wilj/vol30/iss2/11

Benner, A., Crosnoe, R., & Eccles, J. S. (2015). Schools, peers, and prejudice in adolescence. *Journal of Research on Adolescence*, *25*(1), 173–188. https://doi.org/10.1111/jora.12106

Berry, J. W. (1997), Immigration, acculturation, and adaptation. *Applied Psychology*, *46*(1), 5–34. https://doi.org/10.1111/j.1464-0597.1997.tb01087.x

Berry, J. W. (2015). Acculturation. In J. E. Grusec & P. D. Hastings (Eds.), *Handbook of socialization: Theory and research* (pp. 520–538). Guilford Press.

Berry, J. W., & Annis, R. C. (1974). Ecology, culture and psychological differentiation. *International Journal of Psychology*, *9*(3), 173–193. https://doi.org/10.1080/00207597408247102

Betancourt, T. S., Newnham, E. A., Layne, C. M., Kim, S., Steinberg, A. M., Ellis, H., & Birman, D. (2012). Trauma history and psychopathology in war-affected refugee children referred for trauma-related mental health services in the United States. *Journal of Traumatic Stress*, *25*(6), 682–690. https://doi.org/10.1002/jts.21749

Bevan-Brown, J. (2006). Beyond policy and good intentions. *International Journal of Inclusive Education*, *10*(2–3), 221–234. https://doi.org/10.1080/13603110500392775

Billini, A. (2021). *Dreamers: Stories of DACA recipients in higher education during the 2018–2021 political climate* [Doctoral dissertation, Western Michigan University]. ScholarWorks@WMU. https://scholarworks.wmich.edu/cgi/viewcontent.cgi?article=4791&context=dissertations

Bonifacio, L. (2016). *The career development of Latino immigrant youth* [Doctoral dissertation, Columbia University]. Columbia University Libraries. https://academiccommons.columbia.edu/doi/10.7916/D8BR8SGJ

Bronfenbrenner, U. (1977). Toward an experimental ecology of human development. *American Psychologist*, *32*(7), 513–531. https://doi.org/10.1037/0003-066X.32.7.513

Brown, R., & Zagefka, H. (2011). The dynamics of acculturation: An intergroup perspective. *Advances in Experimental Social Psychology*, *44*, 129–184. https://doi.org/10.1016/B978-0-12-385522-0.00003-2

Cadenas, G. A., Campos, L., Minero, L. P., & Aguila, C. (2020, April 20). *A guide to providing mental health services to immigrants impacted by changes to DACA and the COVID-19 pandemic*. Informed Immigrant. https://www.informedimmigrant.com/resources/tps/daca-mental-health-providers/

Capps, R., Fix, M., & Zong, J. (2017). *The education and work profiles of the DACA population* [Policy brief]. Migration Policy Institute. https://www.migrationpolicy.org/research/education-and-work-profiles-daca-population

Cash, T. F., Morrow, J. A., Hrabosky, J. I., & Perry, A. A. (2004). How has body image changed? A cross-sectional investigation of college women and men from 1983 to 2001. *Journal of Consulting and Clinical Psychology*, *72*(6), 1081–1089. https://doi.org/10.1037/0022-006X.72.6.1081

Chang, J., Natsuaki, M. N., & Chen, C.-N. (2013). The importance of family factors and generation status: Mental health service use among Latino and Asian Americans. *Cultural Diversity and Ethnic Minority Psychology*, *19*(3), 236–247. https://doi.org/10.1037/a0032901

Cigrand, D., Fawcett, M. L., Arredondo, P., Miyakuni, R., & Onderak, G. (2022). Experiences of survival and perseverance through dire decisions: A phenomenological study of the immigration journey. *Journal of Counseling & Development*, *100*(2), 157–170. https://doi.org/10.1002/jcad.12413

Cisneros, L. (2013). Undocumented students pursuing higher education. *UC Merced Undergraduate Research Journal, 5*(1). https://escholarship.org/uc/item/9tg09145

Cobb, C. L., & Martínez, C. R., Jr. (2023). Trajectories of depression for Latino immigrant adolescents: The influence of individual, family, and sociocultural factors. *Journal of Psychopathology and Clinical Science, 132*(1), 1–12. https://doi.org/10.1037/abn0000798

Coenders, M., Gijsberts, M., Hagendoorn, L., & Scheepers, P. (2004). Introduction. In M. Gijsberts, L. Hagendoorn, & P. Scheepers (Eds.), *Nationalism and exclusion of migrants: Cross-national comparisons* (pp. 1–25). Routledge.

Cook, A. L., Pérusse, R., & Rojas, E. D. (2015). Promoting college access among Latina/o English language learners: Implications for professional school counselors. *Journal of School Counseling, 13*(18).

Corona, R., Stevens, L. F., Halfond, R. W., Shaffer, C. M., Reid-Quiñones, K., & Gonzalez, T. (2012). A qualitative analysis of what Latino parents and adolescents think and feel about language brokering. *Journal of Child and Family Studies, 21*(5), 788–798. https://doi.org/10.1007/s10826-011-9536-2

Crosnoe, R., & López Turley, R. N. (2011). K-12 educational outcomes of immigrant youth. *The Future of Children, 21*(1), 129–152. https://doi.org/10.1353/foc.2011.0008

Cruz-Santiago, M., & Ramírez García, J. I. (2011). "Hay que ponerse en los zapatos del joven": Adaptive parenting of adolescent children among Mexican-American parents residing in a dangerous neighborhood. *Family Process, 50*(1), 92–114. https://doi.org/10.1111/j.1545-5300.2010.01348.x

Curle, C. (2020, January 24). *Us vs. them: The process of othering.* Canadian Museum for Human Rights. https://humanrights.ca/story/us-vs-them-process-othering

D'Alonzo, K. T., & Greene, L. (2020). Strategies to establish and maintain trust when working in immigrant communities. *Public Health Nursing, 37*(5), 764–768. https://doi.org/10.1111/phn.12764

Der Vang, P. (2013). Generational differences among a small group of Hmong Americans. *Journal of Ethnic & Cultural Diversity in Social Work, 22*(1), 76–92. https://doi.org/10.1080/15313204.2013.759441

Doumit, R., Kazandjian, C., & Militello, L. K. (2020). COPE for adolescent Syrian refugees in Lebanon: A brief cognitive-behavioral skill-building intervention to improve quality of life and promote positive mental health. *Clinical Nursing Research, 29*(4), 226–234. https://doi.org/10.1177/1054773818808114

Drake, K. (2017). Competing purposes of education: The case of underschooled immigrant students. *Journal of Educational Change, 18*(3), 337–363. https://doi.org/10.1007/s10833-017-9302-3

Durand, T. M., & Blackwell, R. (2022). Dimensions of belonging and "othering" in middle school: Voices of immigrant and island-born Puerto Rican adolescents. *Journal of Education for Students Placed at Risk.* https://doi.org/10.1080/10824669.2022.2136179

Eccles, J. S., & Roeser, R. W. (2011). Schools as developmental contexts during adolescence: Schools as developmental contexts. *Journal of Research on Adolescence, 21*(1), 225–241. https://doi.org/10.1111/j.1532-7795.2010.00725.x

Eckstein, K., Miklikowska, M., & Noack, P. (2021). School matters: The effects of school experiences on youth's attitudes toward immigrants. *Journal of Youth and Adolescence, 50*(11), 2208–2223. https://doi.org/10.1007/s10964-021-01497-x

Ellis, B. H., Abdi, S. M., & Winer, J. P. (2020). *Mental health practice with immigrant and refugee youth: A socioecological framework.* American Psychological Association. https://doi.org/10.1037/0000163-000

Ellis, B. H., Lincoln, A. K., Charney, M. E., Ford-Paz, R., Benson, M., & Strunin, L. (2010). Mental health service utilization of Somali adolescents: Religion, community, and school as gateways to healing. *Transcultural Psychiatry, 47*(5), 789–811. https://doi.org/10.1177/1363461510379933

Ellis, B. H., MacDonald, H. Z., Klunk-Gillis, J., Lincoln, A., Strunin, L., & Cabral, H. J. (2010). Discrimination and mental health among Somali refugee adolescents: The role of acculturation and gender. *American Journal of Orthopsychiatry, 80*(4), 564–575. https://doi.org/10.1111/j.1939-0025.2010.01061.x

Enyioha, J. C. (2019). College access for undocumented students and law. *Educational Considerations, 45*(1), Article 7. https://doi.org/10.4148/0146-9282.2168

Erikson, E. H. (1964). *Insight and responsibility.* Norton.

Estrem, T., & Zhang, S. (2010). Prevalence and disproportionality of autism spectrum disorders among English language learners in Minnesota. *Multiple Voices for Ethnically Diverse Exceptional Learners, 12*(2), 5–20. https://doi.org/10.56829/muvo.12.2.0g260k1111482016

Federal Bureau of Investigation. (n.d.). *What we investigate: Gangs*. https://www.fbi.gov/investigate/violent-crime/gangs

Forrest-Bank, S. S., Held, M. L., & Jones, A. (2019). Provider perspectives of services addressing the mental health needs of resettled refugee youth. *Child and Adolescent Social Work Journal, 36*(6), 669–684. https://doi.org/10.1007/s10560-019-00602-1

Gabel, S. L., Curcic, S., Powell, J. J. W., Khader, K., & Albee, L. (2009). Migration and ethnic group disproportionality in special education: An exploratory study. *Disability & Society, 24*(5), 625–639. https://doi.org/10.1080/09687590903011063

Garcini, L. M., Daly, R., Chen, N., Mehl, J., Pham, T., Phan, T., Hansen, B., & Kothare, A. (2021). Undocumented immigrants and mental health: A systematic review of recent methodology and findings in the United States. *Journal of Migration and Health, 4*, Article 100058. https://doi.org/10.1016/j.jmh.2021.100058

Garduno, L. S., & Brancale, J. M. (2017). Examining the risk and protective factors of gang involvement among Hispanic youth in Maryland. *Journal of Community Psychology, 45*(6), 765–782. https://doi.org/10.1002/jcop.21891

Gatt, J. M., Alexander, R., Emond, A., Foster, K., Hadfield, K., Mason-Jones, A., Reid, S., Theron, L., Ungar, M., Wouldes, T. A., & Wu, Q. (2020). Trauma, resilience, and mental health in migrant and non-migrant youth: An international cross-sectional study across six countries. *Frontiers in Psychiatry, 10*, Article 997. https://doi.org/10.3389/fpsyt.2019.00997

Genç, E. (2022). The effectiveness of trauma treatment approaches in refugee children and adolescents: A systematic review. *Children and Youth Services Review, 141*, Article 106602. https://doi.org/10.1016/j.childyouth.2022.106602

George-Jackson, C., & Gast, M. J. (2015). Addressing information gaps: Disparities in financial awareness and preparedness on the road to college. *Journal of Student Financial Aid, 44*(3), Article 3. https://doi.org/10.55504/0884-9153.1540

Georgiades, K., Paksarian, D., Rudolph, K. E., & Merikangas, K. R. (2018). Prevalence of mental disorder and service use by immigrant generation and race/ethnicity among U.S. adolescents. *Journal of the American Academy of Child & Adolescent Psychiatry, 57*(4), 280–287.e2. https://doi.org/10.1016/j.jaac.2018.01.020

Gindling, T. H., & Poggio, S. (2012). Family separation and reunification as a factor in the educational success of immigrant children. *Journal of Ethnic and Migration Studies, 38*(7), 1155–1173. https://doi.org/10.1080/1369183X.2012.681458

Goldberg, C. (2020, September 1). *Legal aid for unaccompanied children in the U.S. illegally*. National Conference of State Legislatures. https://www.ncsl.org/immigration/legal-aid-for-unaccompanied-children-in-the-us-illegally

Gonzales, R. G. (2009). *Young lives on hold: The college dreams of undocumented students*. College Board Advocacy. https://secure-media.collegeboard.org/digitalServices/pdf/professionals/young-lives-on-hold-undocumented-students.pdf

Goodrum, N. M., Chan, W. Y., & Latzman, R. D. (2015). Gang involvement among immigrant and refugee youth: A developmental ecological systems approach. *International Journal of Developmental Science, 9*(3–4), 125–134. https://doi.org/10.3233/DEV-150164

Gorski, P. (2017). *Beyond celebrating diversity: 20 things I will do to be an equitable educator.* Equity Literacy Institute. http://www.edchange.org/handouts/20things.pdf

Groce, L. L., & Johnson, L. V. (2021). School counselors igniting the hope of undocumented students in college access. *The Journal for Specialists in Group Work, 46*(1), 128–142. https://doi.org/10.1080/01933922.2020.1856256

Guan, S., Nash, A., & Orellana, M. (2015). Cultural and social processes of language brokering among Arab, Asian, and Latin immigrants. *Journal of Multilingual and Multicultural Development, 37*(2), 1–17. https://doi.org/10.1080/01434632.2015.1044997

Guzmán, Á., Koons, A., & Postolache, T. T. (2009). Suicidal behavior in Latinos: Focus on the youth. *International Journal of Adolescent Medicine and Health, 21*(4), 431–440. https://doi.org/10.1515/IJAMH.2009.21.4.431

Haft, S. L., Zhou, Q., Stephens, M., & Alkon, A. (2021). Culture and stress biology in immigrant youth from the prenatal period to adolescence: A systematic review. *Developmental Psychobiology, 63*(3), 391–408. https://doi.org/10.1002/dev.22009

Han, Y. (2014). Differential size of the discrimination-depression relationship among adolescents of foreign-born parents in the US. *Child & Youth Care Forum, 43*(6), 763–781. https://doi.org/10.1007/s10566-014-9265-y

Harker, K. (2001). Immigrant generation, assimilation, and adolescent psychological well-being. *Social Forces, 79*(3), 969–1004. https://doi.org/10.1353/sof.2001.0010

Higginson, A., Benier, K., Shenderovich, Y., Bedford, L., Mazerolle, L., & Murray, J. (2018). Factors associated with youth gang membership in low- and middle-income countries: A systematic review. *Campbell Systematic Reviews, 14*(1). https://doi.org/10.4073/csr.2018.11

Higher Ed Immigration Portal. (n.d.). *Portal to the states.* https://www.higheredimmigrationportal.org/states/

Hillekens, J., Baysu, G., & Phalet, K. (2019). Compatible or conflicting? Peer norms and minority and majority adolescents' acculturation patterns. *Journal of Applied Developmental Psychology, 65*, Article 101074. https://doi.org/10.1016/j.appdev.2019.101074

Hong, J. (2010). Understanding Vietnamese youth gangs in America: An ecological systems analysis. *Aggression and Violent Behavior, 15*(4), 253–260. https://doi.org/10.1016/j.avb.2010.01.003

Horowitz, J. M., & Graf, N. (2019). *Most U.S. teens see anxiety and depression as a major problem among their peers.* Pew Research Center. https://www.pewresearch.org/social-trends/2019/02/20/most-u-s-teens-see-anxiety-and-depression-as-a-major-problem-among-their-peers/

Illegal Immigration Reform and Immigrant Responsibility Act of 1996, Pub. L. No. 104-208, 110 Stat. 3009 (1996). https://www.govinfo.gov/content/pkg/STATUTE-110/pdf/STATUTE-110-Pg3009.pdf

Jin, S. S., Dolan, T. M., Cloutier, A. A., Bojdani, E., & DeLisi, L. (2021). Systematic review of depression and suicidality in child and adolescent (CAP) refugees. *Psychiatry Research, 302*, Article 114025. https://doi.org/10.1016/j.psychres.2021.114025

Johnston, A. R., Siler, D., & De Jesús, A. (2022). "The name game": Adolescent racialization in the era of Trump. *Equity & Excellence in Education, 55*(1–2), 105–117. https://doi.org/10.1080/10665684.2021.2010019

Jones, C. J., & Trickett, E. J. (2005). Immigrant adolescents behaving as culture brokers: A study of families from the former Soviet Union. *The Journal of Social Psychology, 145*(4), 405–428. https://doi.org/10.3200/SOCP.145.4.405-428

Juang, L. P., Simpson, J. A., Lee, R. M., Rothman, A. J., Titzmann, P. F., Schachner, M. K., Korn, L., Heinemeier, D., & Betsch, C. (2018). Using attachment and relational perspectives to understand adaptation and resilience among immigrant and refugee youth. *American Psychologist, 73*(6), 797–811. https://doi.org/10.1037/amp0000286

Kayama, M., & Yamakawa, N. (2020). Acculturation and a sense of belonging of children in U.S. schools and communities: The case of Japanese families. *Children and Youth Services Review, 119*, Article 105612. https://doi.org/10.1016/j.childyouth.2020.105612

Kim, K. H., & Zabelina, D. (2015). Cultural bias in assessment: Can creativity assessment help? *International Journal of Critical Pedagogy, 6*(2), 129–147.

Kimber, M., Couturier, J., Georgiades, K., Wahoush, O., & Jack, S. M. (2015). Ethnic minority status and body image dissatisfaction: A scoping review of the child and adolescent literature. *Journal of Immigrant and Minority Health, 17*(5), 1567–1579. https://doi.org/10.1007/s10903-014-0082-z

Kimber, M., Georgiades, K., Couturier, J., Jack, S. M., & Wahoush, O. (2015). Adolescent body image distortion: A consideration of immigrant generational status, immigrant concentration, sex and body dissatisfaction. *Journal of Youth and Adolescence, 44*(11), 2154–2171. https://doi.org/10.1007/s10964-015-0329-6

Kovacs, K. (2022). *College guide for DACA and undocumented students.* Best Colleges. https://www.bestcolleges.com/resources/undocumented-students/college-guide/

Kreisberg, A. N., & Hsin, A. (2020). The higher educational trajectories of undocumented youth in the United States. *Journal of Ethnic and Migration Studies, 47*(17), 3822–3845. https://doi.org/10.1080/1369183X.2020.1750947

Kubik, J., Docherty, M., & Boxer, P. (2019). The impact of childhood maltreatment on adolescent gang involvement. *Child Abuse & Neglect, 96*, Article 104096. https://doi.org/10.1016/j.chiabu.2019.104096

Johnson, S. (n.d.). *The Joy Labs: Projects*. https://www.thejoylabs.com/portfolio-2

Leet-Otley, J. (2020). (Mis)understanding the hijab: The spirit and strength of Somali girls. *Diaspora, Indigenous, and Minority Education, 14*(1), 43–54. https://doi.org/10.1080/15595692.2019.1652814

Lely, J. C. G., Smid, G. E., Jongedijk, R. A. W., Knipscheer, J., & Kleber, R. J. (2019). The effectiveness of narrative exposure therapy: A review, meta-analysis, and meta-regression analysis. *European Journal of Psychotraumatology, 10*(1), Article 1550344. https://doi.org/10.1080/20008198.2018.1550344

Levy, I. P., & Adjapong, E. S. (2020). Toward culturally competent school counseling environments: Hip-hop studio construction. *The Professional Counselor, 10*(2), 266–284. https://doi.org/10.15241/ipl.10.2.266

Lewin, K. (1951). *Field theory in social science: selected theoretical papers* (Dorwin Cartwright, Ed.). Harpers.

Leyva-Flores, R., Infante, C., Gutierrez, J. P., Quintino-Perez, F., Gómez-Saldivar, M., & Torres-Robles, C. (2019). Migrants in transit through Mexico to the US: Experiences with violence and related factors, 2009–2015. *PLOS ONE, 14*(8), e0220775. https://doi.org/10.1371/journal.pone.0220775

Lichter, D. T., & Johnson, K. M. (2020). A demographic lifeline? Immigration and Hispanic population growth in rural America. *Population Research and Policy Review, 39*(5), 785–803. https://doi.org/10.1007/s11113-020-09605-8

Lincoln, A. K., Cardeli, E., Sideridis, G., Salhi, C., Miller, A. B., Da Fonseca, T., Issa, O., & Ellis, B. H. (2021). Discrimination, marginalization, belonging, and mental health among Somali immigrants in North America. *American Journal of Orthopsychiatry, 91*(2), 280–293. https://doi.org/10.1037/ort0000524

Lincoln, A. K., Lazarevic, V., White, M. T., & Ellis, B. H. (2016). The impact of acculturation style and acculturative hassles on the mental health of Somali adolescent refugees. *Journal of Immigrant and Minority Health, 18*(4), 771–778. https://doi.org/10.1007/s10903-015-0232-y

Lorenzo-Blanco, E. I., Meca, A., Unger, J. B., Szapocznik, J., Cano, M. Á., Des Rosiers, S. E., & Schwartz, S. J. (2019). Cultural stress, emotional well-being, and health risk behaviors among recent immigrant Latinx families: The moderating role of perceived neighborhood characteristics. *Journal of Youth and Adolescence, 48*(1), 114–131. https://doi.org/10.1007/s10964-018-0907-5

Lowenhaupt, R., Dabach, D. B., & Mangual Figueroa, A. (2021). Safety and belonging in immigrant-serving districts: Domains of educator practice in a charged political landscape. *AERA Open, 7*. https://doi.org/10.1177/23328584211040084

Lui, P. P. (2015). Intergenerational cultural conflict, mental health, and educational outcomes among Asian and Latino/a Americans: Qualitative and meta-analytic review. *Psychological Bulletin, 141*(2), 404–446. https://doi.org/10.1037/a0038449

Magtoto, J., Cox, D., & Saewyc, E. (2013). Body satisfaction and eating disorder behaviors among immigrant adolescents in North America. *International Journal of School & Educational Psychology, 1*(1), 13–19. https://doi.org/10.1080/21683603.2013.780193

Marrinan, K. (2019). American beauty standards: "Paling" in comparison to the White norm. *Sociology Senior Seminar Papers, 22*. https://creativematter.skidmore.edu/socio_stu_stu_schol/22

Maslow, A. H. (1943). A theory of human motivation. *Psychological Review, 50*(4), 370–396. https://doi.org/10.1037/h0054346

Maynard, B. R., Vaughn, M. G., Salas-Wright, C. P., & Vaughn, S. (2016). Bullying victimization among school-aged immigrant youth in the United States. *Journal of Adolescent Health, 58*(3), 337–344. https://doi.org/10.1016/j.jadohealth.2015.11.013

McCleary, J. S., Shannon, P. J., Wieling, E., & Becher, E. (2020). Exploring intergenerational communication and stress in refugee families. *Child & Family Social Work, 25*(2), 364–372. https://doi.org/10.1111/cfs.12692

McCullough, M. B., Pieloch, K. A., & Marks, A. K. (2020). Body image, assimilation, and weight of immigrant adolescents in the United States: A person-centered analysis. *Journal of Immigrant and Minority Health, 22*(2), 249–254. https://doi.org/10.1007/s10903-019-00892-8

McEwen, C., Alisic, E., & Jobson, L. (2022). Moderating role of moral injury in the mental health of adolescent refugees. *Journal of Clinical Psychology, 78*(7), 1478–1490. https://doi.org/10.1002/jclp.23306

Metzner, F., Adedeji, A., Wichmann, M. L.-Y., Zaheer, Z., Schneider, L., Schlachzig, L., Richters, J., Heumann, S., & Mays, D. (2022). Experiences of discrimination and everyday racism among children and adolescents with an immigrant background—Results of a systematic literature review on the impact of discrimination on the developmental outcomes of minors worldwide. *Frontiers in Psychology, 13*, Article 805941. https://doi.org/10.3389/fpsyg.2022.805941

Mier-Chairez, J., Arellano, B., Tucker, S. E., Marquez, E., & Hooper, L. M. (2019). Theoretical, empirical, and practice literature on language brokering: Family, academic, and psychological outcomes. *Journal of Human Behavior in the Social Environment, 29*(7), 840–860. https://doi.org/10.1080/10911359.2019.1621791

Miklikowska, M., Eckstein, K., & Matera, J. (2021). All together now: Cooperative classroom climate and the development of youth attitudes toward immigrants. *New Directions for Child and Adolescent Development, 2021*(177), 123–139. https://doi.org/10.1002/cad.20414

Mitra, R., & Hodes, M. (2019). Prevention of psychological distress and promotion of resilience amongst unaccompanied refugee minors in resettlement countries. *Child: Care, Health and Development, 45*(2), 198–215. https://doi.org/10.1111/cch.12640

Mohammadifirouzeh, M., Oh, K. M., Basnyat, I., & Gimm, G. (2023). Factors associated with professional mental help-seeking among U.S. immigrants: A systematic review. *Journal of Immigrant and Minority Health, 25*(5), 1118–1136. https://doi.org/10.1007/s10903-023-01475-4

Morrow, C. B., & Krishna, N. (2019). Depression and suicidality in an Afghan refugee: A case report. *Transcultural Psychiatry, 56*(5), 845–852. https://doi.org/10.1177/1363461519847314

Motti-Stefanidi, F., Pavlopoulos, V., & Asendorpf, J. B. (2018). Immigrant youth acculturation and perceived discrimination: Longitudinal mediation by immigrant peers' acceptance/rejection. *Journal of Applied Developmental Psychology, 59*, 36–45. https://doi.org/10.1016/j.appdev.2018.03.001

National Alliance on Mental Illness. (2023, April). *Mental health by the numbers.* https://www.nami.org/mhstats

National Center for Education Statistics. (2023). *Status dropout rates.* https://nces.ed.gov/programs/coe/indicator/coj

National Conference of State Legislatures. (2021). *Tuition benefits for immigrants.* https://www.ncsl.org/immigration/tuition-benefits-for-immigrants

National Policy Board for Educational Administration. (2015). *Professional standards for educational leaders.* https://www.npbea.org/wp-content/uploads/2017/06/Professional-Standards-for-Educational-Leaders_2015.pdf

Navas, M., Rojas-Tejada, A. García, M., & Pumares, P. (2007). Acculturation strategies and attitudes according to the Relative Acculturation Extended Model (RAEM): The perspectives of natives versus immigrants. *International Journal of Intercultural Relations, 31*(1), 67–86. https://doi.org/10.1016/j.ijintrel.2006.08.002

Ngo, H. V., Rossiter, M. J., & Stewart, C. (2013). Understanding risk and protective factors associated with criminal involvement in a multicultural society. *International Journal of Child, Youth and Family Studies, 4*(1), 54–71. https://doi.org/10.18357/ijcyfs41201311838

Nienhusser, H. K., & Romandia, O. (2022). Undocumented college students' psychosocial well-being: A systematic review. *Current Opinion in Psychology, 47*, Article 101412. https://doi.org/10.1016/j.copsyc.2022.101412

Nienhusser, H. K., Vega, B. E., & Carquin, M. C. (2016). Undocumented students' experiences with microaggressions during their college choice process. *Teachers College Record, 118*(2), 1–33. https://doi.org/10.1177/016146811611800208

Office of Juvenile Justice and Delinquency Prevention. (2020). *Gangs in schools.* https://www.nationalgangcenter.gov/Content/Documents/Gangs-in-Schools.pdf

Office of Refugee Resettlement. (2023a). *Unaccompanied children program policy guide: Section 2.* https://www.acf.hhs.gov/orr/policy-guidance/unaccompanied-children-program-policy-guide-section-2

Office of Refugee Resettlement. (2023b). Unaccompanied children released to sponsors by state. https://www.acf.hhs.gov/orr/grant-funding/unaccompanied-children-released-sponsors-state

O'Higgins, A., Ott, E. M., & Shea, M. W. (2018). What is the impact of placement type on educational and health outcomes of unaccompanied refugee minors? A systematic review of the evidence. *Clinical Child and Family Psychology Review, 21*, 354–365. https://doi.org/10.1007/s10567-018-0256-7

Oppedal, B., Keles, S., Cheah, C., & Røysamb, E. (2020). Culture competence and mental health across different immigrant and refugee groups. *BMC Public Health*, *20*(1), Article 292. https://doi.org/10.1186/s12889-020-8398-1

Organisation for Economic Co-operation and Development. (2020). *Enhancing equal access to opportunities for all in G20 countries*. https://www.oecd.org/economy/Enhancing-equal-access-to-opportunities-OECD-background-note-for-G20-Framework-Working-Group-july-2020.pdf

Ortiz, A. M., & Hinojosa, A. (2010). Tenuous options: The career development process for undocumented students. *New Directions for Student Services*, *131*, 53–65. https://doi.org/10.1002/ss.367

Ozdemir, S. B., Sun, S., Korol, L., Ozdemir, M., & Stattin, H. (2018). Adolescents' engagement in ethnic harassment: Prejudiced beliefs in social networks and classroom ethnic diversity. *Journal of Youth and Adolescence*, *47*(6), 1151–1163. https://doi.org/10.1007/s10964-017-0795-0

Pacheco, G. P. (2021). *Building culturally responsive schools: How principals lead secondary public schools with increasing numbers of immigrant students* (Order No. 28644154) [Doctoral dissertation, George Washington University]. ProQuest Dissertations and Theses Global.

Paralta, A. (2010). The art of storytelling: The co-construction of cultural knowledge. *Art Education*, *63*(2), 25–30. https://doi.org/10.1080/00043125.2010.11519058

Park, J. K., Park, J., Elbert, T., & Kim, S. J. (2020). Effects of narrative exposure therapy on posttraumatic stress disorder, depression, and insomnia in traumatized North Korean refugee youth. *Journal of Traumatic Stress*, *33*(3), 353–359. https://doi.org/10.1002/jts.22492

Parker, A. L. (2022, April 28). *US immigration enforcement and US obligations under the international convention on the elimination of racial discrimination (ICERD)*. Human Rights Watch. https://www.hrw.org/news/2022/04/28/us-immigration-enforcement-and-us-obligations-under-international-convention

Partida, J. (1996). The effects of immigration on children in the Mexican-American community. *Child and Adolescent Social Work Journal*, *13*(3), 241–254. https://doi.org/10.1007/BF01875790

Paterson, J. (2010, May 10). Getting inside the gang mentality. *Counseling Today*. https://ct.counseling.org/2010/05/getting-inside-the-gang-mentality/

Perez, W. (2010). Higher education access for undocumented students: Recommendations for counseling professionals. *Journal of College Admission*, *206*, 32–35.

Perez, W., Espinoza, R., Ramos, K., Coronado, H. M., & Cortes, R. (2009). Academic resilience among undocumented Latino students. *Hispanic Journal of Behavioral Sciences*, *31*(2), 149–181. https://doi-org/10.1177/0739986309333

Perreira, K. M., & Ornelas, I. (2013). Painful passages: Traumatic experiences and post-traumatic stress among U.S. immigrant Latino adolescents and their primary caregivers. *International Migration Review*, *47*(4), 976–1005. https://doi.org/10.1111/imre.12050

Pew Research Center. (2016). *The value of a college education*. https://www.pewresearch.org/social-trends/2016/10/06/5-the-value-of-a-college-education/

Pincus, F. L. (2018). From individual to structural discrimination. In F. L. Pincus & H. J. Ehrlich (Eds.), *Race and ethnic conflict: Contending views on prejudice, discrimination, and ethnoviolence* (2nd ed., pp. 120–124). Routledge. (Original work published 1999)

Pivovarova, M., & Powers, J. M. (2019). Generational status, immigrant concentration and academic achievement: Comparing first and second-generation immigrants with third-plus generation students. *Large-Scale Assessments in Education*, *7*(1), Article 7. https://doi.org/10.1186/s40536-019-0075-4

Potochnick, S. (2018). The academic adaptation of immigrant students with interrupted schooling. *American Educational Research Journal*, *55*(4), 859–892. https://doi.org/10.3102/0002831218761026

Potochnick, S. R., & Perreira, K. M. (2010). Depression and anxiety among first-generation immigrant Latino youth: Key correlates and implications for future research. *The Journal of Nervous and Mental Disease*, *198*(7), 470–477. https://doi.org/10.1097/NMD.0b013e3181e4ce24

Prewitt, K. (2005). Racial classification in America: Where do we go from here? *Daedalus*, *134*(1), 5–17. https://doi.org/10.1162/0011526053124370

Pryce, J., Kelly, M. S., Lawinger, M., & Wildman, A. (2018). Conversation club: A promising practice in youth mentoring of migrants and refugees. *Advances in Social Work*, *18*(3), 767–787. https://doi.org/10.18060/21650

Rafieifar, M., & Macgowan, M. J. (2022). A meta-analysis of group interventions for trauma and depression among immigrant and refugee children. *Research on Social Work Practice, 32*(1), 13–31. https://doi.org/10.1177/10497315211022812

Refugee Student Alliance. (n.d.). *About us.* https://ccc.rochester.edu/rsa/home/

Romo, L. F., & Mireles-Rios, R. (2016). Latina immigrant mother-daughter communication about their body self-esteem and weight dissatisfaction: An exploratory video-observational study. *Journal of Latina/o Psychology, 4*(1), 18–31. https://doi.org/10.1037/lat0000044

Rossiter, A., Byrne, F., Wota, A. P., Nisar, Z., Ofuafor, T., Murray, I., Byrne, C., & Hallahan, B. (2015). Childhood trauma levels in individuals attending adult mental health services: An evaluation of clinical records and structured measurement of childhood trauma. *Child Abuse & Neglect, 44*, 36–45. https://doi.org/10.1016/j.chiabu.2015.01.001

Rossiter, M. J., & Rossiter, K. R. (2009). Diamonds in the rough: Bridging gaps in supports for at-risk immigrant and refugee youth. *Journal of International Migration and Integration, 10*(4), 409–429. https://doi.org/10.1007/s12134-009-0110-3

Rowland, K., & Davis, T. (2014). Counseling immigrant students in the schools. *Georgia School Counselors Association Journal, 21*(1).

Ruge, T. R., & Iza, A. D. (2005). Higher education for undocumented students: The case for open admission and in-state tuition rates for students without lawful immigration status. *Indiana International & Comparative Law Review, 15*(2), 257–278. https://journals.iupui.edu/index.php/iiclr/article/view/17838/18009

Sahay, K. M., Thatcher, K., Núñez, C., & Lightfoot, A. (2016). "It's like we are legally, illegal": Latino/a youth emphasize barriers to higher education using photovoice. *The High School Journal, 100*(1), 45–65. https://doi.org/10.1353/hsj.2016.0020

Salas-Wright, C. P., Vaughn, M. G., Goings, T. C., Miller, D. P., & Schwartz, S. J. (2018). Immigrants and mental disorders in the United States: New evidence on the healthy migrant hypothesis. *Psychiatry Research, 267*, 438–445. https://doi.org/10.1016/j.psychres.2018.06.039

Schuchart, C., & Siebel, A. (2023). Counselling of immigrant students in schools: The development of shared understanding between advisers and students. *British Journal of Guidance & Counselling, 51*(5), 820–834. https://doi.org/10.1080/03069885.2021.2009767

Scott, D. (2022). Where you from? Examining the relationship between gang migrants and gang-related homicide. *Societies, 12*(2), Article 48. https://doi.org/10.3390/soc12020048

Segal, U. A. (2018). Education and migrants: A view from the United States of America. *Sisyphus, 6*(1), 120–140. https://doi.org/10.25749/SIS.13797

Shekunov, J. (2017). Immigration and risk of psychiatric disorders: A review of existing literature. *The American Journal of Psychiatry, 11*(2), 3–5. https://doi.org/10.1176/appi.ajp-rj.2016.110202

Staff, J., Yetter, A. M., Cundiff, K., Ramirez, N., Vuolo, M., & Mortimer, J. T. (2020). Is adolescent employment still a risk factor for high school dropout? *Journal of Research on Adolescence, 30*(2), 406–422. https://doi.org/10.1111/jora.12533

Stark, L., Seff, I., Yu, G., Salama, M., Wessells, M., Allaf, C., & Bennouna, C. (2022). Correlates of suicide ideation and resilience among native- and foreign-born adolescents in the United States. *Journal of Adolescent Health, 70*(1), 91–98. https://doi.org/10.1016/j.jadohealth.2021.07.012

Storlie, C. A. (2011). Career development for all students: School counselor advocacy with undocumented immigrant youth. *School Counseling Research & Practice, 3*, 35–42.

Suárez-Orozco, C., Onaga, M., & de Lardemelle, C. (2010). Promoting academic engagement among immigrant adolescents through school-family-community collaboration. *Professional School Counseling, 14*(1). https://doi.org /10.1177/2156759X1001400103

Sue, D. W. (2010). *Microaggressions in everyday life: Race, gender, and sexual orientation.* John Wiley & Sons

Tanaka, H. (2021). Development of the *ibasho* concept in Japanese education and youth work: Ibasho as a place of refuge and empowerment for excluded people. *Educational Studies in Japan: International Yearbook, 15*, 3–15.

Telzer, E. H. (2010). Expanding the acculturation gap-distress model: An integrative review of research. *Human Development, 53*(6), 313–340. https://doi.org/10.1159/000322476

Torres, S. A., Sosa, S. S., Flores Toussaint, R. J., Jolie, S., & Bustos, Y. (2022). Systems of oppression: The impact of discrimination on Latinx immigrant adolescents' well-being and development. *Journal of Adolescent Research, 32*(2), 501–517. https://doi.org/10.1111/jora.12751

Tummala-Narra, P. (2015). Ethnic identity, perceived support, and depressive symptoms among racial minority immigrant-origin adolescents. *American Journal of Orthopsychiatry, 85*(1), 23–33. https://doi.org/10.1037/ort0000022

Tummala-Narra, P. (2020). The fear of immigrants. *Psychoanalytic Psychology, 37*(1), 50–61. https://doi.org/10.1037/pap0000245

Tummala-Narra, P., & Claudius, M. (2013). Perceived discrimination and depressive symptoms among immigrant-origin adolescents. *Cultural Diversity and Ethnic Minority Psychology, 19*(3), 257–269. https://doi.org/10.1037/a0032960

Unger, J. B., Gallaher, P., Shakib, S., Ritt-Olson, A., Palmer, P. H., & Johnson, C. A. (2002). The AHIMSA Acculturation Scale: A new measure of acculturation for adolescents in a multicultural society. *The Journal of Early Adolescence, 22*(3), 225–251. https://doi.org/10.1177/02731602022003001

UNICEF, Division of Policy and Strategy. (2006). *Somalia: Statistical country profile on female genital mutilation/cutting.* https://data.unicef.org:wp-content:uploads:country_profiles:Somalia:FGMC_SOM.pdf

United Nations High Commissioner for Refugees. (2018). *Profiling study on internal mobility due to violence in El Salvador: Final report.* https://www.jips.org/uploads/2018/03/El-Salvador-profiling-report-EN.pdf

United Nations Office on Drugs and Crime. (2022). *Gender-related killings of women and girls (femicide/feminicide).* https://www.unodc.org/documents/data-and-analysis/briefs/Femicide_brief_Nov2022.pdf

University of California at Berkeley. (2023, June 7). *DACA information.* https://undocu.berkeley.edu/legalsupport-overviw3/what-is-daca/

U.S. Citizenship and Immigration Services. (2023, September 18). *Consideration of Deferred Action for Childhood Arrivals (DACA).* https://www.uscis.gov/DACA

U.S. Department of Education, Federal Student Aid. (n.d.). *Many non-U.S. citizens qualify for federal student aid.* https://studentaid.gov/understand-aid/eligibility/requirements/non-us-citizens

U.S. Department of Health and Human Services, Office of Civil Rights. (2023). *Discrimination on the basis of race, color, or national origin (including LEP).* https://www.hhs.gov/guidance/document/discrimination-basis-race-color-or-national-origin-including-lep

U.S. Department of Homeland Security. (2021, November 10). *Deferred Action for Childhood Arrivals (DACA).* https://www.dhs.gov/deferred-action-childhood-arrivals-daca-0

Valenzuela, J. I., Perez, W., Perez, I., Montiel, G. I., & Chaparro, G. (2015). Undocumented students at the community college: Creating institutional capacity. *New Directions for Community Colleges, 2015*(172), 87–96. https://doi.org/10.1002/cc.20166

Velarde Pierce, S., Haro, A. Y., Ayón, C., & Enriquez, L. E. (2021). Evaluating the effect of legal vulnerabilities and social support on the mental health of undocumented college students. *Journal of Latinos and Education, 20*(3), 246–259. https://doi.org/10.1080/15348431.2021.1949990

Victims of Trafficking and Violence Protection Act of 2000, Pub. L. No. 106-386, 114 Stat. 1464 (2000). https://www.govinfo.gov/content/pkg/PLAW-106publ386/pdf/PLAW-106publ386.pdf

Vitoroulis, I., & Georgiades, K. (2017). Bullying among immigrant and non-immigrant early adolescents: School- and student-level effects. *Journal of Adolescence, 61*(1), 141–151. https://doi.org/10.1016/j.adolescence.2017.10.008

Vogt, W.A. (2013). Crossing Mexico: Structural violence and the commodification of undocumented Central American migrants. *American Ethnologist, 40*(4), 764–780. https://doi.org/10.1111/amet.12053

Wambu, G. (2018, September 18). Career decision making of African-immigrant students: What career counselors need to know. *Career Convergence Web Magazine.* https://www.ncda.org/aws/NCDA/page_template/show_detail/185957?model_name=news_article

Wang, C., Do, K. A., Frese, K., & Zheng, L. (2019). Asian immigrant parents' perception of barriers preventing adolescents from seeking school-based mental health services. *School Mental Health, 11*(2), 364–377. https://doi.org/10.1007/s12310-018-9285-0

Watkinson, J. S., & Hersi, A. A. (2014). School counselors supporting African immigrant students' career development: A case study. *The Career Development Quarterly, 62*(1), 44–55. https://doi.org/10.1002/j.2161-0045.2014.00069.x

Weisskirch, R. S., Guan, S.-S. A., & Lazarevic, V. (2021). How language brokering relates to empathy and psychological well-being. *Journal of Social and Personal Relationships, 38*(11), 3061–3077. https://doi.org/10.1177/02654075211020407

William Wilberforce Trafficking Victims Protection Reauthorization Act of 2008, Pub. L. No. 110-457, 122 Stat. 5044 (2008). https://www.congress.gov/110/plaws/publ457/PLAW-110publ457.pdf

Wilson, J., Ward, C., & Fischer, R. (2013). Beyond culture learning theory: What can personality tell us about cultural competence? *Journal of Cross-Cultural Psychology, 44*(6), 900–927. https://doi.org/10.1177/0022022113492889

Wolf, K. M., Zoucha, R., McFarland, M., Salman, K., Dagne, A., & Hashi, N. (2016). Somali immigrant perceptions of mental health and illness: An ethnonursing study. *Journal of Transcultural Nursing, 27*(4), 349–358. https://doi.org/10.1177/1043659614550487

Wolfe, D. (2023). *Femicide: A global tragedy, no matter your gender.* World Vision Canada. https://www.worldvision.ca/stories/gender-equality/femicide-a-global-tragedy-no-matter-your-gender

World Health Organization. (n.d.). *Maternal, newborn, child and adolescent health and ageing data portal.* https://platform.who.int/data/maternal-newborn-child-adolescent-ageing/indicator-explorer-new/mca/adolescent-population-as-percentage-of-total-population

Zagefka, H., & Brown, R. (2002). The relationship between acculturation strategies, relative fit and intergroup relations: Immigrant-majority relations in Germany. *European Journal of Social Psychology, 32*(2), 171–188. https://doi.org/10.1002/ejsp.73

Zeiders, K. H., Nair, R. L., Hoyt, L. T., Pace, T. W. W., & Cruze, A. (2020). Latino early adolescents' psychological and physiological responses during the 2016 U.S. presidential election. *Cultural Diversity and Ethnic Minority Psychology, 26*(2), 169–175. https://doi.org/10.1037/cdp0000301

Chapter 9

Counseling With Immigrant, Refugee, and Birthright Adults

In the research and in news outlets, the stories that most often appear about immigrants and refugees are about adults. They are the ones who have had to plan and carry out the migratory processes for themselves and their families. This is an enormous burden of responsibility, one that is predictably loaded with a range of emotions for successes and failures in their quest for a new life. In Chapter 3, we discussed the various phases or stages of the migration process, pointing out that, all along, individuals are planful, decisive, and goal oriented. If they do not make it into the United States on the first attempt, they try again and again. Refugees may have a different means of entry into the United States; however, extended periods in refugee camps, the loss of family and friends during those confinements, and fleeing to different countries (e.g., Syria to Turkey to France) are also exhausting. Adults generally do not have time to mourn or reflect on the risks and losses, but this does not mean those events evaporate. How and when developmental tasks manifest for adult immigrants and refugees will be discussed through case examples that emerged through our research.

The developmental challenges of young adults, adults, and older adults are addressed in this chapter. Throughout, the complexity of individuals' life situations in the United States will become noteworthy. It is not just the cultural differences that come into play but also the premigration circumstances, immigrant journey, and generation status that play a role in immigrants' identities, relationships, health and mental health concerns, and sense of stability. In the sections that follow, there is valuable knowledge-building material for counselors who will find themselves serving and advocating for immigrants. References to the Multicultural and Social Justice Counseling Competencies (MSJCC; Ratts et al., 2015) will be made where appropriate.

Learning Objectives

- Recognize adult developmental tasks and implications for counseling practices.
- Identify the effects of working on developmental tasks on the mental health of adults (from young adults to older adults).
- Develop multicultural competencies to inform counselors' culturally responsive services in working with adults, across the life span, from a variety of populations.

The following section introduces a self-assessment to gauge your existing knowledge of culturally responsive counseling frameworks designed to address inequities and marginalization, ethical considerations in working with immigrant and refugee populations, and the MSJCC (Ratts et al., 2015) needed to do so. This brief assessment aims to explore your current understanding of key concepts and provide a foundation for further learning. Answering the following questions will better equip you to engage with the content.

Self-assessment: Please respond to the following statements by rating yourself on the following Likert scale: *strongly agree, agree, disagree, strongly disagree,* or *unsure.*

1. I understand the unique needs of adult refugee and immigrant clients postmigration and during the resettlement process.
2. I am aware that I must gain insight about adult developmental issues as they apply to my adult clients who are refugees and immigrants.
3. I feel confident in my work with adult immigrant and refugee clients in working on family, career, spiritual, and financial issues related to mental health.
4. I understand the need for special considerations for adult immigrant and refugee clients of various developmental stages dealing with mental health issues related to the acculturation process.

There is considerable research about immigrant and host populations' developmental markers, such as secondary education, marriage, employment, and parenting. It is important to distinguish between generations of immigrants given that research indicates significant differences in immigrants' and refugees' experiences and types of adjustments through transitions. The "1.25" immigrants migrated between the ages of 13 and 17 years. Individuals who immigrated as children under the age of 13 years, second-generation U.S.-born immigrants with one or both immigrant parents, and third-generation immigrants who have U.S.-born parents are known as "1.5" immigrants (Rumbaut & Komaie, 2010). Discussions about emerging adults and adults in this chapter include literature and research on 1.25 and 1.5 immigrants, and first-generation immigrants.

Immigrant and Refugee Adult Development

As previously discussed, knowledge of developmental stages in life span development is a key ingredient in developing MSJCC competency. *Emerging adulthood* is a term conceptualized by Arnett (2000) to describe a time between adolescence and adulthood, ages 18–25, when young adults explore a plethora of opportunities in relationships, jobs, and personal perspectives about the world. The degree of exploration in these developmental areas is greater during this stage than any other stage of development (Arnett, 2000). Contemporary Americans currently perceive becoming an adult as satisfying three life tasks that are individually oriented (i.e., taking responsibility for oneself, making independent decisions, and having financial independence; Arnett, 1998), although these may not fit emerging adults or all adults with marginalized/minoritized status or families that live in poverty (Berlin et al., 2010). Unlike U.S. emerging adult experiences, many emerging adult immigrants' entries into the workforce occur before high school completion and often align with dropping out of school (Gonzales & Roth, 2015). For example, in 2015 in the United States, 9% of eligible immigrant students were "out of school," working to help support their families (Granados, 2018).

For immigrants and refugees who are searching for a safe place in the world to establish a livable income and meet other developmental tasks (i.e., raise a family), emerging adulthood is often culturally driven by traditions, survival and identity negotiation, and exploration of a scope of adult tasks (Arnett, 2000). However, there are no absolutes in terms of immigrant and refugee developmental milestones, and there is literature that provides frameworks in which immigrants and refugees develop through their process of immigration and settling into a new home and culture. The immigration process is a developmental experience that impacts the process of development during the emerging adult maturation stage (Walsh et al., 2005). Immigrant emerging adults do not have a standard timeline for maturation into adulthood; they gain independence from their parents while at times helping to contribute financially to their family, marry, become employed, and start their own family (Rumbaut & Komaie, 2010). This occurs at various rates with a considerable variation among immigrant groups (Rumbaut & Komaie, 2010). Many immigrants and refugees may get waylaid from engaging in Western-centered, adult development tasks due to dropping out of high school, becoming involved with the legal system, or becoming young parents, which leads to more inequity in the United States (Gonzales & Roth, 2015). One way to look at how some immigrant emerging adults and young U.S.-born adults from lower socioeconomic status (SES) backgrounds may fail to reach adult milestones is a concept known as *cumulative disadvantage*, which is the culmination of experiences of poverty, legal status, community violence, bad schools, and discrimination in employment (Gonzales & Roth, 2015). Whether the focus is on immigrant or U.S.-born populations living in lower SES income brackets, when emerging adults experience so many challenges, it is difficult to manage developmental tasks with much success. For example, individuals who withdraw from school and begin working to help support their family may miss the educational and social milestones of an emerging adult. Having this knowledge increases a counselor's MSJCC development in terms of the counseling relationship and client worldview.

The immigration process is its own developmental experience and impacts the process of maturation during the emerging adult stage of development (Walsh et al., 2005). Migration is known as a stressful and anxious time for immigrants, often challenging their ego identity, with potential threats to one's perspective of continuity over time, one's sense of consistency between one's culture and the self, and a feeling of confirmation of one's identity (Garza-Guerrero, 1974). Akhtar (1999) described immigration as a *psychic flux*, challenging the process of reorganization of the self as one adapts to difficult changes in the new environment postmigration. It is for these reasons that studies of immigrant and refugee developmental processes are important for counselors to understand so that they do not unknowingly make assumptions about immigrants' and refugees' developmental progress, or impairment, based on Western experiences. Far too often comparisons are drawn between "normal" development for nonimmigrants of different economic and education statuses and immigrants and refugees who have different trajectories.

Mexican immigrant adolescents are known to enter adulthood earlier than most adolescents from developed countries because of economic issues (Zenteno et al., 2013). Emerging adult refugees from the former Soviet Union have been found to suffer through migration with the result of an impaired sense of self, low levels of reflectivity on their journey and life experiences, and struggles with a false self, meaning that they carry with them a sense of identity confusion (Walsh et al., 2005). Numerous immigrants from low-income families do not automatically attend secondary education because they lack financial support from parents and must contribute to the family income (Fuligni & Pedersen, 2002). Undocumented emerging adults may struggle with developmental milestones because of their immigration status and restrictions in employment opportunities, voting, and travel; the result is often decision-making about illegal and risky employment (Gonzales & Roth, 2015).

> Julia Bendis (n.d.) came to the United States with her parents when they left the former Soviet Union to flee persecution, discrimination, and antisemitism. She was 13 years old, and her brother was 10 years old. She describes her expectations of better treatment in the United States but quickly found that she was wrong. Once in the United States, she was told to lose her accent and assimilate, but she struggled with letting go of her identity. Her parents were in respected occupations in the former Soviet Union—her father an engineer and her mother a microbiologist. However, once they immigrated to the United States, they were treated like second-class citizens. Her father could only find work drilling cement and her mother could only find work sorting shoes in a warehouse. Her parents' developmental tasks of building on the careers they began in the former Soviet Union were stalled when they were forced to take work in occupational fields unrelated to their previous jobs. Julia's developmental trajectory was interrupted by her "assimilation" in the United States and a perceived sense that she could not be herself. Today, Julia's children respect her differentness and culture and ask her to get her accent back. She feels happy that her children's generation is more open to diversity.

To understand the needs of emerging immigrant adults, there should be more research and discussion about how immigrants and refugees settle once they arrive in the United States and the challenges they face that may delay their development and impact their sense of identity. For example, engaging in community groups and clubs or attending a community college with flexible timeline to completion may help them stay on track with their life goals (Gonzales & Roth, 2015). Resources that help immigrants and refugees are discussed later in this chapter.

> Valleria moved to the Midwest from Mexico in her mid-20s when she decided she wanted to study in the United States and make a good life for herself. She found a community organization that welcomes immigrants and refugees and helps them get established with work, housing, and medical care. This community organization helps hundreds of immigrants and refugees annually to establish their home in the United States and gain academic achievement for a better life than the one they left behind. Valleria's experiences with finding support and resources helped her stay on track in terms of her developmental and professional growth.

Mexican migrants' first trips to the United States typically occur prior to the age of 35, during adolescence and early adulthood (Zenteno et al., 2013). It is also known that Mexican immigrants fare better as adults than their parents in terms of economic success when they immigrate at younger ages due to educational attainment and English proficiency (Stevens, 2004). Age at arrival is considered an important element in understanding varying levels of economic success as age defines developmental tasks such as academic achievement, employment status, and establishment of marriage and family (Rumbaut & Komaie, 2010). Research has also shown that the same is true for Asian immigrants in the United States, in that younger immigrants fared better in language acquisition, educational success, and occupational achievements (S. M. Lee & Edmonston, 2011).

Undocumented immigrant children typically surpass their immigrant parents because of greater educational attainment and language acquisition (Gonzales, 2016). In fact, many emerging adults contribute financially to support their parents (Rumbaut & Komaie, 2010). In terms of academic success, undocumented and documented immigrants are catching up to their U.S.-born counterparts' achievement. By the year 2019, 33% of immigrants held a college degree or more (vs. 33% of nonimmigrants), 19% had some college (vs. 31% of nonimmigrants), 22% held a high school diploma only (vs. 28% of nonimmigrants), and 26% had less than a high school diploma (vs. 8% of nonimmigrants; American Immigration Council, 2021). More Hispanics are graduating from high school than ever before. Hispanic high school graduates increased from 55% in 1997 to 71% in 2017 (Schmidt, 2018). Immigrants seem to be faring better in these areas and balancing their family and school responsibilities successfully. This may be a result of immigrants' understanding that the current job market in the United States requires a minimum of a high school diploma (Schmidt, 2018). Knowledge in this area helps develop MSJCC competency in terms of the counseling relationship when counselors can inspire immigrant and refugee clients to attend and graduate high school.

Immigrant children and adolescents can experience disadvantaged environments (i.e., neighborhoods with high crime rates and poor schools) that result in barriers to success in adulthood (Soehl, 2017). Immigrant emerging adults experience a process of cultural identity development involving factors such as age of migration, engagement with the host culture's educational system, immigration status, and potential values conflicts between the host country and the immigrant's family (Ellis & Chen, 2013). It has been found that immigrants experience less racial discrimination than U.S.-born minorities, perhaps because racial minorities born in the United States have spent more time in the country and thus have more experience with discrimination than immigrants (Polanco-Roman, 2016). This does not mean that immigrants do not experience racial discrimination, bullying in schools and the workplace, and other forms of marginalization based on appearance, language, and color. Research has found that immigrants with more experience with acculturation in the United States report more racial discrimination than those with less acculturation because they may face more opportunities for discrimination as they try to fit into the majority culture (Pérez et al., 2008; Saadi et al., 2020). Understanding the impact of acculturation processes for immigrants and refugees is one of the keys in being culturally competent in working with immigrants and refugees.

College Student Mental Health Counseling

The American College Counseling Association (ACCA) is the national organization for professional counselors, social workers, and psychologists who work with university and college populations to promote mental health and student development. Members of ACCA "enhance the learning experience for students through the promotion of social justice . . . and multidimensional diversity and provide college counseling services that nurture environments where similarities and differences among people are recognized, respected, and honored" (ACCA, 2009, "Diversity Statement").

More than 2 million immigrants and second-generation Americans attend U.S. colleges, representing nearly 20% of all college students in the United States (Zong & Batalova, 2016) and 24% of community college students (Higher Ed Immigration Portal, n.d.). Immigrant students are diverse and in 2018 were shown to be made up of the following: 85% Asian American and Pacific Islander students, 63% Latino students, and 24% Black students (Batalova & Feldblum, 2020). Most immigrant students are U.S. citizens, with 68% being born in the United States and 16% becoming citizens by naturalization (Batalova & Feldblum, 2020).

Typically, immigrants who arrive in the United States prior to the age of 12 years have experiences with language and American educational system norms (Baum & Flores, 2011) and achieve more success in college than older immigrant students (Hernandez et al., 2011). Immigrant students report the following obstacles to success in college: more family responsibilities compared with nonimmigrant students, weak math and English skills, lack of study skills, and feelings of stress (Soria & Stebleton, 2013). Knowing these factors can help career counselors work with immigrants in a more effective way.

Counseling issues specific to immigrant college students include acculturation (Brilliant et al., 2000; Schwartz et al., 2011; Torres et al., 2004), high-risk behaviors related to typical college student behaviors (Warner et al., 2010), documentation challenges, varying levels of academic preparation and difficulty with the English language (Teranishi et al., 2011), identity and self-esteem (Luyckx et al., 2013), and career development (Cadenas et al., 2021; Poon, 2014; Stebleton, 2007). Students must be recognized for their intersecting identities as well. For example, if a student is LGBTQ+, they may have additional stress, and the college counseling center may be their best recourse. Immigrant students who struggle from attempting to cope with stressors and experience anxiety, depression, or social concerns are often drawn to the college counseling office (Hayes et al., 2011).

Counseling Interventions With Immigrant College Students

Narrative therapy is recommended when working with Latinx immigrant college students (Oliver et al., 2011; Taylor et al., 2006) given its cultural sensitivity framework and usefulness in attending to bridging the gap between culture of origin and new culture (Henry et al., 2005). Furthermore, narrative therapy provides counselors with the tools to explore immigration and acculturation issues (Farrell & Gibbons, 2019). Problematic narratives create distress when they conflict with lived experiences (C. Brown & Augusta-Schott, 2007), and narrative therapy helps immigrants to explore oppressive narratives and rewrite narratives that are mentally healthier and more meaningful to their identity (Farrell & Gibbons, 2019). Marginalized and oppressed Latinx immigrant students can express themselves freely and regain their voice that might have been lost through discrimination (Arredondo et al., 2014).

The sub-Saharan African population has increased recently in the United States, and Sub-Saharan African immigrants present many of the same needs as other immigrant college students; however, they are confronted with unique decisions about work, family, and community (Stebleton, 2007). Stebleton (2007) found unique career issues of African immigrant students: the impact of colonialism related to slavery and identity, living in uncertainty due to the influence of contextual issues, and struggling with conflicting messages between African and Western worldviews. Issues related to the long-term effects of colonialism, discrimination, and social injustices may affect their self-esteem and confidence (Stebleton, 2007). Many African immigrants maintain family ties in their home countries (Rendón, 1996) and are unsure about their future and whether they can return home; worry about sending money back home to loved ones; and struggle with depression, anxiety, and fear related to ambiguity (Stebleton, 2007).

Understanding these issues is critical for counselors in terms of working effectively with this client population and in terms of developing MSJCC competency. Traditional decision-making career models and theories are not necessarily meaningful for African students who live in limbo and deal with the impact of discrimination in terms of vocational processes (e.g., job applications and promotions; Stebleton, 2007). Kamya (1997) recommended a developmental-contextual counseling approach. A systems lens developed from a constructivist perspective is more holistic (McMahon, 2005) and offers a framework in which individuals consider interpersonal and social relations when contemplating their vocational plans (Stebleton, 2007). Overall, it is important to use the developmental-contextual and systems approach in counseling to address discrimination, identity development, and decision-making for positive outcomes (Stebleton, 2007).

Counseling Interventions With Undocumented College Students

Immigration policies in the United States prevent undocumented immigrant high school students from achieving naturalization (Gonzales, 2016), gaining work authorization, receiving in-state college tuition, accessing public assistance, and obtaining a driver's license

(Zong & Batalova, 2019). Undocumented students represent 2% of all college students, and a fraction of these students graduate from college (Suárez-Orozco et al., 2015).

Undocumented students can develop protective factors in dealing with discrimination, and one such factor is known as *critical consciousness*, which is the ability to comprehend sociopolitical stressors and develop coping skills to tackle them (Cadenas et al., 2021). Marginalized students possessing critical consciousness develop better mental health, stronger academic ability, and more successful career development and vocational outcomes (Diemer et al., 2016). Moreover, undocumented students tend to cope with racism by developing career motivation and aspirations (Autin et al., 2018). Cadenas et al. (2021) found that coping skills of undocumented students can be strengthened by reconceptualizing existing strategies, becoming involved in activism and self-advocacy that increase their social justice agency and career development, and experiencing university supports for academic achievement (e.g., tutoring, diversity organizations).

Cadenas et al. (2021) suggested that counselors working with undocumented college students use culturally appropriate approaches to facilitate the development of coping skills, student confidence, and positive vocational outcomes. Addressing and affirming discrimination is an important first step in helping students develop awareness of their sociopolitical environment of systemic oppression through values identification and narrative therapy (Cadenas et al., 2021). Additionally, addressing cultural trauma can be accomplished by using a model such as Healing Ethno and Racial Trauma (HEART) for Latinx clients (Chavez-Dueñas et al., 2019). This model provides interventions that increase clients' feelings of empowerment and develops agency. HEART also promotes the idea that client healing is grounded in their reconnecting, strengthening, or staying connected to their ethnoracial roots (Adames & Chavez-Dueñas, 2017).

Immigrant college students have resilience and strength in their cultural identity, and with the help of legislation such as Deferred Action for Childhood Arrivals and the support of college counseling center personnel, they can meet the demands of academia, succeed in vocational planning, and develop agency in the challenges of discrimination.

College and University Career Counseling Services

Career counselors in colleges and universities offer the following services for clients and students: career assessments of beliefs, decision-making, interests, and values; job search skills; professional employment skills; job matching; education sessions; and life skills (Zunker, 2016). Typically, career counselors assess the needs and goals of their client before determining the type of assessments to use and prior to determining interventions to be implemented. Much of career counseling is meeting the client or student where they are in terms of career development, job search needs, decision-making skill development, and vocational identity (Zunker, 2016).

Contextual issues for African immigrants include events such as war, political oppression, disease, natural disaster, and poverty (Vondracek, 1990). Understanding these contextual issues will be critical for a career counselor to help African immigrants explore their perspective about work and career development (Stebleton, 2007). Also important to explore with African immigrant college students are possible grief and loss issues due to separations from family members and the potential guilt related to leaving family in Africa (Espin, 1987). Many students maintain their state of mourning for the loss of family for long periods of time (Nwadiora & McAdoo, 1996). African immigrant students may also present in counseling and career centers with depression and anxiety related to the loss of family, and these mental health symptoms may impact their career development and related decisions (Stebleton, 2007).

College mental health counselors should become familiar with their student population and their cultural identity. Understanding the students' culture and specific mental health and career development needs is important for counselors to support their students' educational aspirations and specific culture-based stressors.

Job and Career

Career theorists note that in the United States, traditional definitions of "career" have described narrow, sequential, and focused occupational positions whereby one might work in one career/job for their entire career (e.g., Savickas, 2019). Contemporary definitions of career involve less predictability and more *boundarylessness*, meaning that many career journeys today involve job opportunities that extend outside the boundaries of specific employment opportunities (Defillippi & Arthur, 1994). Additionally, contemporary careers are seen more as lattice oriented in that one's career has horizontal and diagonal moves, organizational structures are less obvious, and career paths are more difficult to navigate (Neve, 2021).

Jobs are most often acquired by adult immigrants and refugees through family, friends, and acquaintances. Many immigrants and refugees live in a collectivistic system in their ways of cohabiting in multigenerational households, supporting each other financially, and experiencing a fluidness in relationships across extended family members near and at a distance. Finances are typically shared for living expenses and traditional family celebrations that can be costly, between immediate family members and distant relatives, and for supporting families in the country of origin through remittances (Falicov, 2001). Ward and Batalova (2023) reported that immigrants ages 16 and older comprised 37% of the workforce and worked in management, professional, and related occupations. These working-age immigrants have found service and professional jobs and careers with varying levels of difficulty. Many undocumented immigrants, as already mentioned earlier in this chapter, struggle with finding jobs that pay well and are safety conscious, while documented immigrants with more formal education may be hired in a variety of professions.

Salaries for immigrants are very similar to those of U.S.-born employees, with an immigrant household median income of $69,622 in 2021, compared with the household median income of nonimmigrants of $69,734; 14% of immigrants in 2021 had family incomes below the poverty line of $27,500 for a family of four compared with 13% of nonimmigrant households (Ward & Batalova, 2023). In terms of capital resources, an average of 55.2% of immigrant and refugee adults live in owner-occupied homes (housing where homeowners use their property as their primary residence) compared with 64.6% of nonimmigrants, and immigrants often find that home prices are higher in densely populated immigrant communities (Channel, 2022). Additionally, working-age immigrant adults have fewer Social Security benefits than U.S.-born adults, and those over the age of 65 report lower Social Security benefits (Sevak & Schmidt, 2014), meaning that many immigrant adults are contributing to their parents' finances and have fewer resources for their own families (Sweet & Meiksins, 2021).

There are many state resources for immigrants and refugees through programs that target career goals and assist immigrants with postmigration resources. For example, Minnesota State CAREERwise (n.d.) provides information about agencies, services, and web addresses (see Appendix 9A).

Departments of social services offer information about private nongovernment organizations to support national refugee resettlement services (California Department of Social Services, n.d.). Some examples of these organizations are Amnesty International USA, Doctors Without Borders, Episcopal Migration Ministries, Human Rights Watch, and Refugee Council. Accessing resources for immigrants and refugees is important in their resettlement process. These organizations contribute to advocacy efforts as outlined in the MSJCC (Ratts et al., 2015) for immigrants and refugees and their transition to their new life.

Sexual Identity and Marriage

Common markers in adult identity development across cultures include marriage or some type of betrothal (Schlegel & Barry, 1991). In the past 50 years, the United States has seen a transition from early to later age of marriage. In 1960, the median age of marriage for men and women was 22 years and 20 years, respectively; in 1997, the median age of marriage for men and women had risen to 27 years and 25 years, respectively (Arnett et al., 2001). By 2021, the median age of marriage was 30.6 years for men and 28.6 years for women (Statista, 2022). Comparatively, 46% of immigrant women and 35% of immigrant men tend to marry by the age of 24 years (Mayol-García & Gurrentz, 2021).

Marriages in the United States conducted in an individualistic cultural orientation are typically matches made independently between partners. Whether matches are made explicitly or implicitly in collectivistic cultures, many cultures view marriage as a type of arrangement to strengthen the family, but they vary in terms of adult responsibilities and gender roles and expectations. For example, Jewish immigrants view marriage as a means of raising families and preserving cultural values and heritage. Postmarriage, Jewish partners tend to stay connected to their parents, who may continue to see their adult children as dependents who need financial and other resources well into adulthood (Rosen & Weltman, 2005), and up to 32% of young Jewish adults live with their parents (Roberts, 2019). In terms of intermarriage, in the United States, roughly two thirds of Jewish adults are married or living with a partner, with 42% intermarried individuals indicating having a non-Jewish spouse and 98% of Orthodox Jews reporting being married to another Jewish partner (Pew Research Center, 2021).

Greek marriages are often bound by family commitment and strict gender roles. In terms of fidelity, Greek husbands are expected to explore sexual opportunities outside marriage (Killian & Agathangelou, 2005), resulting in 20% of Greek husbands being unfaithful (Chrysopoulos, 2017). Husbands, however, rarely divorce and leave their families for an affair (Killian & Agathangelou, 2005). Greek wives have historically been forbidden from engaging in extramarital affairs (Killian & Agathangelou, 2005); however, more recent trends show that 10% of Greek wives are unfaithful (Chrysopoulos, 2017). Gender role expectations are strict and rigid. Matchmaking was at one time the practice of parents finding ideal partners for their adult children, and although arranged marriages were the order of the day in ancient Greece, traditional matchmaking is no longer considered customary (Harris-Papaioannou, 2022).

Asian families emphasize collectivism and a sense of "we," and individuals are seen as a member of a family of many generations, while passing along important traditions and rituals in child-rearing, customs, and family celebrations, as well as metaphors and stories to illustrate family values (E. Lee & Mock, 2005). Divorce is somewhat rare in Asian families. Compared with other ethnic groups, Asian women and men have the lowest rate of divorce (14% and 11%, respectively; Mayol-García et al., 2021).

Irish women are found to be an exception when it comes to marriage and motherhood. During the emigration from Ireland after the Great Famine, caused by a failure of the potato crop, in the mid-1800s to the United States, Irish women sought to find economic independence and autonomy not available to them in their homeland (Flanagan, 2015). Attitudes toward Irish working women and the unmarried are more acceptable than many other cultures, and Irish immigrant women find employment in health care, higher education, retail, pharmaceutical, banking, hospitality, and education management (Morahan, 2022).

LGBTQ+ Identity and Discrimination

LGBTQ+ immigrant adults are individuals with sexual orientations and gender identities that are not part of the heterosexual and male/female binary perspective. Gender and sexual identities are part of the intersectionality of multiple identities. Intersectionality is a theoretical framework developed by Black women feminists to address and understand the many interwoven forms of disadvantages related to one's many layers of identity (Crenshaw, 1991). It is important to look at intersectionality of adult immigrants and refugees, although immigrant status in the literature does not include sexual identification as an important dimension of study; thus, the topic has not been well researched. Adult immigrants face racism, sexism, heterosexism, and xenophobia, and it is essential that counselors understand the impact of these biases on the adult immigrant and refugee population in the United States. Silva and Evans (2020) researched the intersectional patterning of sexual identity of a national U.S. sample with young adults of varying demographics, including adult immigrants. Their study found substantial variability in women's inclination to identify as exclusively heterosexual but little variability in men's self-identification of heterosexuality across racial/ethnic and immigrant status categories. The reason the researchers believe that individuals may report heterosexism despite identifying as LGBTQ+ is to avoid the multiple layers of discrimination based on race, gender, immigrant status, and SES level (Silva & Evans, 2020).

Research shows that 1.3 million LGBTQ+ immigrant adults live in the United States (Goldberg & Conron, 2021). It is estimated that 3% of the immigrant population identify as LGBTQ+, and of this population, 8.8% of those ages 18–29 years, 3.3% of those ages 30–44 years, 2% of those ages 45–54 years, and 1.1% of those ages 55 years and over identify as LGBTQ+ (Goldberg & Conron, 2021). For undocumented immigrants, it is estimated that 3% of all undocumented individuals identify as LGBTQ+, with 6.5% under the age of 30 years compared with 2.5% ages 30–44 years, 1.5% ages 45–54 years, and less than 1% ages 55 years or older (Goldberg & Conron, 2021). Very little research has focused on an intersectional approach to understanding the lived experiences of LGBTQ+ immigrants (Viruell-Fuentes et al., 2012), and more needs to be done to understand this immigrant population.

Documented and undocumented LGBTQ+ immigrants experience discrimination, cissexism, hate crimes, and microaggressions upon arrival to their new communities (Zwiers, 2010). It is reported that undocumented immigrants are mistreated mentally, physically, and sexually in immigration detention facilities (Lambda Legal, 2011). LGBTQ+ immigrants are often segregated and put in solitary confinement and do not receive medical care (e.g., transgender individuals are not allowed treatment for their ongoing medical needs). In many cases, sending an individual who identifies as LGBTQ+ back to their home country can be a death sentence; deportation can be more dangerous than staying in the United States (D. Ortiz, 2014).

Homosexuality is outlawed in many cultures around the world. Recent research studies find 26 countries where women in particular experience forced marriage, property rights discrimination, and police violence (Human Rights Watch, 2023). In many cultures, LGBTQ+ individuals hide their identity. For example, gay Lebanese and Syrian immigrants often marry heterosexual partners to honor their religion and maintain family honor (Haboush, 2005). Greek LGBTQ+ immigrants may conceal their sexual orientation given the explicitly strong negative attitudes about homosexuality in their cultural value system (Killian & Agathangelou, 2005). In Irish culture, LGBTQ+ individuals are tolerated, and partners are accepted if they are not explicit in their sexual identity (McGoldrick, 2005). Varying behaviors and attitudes among LGBTQ+ immigrants are important for counselors and mental health providers to understand to better serve the personal, marital, and sexual identity needs of their clients.

The term *undocuqueer* is a political identity term acknowledging queer and trans identities of marginalized undocumented immigrants (Seif, 2016). Cisneros and Gutierrez (2018) studied undocuqueer Latinx immigrants and found that they experience systemic violence and degradation in reaction to their gender, sex, and immigration intersectionality identity. Undocuqueer individuals face difficult conditions that exclude them from jobs and policies that focus on criminalization through racializing practices (Cisneros & Gutierrez, 2018). On a more positive note, Gray et al. (2015) reported that LGBTQ+ immigrants found support and affirmation within the LGBTQ+ community. However, Gray et al. also found that when LGBTQ+ individuals experienced a values conflict between their racial identity and sexual orientation, they downplayed their sexual orientation when around family or immigrant community members who were not supportive. Furthermore, LGBTQ+ individuals tended to report positive character and strength in their sexual and gender identities because of challenges and negative experiences in the past (Gray et al., 2015). Gray et al. recommended that counselors view LGBTQ+ immigrants' challenges as a character-building experience. Overall, counselors need to stay up to date on the shifting sociopolitical climate in terms of systemic discrimination and understand the related impact of dehumanization that many undocuqueer and LGBTQ+ individuals experience, as well as empowerment models of viewing adversity as a growth opportunity.

Cross-Cultural Relationships

Cross-cultural relationships and mixed marriages are created by partners from different cultural identities and/or of immigrant and U.S.-born status. There has been a growth in mixed marriages due to the increase in immigration from Latin America, the Caribbean, and Asia since the year 2000 (Mayol-García & Gurrentz, 2021). In 2015, the number of mixed marriages was 17%, up from 7% in the 1980s (Livingston & Brown, 2017). Eight percent of migrant women were in a mixed relationship in their first marriage, and 19% of migrant Asians, Hispanics, and women who identify as "other" were in mixed marriages (Mayol-García & Gurrentz, 2021). Additionally, younger migrant women were more likely to be in a mixed marriage, with young women ages 15–24 years having twice the likelihood of being in a mixed marriage than women ages 55 years and older (Mayol-García & Gurrentz, 2021). The most common cross-cultural marriages are a Hispanic and a White spouse (42%), a White and an Asian spouse (15%), and a White and a multiracial spouse (12%; Livingston & Brown, 2017). Additionally, metropolitan areas, where it seems that attitudes are more open to diverse marriages, have more interracial marriages than rural areas (18% and 11%, respectively; Livington & Brown, 2017).

> Savanna migrated to the United States from Mexico after her then husband who had immigrated ahead of her to the United States quit sending her money and told her he could not support her anymore. She described him drinking up his money and having very little left over for her or his bills. Once she arrived in the United States, she traveled from the West to the East working seasonal jobs at orchards and farms. She found herself in a series of bad relationships with the immigrant men she met, finally settling on a man who was born in the United States who wanted to support and care for her and her family. She reported finally being in a relationship that felt safe to her.

Supportive counselors with knowledge about the issues faced by immigrant and refugee sexual and gender minorities can assist them effectively when they are culturally competent and understand the intersectionality and the layers of their clients' sex and gender identities. For example, Fox et al. (2020) found that asylum seekers who identify as LGBTQ+ experience loneliness and struggle with disclosures about their sexual and gender identity, which has a connection to mental distress. Most of these asylum seekers report mental health goals that include finding an LGBTQ+ community in which they could make friends, mentor an LGBTQ+ individual, and join an actual LGBTQ+ community center

(Fox et al., 2020). Understanding the sexual and relationship issues of immigrants and refugees helps counselors become aware of the nuances of why their clients establish or maintain relations with partners during the migratory process, marriage, and child-rearing period while experiencing discrimination because of their multiple intersectional identities.

Health and Wellness

Immigrants and refugees create demands for health services in the communities in which they reside (Tsoh et al., 2016). Despite great needs, immigrants and refugees tend to encounter barriers to health services, including language, culture, health beliefs, expenses, lack of health insurance, and SES level (Wang & Kwak, 2015), and these barriers are more challenging for older immigrants because of decreased mobility and lower SES (Subedi & Rosenberg, 2014). Furthermore, stigma about mental health issues in many cultures remains a barrier; for example, persons of Asian heritage in need of mental health services often avoid mental health treatment because of fear of stigma (Fancher et al., 2010).

According to the MSJCC (Ratts et al., 2015), knowledge of government policies increases a counselor's ability to serve immigrants and refugees. National events have occurred in the United States that impact immigrant health care and insurance options. Specifically, during the 2016–2020 U.S. presidential administration, changes to immigration policy increased fears among immigrant families in terms of seeking health and mental health services, with stricter policies on limiting immigration, enforcing immigration offenses, and limiting the use of public services by immigrant families (Kaiser Family Foundation, 2023). Since then, the 2020 U.S. administration has taken great strides in reversing policies made in the previous administration, but continuing efforts are needed to encourage immigrant families to engage in services available to them.

Conflicting research findings about mental health status presents a "yes, and" perspective in the current state of the needs of immigrant adult clients. Some studies find minority status to be associated with fewer mental health issues when compared with nonminority data on depression (e.g., J. S. Brown et al., 2007), and other studies have found that immigrants are shown to be healthier than their U.S. counterparts and much less likely to participate in risky behaviors (Alegría et al., 2017). However, undocumented immigrants have been found to have significantly higher rates of mental health issues than their documented counterparts due to the stressors of immigration status and resettlement (Garcini et al., 2017). Nonetheless, Marks et al. (2014) found that studies on physical and mental health indicate that first-generation immigrants have more positive health outcomes than U.S.-born individuals. Interestingly, neighborhoods with a high percentage of immigrants are found to be protective in terms of managing psychological stress (Mair et al., 2010) and lower levels of certain illnesses, such as the Epstein-Barr virus (Ford & Browning, 2015). Studies have shown that immigrants experience substantially fewer incidents of health problems and are less likely to engage in behaviors such as substance use, gambling, and violence (Breslau et al., 2009). Moreover, Alegría et al. (2017) found that foreign-born Hispanic Americans are much healthier than U.S.-born Hispanic Americans, and the U.S. Census Bureau (2016) reports that Mexican Americans experience health benefits in terms of less occurrence of illness than many U.S. ethnic groups. This array of conflicting research findings motivates researchers to conduct more studies on the mental health of immigrants that may guide counselors and mental health professionals in their work with immigrant and refugee adult clients.

The *healthy migrant hypothesis*, a theory about adult immigrant health and resilience, describes positive immigrant health related to self-selection whereby individuals who migrate to pursue a better life are more likely to be more mentally and physically healthy than their U.S.-born counterparts, with less tendency for mental health issues

(Salas-Wright et al., 2019). Suárez-Orozco and Carhill (2008) cautioned against counselors assuming a negative connection between adult immigrant experiences with stressful migration and mental health difficulties. Cigrand et al. (2022) found that although their adult immigrant and refugee sample described horrendous migration journeys to the United States, they also described resilient and impressive coping strategies, and most did not seek out counseling within the 10 years that followed their resettlement.

Older Adult Immigrant and Refugee Mental Health

It is essential for counselors to understand older immigrants' and refugees' mental health needs to understand associated challenges, coping skills, and use of internal and community resources later in life to be MSJCC competent. In 2018, there were 7.3 million immigrants and refugees 65 years and older, representing 13.9% of the older population in the United States (Mizoguchi et al., 2019). Individuals ages 60 years and older, also known as *boomers* in the United States, who were born between 1946 and 1965, are the fastest emergent population in the world (United Nations, 2015). Mental health research on older adult immigrants finds that fewer than one in 11 Latinx individuals with a mental health diagnosis pursues counseling with mental health providers, and that statistic is reduced significantly for Latinx immigrants (National Hispanic Council on Aging, 2016). While only 30%–50% of older adults in need of mental health services seek counseling, even fewer older immigrants and ethnic minorities utilize mental health services at all (Crabb & Hunsley, 2006). Latinx undocumented immigrants avoid health care due to their fear that seeking health services could alert immigration officials to their undocumented status or that their use of health services will impair their ability to obtain legal status (Rhodes et al., 2015).

D. V. Ortiz (2012) found that when mental health clinic administration and counseling practitioners work to understand the unique needs of the immigrant client population, counseling issues can be more effectively identified and addressed. Common counseling topics for older immigrants include loss of social and personal resources because of relocation and family (which is a central conversation topic in counseling, even when family members are not present). D. V. Ortiz also found that when clinics focus on the multicultural competency development of their staff, they impact the cultural climate of the clinic. There seem to be two-way benefits for practitioners and immigrant clients alike.

Cultural competence in working with immigrants and refugees requires knowledge about the respective culture and counseling skills geared toward rapport building and a working relationship between client and counselor (Ratts et al., 2015). D. V. Ortiz (2012) found that focusing on cultural understanding on such elements as *respeto* (respect) for older Latinx clients is an important attending skill demonstrating clinician cultural responsiveness. Miyawaki et al. (2022) found that understanding the importance of the family helps clinicians and mental health programs center their focus on family support to encourage Asian immigrant clients to become more motivated to receive mental health services. The value of collectivism is tied to family interdependence and support.

Senior centers, adult day care centers, and community activities for groups tend to have a positive health benefit for ethnically diverse older adults (Dane et al., 2020). Community programs offer learning, exercise classes, and social programs that can provide older immigrants with opportunities to stay involved socially and learn about mental and physical health practices. For example, Koehn et al. (2016) found that older immigrants attending exercise classes reaped health benefits for physical as well as mental health. Jo et al. (2018) found that a program called Canada Enoch Senior's College provided many benefits to its Korean immigrant older adults: physical strengthening through exercise/dance classes, improved appetite and energy, a motivation to take better care of the self, a feeling of less restriction socially, a sense of emotional support, and opportunities for social connection.

Zhu and Zhang (2019) proposed an active aging model for older Chinese immigrants in Canada and found that their participants engaged in four categories of lifelong learning: learning language and computer skills, culture and history, civic engagement, and leisure and health. These older Chinese immigrants reported experiencing daily challenges but were found to have sought out resources from local governments and nongovernmental agencies to live fuller lives in the four areas of learning. By continuing to engage within their communities, they remain active, learn skills, experience culture, acquire information on health-related topics, and feel more connected to others (Zhu & Zhang, 2019).

Somchai immigrated to the United States after living in a refugee camp in Thailand with his siblings, wife, children, and mother. He had been a farmer by trade and unsuccessful before the Vietnam War, in which his father and brothers fought. His father died during the war. After the war, Somchai found himself with the rest of his family in the refugee camp. After 10 years in the refugee camp, he arrived in the United States with his family and worked for 20 years on farms and in orchards. Now, Somchai is most happy in his retirement after many years in the United States and that his adult children are well educated and bilingual. They support him, take him to the doctor, and generally care for him during his old age. "I don't have to worry about what I am going to eat tomorrow. . . . I am happy to be a citizen. I am an American, and I feel like this is my country now."

Ying immigrated to the United States from Laos after the Vietnam War ended. She immigrated with her mother, two brothers, and two sisters. They were a source of support for her. Ying reports that the U.S. government supported her family with housing, food, and work opportunities. U.S. sponsors were an important resource for Ying and her family when they helped them access food and took them to places in their community to help them settle. Her siblings helped her with language and resettlement issues as their transition was smoother than for Ying as she was very sick much of the time after arriving in the United States. Once settled in the United States, she married and had three children, two boys and a girl. Her children have been able to help Ying in her older age with translations at the doctors' office and when shopping for food. Her own grasp of the English language has been difficult, and she has relied on her children who are "well educated." She is very proud of her children as adults and sees the benefits of immigration from her perspective as an older immigrant.

Counselors are taught to be multiculturally competent in counseling immigrants in their training programs but also need to remember immigrant and refugee clients' amazing tenacity, strength, and faith in working on counseling goals when they do attend counseling sessions. Part of cultural competency development is understanding why immigrants and refugees do not seek out counseling (they do not think about it necessarily and/or they have religious faith that sustains them) and why they do (easy access to services and education about mental health).

The case study below introduces Adam, whose parents are from distinctly different cultures and experienced many challenges as a result. During a time of anti-Semitic attitudes in Europe, many suffered and escaped unsafe communities. Adam's parents met and were able to recognize their differences and resolve their dissimilarities.

CASE STUDY

Adam's grandparents migrated from Morocco to Israel when anti-Semitism was increasing in 1940 (Fine, 2019). Israel was a safe place for Jews at the time, and they built a life there and raised Adam's mother, Rachel. Adam's father, David, and his family immigrated from Poland to the United States when he was a child prior to World War II. He attended Jewish school in Pittsburgh, then visited Israel during college. This is where Rachel and David met and fell in love. Adam describes the differences in Moroccan and Polish Jewish cultures and the intensity of friction between the "two drastically different families and their cultures." Eventually, they resolved their identity and cultural differences together, and Rachel and David migrated to Boston. Adam describes his parents as creating a blend of cultures in their marriage and family as he has worked to make sense of his two cultures.

Reflection Questions

1. How do you understand Adam's developmental growth in terms of milestones?
2. How would you work with Adam if he is struggling with identity issues related to his developmental stage?
3. What is necessary for you to work on that will help you work with Adam?
4. What do you need to learn more about in terms of cross-cultural relationships, and how would you help Adam to negotiate his cultural identity?

Summary

Adult immigrants and refugees have had to plan and carry out the migratory processes for themselves and their families. This process can be an arduous one that encompasses challenges that evoke emotions about their new life unfolding. Depending on the stage of development in adulthood, many factors need to be addressed in counseling. This chapter discussed how and when developmental tasks manifest for adult immigrants and refugees and how these tasks impact their quality of life and mental health issues. Throughout the chapter, we provided valuable knowledge-building material for counselors who will find themselves serving and advocating for immigrants and refugees.

References

Adames, H. Y., & Chavez-Dueñas, N. Y. (2017). *Cultural foundations and interventions in Latino/a mental health: History, theory and within group differences*. Routledge.

Akhtar, S. (1999). *Immigration and identity: Turmoil, treatment, and transformation*. Jason Aronson.

Alegría, M., Álvarez, K., & DiMarzio, K. (2017). Immigration and mental health. *Current Epidemiology Reports, 4*(2), 145–155. https://doi.org/10.1007/s40471-017-0111-2

American College Counseling Association. (2009). *Mission statement*. https://www.collegecounseling.org/Mission-Statement

American Immigration Council. (2021). *Immigrants in the United States* [Fact sheet]. https://www.americanimmigrationcouncil.org/research/immigrants-in-the-united-states

Arnett, J. J. (1998). Learning to stand alone: The contemporary American transition to adulthood in cultural and historical context. *Human Development, 41*(5 6), 295 315. https://doi.org/10.1159/000022591

Arnett, J. J. (2000). Emerging adulthood: A theory of development from the late teens through the twenties. *American Psychologist, 55*(5), 469–480. https://doi.org/10.1037/0003-066X.55.5.469

Arnett, J. J., Ramos, K. D., & Jensen, L. A. (2001). Ideological views in emerging adulthood: Balancing autonomy and community. *Journal of Adult Development, 8*(2), 69–79. https://doi.org/10.1023/A:1026460917338

Arredondo, P., Gallardo-Cooper, M., Delgado-Romero, E. A., & Zapata, A. L. (2014). *Culturally responsive counseling with Latinas/os*. American Counseling Association.

Autin, K. L., Duffy, R. D., Jacobson, C. J., Dosani, K. M., Barker, D., & Bott, E. M. (2018). Career development among undocumented immigrant young adults: A psychology of working perspective. *Journal of Counseling Psychology, 65*(5), 605–617. https://doi.org/10.1037/cou0000280

Batalova, J., & Feldblum, M. (2020). *Immigrant-origin students in U.S. higher education: A data profile* [Fact sheet]. Migration Policy Institute. https://www.migrationpolicy.org/research/immigrant-origin-students-us-higher-education

Baum, S., & Flores, S. M. (2011). Higher education and children in immigrant families. *The Future of Children, 21*(1), 171–193. https://www.jstor.org/stable/41229016

Bendis, J. [@iamanimmigrant] (n.d.). *My immigrant story starts in the former Soviet Union* [Photographs]. Instagram. https://www.instagram.com/p/CsSCI8EOvtk/

Berlin, G., Furstenberg, F. F., Jr., & Waters, M. C. (2010). Introducing the issue. *The Future of Children, 20*(1), 3–18.

Breslau, J., Borges, G., Hagar, Y., Tancredi, D., & Gilman, S. (2009). Immigration to the USA and risk for mood and anxiety disorders: Variation by origin and age at immigration. *Psychological Medicine, 39*(7), 1117–1127. https://doi.org/10.1017/s0033291708004698

Brilliant, J. J. (2000). Issues in counseling immigrant college students. *Community College Journal of Research and Practice, 24*, 577–586. https://doi.org/10.1080/10668920050139721

Brown, C., & Augusta-Schott, T. (Eds.). (2007). *Narrative therapy: Making meaning, making lives.* Sage Publications.

Brown, J. S., Meadows, S. O., & Elder, G. H., Jr. (2007). Race-ethnic inequality and psychological distress: Depressive symptoms from adolescence to young adulthood. *Developmental Psychology, 43*(6), 1295–1311. https://doi.org/10.1037/0012-1649.43.6.1295

Cadenas, G. A., Peña, D., Minero, L. P., Rojas-Araúz, B. O., & Lynn, N. (2021). Critical agency and vocational outcome expectations as coping mechanisms among undocumented immigrant students. *Journal of Latinx Psychology, 9*(2), 92–108. https://doi.org/10.1037/lat0000178

California Department of Social Services. (n.d.). *Private non-governmental organizations.* https://www.cdss.ca.gov/inforesources/refugees/stakeholders/ngos

Channel, J. (2022, May 24). *Foreign-born homeowners are less likely to live in owner-occupied homes and more likely to be housing cost burdened than U.S.-born peers.* LendingTree. https://www.lendingtree.com/home/lendingtree-reveals-the-cities-with-the-most-foreign-born-homeowners/

Chavez-Dueñas, N. Y., Adames, H. Y., Perez-Chavez, J. G., & Salas, S. P. (2019). Healing ethno-racial trauma in Latinx immigrant communities: Cultivating hope, resistance, and action. *American Psychologist, 74*(1), 49–62. https://doi.org/10.1037/amp0000289

Chrysopoulos, P. (2017, February 6). One in five Greek men cheat on their partners. *Greek Reporter.* https://greekreporter.com/2017/02/06/one-in-five-greek-men-cheat-on-their-partners/

Cigrand, D., Fawcett, M. L., Arredondo, P., Miyakuni, R., & Onderak, G. (2022). Experiences of survival and perseverance through dire decisions: A phenomenological study of the immigration journey. *Journal of Counseling & Development, 100*(2), 157–170. https://doi.org/10.1002/jcad.12413

Cisneros, J., & Gutierrez, J. (2018). "What does it mean to be undocuqueer?" Exploring (il)legibility within the intersection of gender, sexuality, and immigration status. *QED, 5*(1), 84–102. https://doi.org/10.14321/qed.5.1.0084

Crabb, R., & Hunsley, J. (2006). Utilization of mental health care services among older adults with depression. *Journal of Clinical Psychology, 62*(3), 299–312. https://doi.org/10.1002/jclp.20231

Crenshaw, K. (1991). Mapping the margins: Intersectionality, identity politics, and violence against women of color. *Stanford Law Review, 43*(6), 1241–1299. https://doi.org/10.2307/1229039

Dane, S., Haslam, C., Jetten, J., Liu, S., Gallois, C., & Tran, T. L. N. (2020). The benefits of ethnic activity group participation on older immigrant well-being and host country adjustment. *International Journal of Intercultural Relations, 77*, 119–124. https://doi.org/10.1016/j.ijintrel.2020.05.006

Defillippi, R. J., & Arthur, M. B. (1994). The boundaryless career: A competency-based perspective. *Journal of Organizational Behavior, 15*(4), 307–324. https://doi.org/10.1002/job.4030150403

Diemer, M. A., Rapa, L. J., Voight, A. M., & McWhirter, E. H. (2016). Critical consciousness: A developmental approach to addressing marginalization and oppression. *Child Development Perspectives, 10*(4), 216–221. https://doi.org/10.1111/cdep.12193

Ellis, L. M., & Chen, E. C. (2013). Negotiating identity development among undocumented immigrant college students: A grounded theory study. *Journal of Counseling Psychology, 60*(2), 251–264. https://doi.org/10.1037/a0031350

Espin, O. M. (1987). Psychological impact of migration on Latinas: Implications for psychotherapeutic practice. *Psychology of Women Quarterly, 11*(4), 489–503. https://doi.org/10.1111/j.1471-6402.1987.tb00920.x

Falicov, C. J. (2001). The cultural meanings of money: The case of Latinos and Anglo-Americans. *American Behavioral Scientist, 45*(2), 313–328. https://doi.org/10.1177/00027640121957088

Fancher, T. L., Ton, H., Meyer, O. L., Ho, T., & Paterniti, D. A. (2010). Discussing depression with Vietnamese American patients. *Journal of Immigrant and Minority Health, 12*(2), 263–266. https://doi.org/10.1007/s10903-009-9234-y

Farrell, I. C., & Gibbons, M. M. (2019). Using narrative therapy to assist college-age Latino immigrants. *Journal of College Counseling, 22*(1), 83–96. https://doi.org/10.1002/jocc.12116

Fine, A. (Creator). (2019). *Adam Fine* [Moving image; oral history]. University of Minnesota, Immigration History Research Center. https://umedia.lib.umn.edu/item/p16022coll554:197?facets%5Bcollection_name_s%5D%5B%5D=Immigrant+Stories

Flanagan, M. S. (2015). *Irish women's immigration to the United States after the potato famine, 1860–1900* (Senior Theses, 42) [Bachelor's thesis, Dominican University of California]. Dominican Scholar. https://doi.org/10.33015/dominican.edu/2015.HIST.ST.01

Ford, J. L., & Browning, C. R. (2015). Exposure to neighborhood immigrant concentration from adolescence to young adulthood and immune function among Latino young adults. *Health & Place, 32*, 59–64. https://doi.org/10.1016/j.healthplace.2014.12.010

Fox, S. D., Griffin, R. H., & Pachankis, J. E. (2020). Minority stress, social integration, and the mental health needs of LGBTQ asylum seekers in North America. *Social Science & Medicine, 246*, Article 112727. https://doi.org/10.1016/j.socscimed.2019.112727

Fuligni, A. J., & Pedersen, S. (2002). Family obligation and the transition to young adulthood. *Developmental Psychology, 38*(5), 856–868. https://doi.org/10.1037/0012-1649.38.5.856

Garcini, L. M., Peña, J. M., Galvan, T., Fagundes, C. P., Malcarne, V., & Klonoff, E. A. (2017). Mental disorders among undocumented Mexican immigrants in high-risk neighborhoods: Prevalence, comorbidity, and vulnerabilities. *Journal of Consulting and Clinical Psychology, 85*(10), 927–936. https://doi.org/10.1037/ccp0000237

Garza-Guerrero, A. C. (1974). Culture shock: Its mourning and the vicissitudes of identity. *Journal of American Psychoanalytic Association, 22*(2), 408–429. https://doi.org/10.1177/000306517402200213

Goldberg, S. K., & Conron, K. J. (2021). *LGBT adult immigrants in the United States.* The Williams Institute, UCLA School of Law. https://williamsinstitute.law.ucla.edu/wp-content/uploads/Adult-LGBT-Immigrants-Feb-2021.pdf

Gonzales, R. G. (2016). *Lives in limbo.* University of California Press.

Gonzales, R. G., & Roth, B. J. (2015). Immigrant children and the transition to adulthood. In R. A. Scott & S. M. Kosslyn (Eds.), *Emerging trends in the social and behavioral sciences: An interdisciplinary, searchable, and linkable resource.* John Wiley & Sons. https://doi.org/10.1002/9781118900772.etrds0173

Granados, A. (2018, November 28). *Education, unsettled: Inside the struggle to keep migrant students in school and out of the fields.* Education Week. https://www.edweek.org/leadership/education-unsettled-inside-the-struggle-to-keep-migrant-students-in-school-and-out-of-the-fields/2018/11

Gray, N. N., Mendelsohn, D. M., & Omoto, A. M. (2015). Community connectedness, challenges, and resilience among gay Latino immigrants. *American Journal of Community Psychology, 55*(1–2), 202–214. https://doi.org/10.1007/s10464-014-9697-4

Haboush, K. L. (2005). Lebanese and Syrian families. In M. McGoldrick, J. Giordano, & N. Garcia-Preto (Eds.), *Ethnicity and family therapy* (3rd ed., pp. 468–486). Guilford Press.

Harris-Papaioannou, S. (2022, February 7). Arranged marriages in Greece: Traditional matchmaking and its legacy. *Greek Reporter.* https://greekreporter.com/2022/02/07/arranged-marriages-greece/

Hayes, J. A., Youn, S. J., Castonguay, L. G., Locke, B. D., McAleavey, A. A., & Nordberg, S. (2011). Rates and predictors of counseling center use among college students of color. *Journal of College Counseling, 14*(2), 105–116. https://doi.org/10.1002/j.2161-1882.2011.tb00266.x

Henry, H. M., Stiles, W. B., & Biran, M. W. (2005). Loss and mourning in immigration: Using the assimilation model to assess continuing bonds with native culture. *Counselling Psychology Quarterly, 18*(2), 109–119. https://doi.org/10.1080/09515070500136819

Hernandez, D. J., Denton, N. A., & Blanchard, V. L. (2011). Children in the United States of America: A statistical portrait by race-ethnicity, immigrant origins, and language. *The Annals of the American Academy of Political and Social Science, 633*(1), 102–127. https://doi.org/10.1177/0002716210383205

Higher Ed Immigration Portal. (n.d.). *2021 national data.* Retrieved November 16, 2023, https://www.higheredimmigrationportal.org/national/national-data/

Human Rights Watch. (2023, February 14). *LBQ+ women face brutal attacks, discrimination at every turn: Research in 26 countries finds forced marriage, property rights violations, police violence.* https://www.hrw.org/news/2023/02/14/lbq-women-face-brutal-attacks-discrimination-every-turn

Jo, E. H., Jo, J. S., Veblen, K. K., & Potter, P. J. (2018). Enoch Senior's College for Korean immigrant seniors: Quality of life effects. *Canadian Journal on Aging, 37*(3), 345–359. https://doi.org/10.1017/S0714980818000211

Kaiser Family Foundation. (2023, September 17). *Key facts on health coverage of immigrants.* https://www.kff.org/racial-equity-and-health-policy/fact-sheet/health-coverage-of-immigrants/

Kamya, H. A. (1997). African immigrants in the United States: The challenge for research and practice. *Social Work, 42*(2), 154–165. https://doi.org/10.1093/sw/42.2.154

Killian, K. D., & Agathangelou, A. M. (2005). Greek families. In M. McGoldrick, J. Giordano, & N. Garcia-Preto (Eds.), *Ethnicity and family therapy* (3rd ed., pp. 573–585). Guilford Press.

Koehn, S., Habib, S., & Bukhari, S. (2016). S4AC case study: Enhancing underserved seniors' access to health promotion programs. *Canadian Journal on Aging/La Revue canadienne du vieillissement, 35*(1), 89–102. https://doi.org/10.1017/s0714980815000586

Lambda Legal. (2011, June 8). *Lambda Legal, immigrants' rights and LGBT groups urge Homeland Security to protect LGBT immigrants' rights in detention facilities.* https://www.lambdalegal.org/news/ny_20110608_lambda-legal-immigrants

Lee, E., & Mock, M. R. (2005). Asian families: An overview. In M. McGoldrick, J. Giordano, & N. Garcia-Preto (Eds.), *Ethnicity and family therapy* (3rd ed., pp. 269–289). Guilford Press.

Lee, S. M., & Edmonston, B. (2011). Age-at-arrival's effects on Asian immigrants' socioeconomic outcomes in Canada and the U.S. *International Migration Review, 45*(3), 527–561. https://doi.org/10.1111/j.1747-7379.2011.00857.x

Livingston, G., & Brown, A. (2017, May 18). *Intermarriage in the U.S. 50 years after Loving v. Virginia.* Pew Research Center. https://www.pewresearch.org/social-trends/2017/05/18/intermarriage-in-the-u-s-50-years-after-loving-v-virginia/

Luyckx, K., Klimstra, T. A., Duriez, B., Van Petegem, S., Beyers, W., Teppers, E., & Goossens, L. (2013). Personal identity processes and self-esteem: Temporal sequences in high school and college students. *Journal of Research in Personality, 47*(2), 159–170. https://doi.org/10.1016/j.jrp.2012.10.005

Mair, C., Diez Roux, A., Osypuk, T., Rapp, S., Seeman, T., & Watson, K. (2010). Is neighborhood racial/ethnic composition associated with depressive symptoms? The Multi-Ethnic Study of Atherosclerosis. *Social Science Medicine, 71*(3), 541–550. https://doi.org/10.1016/j.socscimed.2010.04.014

Marks, A. K., Ejesi, K., & García Coll, C. (2014). Understanding the U.S. immigrant paradox in childhood and adolescence. *Child Development Perspectives, 8*(2), 59–64. https://doi.org/10.1111/cdep.12071

Mayol-García, Y., & Gurrentz, B. (2021, May 3). *Marital histories differ between native-born and foreign-born adults.* U.S. Census Bureau. https://www.census.gov/library/stories/2021/05/marital-histories-differ-between-native-born-and-foreign-born-adults.html

Mayol-García, Y., Gurrentz, B., & Kreider, R. M. (2021). *Number, timing, and duration of marriages and divorces: 2016* (P70-167). U.S. Census Bureau. https://www.census.gov/content/dam/Census/library/publications/2021/demo/p70-167.pdf

McGoldrick, M. (2005). Irish families. In M. McGoldrick, J. Giordano, & N. Garcia-Preto (Eds.), *Ethnicity and family therapy* (3rd ed., pp. 595–615). Guilford Press.

McMahon, M. (2005). Career counseling: Applying the systems theory framework of career development. *Journal of Employment Counseling, 42*(1), 29–38. https://doi.org/10.1002/j.2161-1920.2005.tb00896.x

Minnesota State CAREERwise. (n.d.). *Cultural services for immigrants and refugees.* https://careerwise.minnstate.edu/guide/immigrants/immigrantservices.html

Miyawaki, C. E., Liu, M., Park, V. T., Tran, M. T., & Markides, K. S. (2022). Social support as a moderator of physical disability and mental health in older Vietnamese immigrants in the U.S.: Results from the Vietnamese Aging and Care Survey (VACS). *Geriatric Nursing, 44*, 151–158. https://doi.org/10.1016/j.gerinurse.2022.01.012

Mizoguchi, N., Walker, L., Trevelyan, E., & Ahmed, B. (2019). *The older foreign-born population in the United States: 2012–2016* (ACS-42). U.S. Census Bureau. https://www.census.gov/content/dam/Census/library/publications/2019/acs/acs-42.pdf

Morahan, G. (2022, November 25). *The jobs and industries where Irish women are most represented.* Business Plus. https://businessplus.ie/jobs/women-jobs-industries-represented/

National Hispanic Council on Aging. (2016). *Status of Hispanic older adults: Insights from the field.* http://www.nhcoa.org/wp-content/uploads/2016/09/2016-NHCOA-Status-of-Hispanic-Older-Adults-report-.pdf

Neve, T. (2021, October 29). *What does "career" really mean in the 21st century?* LinkedIn. https://www.linkedin.com/pulse/what-does-career-really-mean-21st-century-tina/

Nwadiora, E., & McAdoo, H. (1996). Acculturative stress among Amerasian refugees: Gender and racial differences. *Adolescence, 31*(122), 477–487.

Oliver, M., Flamez, B., & McNichols, C. (2011). Postmodern applications within Latino/a cultures. *Journal of Professional Counseling, Practice, Theory & Research, 38*(3), 33–48. https://doi.org/10.1080/15566382.2011.12033875

Ortiz, D. (2014, April 2). *Deportation can be a death sentence for LGBT immigrants.* Immigration Equality. https://perma.cc/BJC7-LLL6

Ortiz, D. V. (2012). Structuring mental health within senior services: A case study of an outpatient mental health clinic serving Latinos. *Journal of Gerontological Social Work, 55*(6), 503–518. https://doi.org/10.1080/01634372.2012.673539

Pérez, D. J., Fortuna, L., & Alegría, M. (2008). Prevalence and correlates of everyday discrimination among U.S. Latinos. *Journal of Community Psychology, 36*(4), 421–433. https://doi.org/10.1002/jcop.20221

Pew Research Center. (2021, May 11). *Jewish Americans in 2020.* https://www.pewresearch.org/religion/2021/05/11/jewish-americans-in-2020/

Polanco-Roman, L., Danies, A., & Anglin, D. M. (2016). Racial discrimination as race-based trauma, coping strategies, and dissociative symptoms among emerging adults. *Psychological Trauma: Theory, Research, Practice, and Policy, 8*(5), 609–617. https://doi.org/10.1037/tra0000125

Poon, O. (2014). "The land of opportunity doesn't apply to everyone": The immigrant experience, race, and Asian American career choices. *Journal of College Student Development, 55*(6), 499–514. https://doi.org/10.1353/csd.2014.0056

Ratts, M. J., Singh, A. A., Nassar-McMillan, S., Butler, S. K., & McCullough, J. R. (2015). *Multicultural and social justice counseling competencies.* Association for Multicultural Counseling and Development. https://www.counseling.org/docs/default-source/competencies/multicultural-and-social-justice-counseling-competencies.pdf?sfvrsn=20

Rendón, L. I. (1996). Life on the border. *About Campus, 1*(5), 14–20. https://doi.org/10.1002/abc.6190010504

Rhodes, S. D., Mann, L., Simán, F. M., Song, E., Alonzo, J., Downs, M., Lawlor, E., Martinez, O., Sun, C. J., O'Brien, M. C., Reboussin, B. A., & Hall, M. A. (2015). The impact of local immigration enforcement policies on the health of immigrant Hispanics/Latinos in the United States. *American Journal of Public Health, 105*(2), 329–337. https://doi.org/10.2105/AJPH.2014.302218

Roberts, C. (2019, June 18). *A third of young adults live with their parents.* Israel National News. https://www.israelnationalnews.com/news/264741

Rosen, E. J., & Weltman, S. F. (2005). Jewish families: An overview. In M. McGoldrick, J. Giordano, & N. Garcia-Preto (Eds.), *Ethnicity and family therapy* (3rd ed., pp. 667–679). Guilford Press.

Rumbaut, R. G., & Komaie, G. (2010). Immigration and adult transitions. *The Future of Children, 20*(1), 43–66. https://doi.org/10.1353/foc.0.0046

Saadi, A., & Ponce, N. A. (2020). Worse mental health among more-acculturated and younger immigrants experiencing discrimination: California Health Interview Survey, 2015–2016. *Journal of General Internal Medicine, 35*(5), 1419–1426. https://doi.org/10.1007/s11606-019-05412-w

Salas-Wright, C. P., Vaughn, M. G., Miller, D. P., Hahm, H. C., Scaramutti, C., Cohen, M., Delva, J., & Schwartz, S. J. (2019). Overeating and binge eating among immigrants in the United States: New terrain for the healthy immigrant hypothesis. *Social Psychiatry and Psychiatric Epidemiology, 54*(8), 1007–1017. https://doi.org/10.1007/s00127-019-01677-y

Savickas, M. L. (2019). *Career counseling* (2nd ed.). American Psychological Association. https://doi.org/10.1037/0000105-000

Schlegel, A., & Barry, H., III. (1991). *Adolescence: An anthropological inquiry.* Free Press.

Schmidt, E. (2018, July 31). *For the first time, 90 percent completed high school or more.* U.S. Census Bureau. https://www.census.gov/library/stories/2018/07/educational-attainment.html

Schwartz, S. J., Weisskirch, R. S., Zamboanga, B. L., Castillo, L. G., Ham, L. S., Huynh, Q.-L., Park, I. J. K., Donovan, R., Kim, S. Y., Vernon, M., Davis, M. J., & Cano, M. A. (2011). Dimensions of acculturation: Associations with health risk behaviors among college students from immigrant families. *Journal of Counseling Psychology*, *58*(1), 27–41. https://doi.org/10.1037/a0021356

Seif, H. (2016). "We define ourselves": 1.5-generation undocumented immigrant activist identities and insurgent discourse. *North American Dialogue*, *19*(1), 23–35. https://doi.org/10.1111/nad.12039

Sevak, P., & Schmidt, L. (2014). Immigrants and retirement resources. *Social Security Bulletin*, *74*(1), 27–45. https://www.ssa.gov/policy/docs/ssb/v74n1/v74n1p27.html

Silva, T., & Evans, C. R. (2020). Sexual identification in the United States at the intersections of gender, race/ethnicity, immigration, and education. *Sex Roles*, *83*(1), 722–738. https://doi.org/10.1007/s11199-020-01145-x

Soehl, T. (2017). Social reproduction of religiosity in the immigrant context: The role of family transmission and family formation—Evidence from France. *International Migration Review*, *51*(4), 999–1030. https://doi.org/10.1111/imre.12289

Soria, K. M., & Stebleton, M. (2013). Immigrant college students' academic obstacles. *The Learning Assistance Review*, *18*(1), 7–24. https://www.immigrationresearch.org/system/files/Immigrant_College_Students_Academic_Obstacles.pdf

Statista. (2022, September). *Estimated median age of Americans at their first wedding in the United States from 1998* to *2021, by sex*. https://www.statista.com/statistics/371933/median-age-of-us-americans-at-their-first-wedding/

Stebleton, M. J. (2007). Career counseling with African immigrant college students: Theoretical approaches and implications for practice. *The Career Development Quarterly*, *55*(4), 290–312. https://doi.org/10.1002/j.2161-0045.2007.tb00085.x

Stevens, G. (2004). Using census data to evaluate the critical-period hypothesis in second-language acquisition. *Psychological Science*, *15*(3), 215–216. https://doi.org/10.1111/j.0956-7976.2004.01503012.x

Suárez-Orozco, C., & Carhill, A. (2008). Afterword: New directions in research with immigrant families and their children. *New Directions for Child and Adolescent Development*, *2008*(121), 87–104. https://doi.org/10.1002/cd.224

Suárez-Orozco, C., Katsiaficas, D., Birchall, O., Alcantar, C. M., Hernandez, E., Garcia, Y., Michikyan, M., Cerda, J., & Teranishi, R. T. (2015). Undocumented undergraduates on college campuses: Understanding their challenges and assets and what it takes to make an undocufriendly campus. *Harvard Educational Review*, *85*(3), 427–463. https://doi.org/10.17763/0017-8055.85.3.427

Subedi, R. P., & Rosenberg, M. W. (2014). Determinants of the variations in self-reported health status among recent and more established immigrants in Canada. *Social Science & Medicine*, *115*, 103–110. https://doi.org/10.1016/j.socscimed.2014.06.021

Sweet, S., & Meiksins, P. (2021). *Changing contours of work: Jobs and opportunities in the new economy* (4th ed.). Sage Publications.

Taylor, B. A., Gambourg, M. B., Rivera, M., & Laureano, D. (2006). Constructing cultural competence: Perspectives of family therapists working with Latino families. *The American Journal of Family Therapy*, *34*(5), 429–445. https://doi.org/10.1080/01926180600553779

Teranishi, R. T., Suárez-Orozco, C., & Suárez-Orozco, M. (2011). Immigrants in community colleges. *The Future of Children*, *21*(1), 153–169. https://doi.org/10.1353/foc.2011.0009

Torres, L., & Rollock, D. (2004). Acculturative distress among Hispanics: The role of acculturation, coping, and intercultural competence. *Journal of Multicultural Counseling and Development*, *32*(3), 155–167. https://doi.org/10.1002/j.2161-1912.2004.tb00368.x

Tsoh, J. Y., Sentell, T., Gildengorin, G., Le, G. M., Chan, E., Fung, L., Pasick, R. J., Stewart, S., Wong, C., Woo, K., Burke, A., Wang, J., McPhee, S. J., & Nguyen, T. T. (2016). Healthcare communication barriers and self-rated health in older Chinese American immigrants. *Journal of Community Health*, *41*(4), 741–752. https://doi.org/10.1007/s10900-015-0148-4

United Nations, Department of Economic and Social Affairs, Population Division. (2015). *World population prospects: The 2015 revision: Key findings and advance tables* (Working Paper No. ESA/P/WP.241). http://esa.un.org/unpd/wpp/publications/files/key_findings_wpp_2015.pdf

U.S. Census Bureau. (2016). *Hispanic heritage month 2016*. https://www.census.gov/content/dam/Census/newsroom/facts-for-features/2016/cb16-ff16.pdf

Viruell-Fuentes, E. A., Miranda, P. Y., & Abdulrahim, S. (2012). More than culture: Structural racism, intersectionality theory, and immigrant health. *Social Science & Medicine*, *75*(12), 2099–2106. https://doi.org/10.1016/j.socscimed.2011.12.037

Vondracek, F. W. (1990). A developmental-contextual approach to career development research. In R. A. Young & W. A. Borgen (Eds.), *Methodological approaches to the study of career* (pp. 37–56). Praeger.

Walsh, S., Shulman, S., Feldman, B., & Maurer, O. (2005). The impact of immigration on the internal processes and developmental tasks of emerging adulthood. *Journal of Youth and Adolescence*, *34*(5), 413–426. https://doi.org/10.1007/s10964-005-7259-7

Wang, L., & Kwak, M.-J. (2015). Immigration, barriers to healthcare and transnational ties: A case study of South Korean immigrants in Toronto, Canada. *Social Science & Medicine*, *133*, 340–348. https://doi.org/10.1016/j.socscimed.2014.11.039

Ward, N., & Batalova, J. (2023). *Frequently requested statistics on immigrants and immigration in the United States*. Migration Policy Institute. https://www.migrationpolicy.org/article/frequently-requested-statistics-immigrants-and-immigration-united-states

Warner, T. D., Fishbein, D. H., & Krebs, C. P. (2010). The risk of assimilating? Alcohol use among immigrant and U.S.-born Mexican youth. *Social Science Research*, *39*(1), 176–186. https://doi.org/10.1016/j.ssresearch.2009.07.001

Zenteno, R., Giorguli, S. E., & Gutiérrez, E. (2013). Mexican adolescent migration to the United States and transitions to adulthood. *The Annals of the American Academy of Political and Social Science*, *648*(1), 18–37. https://doi.org/10.1177/0002716213481189

Zhu, Y., & Zhang, W. (2019). Active learning for active ageing: Chinese senior immigrants' lifelong learning in Canada. *Educational Gerontology*, *45*(8), 506–518. https://doi.org/10.1080/03601277.2019.1662933

Zong, J., & Batalova, J. (2016). College-educated immigrants in the United States. *Migration Information Source*. https://www.migrationpolicy.org/article/college-educated-immigrants-united-states-2014#11

Zong, J., & Batalova, J. (2019). *How many unauthorized immigrants graduate from U.S. high schools annually?* [Fact sheet]. Migration Policy Institute. https://www.migrationpolicy.org/research/unauthorized-immigrants-graduate-us-high-schools

Zunker, V. G. (2016). *Career counseling: A holistic approach* (9th ed.). Cengage Learning.

Zwiers, A. (2010). LGBT people and mental health: Healing the wounds of prejudice. *Visions: BC's Mental Health and Addictions Journal*, *6*(2), 10–11.

APPENDIX 9A

List of Immigration Resources

African Development Center
https://www.adcminnesota.org
Provides support to African business owners

Catholic Charities Migration and Refugee Services
https://www.catholiccharitiesusa.org/our-vision-and-ministry/immigration-refugee-services/
Manages cases of new arrivals

Centre for Asian and Pacific Islanders (CAPI)
https://www.volunteermatch.org/search/org95115.jsp
Supports Southeast Asian and East African immigrants and refugees

Center for Victims of Torture
https://www.cvt.org
Helps immigrants and refugees that have been tortured to heal from symptoms of trauma

Comunidades Latinas Unidas en Servicio
https://clues.org/es/
Provides culturally-specific resources to the Latinx community

Hennepin County Office of Multicultural Services
https://www.hennepin.us/residents/human-services/multi-cultural-services
Provides immigrants and refugees services in 32 languages

Hmong American Partnership
https://hmong.org
Helps Hmong adults with technology and English language skill development, jobs assistance, and building academic achievement of Hmong youth

Hmong Cultural Center
https://www.hmongcc.org
Supports the personal development through Hmong education

International Institute of Minnesota
https://iimn.org
Supports fellowship and welfare of immigrants and their families

Jewish Family Services of St. Paul
https://jfssp.org
Provides support for the unemployed, which includes counseling, employment information, older adult services, and bilingual support

Karen Organization of Minnesota
https://www.mnkaren.org
Provides support for refugees

Minnesota Council on Latino Affairs
https://mn.gov/mcla/
Works with the Minnesota Governor to support Minnesota's Chicano Latino community

Minnesota State Career Wise
https://careerwise.minnstate.edu
Exploration of careers, education, and job market

Vietnamese Social Services of Minnesota
https://vssmn.org
Works to maintain the Minnesota Vietnamese community identity

Chapter 10

Counseling With Immigrant and Refugee Families

As previously discussed, immigrants and refugees are in all sectors of society, living across the United States, and employed in a range of work settings depending on their skills and educational level. As immigrant families settle into their new communities and schools, clinical mental health counselors, school counselors, family counselors, and college and career counselors will be called upon to deliver culturally responsive and ethical care to families with mental health needs. Family counseling must be a primary approach because of the collectivistic orientation of many immigrants and refugees.

In school settings, playgrounds, and other locations, children and adolescents may experience bullying and other forms of harm. During counseling, the child or adolescent must be seen with their parents, not alone. In college, first-generation students may have the burden of being academically successful and meeting their family's priorities, including supporting the family financially. Students with Deferred Action for Childhood Arrivals (DACA) and undocumented status have additional emotional dilemmas depending on their college and their state of residence. More often, career counseling becomes important to college-age young adults and adults. Although family counseling is not prevalent in college settings, counselors must inquire about parents' ideas on the student's situation. The student does not make decisions alone. They carry with them their dreams and their family's dreams, all part of the collectivistic mindset and value system. With this circumstance, there must be sensitivity to taking a psychoeducational approach and providing a rationale for services.

This chapter focuses on specific clinical needs of immigrant families and clients in a variety of settings. It includes a discussion of situations that school counselors, clinical mental health counselors, and career counselors often engage in with immigrant students, families, young adults, and children of immigrants. As these examples are presented, there is also attention to individuals' intersecting identities and lived experiences with the stages of immigration. Reference to the Multicultural and Social Justice Counseling Competencies (MSJCC; Ratts et al., 2015) will be made where appropriate.

Learning Objectives

- Recognize premigration circumstances and experiences that may contribute to immigrants' mental health stressors in migration-specific and different postmigration settings.
- Identify the effects of the acculturation process on mental health stressors and how they manifest with different individuals and families.
- Apply the relational-cultural theory model that promotes collectivism in counseling across different settings.
- Develop client- and family-centered interventions based on social justice principles.
- Link cultural and social justice competencies to inform counselors' culturally responsive services in multiple settings and for different presenting issues.

The following section introduces a self-assessment to gauge your existing knowledge of culturally responsive counseling frameworks designed to address inequities and marginalization, ethical considerations in working with immigrant and refugee populations, and the MSJCC (Ratts et al., 2015) needed to do so. This brief assessment aims to explore your current understanding of key concepts and provide a foundation for further learning. Answering the following questions will better equip you to engage with the content.

Self-assessment: Please respond to the following statements by rating yourself on the following Likert scale: *strongly agree*, *agree*, *disagree*, *strongly disagree*, or *unsure*.

1. I am familiar with effective, culturally unique counseling interventions with clients from various countries.
2. I feel comfortable addressing counseling and clinical issues in school, mental health, college counseling, and family settings.
3. I am confident in my ability to distinguish between immigration-related familial challenges.
4. I understand the role collectivism plays in communication with immigrant and refugee clients.

Clinical Mental Health Counseling With Families

The American Counseling Association (ACA) and the Council for Accreditation of Counseling and Related Educational Programs (CACREP) influence the education of clinical mental health counselors in terms of multicultural competency development requirements. The *ACA Code of Ethics* (ACA, 2014) describes guidelines for counselor training to include issues of diversity and competence about their clients' cultures, including a statement to "infuse material related to multiculturalism/diversity into all courses and workshops for the development of professional counselors" (Standard F.7.c.). CACREP (2024) standards for counselor training state a commitment to a unified counselor identity and to the excellence of programs. In the discussion of academic quality (Section 2, p. 8), CACREP stipulates that program missions must reflect counseling practice in a diverse and global society with marginalized populations.

Licensed clinical mental health counselors will likely encounter immigrant families and individuals in community mental health and social service agencies. Immigrants live in all regions of the United States: About two thirds of immigrants live in the West (34%) and South (34%), about one fifth live in the Northeast (21%), and 11% are in the Midwest (Budiman, 2020). In 2018, the immigrant population in the United States reached 44.8 million (Budiman, 2020). As previously noted, most immigrants today come to the United States from China; Central, East, Southwest, and South Asia; the Philippines; and Mexico and El Salvador, among other Latin American countries (Budiman, 2020). A smaller percentage come from African countries.

Torres Stone et al. (2020) studied immigrant mental health needs from community stakeholders and found that immigrants struggle with navigating mental health services, language barriers, scarcity of culturally competent providers, mental health stigma, and lack of non-Western conceptualizations of mental health. To meet the needs of diverse populations, including immigrants, Torres Stone et al. recommended developing a culturally competent mental health team of patient navigators and mental health providers, offering mental health literacy, and providing culturally competent interventions. Patient navigation was created as a service to patients with cancer to help them address barriers to treatment and to help providers reduce cancer disparities (Ko et al., 2016). Patient navigation has been an emerging service in the mental health field (Druss et al., 2010) and aids with patient assessment, screening, education, support, and coordination of care (Wells et al., 2008). Integration of health care with the use of case managers, patient navigators, community health workers, and cultural brokers can create a system of culturally responsive health services that assist the client in dealing with stigma, understanding of mental health language, and logistical issues (Torres Stone et al., 2020).

Latinx Immigrants

Latinx immigrants, like many immigrants in the United States, seek out mental health services at a lower rate than their White counterparts. In efforts to meet the needs of Latinx immigrants, researchers have studied Latinx communities via needs assessments. Corona et al. (2009) conducted such a needs assessment in a Latinx community in Richmond, Virginia, where the immigrants were principally from Central America, Mexico, South America, and the Caribbean. The researchers used the principles of community-based participatory research and conducted surveys with more than 200 Latinx adults and 15 key informants who were community members representing faith-based organizations, schools, law and government, and the media. Corona et al. discovered that participants were concerned about mental health issues and parent-child intergenerational conflict resulting from trauma from the immigration process. Furthermore, Corona and colleagues learned that mental health interventions that emphasize family relationships, teach children positive health behaviors, and underscore continuing connection to Latinx culture are important in providing community mental health services. Learning about mental health interventions that are culturally appropriate helps counselors develop their MSJCC competency.

Hmong Immigrants

Hmong immigrants in the United States numbered 299,000 in 2015 (Budiman, 2021). Hmong have been coming to the United States since 1975 because of their arrangement with the Central Intelligence Agency during the Vietnam War. Budiman (2021) reported that Hmong immigrants have mostly settled in urban areas, with the largest numbers in Minneapolis–St. Paul, Minnesota (80,000); Fresno, California (40,000); and Sacramento, California (30,000). Since 2000, there have been 300,000 Hmong immigrants who have arrived (Budiman, 2021) and settled primarily in Minnesota and Wisconsin (Budiman & Ruiz, 2021).

Studies have found that refugees experience distress in the United States (e.g., Berry, 1998) because of acculturation stress and the lack of control over where they land once they are in the United States. Hmong immigrants have been known to struggle with social disadvantages, significant poverty, and linguistic issues (Pfeifer & Lee, 2005). Acculturation stress has been found to be the strongest predictor of mental well-being among Southeast Asian refugees, including Hmong (Nicholson, 1997). Obstacles to effective communication exist between youth and elders in Hmong families and include language barriers and acculturation differences (Meschke & Juang, 2014). Low educational attainment, language barriers, insomnia, and tension related to depressive symptoms have been known to be mental health issues experienced by Hmong middle-aged adults and older adults (Yang & Mutchler, 2017).

To provide services to Hmong immigrants and remove these barriers, some providers have created urban multiservice centers to meet their needs. For example, a center in Minneapolis, Minnesota, provides services in psychotherapy, medications, psychological assessment, case management, day treatment for adults, and youth support programs (Community-University Health Care Center in Minneapolis, 2001). This program and others like it have created high counseling return rates and longer lengths of treatment for refugee clients in larger cities, but it is difficult to develop such programs in smaller urban areas (Collier et al., 2012). Instead, smaller cities determine the need for mental health services and ways in which to meet the needs of refugees, including Hmong.

Collier et al. (2012) and a community planning committee utilized a community-based participatory research model to engage community professionals to study health problems and culturally responsive interventions of the local Hmong in Eau Claire, Wisconsin. Additionally, they interviewed Hmong refugees about their mental health challenges and what worked for them. Findings about social concerns in the community pointed to intergenerational communication issues, marital conflict, domestic violence, and child abuse (Collier et al., 2012). Findings regarding mental illness included defining mental illness and determining the point at which symptoms become problematic, severe stigma associated with mental illness, psychiatric symptoms, elder status and mental well-being, developmental disabilities and medical problems, and LGBTQ+ concerns (Collier et al., 2012).

Participants in Collier et al.'s (2012) study indicated that successful culturally effective services should include bilingual staff, a shaman, and pastoral counseling and allow for herbal treatment and transportation to and from services. Furthermore, Hmong participants identified arrangements that would help them seek out treatment when needed. These included education about American culture for the elders and youth to better understand each other; all services offered under one umbrella, including crisis intervention; in-home counseling; separate groups for each gender; activity-based support groups; and a hotline with support, information, and anonymity (Collier et al., 2012).

Goodkind (2005) found that using undergraduate student advocates with Hmong adults had a positive impact on the mental health of the refugees. One-on-one cultural exchanges occurred within the structure of learning circles between refugees and undergraduate students. In addition to cultural exchanges, advocacy between undergraduate students and refugee adults led to better connections to community resources. Over the 6 months of weekly meetings that lasted 6–8 hours, refugees reported an improved quality of life, satisfaction with resources, English proficiency, and increased knowledge of the U.S. citizenship test (Goodkind, 2005). Improved satisfaction with community resources was determined to be a factor in the lessening of distress (Goodkind, 2005); this finding was supported by Cigrand et al. (2022), who indicated that immigrants prioritize finding resources to support their transition and resettlement over working on a counselor's assessment of their need for mental health services.

Advocacy efforts, community connections, patient navigation services, and mental health services can meet the needs of immigrant clients through cultivating an understanding of the unique needs of Latinx and Hmong clients and assist counselors in their development of MSJCC competency. Clinical mental health counselors can evaluate the needs of their immigrant populations by listening to clients' stories of resettlement challenges and providing immigrant clients with community resources that will enhance their lived experiences in the United States.

Creative Interventions With Refugees and Immigrants

Refugees' and immigrants' sense of homesickness has been a subject of research with regard to how counselors and mental health professionals can help ease their discomfort and find ways to lessen the impact of a sense of loss of place (Dieterich-Hartwell & Koch, 2017). Creative arts therapies include a range of artistic expression through drama, dance, music, and physical movement and provide children, adolescents, and adults ways in which to explore their mental health issues in creative and productive ways (Dieterich-Hartwell & Koch, 2017). For example, researchers have discovered that counselors may assist refugee adolescents to engage in a theater program to share group stories (Rousseau & Guzder, 2008) and make space for adults to listen to the music from their home country (Badakhshan, 2017). Expressive arts therapy also assists in helping refugees explore issues related to resilience (Kalaf & Plante, 2019) and treats refugees' trauma by instilling hope for a future (Meyer DeMott et al., 2017). Expressive arts therapy is showing itself to be an effective intervention to use with children, adolescents, and adults of various ethnic identities on a variety of counseling issues.

Family Counseling

The American Association for Marriage and Family Therapy (AAMFT) is the overarching professional organization for licensed individuals who work with couples and families (e.g., marriage and family therapists, pastors, psychiatrists, psychiatric nurses). AAMFT provides ethical guidelines that focus on ethical professional standards, including statements about potential bias toward clients and families. Standard 1.1 in the AAMFT *Code of Ethics* focuses on nondiscrimination based on race, age, ethnicity, socioeconomic status, disability, gender, health status, religion, national origin, sexual orientation, gender identity, or relationship status (AAMFT, 2015). Furthermore, AAMFT members aspire to commit to diversity and equity excellence in clinical practice, research, education, and administration (AAMFT, 2015). Immigrant and refugee status is not cited among the different statuses.

Globally, approximately 244 million people reside in a country different from where they were born (International Organization for Migration, 2017). Families are impacted by migration whether they move together or are separated when some members stay in the country of origin and some move to a new country. Forms of immigration include permanent, where members join a family member in a destination setting, and circular, where immigrants return seasonally to their home country (Van Hook & Glick, 2020). Migrants tend to sustain connections with families, and circular migrant workers are most likely to do so in the form of sending remittances back home to support the family. Relationships between family members separated by distance can be challenging, as there are tradeoffs as immigrants and family members left behind must consider new ideas about potentially different family norms and expectations, which can create familial stress (Levitt, 1998).

The following sections of the chapter focus on working with Latinx immigrant families from Mexico, Central America, and South America; African immigrant families primarily from the countries of Ghana, Nigeria, Ethiopia, Kenya, Guyana, and Somalia; and Asian immigrant families. Each culture as well as each family has its own unique family system and counseling needs.

Latinx Families

Family counseling with Latinx families must take into consideration roles, rules, and responsibilities for women and men, and even children (Arredondo et al., 2014). It is important for family counselors to understand the impact of gender roles on the family system and structure. Latinx immigrant families typically abide by traditional gender roles wherein husbands are the providers and wives are the caretakers. This worldview, however, does not persist, particularly when women are the immigrants, bringing along children. Even in their home country, Latinas must work to sustain the family.

In traditional Latino cultural worldviews, men identify with *machismo* and manliness (Melendez & McDowell, 2008). Machismo indicates that Latino men are expected to provide for their families (Zagelbaum, 2011). Driven by poverty and lack of work in their home country, men immigrate to the United States to obtain sustainable work and often leave their families behind until they can afford to bring them to their new home, a process that can take years (Zagelbaum, 2011). There is substantial stress for these men, who face many obstacles to finding work and experience discrimination (Melendez & McDowell, 2008). Additionally, the employment available for them is generally low-paying and back-breaking, as many are agricultural workers or work in the meat-packing industry. Although some immigrants have work visas, others do not; they work in the shadows, marry, have children, and make their contributions to the U.S. economy without documentation. An issue for long-term residents without documentation status is their inability to collect Social Security when they leave their employment.

Protective factors for Latinx families include loyalty to family or *familismo*. Familismo is known as the inclination to depend on family and relatives for emotional support, solidarity, and attachment (Unger et al., 2006). Latinx families engage in familismo as a resource for identity and self-worth (Parra-Cardona et al., 2006). Although familismo has been found to have protective factors for family members in dealing with external stressors (Germán et al., 2009), familismo can also be maladaptive when stress occurs from within the family (Hernández et al., 2010). When stressors stem from intrafamily conflict (such as the case of parent-child disagreement), familismo and family harmony can be threatened. It is imperative that counselors understand the importance of familismo and determine from where mental health stressors originate—within or outside of the family.

Protective factors may also include cultural retention of one's primary culture, which can provide immigrants with coping skills to deal with stressors (Sabina et al., 2015). Keeping to traditional values strengthens familial bonds and reduces the incidence of potential issues like domestic violence (Curry et al., 2018). Higher rates of acculturation are linked to higher rates of alcohol use (Lara et al., 2005), separation from family and friends, and a decrease in cultural practices and values (Schwartz et al., 2010). Acculturation and related issues are important for family counselors to explore when working with Latino men. For example, working with Latino men on their identity related to work and their role in the family can be helpful in determining their values and priorities and how it matters to their sense of duty and life satisfaction.

Marianismo is an important framework in the Latinx family in terms of what is expected of women, according to a study by Gil and Vázquez (1996). Marianismo is based on expectations that women are to be self-sacrificing, submissive, and pure in their relationships, particularly premarriage (Gil &Vázquez, 1996), although many women currently do not agree with these expectations, nor do they practice them. According to the concept of marianismo, priorities for Latinas are family, child-rearing, and intergenerational care. Latinas are expected to put their family's needs over their own and to have a strong desire for marriage and childbearing (Ruiz et al., 2017). These gender role expectations impact women's self-efficacy and the balance of power in relationships (Miville et al., 2017). More than half of the Latina population that migrates to the United States is employed in a gender-specific worker role, most often in agriculture, food service, and domestic care (Gonzales, 2008). With employment comes empowerment for Latinas. Many Latina immigrants already having developed egalitarian attitudes (Bejarano et al., 2011) and are likely to integrate new ideas about gender roles from their host country (Villalba et al.,

2018). As they settle in the United States, they are more likely to express their egalitarian attitudes, sense of personal empowerment, and less acceptance of traditional gender roles (Ruiz et al., 2017), which can create tension in the marital arrangement. A counselor's knowledge of their clients' worldview is important in developing their MSJCC competency.

Family counselors also need to understand the expected roles and responsibilities for Latinx immigrant youth. In many ways, Latinx children and adolescents struggle in much the same way their parents do in their acculturation process, with younger children dependent on their parents' guidance and controls while many adolescents deal with more complicated issues related to social stress, identity conflicts, and academic stress (Zagelbaum, 2011). Protective factors for youth include familismo (Stein et al., 2014), which has been found to correlate with healthy youth development, including fewer symptoms related to depression (Piña-Watson et al., 2019) and higher levels of self-esteem (Romero et al., 2020).

Often, Latinx parents and children arrive in the United States separately, as the adults migrate first to find work and housing and send for their children later, sometimes more than 10 years later (Artico, 2003). Symptoms of psychopathology in immigrant youth have been found to be directly related to war trauma, family separation, social network disruption, and impoverishment (Arroyo, 1997; Edberg et al., 2021). Once arriving in the United States, Latinx youth are exposed to violence and stressful experiences at higher rates than U.S.-born youth (Edberg et al., 2021; Porter & Haslam, 2005). In working with children who have been separated from their parents, counselors should expect to work on trust issues and significant stress between parent and child (Artico, 2003). Children report that parents do not recognize their current needs, which are different from their preseparation needs. Furthermore, many children report resentment about their parents' poverty despite working two or three jobs, and their parents' lack of time and attention because of busy work schedules. Children in these cases struggle with identity confusion and relationship development as they attempt to engage with parents whom they barely know. In some situations, a parent may establish a family in the United States and present with new siblings. This is another source of stress for the youth who rejoins their parents after a long separation. They question whether they really belong.

Adolescents need to be listened to and affirmed in their culture; family counselors need to talk about values, family events, and familismo (Ivey et al., 2004). Family counselors also need to recognize the cultural strengths teens bring to their conversation (identify values that are important and notice how they live their values), share with the teen how the school or community is responsible for handling instances of racial harassment (rather than blaming the victim), involve parents in talking with adolescents when possible, and realize that teens will be in various stages of acculturation—some will maintain attachments to traditional cultural values whereas others will adapt to new cultural attitudes in their host country (Ivey et al., 2004). Another area of difficulty with varying acculturation levels is that immigrant parents may make different rules for their children than nonimmigrant parents, resulting in the children comparing themselves with their host country friends and feeling frustrated about their parents' expectations (Ivey et al., 2004).

Use of Interpreters With Latinx Families

The use of interpreters with families is considered best practice when families struggle with the English language. Counselors should identify and arrange for professional interpreters to be paid by insurance or through community services, when available. When professional interpreters are arranged through insurance companies, in-person interpretation is recommended rather than telephonic interpretation, which insurance companies are likely to prefer (Elbalghiti-Williams, 2022). Counselors are advised not to use family members as translators except in the case of emergency, because there may be power differentials whereby family members can get in the way of the counseling process and may withhold important information from the counselor (Amodeo et al., 1997; Elbalghiti-Williams, 2022).

Preparation with professional interpreters must take place prior to family counseling to make sure the interpreter understands their role and know when to translate verbatim and when to elaborate on what they are hearing to help the counseling process (Elbalghiti-Williams, 2022; Potocky & Naseh, 2019). Three types of communication distortions by interpreters may occur based on deficient linguistic skills, lack of clinical awareness, and the interpreter's negative attitudes toward the client (Egli, 1991). These types of problems can lead to misunderstandings of terms or expressions, omission of details, and distortion of a counselor's question (Egli, 1991). The best approach to avoid these issues is for the family counselor to develop strong, long-term relationships with interpreters who have excellent linguistic skills and train them in clinical issues and the technical aspect of interpretation (Egli, 1991). Using the same interpreter with the same family is recommended for consistency (Elbalghiti-Williams, 2022).

In terms of specific logistics for interpretation services, it was once believed that the interpreter should sit behind the counselor and the counselor should focus their eye contact and attention to the client and family directly (Ivey et al., 2004). Recently, it has been found that including the interpreter in a circular sitting pattern is effective in allowing the interpreter to be part of the session, with the understanding that they abide by their role in the session and all eye contact is between counselor and family members (Elbalghiti-Williams, 2022). Short phrases are also recommended so that the interpreter does not get lost, and to keep the conversation as simple as possible for all involved (Ivey et al., 2004). For example, an interpreter and counselor should meet prior to a family's arrival at a session and discuss the role of the interpreter, sitting arrangements, and expectations. As the family arrives, each member is introduced to the interpreter, and all sit in a circular pattern for better communication. When the counselor or one of the family members speaks, the counselor should maintain eye contact with the client and allow the interpreter to translate the words spoken. The use of an interpreter enhances counselor-client relationships, an important competency in the MSJCC (Ratts et al., 2015).

Counseling Interventions With Latinx Families

Narrative therapy is one of the most common and effective counseling approaches in working with Latinx families (Falicov, 2007). Being able to share stories about migration and resettlement with a counselor helps the client feel attended to and assists the counselor in understanding the client's narrative and experience (Zagelbaum, 2011). There are four contexts the counselor must be aware of in working with Latinx clients through the framework of narrative therapy: relational, community, cultural, and sociopolitical (Falicov, 2007).

Relational context refers to the intimate relationships that people have with family and close, intimate friends (Falicov, 2007). Community context represents the network of relationships in one's community, including the new one during resettlement and the old one in the country of origin with family and friends left behind. Cultural and sociopolitical contexts have to do with social justice, and counselors can explore immigrants' opinions of the host culture and how it affects family and generational relationships. Exploring immigrants' opinions about the host country and experiences with discrimination may be difficult as immigrants tend to be reticent in mentioning these with a counselor for fear of being seen as ungrateful or disrespectful (Falicov, 2007).

The exploration with a family of their cultural values and how they may or may not have shifted during the migration and resettlement gives the family an opportunity to connect with each other and understand how they are doing with the transition, and it allows for issues regarding parenting, spiritual practice, and social stress to be shared (Zagelbaum, 2011). Using *dichos*, or sayings or proverbs, is another area of work with Latinx family members, whereby counselors can explore meaningful dichos and apply them to current situations (Zagelbaum, 2011). A counselor's learning of some phrases in the family's language can help build rapport if the counselor is not bilingual. Through easy access to the internet, counselors can download a list of dichos and share these with families. This approach may be another way to build trust. Learning about the culture of the family, the history of their migration, and important family rituals related to a family's culture will enable a family counselor to provide services to a family that are congruent with their ethnicity (Zagelbaum, 2011).

West African Immigrant Families

The term *African immigrant* refers to people of African descent who have voluntarily immigrated to the United States (Lombe et al., 2016). African immigration to the United States began in the 1980s, and between 2000 and 2010, about 1.5 million documented Africans moved to the United States (Osirim, 2008). Most African immigrants come from Ghana, Nigeria, Ethiopia, Kenya, Guyana, and Somalia (Tamir, 2022). Cultures between and within countries vary greatly; however, the reasons why people migrate to the United States are similar: to avoid the rampant spread of HIV, malaria, and other diseases; to obtain economic opportunities; to escape oppression; to improve their education; and to financially support families left in their home countries (Brammer, 2011). Through the resettlement process and afterward, African immigrants struggle to develop an identity of their own, as most do not identify with African Americans even though most Americans typically categorize these two groups together (Wamwara-Mbugua et al., 2008). Families struggle with varying levels of acculturation, and second-generation Africans face challenges because they do not speak their native language and do not comprehend family traditions and cultural aspects of their heritage (Brammer, 2011).

African cultures share a socioreligious philosophy whereby persons look to themselves, their tribe, and their community to understand the world (van Dyk, 2001). Many Africans believe that everything has a cause and that to treat an illness is to understand who or what caused the disease (van Dyk, 2001). Spirits and ancestors play a role in day-to-day life (Vontress, 1991) and likely intercede in life situations when necessary (van Dyk, 2001). Healers are skilled psychotherapists (Berg, 2003) in African communities, and they are trained in "rigorous preparation and ancestral approval" (Brammer, 2011, p. 107). A typical reason for seeking out a healer is to receive support for an event or for a concern. The healer often works to bring spirits to the one needing help (Brammer, 2011). Healers use dream interpretation, dance, pharmacotherapy, shock therapy, exorcisms, and music (Herring & Salazar, 2002). Havenaar et al. (2008) found that Africans sought traditional healers to help with mental health issues such as alcoholism, and South Africans pursued visits with healers for dreamwork, job loss, physical concerns, and cultural issues.

Despite cultural differences between Africans from different countries, there are similarities that are important to note. Many Africans have an allegiance to their tribe before they identify with their country of origin (Lombe et al., 2016), and they feel a sense of loss of tribal identity when their country of origin transitioned from a tribal to a national government (McGoldrick et al., 2005). Many Africans are deeply rooted in their religion; North Africans tend to identify as Muslim, whereas Central, East, and Southern Africans are more likely to be Christians (Lombe et al., 2016). Africans believe in both natural and spiritual realms of existence, and Westerners may see their religion as pagan. A perception of superior European or American religions exists in Western cultures, and this creates difficulty for Africans (McGoldrick et al., 2005). This cultural knowledge about religious differences is essential to counselors.

Africans typically live in a collectivistic society where family (immediate and extended) is highly regarded (Lombe et al., 2016; McGoldrick et al., 2005). Extended family may include kin relationships with members of a tribe or clan (McGoldrick et al., 2005). Africans value communalism for security and identity (Lombe et al., 2016); they include the living and the dead as part of their community (McGoldrick et al., 2005). Africans attempt to combine the secular and religious in their community living (Mbiti, 1970). Spirituality for Africans involves spiritual beings, which are a significant part of African culture. Purpose and meaning are derived from the relationships in the community, including spirits, which serve as guides on living well (Mbiti, 1970).

Recommendations for working with African immigrants include knowing as much about a client's specific tribe/country of origin as possible to fully understand their cultural identity and value system (Lombe et al., 2016). For example, greetings are extremely important and will set the tone for the rest of the counseling relationship. Knowledge of how to greet children is important, and a counselor's comfort with children is extremely meaningful to parents (Lombe et al., 2016).

Counselors should also pay attention to practical matters within families to enhance their counselor-client relationship, according to the MSJCC (Ratts et al., 2015). Of particular importance is

- Helping families manage connections to social networks to reduce social isolation,
- Understanding parenting practices and educating parents on laws and policies in the United States,
- Introducing parents to the concept of listening to their child or adolescent and their needs,
- Advocating for enculturation to balance the acculturation process,
- Educating the school system about the lack of parental involvement,
- Not assuming parental neglect, and
- Working with children to understand their parents' stress in living in a different cultural context. (Lombe et al., 2016)

Counseling Interventions With West African Families

As previously noted, narrative therapy is recommended for work with African families because stories and storytelling are particularly important (Semmler & Williams, 2000) as Africans use stories and proverbs to pass along cultural values to their young (McGoldrick et al., 2005). This type of narrative work in counseling is not insight-oriented; counselors must recognize that African clients and families go to counseling for advice or suggestions. Understanding these priorities will drive the counseling session more effectively than waiting for the client to find their own answers (Lombe et al., 2016).

Counselors working with African immigrant clients and families must convey comfort and genuineness as African immigrants can sense the slightest nonverbal behaviors of discomfort (Lombe et al., 2016). Counselors must pay careful attention to connect with African immigrants in an authentic manner; this will go a long way in terms of building rapport.

Nwoye (2006) recommended five types of listening with African families and clients: empathic listening, credulous listening, deconstructive listening, unpacking, and hermeneutic listening. Empathic listening focuses on feelings; credulous listening refers to allowing time in the session for the client to tell their story; deconstructive listening explores untold nuggets of a story; unpacking is processing and checking a narrative's negative issues; and hermeneutic listening is identifying personal meanings to content and events (Nwoye, 2006).

Separating the family members in treatment is recommended (Nwoye, 2006) to honor African patrilineal culture, and in such a process, the father is interviewed first, followed by the mother, followed by the children. However, it is wise to ask the parents if this is their preference. Metaphors and cultural phrases are encouraged to enrich the treatment process and help the family counselor connect with the family (Lombe et al., 2016).

Counselors may engage in play therapy with African immigrant children using African games, in particular a game known as Masekitlana (Kekae-Moletsane, 2008). One person at a time tells a story and acts out the feelings of the story while others in the room listen. In this way, everyone is engaged, and counselors can sort through the stories to relate them to current issues faced by the family. Masekitlana is a nondirective game, as African immigrants feel most comfortable with a type of comradeship with everyone involved in the counseling process; directiveness, or confrontation, will be ineffective (Lombe et al., 2016).

Counselors should seek supervision with someone familiar with African culture when working with African immigrant families. Learning about specific regions from which their clients come, cultural beliefs and values, and recommended ways to address the differentness in counselor and client at the outset of counseling is important to the effectiveness of family counseling (Lombe et al., 2016).

Middle East and North Africa Immigrants

Middle East and North Africa (MENA) immigrants come to the United States from countries including Egypt, Iran, Iraq, Jordan, Kuwait, Lebanon, Morocco, Saudi Arabia, Sudan, Syria, and Yemen, among others (Harjanto & Batalova, 2022). Iraq, Egypt, and Lebanon are the countries from which most MENA immigrants emigrate to the United States (Harjanto & Batalova, 2022). Although populations of these countries differ in cultural identity, values, religions, and reasons to migrate, the following discussion provides information about working with these MENA immigrants in counseling.

Cultural values of Middle Eastern immigrants are embedded in religions of Christianity, Judaism, or Islam (Nobles & Sciarra, 2000). Religion, to Middle Eastern immigrants, is seen as their way of life (Husain et al., 2016). For many Muslims, major decisions, daily activities, and relationships are aspects of a religious life, and their religious practice is not solely connected to activities one day a week or during special holiday celebrations a few times a year as in Christianity (Nobles & Sciarra, 2000). Variations in Islamic practice include some Muslims keeping distance between religious identity and state and others strictly following Islam in all aspects of their lives (Abi-Hashem, 2011). In some cases, contemporary Islam is evolving to include ideas and values of globalization. In other cases, extremists try to integrate strict ideology with global politics, rejecting Western beliefs and values and moving to preserving a fundamental and set convention (Sivan, 1985). Counselors working with this population would do well to explore religious beliefs and check with their immigrant client and family on how to best include their religious beliefs and values into the counseling session.

Collectivism is an inherent value for Middle Eastern immigrants, surpassing religious faith and country-of-origin identity (Husain et al., 2016); all counseling needs to integrate family (including extended) and community or tribal association (Al-Krenawi & Graham, 2000).

Stressors for Arab families include more restrictive immigration policies in the United States since September 11, 2001, and an increase in discrimination. One such policy is the USA PATRIOT Act, which directly targets Arabs (U.S. Department of Justice, n.d.):

> Through this action, 25 of the 37 known government security initiatives implemented between September 12, 2001, and mid-2003 either explicitly or implicitly targeted U.S. Arabs and Muslims. These measures included mass arrests, secret and indefinite detentions, prolonged detention of "material witness," closed hearings, secret evidence, government eavesdropping on attorney/client conversations, FBI [Federal Bureau of Investigation] interviews, wiretapping, seizures of property, removals of aliens with technical visa violations and mandatory special registration. (Cainkar, 2006, p. 255)

Other stress factors include some members of a family being documented while others are not. Members of the same family may have different levels of access to resources, and this can cause tensions within the family (Husain et al., 2016).

Counseling Interventions With MENA Families

Counseling interventions should include connecting MENA families to community resources, many of which are designed for these families in large cities across the United States. States with the largest number of Arab immigrants began the development of social service agencies specifically for this population (Husain, 2016). The largest and longest running agency is Arab Community Center for Economic and Social Services (ACCESS), which has eight locations within Michigan offering social, health, economic, and education services (ACCESS, n.d.). Additionally, there are national programs: Arab American National Museum, Center for Arab American Philanthropy, and National Network for Arab American Communities (see ACCESS, n.d.).

Husain (2016) recommended the following for counselors working with families and individuals of Arab, Muslim, or Middle Eastern cultural identity:

- Remember the names of people you are working with and ask about the meaning of their names, and practice difficult names to avoid mispronunciation.
- Maintain a short distance in personal space; do not back up or stand at a distance.
- Greet others with your right hand.
- Crossing your legs with your shoes facing your client is offensive; keep both feet on the floor.
- Dress business-like to reflect the seriousness of your work together.
- Be aware of hand gestures that might offend (thumbs up or pointing are offensive) and use an open palm to invite conversation.
- Use a label or title and surname; never use a client's first name alone.
- Keep women and men together during early work.
- Take care in hugging and shaking hands with women; wait until they initiate contact and watch for excessive eye contact.
- Female family therapists are allowed to shake hands with Muslim men if the woman extends her hand first.
- Handshakes with men last a long time; touching on the shoulder is common; kisses on both cheeks are normal in this culture.
- Respect the Muslim season of Ramadan, which involves fasting and engaging in purification, by not eating or drinking in front of them.
- Unlike Westerners, who consider dogs as pets, Middle Easterners and Arabs consider them as protectors and as "it" (not he or she); avoid talking about your dog in endearing ways.
- Learn a few phrases in Arabic and use them periodically.
- Cordially accepting gifts is important to the relationship, and refusing them can cause more harm and serious feelings of rejection.

The most effective counseling practice is when the family counselor uses an interactive, creative, and integrative approach and applies a sociocultural perspective as a guiding principle in the counseling relationship (Abi-Hashem, 2008). A sociocultural approach can enhance the counselor relationship, which is an important aspect of the MSJCC (Ratts et al., 2015).

South Asian Families

Immigrants from South Asia are individuals and families who come to the United States from Bangladesh, Bhutan, India, Maldives, Nepal, Pakistan, and Sri Lanka. The main religions of South Asia are Hinduism, Islam, and Buddhism. Hindu is the main culture among South Asian immigrants from India and serves as a religion (Gordon et al., n.d.). Important facts to know about South Asian families are the following: Muslims are a heterogeneous group basing their beliefs on a wide spectrum of cultural, spiritual, ethnic, and political principles; patriarchy varies among and within groups; Islam is a fast growing religion in the United States; and Islamic beliefs range from intense fundamentalism to conservatism to liberalism (Almeida, 2005).

Asian Hindus tend to be more conservative than Christians with regard to adolescent development in restricting social activities, dating, diet, and wardrobe (Almeida, 2005). In addition, more conservative families' restrictions on dating and career choice narrow decisions made independently by the adolescent, and reliance on parental influence is common (Graf et al., 2008). These restrictions can affect parent-child relationships and cause distress for adolescents experiencing acculturation and comparing their experiences with those of their U.S. peers.

When Hindu families have a child or adolescent with an intellectual or developmental disability, they may see the disability as a blessing or as the result of the parent or child suffering a *karma* event who is now paying for past behaviors (John, 2012) or as bad karma on the part of the parent (Zechella & Raval, 2016). When this occurs, family therapists can assist the family in processing and creating a ritual about karmic fate to absolve them of their past behaviors (Almeida, 2005).

Disabilities are viewed as stigmatized in South Asian culture; however, positive factors identified through research that assist parents in managing their children's medical issues include being educated, having strong religious faith, and experiencing support from extended family members and social relationships (Venkatesh, 2008). Participants in Zechella and Raval's (2016) study reported that they struggled with their child's diagnosis at first but received strength through many resources, familial and social sources of support, and a wider acceptance of disability in the United States than in India.

Counseling Interventions With South Asian Families

Family therapy is seen by South Asians as necessary only for the unsuccessful (Almeida, 2005). Presenting concerns in counseling include child-related issues, disagreements between teens and parents regarding dating and sexuality, domestic violence, and distress in caring for older family members (Almeida, 2005). Much family therapy seems to be grounded in pastoral care and psychotherapy, with a focus on these and other issues including alienation from family that remained in India, cultural conflict between generations, and a Western perspective of identity development (individualistic vs. the collective; Varughese, 2018). Pastoral counseling aligns well with South Asian views in religious practices and beliefs. Almeida (2005) recommended the following for family therapy with this population: explore family connections, inquire about family cultural beliefs and traditions, offer direct suggestions in terms of role structure when necessary to address issues related to extended family living within the home, and address the life stage of the family's cultural identity and acculturation process. Working with South Asian clients can be fulfilling when a counselor sees the impact of problem-solving and healing in the family.

Asian Families

Discussion of Asian families is challenging given the many diverse sectors of Asian culture and the multitude of countries in Asia, with the focus here primarily on immigrant families from East Asia and Southeast Asia. Despite the vast diversity, there are many commonalities in terms of centrality of the familial cultural identity (collectivism), immigration histories, experiences with trauma from war and political turmoil, dealing with the stereotype of the model minority image, experiences with racism and discrimination, views of mental health and psychopathology, and use of mental health services (Lee & Mock, 2005).

Clinicians working with Asian clients need to focus on issues related to family systems and subsystems, external factors, family history and migration stories, the impact of war, culture shock and discrimination, and employment (Lee & Mock, 2005). Specific counseling foci should address immigration status, marriage (arranged or romantic), gender roles, child-rearing, and family communication patterns (Lee & Mock, 2005).

In terms of Asian adolescent development, Atkin and Yoo (2021) found patterns of cultural identity development based on parent guardedness, passive socialization, and active socialization. The more guarded Asian parents tended to be, the more their adolescents were restrictive in maintaining their heritage and culture and the more they avoided socializing with outside groups. Asian adolescents raised by parents who encouraged active versus passive socialization were supported to become more Americanized and engage with outside groups to different degrees. Adolescents with an active integration identity reported significantly higher levels of cognitive confidence and pride concerning their racial/ethnic identity (Atkin & Yoo, 2021). Understanding parental perspectives on child-rearing assists counselors in their choice of interventions in working with Asian families.

Counseling Interventions With Asian Families

In working with Asian families, counselors should engage the family in a particular way to ensure success in connecting with everyone in the family unit. At the outset, engaging the family in terms of setting an initial appointment should be made through the patriarch; using informed consent is important to educate the family on the role of the counselor; providing the family with a formal but warm stance helps clients ease into the counseling process; being willing to appropriately self-disclose helps Asian family members build trust with the counselor; and asking nonthreatening personal questions of the family will engage clients in small talk, which is helpful at the outset (Lee & Mock, 2005). Counselors using lengthy evaluation processes in family counseling need to educate the family on the reasons behind the evaluation for the Asian family to trust the process and not worry about their information being used politically or for immigration purposes (Lee & Mock, 2005).

Counseling Asian families often involves including family members in therapy, setting goals mutually, paying attention to the problems presented by the family, using a psychoeducational approach, assuming multiple helping roles, being indirect in problem-solving, reframing when necessary, focusing on family and community support, learning the family's communication style, and planning for termination (Lee & Mock, 2005). Being respectful of how Asian American families work together and solve problems is essential for counselors to support the work of the family.

Counselors need to pay attention to current events in the media to appreciate the many layers of discrimination that exist and how they impact the mental health of all immigrant clients. For example, during the COVID-19 pandemic, Asian Americans experienced direct and indirect racism related to being blamed for the coronavirus, and the number of individuals who blame Asian Americans has doubled since 2021 (Bellamy-Walker, 2022). In a study conducted by Liu et al. (2022), it was found that both direct and indirect discrimination were significantly associated with Asian Americans' depressive, anxiety, and somatic symptoms. In first-generation Asian Americans, internalized racism aggravated the effect of COVID-19-related racism on somatic symptoms. Liu et al.'s findings showed ways in which immigrants' racial identity status and internalized racism created a link between COVID-19-related racism and psychological well-being and impact on the family.

Family counseling can be effective with the caveats discussed in this chapter for this diverse group. Culturally competent counselors can navigate working with their Asian American clients by respecting the cultural nuances and family structure, being willing to appropriately self-disclose personal qualities to develop effective counseling relationships, and understanding the many nuances of family communication and functioning.

CASE STUDY

This case study is about Maria, who as a student struggled with differences in cultural perspective with her parents, who expected her to abide by rules and expectations common in Mexico but different from those of her U.S. friends. Maria took care of her parents in social situations in terms of language and translations. She worked hard to obtain her DACA status to navigate college and met her goals of becoming a U.S. citizen and, ultimately, a doctor.

> Maria sought counseling when she was a sophomore in high school. She moved from Mexico to the United States with her parents when she was 8 years old. They traveled across the desert with a coyote to get into the United States and made their way to Minnesota, where family members had already settled. Her father was a farmer, and her mother raised her younger siblings. Both parents struggled with the English language, so Maria found herself translating for them often at stores and in medical appointments. At school, Maria struggled with career counseling sessions because she had few job options as an undocumented immigrant. She wanted to be a doctor and was able to attend college as an in-state student because of her DACA status but saw the futility of going to college if she could not eventually work in the medical profession. The only work options seemed to be working on a farm or in the local chicken factories. Maria presented as happy to be in the United States and grateful for the work, but sad that she couldn't work in a profession in which she longed to work. Other counseling issues included friction with her parents over differing acculturation experiences. Maria wanted to be a "typical American teenager" and wear clothes popular with her peers, whereas her parents wanted her to dress more conservatively. Maria also wanted to stay out later than her parents allowed. These conflicts created issues between Maria and her parents that she did not know how to resolve. The school counselor worked with Maria and her parents to negotiate rules in the house and new clothing options.
>
> Maria eventually worked with her school counselor to obtain DACA status and applied and was accepted into college as a pre-med major. While in college, she applied for citizen status and received her certificate of citizenship. She is a doctor today.

Reflection Questions

1. What are your biases about immigrants working for citizenship that may get in the way of counseling Maria and her family?
2. In what ways do you feel counseling helped Maria in the case study?
3. What do you need to do to develop your MSJCC competency to better prepare for working with immigrants like Maria in the future?
4. What considerations are important to keep in mind for family counseling for Maria and her family?

Summary

Immigrants and refugees in all sectors of society work and live in a variety of settings. In this chapter, we discussed issues related to counseling immigrants and their families in different settings, and we introduced how mental health issues may impact different immigrants and refugees. Settings discussed include family counseling centers, school settings, behavioral health programs, and career counseling community centers. Clients seen in these settings require unique services that must be understood by counselors and mental health professionals.

References

Abi-Hashem, N. (2008). Arab Americans: Understanding their challenges, needs, and struggles. In A. J. Marsella, J. L. Johnson, P. Watson, & J. Gryczynski (Eds.), *Ethnocultural perspectives on disaster and trauma: Foundations, issues, and applications* (pp. 115–174). Springer Science + Business Media.

Abi-Hashem, N. (2011). Working with Middle Eastern immigrant families. In A. Zagelbaum & J. Carlson (Eds.), *Working with immigrant families: A practical guide for counselors* (pp. 151–180). Routledge.

Al-Krenawi, A., & Grajam, J. R. (2000). Culturally sensitive social work practice with Arab clients in mental health settings. *Health & Social Work, 25*(1), 9–22. https://doi.org/10.1093/hsw/25.1.9

Almeida, R. (2005). Asian Indian families. In M. McGoldrick, J. Giordano, & N. Garcia-Preto (Eds.), *Ethnicity and family therapy* (3rd ed., pp. 377–406). Guilford Press.

American Association for Marriage and Family Therapy. (2015) *Code of ethics*. https://aamft.org/Legal_Ethics/Code_of_Ethics.aspx

American Counseling Association. (2014). *ACA code of ethics*. https://www.counseling.org/resources/aca-code-of-ethics.pdf

Amodeo, J., Grigg-Saito, D., & Robb, N. (1997). Working with foreign language interpreters: Guidelines for substance abuse clinicians and human service practitioners. *Alcoholism Treatment Quarterly, 15*(4), 75–87. https://doi.org/10.1300/J020v15n04_06

Arab Community Center for Economic and Social Services. (n.d.). *Our roots*. https://www.access-community.org/about

Arredondo, P., Gallardo-Cooper, M., Delgado-Romero, E. A., & Zapata, A. L. (2014). *Culturally responsive counseling with Latinas/os*. American Counseling Association.

Arroyo, W. (1997). Central American children. In G. Johnson-Powell, J. Yamamoto, G. E. Wyatt, & W. Arroyo (Eds.), *Transcultural child development: Psychological assessment and treatment* (pp. 80–91). John Wiley & Sons.

Artico, C. I. (2003). *Latino families broken by immigration: The adolescent's perceptions*. LFB Scholarly Publishing.

Atkin, A. L., & Yoo, H. C. (2021). Patterns of racial-ethnic socialization in Asian American families: Associations with racial-ethnic identity and social connectedness. *Journal of Counseling Psychology, 68*(1), 17–26. https://doi.org/10.1037/cou0000435

Badakhshan, P. (2017). *Unterstützungsangebote für Migranten mit Fluchterfahrungen—Eine Bedarfserhebung für Ein Musiktherapeutisches Konzeptdesign* [Support offers for migrants with refugee experience: A needs assessment for a music therapy concept design] [Unpublished bachelor's thesis]. SRH University Heidelberg.

Bejarano, C. E., Manzano, S., & Montoya, C. (2011). Tracking the Latino gender gap: Gender attitudes across sex, borders, and generations. *Politics & Gender, 7*(4), 521–549. https://doi.org/10.1017/S1743923X11000341

Bellamy-Walker, T. (2022, May 5). *More people now incorrectly blame Asian Americans for Covid than at height of pandemic*. NBC News. https://www.nbcnews.com/news/asian-america/people-now-incorrectly-blame-asian-americans-covid-height-pandemic-rcna27359

Berg, A. (2003). Ancestor reverence and mental health in South Africa. *Transcultural Psychiatry, 40*(2), 194–207. https://doi.org/10.1177/1363461503402004

Berry, J. W. (1998). Acculturation and health: Theory and research. In S. S. Kazarian & D. R. Evans (Eds.), *Cultural clinical psychology: Theory, research, and practice* (pp. 39–57). Oxford University Press.

Brammer, R. (2011). Working with African immigrant families. In A. Zagelbaum & J. Carlson (Eds.), *Working with immigrant families: A practical guide for counselors* (pp. 103–120). Routledge.

Budiman, A. (2020, August 20). *Key findings about U.S. immigrants*. Pew Research Center. https://www.pewresearch.org/fact-tank/2020/08/20/key-findings-about-u-s-immigrants/

Budiman, A. (2021, April 29). *Hmong in the U.S. fact sheet.* Pew Research Center. https://www.pewresearch.org/social-trends/fact-sheet/asian-americans-hmong-in-the-u-s/

Budiman, A., & Ruiz, N. G. (2021, April 29). *Key facts about Asian origin groups in the U.S.* Pew Research Center. https://www.pewresearch.org/fact-tank/2021/04/29/key-facts-about-asian-origin-groups-in-the-u-s/

Cainkar, L. (2003, March 14). Targeting Muslims, at Ashcroft's discretion. *Middle East Report Online.* https://merip.org/2003/03/targeting-muslims-at-ashcrofts-discretion/

Cainkar, L. (2006). The social construction of difference and the Arab American experience. *Journal of American Ethnic History, 25*(2–3), 243–278. https://doi.org/10.2307/27501698

Cigrand, D. L., Fawcett, M., Miyakuni, R., Arredondo, P., & Onderak, G. (2022). A phenomenological study of perseverance and resilience through the migration journey. *Journal of Counseling & Development, 100*(2), 157–170. https://doi.org/10.1002/jcad.12413

Collier, A. F., Munger, M., & Moua, Y. K. (2012). Hmong mental health needs assessment: A community-based partnership in a small mid-western community. *American Journal of Community Psychology, 49*(1–2), 73–86. https://doi.org/10.1007/s10464-011-9436-z

Community-University Health Care Center in Minneapolis. (2001). An integrated program of culture-sensitive health care for refugees and immigrants: The Mental Health Division of the Community-University Health Care Center in Minneapolis. *Psychiatric Services, 52*(10), 1387–1389.

Corona, R., Gonzalez, T., Cohen, R., Edwards, C., & Edmonds, T. (2009). Richmond Latino needs assessment: A community-university partnership to identify health concerns and service needs for Latino youth. *Journal of Community Health, 34*(3), 195–201. https://doi.org/10.1007/s10900-008-9140-6

Council for Accreditation of Counseling and Related Educational Programs. (2024). *2024 CACREP standards.* https://www.cacrep.org/wp-content/uploads/2023/06/2024-Standards-Combined-Version-6.27.23.pdf

Curry, T. R., Morales, M. C., Zavala, E., & Hernandez, J. L. (2018). Why is family violence lower among Mexican immigrants? The protective features of Mexican culture. *Journal of Family Violence, 33*(3), 171–184. https://doi.org/10.1007/s10896-017-9947-y

Dieterich-Hartwell, R., & Koch, S. C. (2017). Creative arts therapies as temporary home for refugees: Insights from literature and practice. *Behavioral Sciences, 7*(4), Article 69. https://doi.org/10.3390/bs7040069

Druss, B. G., von Esenwein, S. A., Compton, M. T., Rask, K. J., Zhao, L., & Parker, R. M. (2010). A randomized trial of medical care management for community mental health settings: The Primary Care Access, Referral, and Evaluation (PCARE) study. *The American Journal of Psychiatry, 167*(2), 151–159. https://doi.org/10.1176/appi.ajp.2009.09050691

Edberg, M., Benavides-Rawson, J., Rivera, I., Shaikh, H., Monge, R., & Grinker, R. (2021). Transnational determinants of health for Central American migrants to the U.S.: Results of a qualitative study. *Global Public Health, 16*(3), 415–430. https://doi.org/10.1080/17441692.2020.1779329

Egli, E. A. (1991). Bilingual workers. In J. Westermeyer, C. L. Williams, & A. N. Nguyen (Eds.), *Mental health services for refugees* (pp. 90–110) (DHHS Publication No. [ADM] 91-1824). U.S. Government Printing Office.

Elbalghiti-Williams, M. (2022, February 26). *Interpreter assisted therapy 101 for the culturally-conscious clinician* [Workshop session]. Maryland Association for Multicultural Counseling and Development, Eldridge, MD, United States.

Falicov, C. J. (2007). Working with transnational immigrants: Expanding meanings of family, community, and culture. *Family Process, 46*(2), 157–171. https://doi.org/10.1111/j.1545-5300.2007.00201.x

Germán, M., Gonzales, N. A., & Dumka, L. (2009). Familism values as a protective factor for Mexican-origin adolescents exposed to deviant peers. *The Journal of Early Adolescence, 29*(1), 16–42. https://doi.org/10.1177/0272431608324475

Gil, R. M., & Vázquez, C. I. (1996). *The Maria paradox: How Latinas can merge Old World traditions with New World self-esteem.* G. P. Putnam's Sons.

Gonzales, F. (2008). *Hispanic women in the United States, 2007* [Fact sheet]. Pew Research Center. https://www.pewresearch.org/hispanic/2008/05/08/hispanic-women-in-the-united-states-2007/

Goodkind, J. R. (2005). Effectiveness of a community-based advocacy and learning program for Hmong refugees. *American Journal of Community Psychology, 36*(3–4), 387–408. https://doi.org/10.1007/s10464-005-8633-z

Gordon, S., Bernadett, M., Evans, D., Shapiro, N. B., & Patel, U. (n.d.). *Asian Indian culture: Influences and implications for health care*. Molina Healthcare. https://www.molinahealthcare.com/~/media/Molina/PublicWebsite/PDF/providers/fl/Medicaid/resource_FL_AsianIndianCulture_InfluencesAndImplicationsForHealthCare.pdf

Graf, S. C., Mullis, R. L., & Mullis, A. K. (2008). Identity formation of United States American and Asian Indian adolescents. *Adolescence*, *43*(169), 57–69.

Harjanto, L., & Batalova, J. (2022). *Middle Eastern and North Africa immigrants in the United States.* Migration Policy Institute. https://www.migrationpolicy.org/article/middle-eastern-and-north-african-immigrants-united-states

Havenaar, J. M., Geerlings, M. I., Vivian, L., Roberston, B., Collinson, M., & Robertson, B. (2008). Common mental health problems in historically disadvantaged urban and rural communities in South Africa: Prevalence and risk factors. *Social Psychiatry and Psychiatric Epidemiology*, *43*(3), 209–215. https://doi.org/10.1007/s00127-007-0294-9

Hernández, B., Ramírez García, J. I., & Flynn, M. (2010). The role of familism in the relation between parent-child discord and psychological distress among emerging adults of Mexican descent. *Journal of Family Psychology*, *24*(2), 105–114. https://doi.org/10.1037/a0019140

Herring, R. D., & Salazar, C. (2002). Non-Western helping modalities. In J. Trusty, E. J. Looby, & D. S. Sandhu (Eds.), *Multicultural counseling: Context, theory and practice, and competence* (pp. 283–318). Nova Science Publishers.

Husain, A., Nashwam, A., & Howard, S. (2016). Middle Eastern immigrant and refugee children and families. In A. J. Dettlaff & R. Fong (Eds.), *Immigrant and refugee children and families: Culturally responsive practice* (pp. 247–281). Columbia University Press.

International Organization for Migration. (2017). *World migration report 2018*. https://www.iom.int/sites/g/files/tmzbdl486/files/country/docs/china/r5_world_migration_report_2018_en.pdf

Ivey, M. B., Vazquez, E., & Vázquez, L. A. (Writers/Therapists). (2004). *Counseling Latino children and adolescents: Cross-cultural issues* [Film; educational DVD]. Microtraining Associates. https://video.alexanderstreet.com/watch/counseling-latino-children-and-adolescents-cross-cultural-issues

John, A. (2012). Stress among mothers of children with intellectual disabilities in urban India: Role of gender and maternal coping. *Journal of Applied Research in Intellectual Disabilities*, *25*(4), 372–382. https://doi.org/10.1111/j.1468-3148.2011.00672.x

Kalaf, L., & Plante, P. (2019). The lived experience of young Syrian refugees with an expressive arts workshop about resilience. *Canadian Art Therapy Association Journal*, *32*(1), 18–30. https://doi.org/10.1080/08322473.2019.1600895

Kekae-Moletsane, M. (2008). Masekitlana: South African traditional play as a therapeutic tool in child psychotherapy. *South African Journal of Psychology*, *38*(2), 367–375. https://doi.org/10.1177/008124630803800208

Ko, N. Y., Snyder, F. R., Raich, P. C., Paskett, E. D., Dudley, D. J., Lee, J.-H., Levine, P. H., & Freund, K. M. (2016). Racial and ethnic differences in patient navigation: Results from the Patient Navigation Research Program. *Cancer*, *122*(17), 2715–2722. https://doi.org/10.1002/cncr.30109

Lara, M., Gamboa, C., Kahramanian, M. I., Morales, L. S., & Hayes Bautista, D. E. (2005). Acculturation and Latino health in the United States: A review of the literature and its sociopolitical context. *Annual Review of Public Health*, *26*, 367–397. https://doi.org/10.1146/annurev.publhealth.26.021304.144615

Lee, E., & Mock, M. R. (2005). Asian families. In M. McGoldrick, J. Giordano, & N. Garcia-Preto (Eds.), *Ethnicity and family therapy* (3rd ed., pp. 269–289). Guilford Press.

Levitt, P. (1998). Social remittances: Migration driven local-level forms of cultural diffusion. *International Migration Review*, *32*(4), 926–948. https://doi.org/10.1177/019791839803200404

Liu, T., Liu, C., & Chang, Y. J. (2022). Asian American mental health amidst COVID-19 anti-Asian racism: Internalized racism and generational status as moderators. *Asian American Journal of Psychology*, *13*(4), 328–338. https://doi.org/10.1037/aap0000284

Lombe, M., Mufunde, C., & Mabikke, H. (2016). African immigrant and refugee children and families. In A. J. Dettlaff & R. Fong (Eds.), *Immigrant and refugee children and families: Culturally responsive practice* (pp. 214–248). Columbia University Press.

Mbiti, J. S. (1970). *African religions and philosophy*. Doubleday.

McGoldrick, M., Giordano, J., & Preto, N. G. (Eds.). (2005). *Ethnicity and family therapy* (3rd ed.). Guilford Press.

Melendez, T., & McDowell, T. (2008). Race, class, gender, and migration: Family therapy with a Peruvian couple. *Journal of Systemic Therapies, 27*(1), 30–43. https://doi.org/10.1521/jsyt.2008.27.1.30

Meschke, L. L., & Juang, L. P. (2014). Obstacles to parent-adolescent communication in Hmong American families: Exploring pathways to adolescent mental health promotion. *Ethnicity & Health, 19*(2), 144–159. https://doi.org/10.1080/13557858.2013.814765

Meyer DeMott, M. A., Jakobsen, M., Wentzel-Larsen, T., & Heir, T. (2017). A controlled early group intervention study for unaccompanied minors: Can expressive arts alleviate symptoms of trauma and enhance life satisfaction? *Scandinavian Journal of Psychology, 58*(6), 510–518. https://doi.org/10.1111/sjop.12395

Miville, M. L., Mendez, N., & Louie, M. (2017). Latina/o gender roles: A content analysis of empirical research from 1982 to 2013. *Journal of Latina/o Psychology, 5*(3), 173–194. https://doi.org/10.1037/lat0000072

Nicholson, B. L. (1997). The influence of pre-emigration and postemigration stressors on mental health: A study of Southeast Asian refugees. *Social Work Research, 21*(1), 19–31. https://doi.org/10.1093/swr/21.1.19

Nobles, A. Y., & Sciarra, D. T. (2000). Cultural determinants in the treatment of Arab Americans: A primer for mainstream therapists. *American Journal of Orthopsychiatry, 70*(2), 182–191. https://doi.org/10.1037/h0087734

Nwoye, A. (2006). A narrative approach to child and family therapy in Africa. *Contemporary Family Therapy, 28*(1), 1–23. https://doi.org/10.1007/s10591-006-9691-6

Osirim, M. J. (2008). African women in the new diaspora: Transnationalism and the (re)creation of home. *African and Asian Studies, 7*(4), 367–394. https://doi.org/10.1163/156921008X359588

Parra-Cardona, J. R., Bulock, L. A., Imig, D. R., Villarruel, F. A., & Gold, S. J. (2006). "Trabajando duro todos los dias": Learning from the life experiences of Mexican-origin migrant families. *Family Relations, 55*(3), 361–375. https://doi.org/10.1111/j.1741-3729.2006.00409.x

Pfeifer, M., & Lee, T. (2005). Hmong population, demographic, socioeconomic, and educational trends in the 2000 Census. In B. Thao, L. Shein, & M. Niedzweicki (Eds.), *Hmong 2000 Census publication: Data and analysis* (pp. 3–11). Hmong National Development; Hmong Cultural and Resource Center.

Piña-Watson, B., Gonzalez, I. M., & Manzo, G. (2019). Mexican-descent adolescent resilience through *familismo* in the context of intergeneration acculturation conflict on depressive symptoms. *Translational Issues in Psychological Science, 5*(4), 326–334. https://doi.org/10.1037/tps0000210

Porter, M., & Haslam, N. (2005). Predisplacement and postdisplacement factors associated with mental health of refugees and internally displaced persons: A meta-analysis. *JAMA, 294*(5), 602–612. https://doi.org/10.1001/jama.294.5.602

Potocky, M., & Naseh, M. (2019). *Best practices for social work with refugees and immigrants* (2nd ed.). Columbia University Press.

Ratts, M. J., Singh, A. A., Nassar-McMillan, S., Butler, S. K., & McCullough, J. R. (2015). *Multicultural and social justice counseling competencies.* Association for Multicultural Counseling and Development. https://www.counseling.org/docs/default-source/competencies/multicultural-and-social-justice-counseling-competencies.pdf?sfvrsn=20

Romero, A. J., White, R. M. B., Anguas, M. M., Curlee, A., & Rodas, J. M. (2020). Resilience of Mexican descent youth in a low-income neighborhood: Examining family and neighborhood factors. *Journal of Latinx Psychology, 8*(4), 265–279. https://doi.org/10.1037/lat0000149

Rousseau, C., & Guzder, J. (2008). School-based prevention programs for refugee children. *Child and Adolescent Psychiatric Clinics of North America, 17*(3), 533–549. https://doi.org/10.1016/j.chc.2008.02.002.

Ruiz, A. L., Bartkowski, J. P., Ellison, C. G., Acevedo, G. A., & Xu, X. (2017). Religion and gender ideologies among working-age U.S. Latinas/os. *Religions, 8*(7), Article 121. https://doi.org/10.3390/rel8070121

Sabina, C., Cuevas, C. A., & Zadnik, E. (2015). Intimate partner violence among Latino women: Rates and cultural correlates. *Journal of Family Violence, 30*(1), 35–47. https://doi.org/10.1007/s10896-014-9652-z

Schwartz, S. J., Unger, J., Zamboanga, B. L., & Szapocznik, J. (2010). Rethinking the concept of acculturation: Implications for theory and research. *American Psychologist, 65*(4), 237–251. https://doi.org/10.1037/a0019330

Semmler, P. L., & Williams, C. B. (2000). Narrative therapy: A storied context for multicultural counseling. *Journal of Multicultural Counseling and Development, 28*(1), 51–62. https://doi.org/10.1002/j.2161-1912.2000.tb00227.x

Sivan, E. (1985). *Radical Islam: Medieval theology and modern politics.* Yale University Press.

Stein, G. L., Cupito, A. M., Mendez, J. L., Prandoni, J., Huq, N., & Westerberg, D. (2014). Familism through a developmental lens. *Journal of Latina/o Psychology, 2*(4), 224–250. https://doi.org/10.1037/lat0000025

Tamir, C. (2022, January 27). *Key findings about Black immigrants in the U.S.* Pew Research Center. https://www.pewresearch.org/fact-tank/2022/01/27/key-findings-about-black-immigrants-in-the-u-s/

Torres Stone, R. A., Cardemil, E. V., Keefe, K., Bik, P., Dyer, Z., & Clark, K. E. (2020). A community mental health needs assessment of a racially and ethnically diverse population in New England: Narratives from community stakeholders. *Community Mental Health Journal, 56*(5), 947–958. https://doi.org/10.1007/s10597-020-00562-2

Unger, J. B., Shakib, S., Gallaher, P., Ritt-Olson, A., Mouttapa, M., Palmer, P. H., & Johnson, C. A. (2006). Cultural/interpersonal values and smoking in an ethnically diverse sample of Southern California adolescents. *Journal of Cultural Diversity, 13*(1), 55–63.

U.S. Department of Justice. (n.d.). *The USA PATRIOT Act: Preserving life and liberty.* https://www.justice.gov/archive/ll/highlights.htm

van Dyk, A. C. (2001). Traditional African beliefs and customs: Implications for AIDS education and prevention in Africa. *South African Journal of Psychology, 31*(2), 60–66. https://doi.org/10.1177/008124630103100208

Van Hook, J., & Glick, J. E. (2020). Spanning borders, cultures, and generations: A decade of research on immigrant families. *Journal of Marriage and Family, 82*(1), 224–243. https://doi.org/10.1111/jomf.12621

Varughese, E. D. (2018). *Visuality and identity in post-millennial Indian graphic narratives.* Palgrave Macmillan. https://doi.org/10.1007/978-3-319-69490-0_4

Venkatesh, K. G. (2008). Psychological stress and coping strategies of the parents of mentally challenged children. *Journal of the Indian Academy of Applied Psychology, 34*(2), 227–231.

Villalba, K., Ramirez-Ortiz, D., Dévieux, J. G., Attonito, J., & Rojas, P. (2018). Gender-role attitudes among immigrant Latinas: Empowering women. *World Medical and Health Policy, 10*(4), 401–414. https://doi.org/10.1002/wmh3.288

Vontress, C. E. (1991). Traditional healing in Africa: Implications for cross-cultural counseling. *Journal of Counseling & Development, 70*(1), 242–249. https://doi.org/10.1002/j.1556-6676.1991.tb01590.x

Wamwara-Mbugua, L. W., Cornwell, T. B., & Boller, G. (2008). Triple acculturation: The role of African Americans in the consumer acculturation of Kenyan immigrants. *Journal of Business Research, 61*(2), 83–90. https://doi.org/10.1016/j.jbusres.2007.04.011

Wells, K. J., Battaglia, T. A., Dudley, D. J., Garcia, R., Greene, A., Calhoun, E., Mandleblatt, J., Paskett, E. D., Raich, P. C., & Patient Navigation Research Program. (2008). Patient navigation: State of the art or is it science? *Cancer, 113*(8), 1999–2010. https://doi.org/10.1002/cncr.23815

Yang, M. S., & Mutchler, J. E. (2017). Mental health status of middle-aged and older Hmong refugees in the U.S. *Innovation in Aging, 1*(Suppl. 1), 124. https://doi.org/10.1093/geroni/igx004.506

Zagelbaum, A. (2011). Working with Hispanic/Latino(a) immigrant families. In A. Zagelbaum & J. Carlson (Eds.), *Working with immigrant families: A practical guide for counselors* (pp. 59–74). Routledge.

Zechella, A. N., & Raval, V. V. (2016). Parenting children with intellectual and developmental disabilities in Asian Indian families in the United States. *Journal of Child and Family Studies, 25*(4), 1295–1309. https://doi.org/10.1007/s10826-015-0285-5

EPILOGUE

To write about immigrants and refugees involves an accounting of U.S. history, an overview of the current state of affairs for receiving and accepting these populations from diverse countries and with intersecting identities, and an opportunity to project into the future. I (Arredondo) believe that the narratives and case examples in this book illustrate the dilemmas faced by newcomers along with their hopes and aspirations in all three phases of the migration journey. Insomuch as the United States continues to be viewed as the destination for individuals seeking to improve their lives and those of family members, the arrival of immigrants and refugees will never cease. In real time, counselors can read about and see the buoys attempting to impede passage across the Rio Grande. Images of people wading into the water with little children may seem foolhardy to us in our comfortable offices and homes, but as has been discussed in the book, these are risks taken by desperate individuals hoping for a better future. Can we as counselors judge these actions? By engaging in perspective taking, a practice embodied in the Multicultural and Social Justice Counseling Competencies (MSJCC; Ratts et al., 2015), and trying to learn about others' worldviews, counseling professionals may appreciate how desperation leads to life-altering decisions. This is about our shared humanity and dignity, and as counselors, we chose this profession because we want to help others.

The sociopolitical climate in many countries continues to be hostile and oppressive, leaving little recourse for individuals but to seek freedom, economic well-being, and a chance to live in safety. This has always been the storyline for those who arrive to the United States of their own "will," not enslaved, since the days of the *Mayflower*, and it will likely not change. Counselors need to recognize the similarity of push and pull factors for the past 3 to 4 centuries. The refugees and immigrants of tomorrow will have similar stressors in their home country motivating them to walk hundreds of miles, get into flimsy boats, try to swim across rivers, pay a coyote, and make difficult decisions about when to leave, which child to take, and where to go. Refugee camps will continue to exist, natural disasters will occur, and global domestic warfare will make individuals and families targets of elimination. Although there is no certainty about where refugees will come from, it is predictable that they will look to the United States as their beacon of hope. And as has been the practice for decades, the United States will try to rescue and accommodate refugees and immigrants, looking at their situation as a humanitarian cause.

Current projections and trends for future immigration are based on 2020–2021 census data and reports from federal agencies such as the Congressional Budget Office (CBO, 2023). Other data sources, such as the Migration Policy Institute, National Intelligence Council, and Pew Research Center, provide insights about what might be expected (i.e., from what countries and the rationale). There are different scenarios about immigration trends with ebbs and flows precipitated by push factors previously discussed. These include warfare, natural disasters, governmental oppression, and other circumstances that deny people their freedoms and basic human rights. The CBO (2023) reports that U.S. immigration will begin to decline in 2035 although it will never get to zero for very practical reasons; according to the CBO, the only way the country's population will grow is through immigration. The CBO predicts U.S. population growth from 336 million in 2023 to 373 million in 2053, driven by net immigration, which will account for all population growth because of the decrease of fertility rates. On average, immigrants have larger families, and this will offset the decrease in births of the White population in particular.

Furthermore, discussions about the United States becoming a majority-minority country are not that far off and should also get the attention of counseling professionals. According to projections from the U.S. Census Bureau, the U.S. population will grow to 400 million in 2058, with the non-Hispanic White population declining and the "two or more races" (multiracial) group becoming the fastest growing ethnic demographic group. The multiracial category already appears on the census forms. Additionally, by 2060, the Asian population is expected to grow by 101% and the Latinx population by 93.5%; the foreign-born population is projected to increase by 16.49% by 2045 (Budiman & Ruiz, 2021).

A report by the Pew Research Center provides projections through 2065 (Cohn, 2015). Its data indicate that new immigrants and their descendants will drive most U.S. population growth in the coming 50 years, as they have for the past half century. And of the projected 441 million Americans in 2065, 78 million will be immigrants, and 81 million will be people born in the United States to immigrant parents (Cohn, 2015).

The reality of communities that are no longer a White majority is seen in states such as California, Texas, Arizona, and Florida. These demographics have implications for who will be the electorate; the increase in education levels, particularly of children of immigrants; and a shift in birth patterns. As is already evident, those who are foreign born are already more numerous throughout the country, and counselors need to take note of this fact for their professional practice.

Employment of both skilled and unskilled immigrants will continue for several reasons, including the decline in employment of the White male population and the growth of particular industries in this country. According to the Bureau of Labor Statistics (Dunn, 2022), although White men were least affected by the COVID-19 pandemic, they "recovered only about half of their 2020 employment losses in 2021, while other groups recovered about three-fourths or more of their losses" (p. 4). Some of the workplaces where immigrants find employment and are needed have been mentioned in this book. Those without a high school diploma may work in construction, home care for older adults, childcare, the hospitality industries, and the service sectors such as cleaning offices, landscaping, and agriculture. However, there are also skilled immigrants, although they are often not recognized. Some earn their college degrees in the United States, and others arrive as professionals, ready to move into their profession if possible. Counselors may work with undergraduate and graduate students of immigrant backgrounds, as well as faculty who are immigrants or refugees. Wherever one turns, there will be immigrants, children of immigrants, and grandchildren of immigrants living and working around us.

As discussed in this book, counselors will be meeting with individuals and families in different contexts, including professional, social, and community based. Thus, counselors are encouraged to deepen their cultural competency development—that is, their awareness, knowledge, and skill building, as well as grounding in the MSJCC (Ratts et al., 2015). The MSJCC model emphasizes the concepts of privilege and marginalization status for both counselors and clients. Nevertheless, with respect to counseling with immigrants and refugees, it is important that counselors recognize their privilege of education, degree, title, and other assets that may also pose a barrier. Case studies in this book have described individuals who are afraid to speak up but who are also polite in their manner when engaging with authority figures such as counselors, teachers, and others (see also Arredondo et al., 2014; Torres-Fernandez et al., 2015). Deference and humility should not be equated with helplessness.

The discussion about internal locus of control and internal locus of responsibility frames the choices and behaviors immigrants make. Intentionality, determination, and future thinking are qualities immigrants and refugees possess. At the same time, the experiences as described through the Bronfenbrenner (1977) socioecological systems model are also reminders of forces that may lead immigrants and refugees to externalize their control as they depend on legislation and other institutional practices at the state and federal levels that may limit their pragmatic goals.

An issue out of their control, for example, is the "great replacement" theory, as it is called and promulgated with messaging by Republicans that immigrants will replace White voters. In Texas, the governor invoked an "invasion clause" to criminalize access to the U.S.-Texas border (Miller & Kieffer, 2023). Anti-immigration hate groups throughout the country foster xenophobic messages about the great replacement conspiracy. It behooves counselors to know what groups are in their respective states. Are these hate, antigovernment, anti-LGBTQ+ groups? What is sad about these scenarios is the fact that many immigrants and refugees have fled their home countries because of hostilities and violence; in the United States, it may happen again. The hardships and barriers experienced by immigrants and refugees will require counselors to engage in advocacy efforts.

The MSJCC (Ratts et al., 2015) stipulate counseling and advocacy interventions. Specifically, counselors are encouraged to intervene with but also on behalf of their clients with respect to public policy and at community and institutional levels. This statement suggests counselor leadership working from empowerment theories and perspectives to lend support to those whom counselors believe cannot go it alone. Immigrants and refugees need to be affirmed about their rights and privileges within the United States. As mentioned in Chapter 6, the state of Florida passed a law in 2023 prohibiting individuals to drive in Florida with an out-of-state license. Counselors require awareness and knowledge about state laws affecting immigrants so that they can take action as needed on their behalf. In short, counselors need to put their "privilege to work."

For centuries, immigrants have demonstrated their determination, resilience, and commitment to start over and to give back. We have so much to learn from these brave individuals who care about freedom, family values, and bringing others along. Their collectivistic mindset and behaviors allow them to succeed, bringing economic growth to communities that need their labor and willingness to do the hard work not readily done by U.S. citizens. As counselors, we need to reflect on what we can learn from the examples of change, transitions, and other adaptations immigrants and refugees make and incorporate these lessons into our minds and hearts.

References

Arredondo, P., Gallardo-Cooper, M., Delgado-Romero, E. A., & Zapata, A. L. (2014). *Culturally responsive counseling with Latinas/os*. American Counseling Association.

Bronfenbrenner, U. (1977). Toward an experimental ecology of human development. *American Psychologist, 32*(7), 513–531. https://doi.org/10.1037/0003-066X.32.7.513

Budiman, A., & Ruiz, N. G. (2021). *Asian Americans are the fastest-growing racial or ethnic group in the U.S.* Pew Research Center. https://www.pewresearch.org/short-reads/2021/04/09/asian-americans-are-the-fastest-growing-racial-or-ethnic-group-in-the-u-s/

Cohn, D. (2015, October 5). *Future immigration will change the face of America by 2065*. Pew Research Center. https://www.pewresearch.org/short-reads/2015/10/05/future-immigration-will-change-the-face-of-america-by-2065/

Congressional Budget Office. (2023). *The demographic outlook: 2023 to 2053*. https://www.cbo.gov/system/files/2023-01/58612-Demographic-Outlook.pdf

Miller, C., & Kieffer, C. (2023). *Hate and extremism—In the mainstream and on the Main Street*. Southern Poverty Law Center. https://www.splcenter.org/year-hate-extremism-2022/introduction#hateextremism

Ratts, M. J., Singh, A. A., Nassar-McMillan, S., Butler, S. K., & McCullough, J. R. (2015). *Multicultural and social justice counseling competencies*. Association for Multicultural Counseling and Development. https://www.counseling.org/docs/default-source/competencies/multicultural-and-social-justice-counseling-competencies.pdf?sfvrsn=20

Torres-Fernandez, I., Chavez Dueñas, N., & Consoli, A. (2015). Guidelines for the treatment of unaccompanied asylum-seeking minors: What mental health professionals and detention center personnel can do. *Latino Psychology Today*, *2*(1), 44–54.

GLOSSARY

access gaps. Disparities or inequalities in accessing essential resources, services, or opportunities among different individuals, groups, or communities.

acculturation. The dual process of cultural and psychological change that takes place as a result of contact between two or more cultural groups and their individual members.

acculturation gap-distress theory. The theory that immigrant children acculturate to their new culture at a quicker pace than their parents, leading to family conflict and youth maladjustment.

acculturative stress. The dissonance between beliefs, behaviors, values, and attitudes that can lead to long-term strain marked by negative psychological and physical outcomes.

adverse childhood experiences (ACEs). Traumatic or negative events that occur during childhood and that can have lasting effects on a person's physical, emotional, and mental health throughout their life.

alien; illegal alien. A legal term used to describe a person who is not a citizen or national of the United States.

Alien Acts of 1798. Composed of two separate acts: the Alien Friends Act, which empowered the president to deport any alien whom they considered dangerous, and the Alien Enemies Act, which allowed the deportation of any alien who hailed from a country at war with the United States.

American Association for Marriage and Family Counseling (AAMFT). The overarching professional organization for licensed individuals who work with couples and families (e.g., marriage and family therapists, pastors, psychiatrists, psychiatric nurses).

American College Counseling Association (ACCA). The national organization for professional counselors, social workers, and psychologists who work with university and college populations to promote mental health and student development.

American dream. The ideal that every citizen of the United States should have an equal opportunity to achieve success and prosperity through hard work, determination, and initiative.

anchor baby. A child born to a noncitizen parent in a country that has birthright citizenship who may help a parent or another family member gain legal residency.

asylum seeker. A person who has left their country and is seeking protection from persecution and serious human rights violations in another country, but who has not yet been legally recognized as a refugee and is waiting to receive a decision on their asylum claim.

attachment theory. A psychological framework developed by British psychologist John Bowlby in the mid-20th century. It focuses on the emotional bonds and connections formed between individuals, particularly between children and their primary caregivers, typically parents.

biopsychosocial model. A model that provides a comprehensive overview of biological, social, environmental, and psychological factors that may be in play simultaneously.

birthright citizen. A person born to an immigrant who acquires citizenship status in the immigrant's host country.

Black code. A series of laws that the southern states invented to criminalize free African Americans in order to maintain social control after the Civil War. The Black codes had their roots in slave codes and functioned as a way to maintain subjugation of free Black people and forced them into prison labor in the form of convict leasing, from which many corporations profited.

***Chae Chan Ping v. United States* (1889).** A landmark U.S. Supreme Court decision in 1889 that upheld the constitutionality of the Chinese Exclusion Act of 1882. Also known as the Chinese Exclusion Case.

Chinese Exclusion Act of 1882. A significant piece of legislation in the United States that marked the first time the country restricted immigration based on a specific nationality. It was passed by Congress and signed into law by President Chester A. Arthur on May 6, 1882.

chronosystem. A "space" where the relationship between time, events, and conditions (outside of one's control) affects one's development and plans.

community-based participatory research (CBPR). An approach to research that actively involves community members, stakeholders, and researchers as equal partners in all stages of the research process. It seeks to address community issues and concerns by collaboratively designing and conducting studies that are relevant, culturally appropriate, and beneficial to the community.

contextual factors. The various environmental elements and circumstances that surround and influence an individual, a group, or a situation.

convict leasing. The practice of the southern states after the Thirteenth Amendment abolished slavery except for conviction crimes. The southern states imprisoned mainly Black men, often for minor crimes (i.e., Black code), and then leased them out to plantations and corporations (e.g., the Tennessee Coal, Iron and Railroad company) for years, even decades, at a time under cruel and inhumane conditions. The death rates were as high as 40%.

Council for Accreditation of Counseling and Related Educational Programs (CACREP). The premier accrediting body responsible for evaluating the excellence and legitimacy of graduate counseling programs. This council plays a pivotal role in ensuring the quality and credibility of these educational initiatives.

creative arts therapies (CAT). Include a range of artistic expression through drama, dance, music, and physical movement and provide children, adolescents and adults ways to explore their mental health issues in creative and productive ways.

cross-cultural relationships. Relationships created by partners from different cultural identities and/or of immigrant and citizen status.

cultural brokering. Involves immigrant youth mediating a new culture for their family.

culture shock. A process consisting of five stages: honeymoon, disintegration, reintegration, autonomy, and interdependence.

cumulative disadvantage. The culmination of experiences within poverty, legal status, community violence, bad schools, and discrimination in employment.

decolonize. Critically examine traditional counseling theories that approach work with clients from a White, Eurocentric viewpoint to avoid further marginalization of those clients, as well as consider alternative theories and counseling practices that may better align with clients' cultural beliefs.

Deferred Action for Childhood Arrivals (DACA). An administrative relief program that protects eligible immigrant youth from being deported.

deportation. The action of forcing a noncitizen to leave a country where they currently reside and may face these legal proceedings without representation.

dichos. Meaningful Latinx cultural sayings and proverbs, which can apply to current situations.

dimensions of personal identity model. A model that partitions identity into three dimensions: A, B, and C. The A dimensions include age/generational status, culture, ethnicity, gender, language, physical/mental status, race, sexual orientation, and social class. The B dimensions are less visible and are developmental in nature. They include educational background, geographic location, hobbies/recreation, military experience, relationship status, religion/spirituality, work experience, and health care practices/beliefs. The C dimensions emphasize historical contexts and external forces that individuals and families must deal with.

***Dred Scott v. Sandford* (1856).** The court ruled that "a negro, whose ancestors were imported into [the United States], and sold as slaves," could not be an American citizen and held portions of the Missouri Compromise unconstitutional in violation of the Fifth Amendment, treating Scott as property, not as a person.

dual consciousness. A term used to describe the worldview of people who simultaneously hold two apparently inconsistent sets of beliefs.

ego identity. A concept developed by psychologist Erik Erikson as part of his psychosocial theory of development. It refers to a person's sense of self and how they perceive and understand themselves in relation to the world around them.

Emergency Quota Law. A United States federal law passed on May 19, 1921. It was the country's first major attempt to establish numerical limits on immigration and marked a significant shift in immigration policy. Also known as the Emergency Immigration Act of 1921.

emerging adulthood. The period between adolescence and adulthood (ages 18–25) when young adults explore a plethora of opportunities in relationships, jobs, and personal perspectives about the world.

emigration. Leaving one country to move to another.

exosystem. The external environments or systems that indirectly influence an individual's development, encompassing societal institutions and factors beyond immediate interactions. It includes elements such as community resources, policies, and cultural contexts.

Extension of Chinese Exclusion Act of 1904. An extension and reinforcement of the original Chinese Exclusion Act of 1882. The primary purpose of this 1904 act was to strengthen the exclusionary measures against Chinese immigrants.

external migrant. A person who moves to a different state, country, or continent.

familial contextual factors. Various influences and elements within a family setting that can shape and impact an individual's development, behavior, and overall well-being.

familismo. A central Latin cultural value involving dedication, commitment, and loyalty to family.

family, friend, and neighbor (FFN) care. A type of care that is used when immigrant parents, especially those who are undocumented, lack reliable childcare options.

femicide. The killing of a woman or girl by a man on account of her gender.

first-generation immigrant child. A foreign-born child with at least one foreign-born parent.

five stages of death and dying. A model that describes a series of emotional stages that individuals may experience when facing their own mortality or dealing with the impending death of a loved one. The stages include denial, anger, bargaining, depression, and acceptance.

***Fred T. Korematsu v. United States* (1944).** A landmark U.S. Supreme Court case in 1944 that dealt with the constitutionality of the forced relocation and internment of Japanese Americans during World War II. The case addressed the legality of Executive Order 9066, which authorized the removal and incarceration of over 120,000 Japanese Americans, two thirds of whom were U.S. citizens.

generativity. The concern and sense of responsibility that adults have for the well-being and development of future generations.

Gentlemen's Agreement of 1907. An informal agreement between the United States and the Empire of Japan, designed to address the increasing tensions and discrimination faced by Japanese immigrants in the United States. The agreement was reached through negotiations between the two countries' governments and was not a formal treaty.

haram. Something forbidden by Islamic law.

H-2A visa. A nonimmigrant visa designed to help temporary or seasonal agricultural workers enter the United States to work in the agriculture sector.

ibasho. An emerging Japanese educational concept of a physical and psychological place where individuals feel a sense of acceptance, freedom, and security.

illegal immigrant. A colloquial term used to describe a person who is not a citizen or national of the host country.

immigrant. From the perspective of the country of arrival, a person who moves into a country other than that of their nationality or usual residence, so that the country of destination effectively becomes their new country of usual residence.

immigrant paradox. The concept suggesting that first-generation immigrants' developmental outcomes tend to be better than their second- or third-generation peers. It is still being studied in earnest, as there appears to be high variability based on factors such as acculturation, race, and academic and behavioral outcomes measured.

immigration. Moving into a new country.

Immigration Act of 1917. Reflecting the prevailing sentiment of the time, an act that sought to restrict immigration and preserve the perceived cultural and racial makeup of the United States. This act contributed to a more selective and exclusionary approach to immigration policy that persisted throughout the early 20th century.

Immigration Act of 1924. An act that significantly limited the number of immigrants, particularly from Southern and Eastern Europe, and reinforced the discriminatory practices against Asian immigrants. This act had a profound impact on immigration patterns to the United States for decades to come.

Indian Citizenship Act of 1924. An act that imposed strict quotas on immigration to the United States. It significantly reduced arrivals from Southern and Eastern Europe, while also reinforcing discriminatory measures against Asian immigrants. This legislation had a lasting impact on U.S. immigration patterns for decades. Also known as the Johnson-Reed Act.

information gaps. The missing or incomplete information that prevents individuals, organizations, or researchers from fully understanding a particular subject or problem.

intergenerational cultural conflict (ICC). Disagreements that occur as a result of acculturation gaps between parents and children, often leading to a clash in values and beliefs.

internal migrants. People who move within a state, country, or continent.

intersectionality. Differentiating aspects of a person's experiences based on the complex interplay of attributes such as race, gender, and country of origin.

Jim Crow. A series of laws and social customs invented in the southern states to maintain social control and oppression of African Americans. Schools, theaters, restaurants, and transportation vehicles were segregated. Poll taxes, literacy requirements, and grandfather clauses prevented Blacks from voting and serving on juries or running for office.

karma. The concept that one's actions have consequences. It embodies the idea that moral and ethical actions contribute to the cycle of cause and effect.

la bestia. A train that accelerates immigrant travel from Central American countries through Mexico.

la migra. Refers to ICE (see U.S. Immigration and Customs Enforcement), the body that chases down individuals in the country to remove them, sometimes unlawfully.

language brokers. Children or young people who translate or interpret on behalf of adult family members, siblings, or peers who do not speak the local language.

legally illegal. A term that connotes the limbo immigrants face, expressing in derogatory terms the idiosyncratic characteristics of DACA recipients in a society where they are allowed to be present but have no pathway to citizenship or residency.

LGBTQ+ immigrant adults. Individuals with sexual orientation and gender identities that are not part of the heterosexual and male/female binary perspective.

macrosystem. The system that imposes on individuals and families because it includes the overarching, intrusive, and controlling governmental and legislative bodies.

marianismo. An important framework in the Latinx family in terms of what is expected of women.

mass incarceration. The expansive network of people and parties with vested interests in profiting from mass incarceration to fill prisons. People of color are incarcerated at disproportionately higher rates than White people since the war on drugs that began in the late 1960s.

McCarran-Walter Act (Immigration and Nationality Act of 1952). A significant piece of legislation in the United States that reformed and consolidated immigration laws.

mesosystem. The system in which a child's immediate influences (family, school, community, church, etc.) interact.

Mexican-American War. A conflict that took place between the United States and Mexico from 1846 to 1848. The war was triggered by territorial disputes and issues surrounding the annexation of Texas to the United States in 1845. The outcome of the war resulted in significant territorial changes, with Mexico ceding a vast amount of land to the United States.

microaggressions. Everyday verbal, nonverbal, and environmental slights, snubs, and insults, whether intentional or unintentional, that communicate hostile, derogatory, or negative messages to target people based solely on their marginalized group membership.

microsystem. A system of people, groups, and institutions that play an immediate and explicit role in a child's life. Examples include the family, neighborhood, religious community, school, and peers.

migrant. Any person who is moving or has moved across an international border or within a state away from their habitual place of residence, regardless of (a) the person's legal status, (b) whether the movement is voluntary or involuntary, (c) what the causes for the movement are, or (d) what the length of the stay is.

migratory loss. A term used to describe the emotional and psychological challenges experienced by individuals or communities that have been displaced or forced to move from their original homes to a new location.

model minority. A minority demographic (whether based on race, ethnicity, or religion) whose members are perceived as achieving a higher degree of socioeconomic success than the population average, thus serving as a reference group to out-groups.

narrative therapy. A form of therapy that aims to separate the individual from the problem, allowing the individual to externalize their issues rather than internalize them. It relies on the individual's own skills and sense of purpose to guide them through difficult times.

National Emergencies Act (NEA) of 1976. A United States federal law that governs the declaration and termination of national emergencies by the president. The NEA was passed by Congress and signed into law by President Gerald Ford on September 14, 1976, in response to concerns about the proliferation of emergency declarations without clear guidelines or oversight.

National Security Entry-Exit Registry (NSEER). A U.S. immigration program that was implemented in the aftermath of the September 11, 2001, terrorist attacks. It was introduced as part of the efforts to enhance national security and track individuals from certain countries with potential security concerns. The NSEER program faced criticism from civil liberties and immigrant rights advocates who argued that it unfairly targeted individuals based on their nationality and religion rather than on specific evidence of wrongdoing. Also known as the Special Registration program.

naturalization. The process to become a U.S. citizen if you were born outside of the United States. If you meet certain requirements, you may become a U.S. citizen either at birth or after birth.

Naturalization Act of 1790. One of the earliest pieces of U.S. legislation regarding citizenship and naturalization. It was the first uniform rule enacted by Congress for granting citizenship to foreign-born individuals.

Naturalization Act of 1870. An important piece of legislation in the United States that made significant changes to the naturalization process and expanded citizenship eligibility to include certain groups of immigrants who were previously excluded. The act was signed into law by President Ulysses S. Grant on July 14, 1870.

naturalized citizen. A migrant person who has completed the process to become a citizen in their host country.

nonnormative influences. Events that are not typical but affect development, such as trauma, divorce, illness, and other challenges to development.

normative influences. Biological and environmental factors that associate with a specific historical era.

numeracy skills. The ability to understand, use, and interpret numerical information effectively in various real-life situations.

Office of Refugee Resettlement (ORR). A U.S. government agency under the Department of Health and Human Services. ORR is responsible for the care and placement of unaccompanied immigrant minors, including their resettlement and reunification with family members.

ontogenesis. Individual development and growth from conception to maturity, encompassing various stages of biological and behavioral evolution. It involves the unfolding and realization of the organism's inherent potential over time.

othering. Focusing on differences to dismantle connectedness between people, due to political, sociocultural, and other motives, which can lead to discrimination, bullying, and acculturation issues for immigrant adolescents.

Passenger Cases of 1849. A collective term referring to a group of five U.S. Supreme Court cases that were decided together in 1849. These cases were instrumental in shaping the understanding of the Commerce Clause of the U.S. Constitution and its implications for regulating interstate and international commerce.

person-environment fit. A concept, described formulaically as $B = f(P, E)$, that has been used to explain group phenomena, where a member's personal characteristics (P) interact with the environmental factors (E) of the group, its members, and the situation to elicit behavior (B).

prison industrial complex (PIC). A term that, according to the abolitionist organization Critical Resistance, describes the overlapping interests of government and industry that use surveillance, policing, and imprisonment as solutions to economic, social, and political problems. PIC thrives on and profits from criminalization of and mass incarceration of mainly Black and Brown bodies. There is a growing network of privatized immigration detention centers to detain "illegal immigrants."

protective factors. Elements or characteristics that contribute to a person's resilience and ability to cope with adversity, stress, or challenging life circumstances.

psychological first aid (PFA). An evidence-based intervention recommended for children who have recently migrated and experienced traumatic incidents.

pull factors. Circumstances in the destination country that make it a more desirable place to live than one's home country. Some examples include safety, a desire for greater stability, freedom, better wages, family reunification, increased quality of life, and availability of basic needs and other services.

push factors. Conditions or events that lead people to consider a life-changing move. Some examples include escaping violence, femicide, poverty, political corruption, lack of employment, environmental degradation, natural disasters, limited access to quality health care and education, drug cartels, and religious oppression.

qualified immigrants. Include the following: (a) lawful permanent residents, or LPRs (people with green cards); (b) refugees, people granted asylum or withholding of deportation/removal, and conditional entrants; (c) people granted parole by the U.S. Department of Homeland Security for a period of at least 1 year; (d) Cuban and Haitian entrants; (e) certain abused immigrants, their children, and/or their parents; (f) certain survivors of trafficking; and (g) individuals residing in the United States pursuant to a Compact of Free Association (for Medicaid purpose only).

racial/ethnic socialization (RES). The process through which parents contribute to their children's learning about their culture and their relationships with others outside their ethnic group.

***Rajah v. Mukasey* (2008).** A significant U.S. federal court case that addressed the issue of asylum for individuals facing persecution based on their sexual orientation.

refugee. A person who has left their country of origin for fear of "persecution, conflict, generalized violence, or other circumstances that have seriously disturbed public order and, as a result, require[s] international protection" (United Nations, 1951) and who has been granted legal refugee status by the host country.

relational context. Refers to the intimate relationships that people have with family and close, intimate friends.

respeto. An important attending skill demonstrating clinician cultural responsiveness.

return migration. Moving back to where one came from.

Rodriguez's case in 1897. A court case in 1896 involving Ricardo Rodríguez that brought attention to questions of citizenship and voting rights for Mexican Texans.

scaffolding. Refers to having a supportive teacher or other individual.

seasonal migration. Moving with each season or in response to labor or climate conditions.

second-generation immigrant child. Typically refers to U.S.-born children with at least one foreign-born parent.

separation and individualization theory. A theory that explores the process through which infants transition from a state of symbiotic dependence with their primary caregiver to becoming separate individuals with a sense of self.

social support. Reciprocal, accessible, and reliable social relationships that provide resources and assistance with stressors.

Special Immigrant Juvenile Status (SIJS). An immigration classification available to certain undocumented immigrants under the age of 21 who have been abused, neglected, or abandoned by one or both parents. SIJS allows immigrant youth under the age of 21, who need protection from the state juvenile court, to obtain lawful permanent immigration status.

sponsors. People (usually family members) willing to provide food, housing, and medical and mental health care to unaccompanied immigrant youth and who have completed a background check and met other eligibility criteria to be granted placement.

Supplemental Nutrition Assistance Program (SNAP). The largest federal nutrition assistance program. SNAP provides food benefits to low-income families to supplement their grocery budget so that they can afford the nutritious foods essential to health and well-being.

temporary protected status (TPS). A transitory immigration status for specific countries confronting an ongoing armed conflict or environmental disaster.

totems. Symbols or representations used within human affiliations.

Treaty of Guadalupe Hidalgo of 1848. A peace treaty signed on February 2, 1848, between the United States and Mexico officially ending the Mexican-American War.

***Trump v. Hawaii* (2018).** A landmark case (decided by the U.S. Supreme Court in 2018) that addressed the constitutionality of the third version of President Donald Trump's travel ban, also known as the "Muslim Ban." The decision generated criticism from opponents who argued that the travel ban amounted to religious discrimination and undermined the country's values of religious freedom and inclusivity.

T-visa. A visa, or temporary legal status in the United States for up to 4 years under the Victims of Trafficking and Violence Protection Act (2000), that may be granted to unaccompanied immigrant youth who have been abused, neglected, or trafficked or who have a disability.

unaccompanied children. Children (under the age of 18) who enter the United States without lawful immigration status and without an accompanying parent or legal guardian.

undocumented. A foreign-born person who does not possess a valid visa or other immigration documentation.

undocumented students. Students who were not born in the United States but who immigrated, live, and attend school in the United States.

undocuqueer. A political identity term acknowledging queer and trans identities of marginalized undocumented immigrants.

universal screening. Should be considered a best practice to improve the likelihood that immigrant families receive early intervention for their children who need it.

USA PATRIOT Act. An act that increased the penalties for those who commit terrorist crimes.

U.S. Border Patrol. A federal law enforcement agency within U.S. Customs and Border Protection tasked with securing and patrolling the U.S. border to prevent illegal entry, smuggling, or other border-related responsibilities. Their primary function is to enforce immigration laws and border security.

U.S. Citizenship and Immigration Services (USCIS). The federal agency responsible for administering and overseeing immigration and naturalization services in the United States.

U.S. Customs and Border Protection. The federal agency within the Department of Homeland Security responsible for securing the U.S. borders and supporting lawful trade and travel, including enforcing customs and immigration laws.

U.S. Department of Homeland Security (DHS). The federal agency established to safeguard the United States against various threats, including terrorism, natural disasters, and other emergencies.

U.S. Immigration and Customs Enforcement (ICE). The federal agency within the Department of Homeland Security responsible for enforcing laws governing border control, customs, trade, and immigration.

William Wilberforce Trafficking Victims Protection Reauthorization Act (TVPRA). A law that was passed in 2008 that strengthened federal trafficking laws and added provisions that govern the rights of unaccompanied immigrant children who enter the United States.

xenophobia. The fear of foreigners, which can fuel negative and hostile attitudes and behaviors toward perceived outsiders in the United States.

zero-tolerance policy. Adopted by the United States in 2018 requiring children to be separated from adults who were accompanying them for the purpose of prosecuting the adults.

zone of proximal development. Refers to the environment of learning whereby a student develops cognitive growth by communicating with others and being exposed to the process of learning.

INDEX

Figures and tables are indicated by "f" and "t" following the page numbers.

www.ingramcontent.com/pod-product-compliance
Lightning Source LLC
LaVergne TN
LVHW060030210926
848481LV00013B/3824
* 9 7 8 1 5 5 6 2 0 4 1 8 0 *